Love, Divine and Human

Love, Divine and Human

Contemporary Essays in Systematic and Philosophical Theology

Edited by
Oliver D. Crisp, James M. Arcadi,
and Jordan Wessling

t&tclark
LONDON • NEW YORK • OXFORD • NEW DELHI • SYDNEY

T&T CLARK
Bloomsbury Publishing Plc
50 Bedford Square, London, WC1B 3DP, UK
1385 Broadway, New York, NY 10018, USA
29 Earlsfort Terrace, Dublin 2, Ireland

BLOOMSBURY, T&T CLARK and the T&T Clark logo are trademarks of Bloomsbury Publishing Plc

First published in Great Britain 2020
This paperback edition published in 2021

Copyright © James M. Arcadi, Oliver D. Crisp, Jordan Wessling and contributors, 2020

James M. Arcadi, Oliver D. Crisp and Jordan Wessling have asserted their right under the Copyright, Designs and Patents Act, 1988, to be identified as Editors of this work.

For legal purposes the Acknowledgments on p. viii constitute an extension of this copyright page.

Cover image © *Tide at Walker Creek* © Bruce Herman, 2011,
oil on wood panels, 60" x 72". Courtesy of the artist: www.bruceherman.com

All rights reserved. No part of this publication may be reproduced or transmitted in any form or by any means, electronic or mechanical, including photocopying, recording, or any information storage or retrieval system, without prior permission in writing from the publishers.

Bloomsbury Publishing Plc does not have any control over, or responsibility for, any third-party websites referred to or in this book. All internet addresses given in this book were correct at the time of going to press. The author and publisher regret any inconvenience caused if addresses have changed or sites have ceased to exist, but can accept no responsibility for any such changes.

A catalogue record for this book is available from the British Library.

A catalog record for this book is available from the Library of Congress.

ISBN: HB: 978-0-5676-8773-9
PB: 978-0-5676-9889-6
ePDF: 978-0-5676-8774-6
ePUB: 978-0-5676-8776-0

Typeset by Deanta Global Publishing Services, Chennai, India

To find out more about our authors and books visit www.bloomsbury.com and sign up for our newsletters.

To our families

Contents

Acknowledgments	viii
Introduction *Jordan Wessling*	1
1 Love Without Measure? John Webster's Unfinished Dogmatic Account of the Love of God, in Dialogue with Thomas Jay Oord's Interdisciplinary Theological Account *Kevin J. Vanhoozer*	7
2 Analogies of Love between God and Creatures: A Response to Kevin Vanhoozer *Thomas Jay Oord*	27
3 Divine Love and Personality *Michael C. Rea*	43
4 The Hidden Love of God and the Imaging Defense *Sameer Yadav*	63
5 The Limits of Divine Love *Jeff Jordan*	81
6 In Defense of the Loving Parent Analogy *Thomas Talbott*	97
7 What Wideness, Whose Strictness? The Scope and Limits of Divine Love for Humankind *Marilyn McCord Adams*	113
8 Impassibility, Omnisubjectivity, and the Problem of Unity in Love *R. T. Mullins*	127
9 A Love that Speaks in Harsh Tones: On the Superiority of Divine Communicative Punishment *Jordan Wessling*	145
10 The Indwelling of the Holy Spirit as Love *Adonis Vidu*	165
11 Love and Resentment *Leigh Vicens*	187
12 Is There a Christian Duty to Love? *Kent Dunnington*	199
13 "Sex Is Really about God": Sarah Coakley and the Transformation of Desire *Erin Dufault-Hunter*	215
14 Perfect Obedience, Perfect Love, and the (So-Called) Problem of Heavenly Freedom *James T. Turner, Jr.*	235
List of Contributors	255
Index	256

Acknowledgments

Most of the chapters contained in this volume began as research seminar presentations given as part of a John Templeton Foundation grant, "Analytic Theology for Theological Formation," which was hosted at Fuller Theological Seminary from 2015 to 2018. The "Fuller AT Project," as we called it, was a great gift to all those involved with it. In addition to the editors of this volume, the Fuller AT Project team included Jesse Gentile, Steven Nemes, Martine Oldoff, Dr. J. T. Turner, Jr., Allison Wilshire, and Christopher Woznicki. We gratefully acknowledge the generosity of the Templeton Foundation, the dean and faculty of the School of Theology, Fuller Theological Seminary, and the staff of the STAR Office, who hosted the grant and helped make it such a great success. Thanks are also due to Anna Turton, our editor at T&T Clark, and the team there, who have shepherded this volume through the publication process. We are also grateful to Steven Nemes for his work on the index of this volume.

We would like to acknowledge that in addition to being presented at the Fuller AT Project seminars, versions of two of the chapters in this volume appear elsewhere. Kevin J. Vanoozer's chapter appears in a special issue of the *International Journal of Systematic Theology* dedicated to the work of the late John Webster, vol. 19 no. 4 (2017), pp. 505–26. Michael C. Rea's chapter appears in his monograph, *The Hiddenness of God* (Oxford: Oxford University Press, 2018). We are grateful to Wiley and Oxford for the ability to reprint these chapters here.

Finally, all research is done in community. This book is no different in that regard. Our families are the part of the community that made this work possible in all sorts of practical ways. We are very grateful to them for supporting us in our work on the Fuller AT Project and on this volume. It seems fitting in a volume focused on exploring human and divine love to dedicate this work to those whose love and care for us have made this volume possible.

Introduction

Jordan Wessling

In his widely read historical exploration of the concept of love, Irving Singer writes that "only Christianity . . . defines itself as *the* religion of love," in that Christianity "alone has made love the dominant principle in all areas of dogma."[1] Although Singer might be accused of exaggerating the emphasis Christians have historically placed on love, there is no denying that love rests at the center of the standard Christian vision of reality. According to that vision, the Triune God who is love within Himself graciously creates the world out of love, identifies with the world in general and humanity in particular by taking on flesh, and dies a criminal's death to free men and women from sin so that they might be eternally united with Him. Moreover, God calls humans to love as He loves Christ, to love their friends and enemies as they do themselves, and to be willing to die for others as Christ was willing to die for the church. This theological depiction of reality raises a number of questions concerning how Christians might think about the nature and scope of God's love, and how they might imitate God's love in their limited, creaturely ways. To be sure, Christian theologians and philosophers are currently engaged in the examination of such issues, but this is regularly done in disciplinary isolation from one another, which can only impair the quality of the examination results. For while theologians are typically expert in the history, development, and unity of doctrine, philosophers excel in analyzing concepts and presenting rigorous arguments for well-defined conclusions. However, both strengths are needed if we are to arrive at a rich contemporary Christian theology of love that approximates the truth. For this reason, the present book brings together a thoughtful cast of philosophers and theologians to advance a number of debates within the current study of the theology of love.

Chapter 1 comes from Kevin J. Vanhoozer, "Love Without Measure? John Webster's Unfinished Dogmatic Account of the Love of God, in Dialogue with Thomas Jay Oord's Interdisciplinary Theological Account." In this contribution, Vanhoozer compares and contrasts the late John Webster's treatment of the love of God with that of Thomas Jay Oord's. Vanhoozer contends that the central difference between these theologians concerns whether God stands in a "real" relation with the world, where, roughly, God stands in a real relation with some creature only if God is somehow changed or modified by the creature (e.g., God's emotional life is different than it otherwise would have been). Whereas Webster denies that God has any real relations to creation, Oord affirms that God's mental and emotional life is affected by creation's ebbs and flows. On this issue, Vanhoozer sides with Webster, arguing that Webster's retrieval of St. Thomas Aquinas's

---

[1] Irving's emphasis, *The Nature of Love: Plato to Luther*, 2nd ed. (Chicago, IL: The University of Chicago Press, 1984), 159.

denial that God bears real relations with creation is a necessary condition for understanding the fullness of God's love for the world. In addition, Vanhoozer fears that Oord's theological method and resulting conception of God appears to be little more than a kind of Feuerbachian projection of human wishes onto the clouds.

Thomas Jay Oord responds to these charges in Chapter 2. He argues that Scripture depicts God as giving and receiving from creatures on account of His love and that this biblically oriented and relational conception of God's love fits neatly with human experiences of love. Oord furthermore fleshes out his own understanding of divine love, according to which God essentially gives of Himself and never controls the behavior of His creatures, and Oord submits that this conception is compatible with the claim that God performs miraculous actions. Finally, Oord criticizes Vanhoozer and Webster for failing to take overcoming the problem of evil as a primary theological task, and he answers five conceptual questions related to the theology of God's love which Vanhoozer asks of him.

Like Vanhoozer and Oord, the philosopher Michael C. Rea has readers consider methodological questions about how the doctrine of divine love should be approached, only Rea does this with an eye to addressing the problem of divine hiddenness. Rea's contention is that certain theologians and philosophers are mistaken to think of God's love in terms of a kind of idealized human love, whereby God seeks the good of and/or union with His rational creatures to a maximal degree. On the contrary, since God is a personal being, He is bound to have His own goals for creation that do not involve realizing or deepening His love relationship with His creatures. Rea then argues that this conclusion undercuts a key premise in the hiddenness argument against God's existence.

Sameer Yadav also seeks to undercut the argument from divine hiddenness in his contribution to this volume. Similar to Rea, Yadav contends that it is mistaken to think of God's love as strongly analogous to human love, only free from creaturely limitations. Unlike Rea, however, Yadav reaches this conclusion on biblical-theological grounds rather than from what might be construed as Rea's philosophical grounds, and, in addition, Yadav proposes a different understanding of God's love. Yadav maintains that God wants a unique sort of love relationship with humans, namely, a relationship whereby humans "image" the divine in creation.

In their own ways, Yadav, Rea, and Vanhoozer each seek to correct what they deem to be overly anthropomorphic and anthropocentric conceptions of God's love. In Chapter 5, "The Limits of Divine Love," the philosopher Jeff Jordan likewise seeks to correct what he deems to be widespread misconceptions about God's love. Some philosophers and theologians suppose that God loves every person in an equal and impartial way as deeply as possible, whereas others suppose that God's love is equal and impartial but not as deep as it possibly could be. Against these two understandings of the nature and scope of God's love, Jordan argues that although God loves all human persons, God loves some humans more than others. The reason for this inequality is that not even a perfect being can in-principle love each human at the same deep level, since it is impossible to identify with the conflicting interests of different human persons that inevitably emerge. However, a perfect being would have to love some humans to the highest possible degree. So God, as a perfect being, must distribute His love for humans unequally. An implication of this model of love, Jordan submits, is that it hamstrings two prominent atheistic arguments, the evidential argument from human suffering and the argument from divine hiddenness.

In Chapter 6, Thomas Talbott objects to the limits that Jordan places on God's love. Talbott first argues that Jordan never proposes a coherent account of God's love. Instead of supposing with Jordan that God must comprehensively identify with each person's interests in order to love fully, Talbott contends that we should understand God's love for a human as that which wills the very best for that individual over the long run. But this kind of love, says Talbott, cannot come in degrees, and so if it rests on every human, it must rest on them equally. Finally, Talbott maintains that Jordan fails to appreciate the way in which real love binds the interests of persons together such that a conflict of interests at the deepest conceivable level is logically impossible.

In Chapter 7, the late Marilyn McCord Adams joins Talbott in arguing for, even proclaiming, a conception of God who loves each and every human equally and deeply. This conception of God leads Adams to affirm universalism (i.e., the doctrine that all persons will one day be redeemed), the positive value of which is said not only to balance off the negative value of evils that are particularly horrendous but to swamp them entirely.

Adams's chapter was originally intended to be a talk at Fuller Theological Seminary, but, sadly, she fell seriously ill and was prevented from delivering that talk. Nevertheless, dutifully and despite having several reasons to do otherwise, Adams sent her chapter to the editors of this volume, knowing that it was the goal of the editors to include her chapter in the present book. Just months later, that illness took her life, making her contribution to this book perhaps the last piece of writing before her passing. The editors have chosen to keep Adams's chapter in its original form, which, though eminently readable and thought-provoking, is clearly designed to be heard rather than read in silence.

Adams's contribution is the final chapter in the volume which explicitly links the discussion of the nature and scope of God's love with ways of treating the problem of evil or divine hiddenness. It is worth noting that unlike Rea, Yadav, and Jordan, who each seek to undermine challenges to Christian theism by correcting what they see as inflated or ill-conceived understandings of God's love for humans, Adams, alongside Talbott, leans into the idea that God's love for humans is stronger than many imagine and is able to welcome and save all.[2] Readers are left to judge which emphasis provides a more compelling and theologically faithful conception of God, and they are invited to join these authors in crystalizing certain ways of approaching and thinking about the love of God.

In Chapter 8, R. T. Mullins examines the tenability of the classical doctrine of divine impassibility in light of the doctrine of divine love. Whereas proponents of divine passibility regularly contend that the nature of love entails the capacity to suffer with the beloved, advocates of divine impassibility are usually careful to opt for an

---

[2] Interestingly, the proposal of Adams, and to some degree Talbott, differs from Oord's proposal in a significant manner as well. While Oord supposes that God loves each person deeply, Oord is quick to claim that God's love is subject to certain logical and nomological limits which render God's love ineffectual in crucial respects. Against this, Adams in particular (at least in the present volume) stresses that God is able to bring about His loving ends for all creation.

understanding of love that does not obviously preclude impassibility. Mullins's strategy is to grant the impassibilist what he perceives as a favored account of love and to show that this account can only be satisfied by a passible God who not only is aware of each beloved human's first-person perspective but also experiences each of these perspectives from the "inside" in fine-grained detail.

Jordan Wessling, in Chapter 9, also argues against a widely held theological position. This time, however, the concern is not with God's emotional life but with the interrelation between God's love and punitive wrath. While Wessling agrees with theologians who adhere to what he calls the "unitary account," the claim that God's punishment is at bottom an expression of love for the one punished, Wessling rejects a common way in which God is said to penalize wrongdoers in love. The view with which Wessling takes issue is the idea that God does not impose external penalties on wrongdoers through special divine action, but simply allows sinful humans to undergo the terrible yet eventually inevitable consequences of their own behavior. Proponents of this "natural consequences view" of divine punishment often maintain that this manner of dealing with human sin is loving insofar as it enables God to respect the freedom and choices of His creatures. Against the natural consequences view, Wessling defends an alternative version of the unitary account which he claims is superior in various respects.

In his chapter, "The Indwelling of the Holy Spirit as Love," Adonis Vidu considers an under-discussed topic in contemporary theology, the inhabitation of the Holy Spirit in the believer. In particular, Vidu seeks to reconcile the notion of inhabitation as a work proper to the Holy Spirit with the doctrine of the inseparable operations of the Trinity. To that end, he argues that Aquinas's understanding of love as the form by which the Holy Spirit indwells believers is preferable to Karl Rahner's proposal that love is the consequence, not the form, of the "quasi-formal" presence of the Holy Spirit in the believer.

Vidu's chapter on the indwelling of the Spirit within believers provides something of a conceptual bridge between chapters focused on issues pertaining to divine love (as exemplified by Vanhoozer, Oord, Rea, Yadav, Jordan, Talbott, Adams, Mullins, and Wessling) and chapters focused on human love (as found in the remaining chapters). Leigh Vicens represents the first contribution of the latter sort. She notes that since the publication of Peter Strawson's seminal essay, "Freedom and Resentment," a number of philosophers have affirmed Strawson's claim that loving human relationships necessarily involve a susceptibility to resentment on the part of the lovers. In contradiction to this, Vicens argues that there is no necessary connection between love and resentment and that resentment-free love is a realistic and attainable ideal for humans. Clearly, Vicens's chapter has implications for how Christians should conceive of Christ's command to love one's neighbor as oneself.

In his contribution, Kent Dunnington likewise considers an issue that bears upon the love of neighbor. He raises the question "Is there a Christian *duty* to love one's neighbor as oneself?" Whereas most Christians maintain that the answer to this question is an obvious "yes" in light of Christ's second love command, Dunnington argues for the striking claim that this is not the case. Whatever Jesus was doing when he enjoined his disciples to love their neighbors as themselves, he was not, in Dunnington's view, declaring that the disciples have the moral obligation or duty to love in this way. To argue this point, Dunnington begins by defending and developing the notion that divine love is the regulative ideal for Christian ethics. But, he claims, to suppose that divine love is the ideal for human action and motivation does not entail that Christians have the *duty* to love their neighbors as they do themselves. Realizing that his thesis is deeply controversial, Dunnington devotes a substantial section of his chapter to perceived objections to his thesis before concluding with some of the proposal's practical social implications.

No collection of essays on the theology of love would be complete without a chapter on sex, specifically a chapter that relates, as it were, *eros* to *agape*. Erin Dufault-Hunter's contribution occupies this important space. Building upon Sarah Coakley's reminder that humans are embodied creatures that have been constructed for ecstatic communion with God, Dufault-Hunter contends that the human sex drive is at root a kind of longing for God and that sexual desire, even that which is unwanted, provides a kind of vehicle by which one can be brought into rich communion with God.

James T. Turner, Jr. concludes this book with a chapter on love and last things. Turner argues against recent philosophical theologians who maintain that virtuous character formation provides a central causal link between libertarian free will in pre-heavenly existence and moral impeccabiliy in the eschatological state. Such a position is mistaken, Turner submits, because there is reason to suppose that one cannot form one's character from morally peccable to morally impeccable through a history of choices. And even if this can be done, Turner claims that given the eschatological storyline presented in Scripture, there is a particular class of redeemed humans that simply do not have sufficient time to form their characters through a myriad of free decisions into a morally impeccable state prior to the eschaton. In place of that way of reconciling human freedom with redeemed creation, Turner proposes an exegetically grounded reason for maintaining that genuine love entails obedience to God, and further, that gloried human bodies, which are given rather than developed, explain perfect human love and obedience to God in the New Heavens and Earth.

The chapters in this volume certainly do not exhaust the issues related to divine and human love. Nevertheless, the topics treated herein may be viewed as a window into certain extant debates within the theology of love, while also paving the way for new avenues of inquiry. Indeed, if love is of the central importance that Christians routinely ascribe to it, few theological topics are more worthy of our attention than love, both divine and human.

1

Love Without Measure? John Webster's Unfinished Dogmatic Account of the Love of God, in Dialogue with Thomas Jay Oord's Interdisciplinary Theological Account

Kevin J. Vanhoozer

1 Introduction

"God is love" (1 Jn 4:8). This is a well-formed proposition of the type analytic theologians love—assuming they know what love means. Suggestions abound: "Love makes the world go round" and "Love came down from heaven"—two statements set forth in songs that, taken together, speak of an apparently powerful yet condescending force. Scripture adds two more measures to these metaphysical generalities: neither "height nor depth, nor anything else in all creation, will be able to separate us from the love of God in Christ Jesus our Lord" (Rom. 8:39). What kind of force, then, is the love of God? Can science verify it and, if not, can we still assert its reality? In particular, can we give a Christian dogmatic account of the love that is from God, is God, and is for us in Jesus Christ?

2 "For God *so* loved the world": One faith, five loves, two models

2.1 One faith

Christian theology is the "one faith" seeking understanding of the "one God" and all things in relation to him who is "over all and through all and in all" (Eph. 4:5-6). The doctrine of God is both the theologian's "reasonable worship" (Rom. 12:1) and possible waterloo: worship, because the more we come to understand the God who is love the more we are inclined to love and ascribe worthiness to him; waterloo, because to go wrong in one's doctrine of God is to go wrong everywhere else in theology. As John

Webster reputedly cautioned one of his students, "If your doctrine of God doesn't scare the bejeebers out of you, then you've missed the point."[1]

Although Webster's later work never strayed too far, or for too long, from the theme of God's immanent triune perfect life, the only divine attribute to which he devoted an entire monograph was holiness.[2] Conspicuous by its relative absence is the theme of the love of God. Even his 2004 essay "The Holiness and Love of God" is primarily about holiness.[3] By way of contrast, the love of God has become one of the, if not the most, prominent themes in contemporary systematic theology, where it is often paired with the theme of suffering and divine possibility.[4]

Theologians must be ever vigilant lest, in catching the prevailing intellectual and cultural winds, they sail into idolatry. Ludwig Feuerbach made this idolatrous exception the rule, claiming that *all* God-talk is actually only talk about human beings: "The truly religious man unhesitatingly assigns his own feelings to God. . . . the divine love is only human love made objective, affirming itself."[5] To follow Feuerbach and project human understandings of love onto the divine is to exchange the truth about God for a sigh. Contemporary theologians often make such Feuerbachian slips, particularly when they talk of God's love. D. A. Carson laments the tendency for culturally distorted pictures of love to replace the biblical picture: "The love of God has been sanitized, democratized, and above all sentimentalized."[6]

Theological realists nevertheless maintain that God's love is independent of our best attempts to speak and think about it. Theological realism means that it is possible to go wrong in our descriptions of God's love. Sadly, it is possible to exchange the truth of God's love for the lie of pie in the sky. As in so many disputes, the key issue is definition: Is the love of God an aspect of God's being or a quality of his work? Is the love of God an attribute, action, relation, all of the above, or something else altogether? And how can we convince others that our definition of the love of God is more than merely stipulative?[7]

2.2 Five loves

Words for love abound. C. S. Lewis wrote a whole book about four of them: *eros* or desire, *philia* or friendship, *storge* or affection, and *agape* or charity.[8] Thanks to recent

---

[1] http://blog.lexhampress.com/blog/2016/6/20/john-webster-19552016-surveying-a-man-and-his-mtier (accessed May 9, 2017).
[2] John Webster, *Holiness* (London: SCM, 2003).
[3] John Webster, *Confessing God* (London and New York: T&T Clark International, 2005), 109–30.
[4] In addition to Oord's several books, see inter alia, Vincent Brümmer, *The Model of Love: A Study in Philosophical Theology* (Cambridge: Cambridge University Press, 1993); Ronald Goetz, "The Suffering God: The Rise of a New Orthodoxy," *Christian Century* 103, no. 13 (April 16, 1986): 385–89; Jürgen Moltmann, *The Trinity and the Kingdom of God: The Doctrine of God* (London: SCM Press, 1981); and *The Work of Love: Creation as Kenosis*, ed. John Polkinghorne (Grand Rapids, MI: Eerdmans, 2001).
[5] Ludwig Feuerbach, *The Essence of Christianity*, trans. George Eliot (Buffalo, NY: Prometheus Books, 1989), 55–56.
[6] D. A. Carson, *The Difficult Love of God* (Wheaton, IL: Crossway, 2000), 11.
[7] For a review of the issues involved in defining and locating God's love, see my "The Love of God: Its Place, Meaning & Function in Systematic Theology," in *First Theology: God, Scripture, & Hermeneutics* (Downers Grove, IL: InterVarsity Press, 2001), 71–95.
[8] C. S. Lewis, *The Four Loves* (New York: Harcourt, Brace, 1960).

work in the semantics of biblical love language, however, we now recognize the fluidity of the Bible's terminology and the overly simplistic view of Anders Nygren that *agape* monolithically refers to a distinct kind of unilateral, unconditional, altruistic love unique to God.[9] Jn 3:35 uses *phileo* to speak of the Father's love for the Son, for example.[10] There are other important terms, like *hesed* ("steadfast love"), to consider too.

Carson waxes almost analytic when he examines, like an ordinary philosopher might, the different ways the Bible speaks of the love of God. The result is a helpful conceptual clarification of what we might call the "five loves" of God: (1) the peculiar love of the Father for the Son and the Son for the Father; (2) God's providential love over all he has made; (3) God's general love for the fallen world; (4) God's particular, "selecting" love toward the elect; and (5) God's conditional covenant love that waxes or wanes in proportion to people's obedience or disobedience.[11] This analysis is helpful as far as it goes, but we still do not have a definition. What *is* the love that God is?

Definitions are difficult. If the history of philosophy is a series of footnotes to Plato, it is largely because Plato worked so hard in his dialogues to define fundamental notions that are as elusive as they are familiar: "What is justice?"; "What is knowledge?"; and, we might add, "What is definition?" There are two broad types of the latter: intensional definitions express the essence or core meaning of a term or concept. This is a more deductive "from above" approach to definition that sets forth the necessary and sufficient conditions that must be met for something to fall under a particular concept. Extensional definitions proceed "from below," that is, by listing all the things that display what is being defined.

Scripture encourages us to think of God's love in a peculiarly extensional way. Rather than listing various examples, we are given a definitive paradigm, a Christologically intensive extension, as it were: "In *this* the love of God was made manifest . . . that God sent his only Son into the world. . . . In *this* is love . . . that [God] loved us and sent his Son to be the propitiation for our sins" (1 Jn 4:9-10).[12] We can make the definition more intensional by recalling Jesus's own teaching: "Greater love has no one than this, that someone lay down his life for his friends" (Jn 15:13; cf. 1 Jn 3:16). The cross shows us a love of which there is nothing greater nor better, for God lays down his life for friends and enemies alike: "God shows his love for us in that while we were still sinners, Christ died for us" (Rom. 5:8).

2.3 Two models

Everyone agrees *that* God is love, but not about what love means, or about what God was doing in Christ. John Peckham calls the two prevailing models "transcendent-voluntarist" (classical theism and its variations) and "immanent-experientialist"

---

[9] See John C. Peckham, "*Agape* Versus *Eros*? The Biblical Semantics of Divine Love," in *The Love of God: A Canonical Model* (Downers Grove, IL: InterVarsity Press, 2015), chap. 3, 68–88.
[10] D. A. Carson, *The Difficult Doctrine of the Love of God* (Wheaton, IL: Crossway Books, 2000), 27.
[11] Ibid., 16–20.
[12] Cf. Brunner: "The *idea*, the understanding of love—the Agape of the New Testament can only be understood from what *happens* in revelation." Emil Brunner, *The Christian Doctrine of God* (London: Lutterworth Press, 1949), 185.

(process theism and its variations).[13] They differ on several points, such as whether God's love is volitional or essential, whether or not God is emotionally invested in the world, and whether God is in a reciprocal relationship with the object of his love. The underlying issue is "whether the God-world love relationship is unilateral or bilateral,"[14] and what those options mean and entail.

In the eye of this love-storm is the issue of the nature of the God-world relationship itself. From the immanent-experientialist perspective common to process and relational thinkers, love makes God and the world in some sense codependents.[15] In their view, the transcendent-voluntarist model of a God who is unilaterally benevolent scores too low on the scale of emotional intelligence. Charles Hartshorne dismisses the classical theistic picture as "metaphysical snobbery toward relativity, dependence, or passivity."[16] Exhibit #1: Thomas Aquinas's claim that there is no "real relation" between God and the world: "In God there is no real relation to creatures, but a relation only in idea."[17] This disagreement about the metaphysical status of God's relationship to the world brings us to the heart of the definitional problem: Does God's love entail "real relations"—and does Aquinas mean the same thing as contemporary "relational" theists?[18]

What follows attempts to clarify whether God's love entails a real relation to the world by examining the work of two contemporary theologians, Thomas Oord and John Webster. In each case, I will pay special attention to the way in which they define God's love, first, *in se*, that is in relation to his own life and, second, to the way in which God's love gets worked out toward the world, *ad extra*, in creation, Christ, and providence. The aim is to clarify what is involved in giving a properly dogmatic account of the love of God: a speculative metaphysic (i.e., of perfect being), a scriptural history (i.e., of Jesus's passion), some combination of each, or something else besides.[19]

Why these two theologians? Both merit our attention: Oord, because he has come to be known as the "love theologian" and has also written prolifically on love in connection with philosophy and science; Webster, because his references to God's love, though

---

[13] Peckham, *Love of God*, 15–16.
[14] Ibid., 16.
[15] Cf. Brümmer: "Love must by its very nature be a relationship of free mutual give and take, otherwise it cannot be love at all." *The Model of Love*, 161.
[16] Charles Hartshorne, *Reality as Social Process: Studies in Metaphysics and Religion* (Glencoe, IL: The Free Press and Boston, MA: Beacon Press, 1953), 135.
[17] Aquinas, *Summa Theologiae* [hereafter *ST*] 1.13.7 (cf. 1.45.3). Context, however, is everything. Aquinas was part of a lively medieval conversation about relations that sought to work out God's intra-trinitarian relations as well as God's relation to the world with Aristotle's metaphysical category of relation, a "being toward something": "A relation is essentially what is towards another" (Aquinas, *ST*, 1.40.2. For helpful background to the discussion, see Najeeb Awad, "Thomas Aquinas' Metaphysics of 'Relation' and 'Participation' and Contemporary Trinitarian Theology," *New Blackfriars* 93, no. 1048 (2012): 652–70; Brian Davies, *The Thought of Thomas Aquinas* (Oxford: Clarendon Press, 1992), 75–79; Mark H. Hanninger, *Relations: Medieval Theories, 1250–1325* (Oxford: Clarendon Press, 1989); and Earl Muller, "Real Relations and the Divine: Issues in Thomas's Understanding of God's Relation to the World," *Theological Studies* 56 (1995): 673–95.
[18] On relational, "open," or process theists, see my *Remythologizing Theology: Divine Action, Passion, and Authorship* (Cambridge: Cambridge University Press, 2010), 117–24, 158–60.
[19] Space constraints prevent me from dealing here with two related questions: (1) Does the Son have a real relation to his humanity? (2) Does Jesus Christ have a real relationship to the world? For a possible answer that draws upon the *communicatio idiomatum*, see Muller, "Real Relations and the Divine," 679–94.

infrequent, represent an important dogmatic correction to several contemporary theological trends (many of which may be found in Oord). Though neither thinker explicitly picks up the mantle of analytic theology, each makes important use of conceptual distinctions. In particular, each takes up the question of real relation, but in very different ways. Contrasting these two in particular will help us better see where the conflict between the two approaches really lies.

3 Thomas Oord: God's love as essential *kenosis*

Thomas Jay Oord is a "relational" theologian in the Wesleyan tradition with interests in science and postmodernity whose overriding passion for several years has been love, which he has dutifully studied from all angles: philosophical, cosmological, biological (e.g., altruism), sociological, and, of course, theological. He offers a clear definition and a creative constructive proposal, for which he has a special name: "essential kenosis."[20] He is concerned to be biblical, and so heartily affirms that God's love for the world is a "real" relation.

3.1 The love of God: A metaphysical account

Oord opens his book *Defining Love* with a chapter on "love and the science-and-theology symbiosis." Love has become a topic of scientific investigation in, for example, the Institute for Research on Unlimited Love (founded 2001), whose mission is to increase public awareness of the dialogue taking place between various spiritualties and sciences (including evolution, genetics, neurology, and psychology) and of "the emotional and health benefits of love, both for those who give it and receive it."[21] The Institute traces its origins back to Sir John Templeton, who first suggested it and whose book *Pure Unlimited Love* became its unofficial charter. Unlimited love refers to both scope (everyone) and source ("a hidden reality or energy that underlies all that is good in the universe").[22] It is this force that arrests Oord's attention, and if I belabor the point it is to put his definition of love into context, namely, this newly emergent research program that he terms the "love, science, and theology symbiosis."[23]

Oord wants his definition to be adequate across the range of academic disciplines: "To love is to act intentionally, in sympathetic response to others . . . to promote overall well-being."[24] *Intentional action* speaks to the element of self-determination or freedom

---

[20] In what follows I will be drawing on mainly three of Oord's books: *Defining Love: A Philosophical, Scientific, and Theological Engagement* (Grand Rapids, MI: Brazos, 2010); *The Nature of Love: A Theology* (Danvers, MA: Chalice Press, 2010); and *The Uncontrolling Love of God: An Open and Relational Account of Providence* (Downers Grove, IL: IVP Academic, 2015).

[21] http://unlimitedloveinstitute.org/about.php (accessed May 10, 2017). Their definition of "unlimited love" is also noteworthy: "When the happiness, security, and well-being of another feels as meaningful and real to us as our own, or perhaps more so, we love that person."

[22] Oord, *Defining Love*, 4.

[23] Ibid.

[24] Ibid., 15.

inherent in love.[25] *Sympathetic response* means that love involves actual relations, relations that involve "genuine sway or effect of one agent on another."[26] Whitehead's "fellow-sufferer who understands" makes a similar point.[27] So does Vincent Brümmer, who calls love "a reciprocal relation."[28] Oord adds to this "mutuality tradition" a third element, namely, the *promotion of overall well-being*.

Jesus lived a life of love, and said many things about it, yet Oord claims that neither Jesus nor any other biblical author ever defines love.[29] As to the biblical passage cited previously ("We know love by this, that he laid down his life for us"; 1 Jn 3:16, NRSV), Oord comments that not all love as he defines it need to be self-sacrificial, a point on which feminist theologians as well often insist.[30]

Oord's "full-orbed" concept of love maintains not simply that God loves here and there or from time to time, but rather that God *is* love—love by nature; *essentially* love—and thus loves *necessarily*: "There are no possible circumstances in which God exists and yet does not express love."[31] God's love logically precedes God's will; the only choice is not whether but *how* to love. Oord's full-orbed concept of love involves both divine necessity and freedom. "God cannot not love."[32] God must act intentionally in sympathetic response to others to promote overall well-being. Yet there is contingency as well as necessity, for the *form* that love takes depends upon creaturely actions and responses. Call it "full-Oord" love: *that* God loves others is a foregone conclusion, but "*how* God loves others is a free choice on God's part."[33] God always acts to promote overall well-being, but his sympathetic response may take various forms. This helpful distinction goes a long way toward accounting for the diverse biblical senses of love we previously examined.

Love, for Oord, is essential to not only God's nature but also God's "foremost and governing attribute."[34] This elevation of love to first among equals in the pantheon of divine attributes is a move of no little consequence, for in making it, Oord departs from the traditional doctrine of divine simplicity, according to which God is the whole of his divine perfections. To rank love over other divine attributes is to suggest that God is made up of different parts, or properties, that jostle to sit as it were at the right hand of God's being. The warrant for Oord's claim is not transparent: Is it Scripture (the biblical narrative), metaphysics (the idea of an infinitely perfect being), or some hybrid of the two? What is clear is that, whatever occupies the driver's seat of his theological method, it is the problem of evil in the rearview mirror that he is working hard to escape. Neither classical nor open theism "provide[s] a satisfactory

---

[25] Ibid., 17.
[26] Ibid., 19.
[27] This is Alfred North Whitehead's description of God in his 1927 Gifford Lectures, published as *Process and Reality*.
[28] Brümmer, *The Model of Love*, 162.
[29] Oord, *The Nature of Love*, 15.
[30] Ibid., 28.
[31] Ibid., 55.
[32] Oord, *Defining Love*, 189.
[33] Ibid., 190.
[34] Oord, *The Uncontrolling Love of God*, 144.

answer to why a loving God capable of controlling others . . . fails to prevent genuine evil."[35]

3.2 Essential *kenosis*: Creation, Christ, and Trinity

Oord is critical of openness theologians like Clark Pinnock and John Sanders who hold that God *could* prevent evil but does not, out of respect for creaturely freedom and a lawfully regulated world. Voluntary self-restraint makes for terrible theodicy: "The God who could prevent any genuine evil unilaterally is responsible for *allowing* genuine evil."[36] Oord takes another route: "God's loving nature requires God to create a world with creatures God cannot control"[37]—hence Oord's concept of the "uncontrolling" love of God.

"Solving" the problem of evil requires rejecting creation ex nihilo, a concept that implies God has unlimited power, including the capacity to coerce. Coercion assumes "a nonrelational view in which one agent unilaterally controls others"[38] and is thus incompatible with love. Creation ex nihilo makes it difficult to say that God's love for the world expresses an essential aspect of God's nature. How could it if "there was a time when it [the world] was not?" Oord thus asserts God's necessary but uncontrolling love for creation, largely because of pressure from the problem of evil.

Interestingly, Oord resists the temptation to explain God's essentially loving nature by appealing to the Trinity. In an essay responding to Keith Ward's *Christ and the Cosmos: A Reformulation of the Trinitarian Doctrine*,[39] Oord associates the idea that God is intra-trinitarian love with the idea of the social Trinity, only to reject it on the grounds that it tends toward tritheism. How, then, can God be essentially, in himself, love? Oord's answer: God is essentially love because he creates *and has always been* creating creaturely "others" whose well-being he then desires to promote. In other words, the ground of God's loving relationality is not his triune life *ad intra* but his everlasting creation of others *ad extra*. Oord makes clear that this is not creation ex nihilo but what he calls *creatio ex creatione en amore* (creation out of what God previously created in love).[40]

Is this view—that God's loving nature requires him to always be creating creatures he cannot control—*Christian* theology? Oord certainly thinks so: "Jesus Christ is the center of a Christian theology that makes love central."[41] The position also has a proof

---

[35] Oord, *The Nature of Love*, 113.
[36] Oord, *The Uncontrolling Love of God*, 142.
[37] Ibid., 146.
[38] Oord, *The Nature of Love*, 103.
[39] (Cambridge: Cambridge University Press, 2015).
[40] See Thomas Jay Oord, "Can God Be Essentially Loving without Being Essentially Social? An Affirmation of and Alternative for Keith Ward," *Philosophia Christi* 18, no. 2 (2016): 353–61; and "God Always Creates out of Creation in Love: *Creatio ex Creatione a Natura Amoris*," in *Theologies of Creation: Creatio ex Nihilo and Its New Rivals*, ed. Thomas Jay Oord (New York: Routledge, 2014), 109–22. Oord apparently believes that God creates the universe out of antecedent universes (see the chapter "Love and Cosmology," in *Defining Love: A Philosophical, Scientific, and Theological Engagement* (Grand Rapids, MI: Brazos, 2010), 137–72.
[41] Oord, *The Nature of Love*, 122.

text (Phil. 2:5-11), though what Oord does with it is worth examining.[42] To recast his argument in the form of a syllogism:

(1) The person and work of Jesus Christ reveal God.
(2) Phil. 2:5-11 describes Christ's person and work in terms of *self-giving* (Oord's preferred translation for the verb *ekenosen* in v. 7, usually rendered "he emptied himself") action (and passion) for the well-being of others (i.e., love).
(3) Therefore, God is (necessarily) love, which is to say, essentially kenotic (self-giving).

Let me make two observations about this argument.

In the first place, Oord jumps on the bandwagon of what I have elsewhere termed kenotic-perichoretic relational theology by viewing *kenosis* as pertaining to the doctrine of God proper rather than to Christology in particular: "Theologians today use *kenosis* primarily to describe how Jesus *reveals* God's nature."[43] *Kenosis* now chiefly explains not the relation between the human and divine natures of Christ but the God-world relationship itself. Creation is kenotic, involving a constriction of or limitation on God's power and agency. Elsewhere I have criticized those who export without theological license concepts that originate in one doctrine to another, thus risking dogmatic disorder.[44] In particular, Oord exports *kenosis* from Christology to the doctrine of God: Jesus's humbling himself by assuming the form of a servant morphs into the metaphysical suggestion "that God's power is essentially persuasive and vulnerable, not overpowering and aloof."[45]

Second, Oord draws from Phil. 2:5-11 a distinction between voluntary and involuntary divine self-limitation, between volitional and essential *kenosis*. Many open theists follow Friedrich Schelling, Jürgen Moltmann, and others in arguing that God, in creating a world of free creatures, voluntarily limits his own power and agency, in some sense "sacrificing" himself as an indispensable condition for free and meaningful creaturely existence.[46] Oord will have none of it, however, and one reviewer commends him for rejecting "one of the silliest ideas ever promulgated . . . the notion that although, *in se*, God is omnipotent and sovereign, God has freely chosen not to exercise divine power in order to secure creaturely freedom."[47] What Oord finds objectionable in voluntary kenotic creation theology is the idea that God *could* prevent evil but chooses not to: "A God who voluntarily self-limits ought to become un-self-limited periodically,

---

[42] Oord's most extended engagement with Phil. 2:5-11 is in *The Uncontrolling Love of God*, 153–60.
[43] Oord, *Uncontrolling Love*, 155. For more on kenotic-perichoretic relational theology, see my *Remythologizing Theology*, chap. 3.
[44] For example, viewing the God/world relation as perichoretic is an instance of "illegitimate Trinitarian transfer," that is, exporting a truth about the immanent Trinity to God's relation to the world (see my *Remythologizing Theology*, 130–31, 157–61).
[45] Oord, *Uncontrolling Love*, 155.
[46] On Schelling, see Philip Clayton, *The Problem of God in Modern Thought* (Grand Rapids, MI: Eerdmans, 2000), chap. 9. See also Jürgen Moltmann, "God's Kenosis in the Creation and Consummation of the World," in *The Work of Love: Creation as Kenosis*, ed. John Polkinghorne (Grand Rapids, MI: Eerdmans, 2001), 137–51.
[47] Samuel Powell, review of Oord, *Uncontrolling Love of God*, *Wesleyan Theological Journal* 51.1 (Spring, 2016), 267.

in the name of love, to prevent genuine evil from occurring."[48] The God of voluntary kenoticism is an imperfect lover.

Oord reads Phil. 2:5-11 as a lesson about God's essential nature, a metaphysical rather than a Christological hymn. Kenotic love derives not from a voluntary divine decision, or from some external constraint, but from God's eternal and unchanging nature: "The gift of Godself to creation is essential to what it means to be God. God necessarily relates with and gives to creatures, because necessarily loves us."[49] Oord interprets *kenosis* not as a verb that signals a covenantal initiative and subsequent history, with a before and after, but as a noun that pictures the God/world relation as permanent, essential, and metaphysical. Oord does speak of God's "love covenant" with creation in connection with the Hebrew term *hesed* ("steadfast love"), but he goes on to say, somewhat confusedly, that, "God's covenant with creation is part of God's eternal nature."[50]

3.3 Providence and the uncontrolling love of God

Oord has no wish to abandon the Creator/creature distinction: God is the *only* creative agent who necessarily and everlastingly exists; God has *more* creative power than any other agent ("God is the mightiest being that exists"[51]); God is the *singular* creative agent whose nature is love.[52] As to divine providence, it is essentially a work of love whereby God gives freedom to creatures and works with them noncoercively to maximize well-being. Oord is to be commended for tackling some of the most intractable problems of Christian theology, yet his thesis may raise more questions than it answers, for the only problem it really resolves is why there is evil in the world if God is essentially love. The answer (spoiler alert!) is that God's hands are essentially tied by his uncontrolling loving nature: "God *cannot* unilaterally prevent genuine evil,"[53] for God *cannot* coerce creaturely agency or human freedom.[54]

What, however, does God's love actually *do*? If it is real, it should make a difference, but what kind of difference does it make? *Uncontrolling* suggests what love is not (viz., coercive); it does not specify what positive force love has. If to love is "to act intentionally, in sympathetic response to others . . . to promote overall well-being," then how does God providentially promote overall well-being?

Oord affirms God's causal force and action. God sustains creation, everlastingly providing capacity to every creature after its own kind as well as law-like regularity to creation as a whole. The third traditional aspect of providence—*gubernatio* (governance)—proves trickier for Oord to describe. God gives humans guidance through the law and, in Christ, an example to follow, but guidance is not yet governance.

---

[48] Oord, *The Nature of Love*, 124.
[49] Ibid, 125.
[50] Ibid., 131.
[51] Ibid., 128.
[52] Ibid., 137.
[53] Oord, *Uncontrolling Love of God*, 167. Emphasis in original.
[54] Oord says he is using *coercion* in the "metaphysical sense" of "complete control" or "unilateral determination in which the one coerced loses all capacity for causation, self-organization, agency or free will" (*Uncontrolling Love of God*, 180–86).

Oord finds it difficult to explain how God, who is "spirit" (Jn 4:24), can exert causal force upon creation. God does not have a localized body, yet he can "marshal through persuasion those with localized bodies" to exert causal force.[55] What kind of causal force? Jesus exerted force in cleansing the temple, but Oord insists that even that was not coercive.[56] God's love is not coercive but cruciform: it has attractive power, the lure of goodness.[57] God's love is a pervasive, persuasive, though not necessarily efficacious influence: "All creatures feel God's direct, causal call."[58] "Call" is the operative term and always involves an invitation for creatures to act in ways that optimize overall well-being. God thus loves creatures not by strongly causing (i.e., determining) good things, but rather by constantly issuing non-effectual calls, thus weakly causing good things (when they happen). Can divine providence ever do more than cast its lure? Can God ever catch the profane fish?

Oord offers two examples that repay examination. The first, nature miracles, appears at first blush to be conclusive evidence that God *does* sometimes control situations. Oord nevertheless demurs, maintaining that God is always present to and active in creation and hence never needs to intervene.[59] Oord rejects the slightest whiff of divine intervention, for even benevolence, if it results in unilateral causation, would be coercive. Hence, while a miracle is "an unusual and good event that occurs through God's special action in relation to creation,"[60] this "special action" must be something other than intervention (though I know not what).

Essential *kenosis* "presumes that creaturely causation of some kind is present in all miracles, even when biblical narratives do not identify the creaturely causes."[61] Consider, for example, the great saving event of the Old Testament, the parting of the Red Sea. Oord acknowledges the challenge of having to explain this event without appealing to divine intervention: "Admittedly, the idea that miracles require creaturely cooperation is more difficult to fathom when we consider the cooperation of aggregate entities such as waves [and] wind. . . . At a minimum, my proposal requires that God not coerce wind [and] waves, in the sense of totally controlling them."[62] God may have foreknown with high probability that winds would push back the water, and coordinated this prediction with an invitation to Israel to pass through the Red Sea.[63] Tellingly, however, Oord fails to deal with the episode where Jesus works a miracle that elicits the astonished response, "Who is this, that even the wind and the sea obey him?" (Mk 4:41).

---

[55] Oord, *Uncontrolling Love*, 179.
[56] Ibid., 184.
[57] See Gregory A. Boyd, *The Crucifixion of the Warrior God: Interpreting the Old Testament's Violent Portraits of God in Light of the Cross* (Minneapolis, MN: Fortress Press, 2017), vol. 1, chap. 4, 143–56.
[58] Oord, *Defining Love*, 194.
[59] Ibid., 195.
[60] Ibid., 196.
[61] Oord, *Uncontrolling Love*, 207.
[62] Ibid., 176, n. 59.
[63] He also appeals to the butterfly effect and says that some action by Moses or Pharaoh may have triggered a chain of events that eventually affected the system of Nature that is the Red Sea (Ibid., 209).

To this point, Oord has not adequately distinguished God's special action from his constant loving activity to all creation. This brings us to a second example: Oord's account of God's raising Jesus from the dead. The biblical authors testify that God raised Jesus from the dead (Acts 2:24, 4:10, 13:30; Gal. 1:1; Col. 2:12; 1 Thess. 1:10). Oord agrees, with the qualification that Jesus's resurrection did not involve coercion. Cells, organs, and other parts can resist God's offer of new possible ways of being: "Our bodies may not cooperate with God's healing plans."[64] Oord therefore takes seriously the "limited freedom" of Jesus's dead body: "Even dead bodies—Jesus's dead body in particular—retain some degree of responsiveness to stimuli."[65] Even here, then, at the highpoint of the Father's love for the Son—arguably the greatest mighty act of God in the New Testament—Oord says that "the creaturely side of Jesus conceivably played a cooperative role."[66] Whether this approach does justice to biblical affirmations like Acts 13:30 ("But God raised him from the dead") no doubt remains a talking point.[67]

God's love for the world is, for Oord, clearly a real relation. What is less clear is what kind of reality it is. I am left with five questions: (1) How does Oord reconcile his definition of love as intentional action with his insistence that God necessarily loves everyone, everywhere, all the time? (2) Does Oord truly preserve the Creator/creature distinction, or is God on the same metaphysical level with the rest of created reality? If the call to love that God gives each creature is in one sense "no different from the causal influence that other creatures exert,"[68] then doesn't God exist on the same plane of being as everything else? (3) Does Oord derive his definition of love from the event of Jesus Christ or from somewhere else? (4) In "solving" the problem of evil by stipulating God's nature as uncontrolling love, does Oord render insoluble the equally important question, "What may we hope?" Oord stresses the importance of human participation in what he calls "participatory eschatology": "God's kenotic love invites creatures to participate in securing victory."[69] But why think that the entropic universe, much less rebellious children, will come around to God's way at the end of time? Does not this solution to the problem of evil render evil metaphysically unavoidable and necessary? (5) If Oord is right, is the God who is uncontrolling love more deserving of our worship or sympathy?

4 John Webster: God's love as essential *plerosis*

To move from Oord to John Webster is to discover a different landscape with a properly theological atmosphere, less apologetic than dogmatic. Elsewhere I have written on how Webster roused me from my own nondogmatic slumbers, awakening me to

---

[64] Oord, *Uncontrolling Love*, 213.
[65] Oord, *Nature of Love*, 151.
[66] Ibid. Oord also suggests that the divine Son would cooperate with God's persuasive call to rise from the dead.
[67] It also puts a different spin on what we think will happen to our own bodies on the Day of the Lord. I just hope my cells will be in a cooperative mood!
[68] Oord, *Defining Love*, 194.
[69] Oord, *Nature of Love*, 152.

the possibility of a theological theology that goes against the grain of much modern theology, with its concern for the intellectual respectability of God-talk, perhaps by attending to the theology-and-science symbiosis, a concern Webster did not share.[70]

4.1 The love of God: A dogmatic account

The stark contrast between the form and content of Webster and Oord's approaches is apparent from the start. Where Oord begins with the interdisciplinary dialogue about love, Webster focuses on the intra-trinitarian dialogue, namely, the eternal fellowship of Father, Son, and Spirit. A well-ordered Christian dogmatics first treats God in relation to himself, and only then God in relation to creatures. To begin anywhere else than God in relation to himself is to court dogmatic disorder and untheological theology. This is as true of love as any other perfection: "Christian faith and theology begin their talk about love, as they begin their talk about all things, by talking of God's nature and his inner and outer works."[71] Webster's prose falls prostrate as he moves from dogmatic indicative to doxological exclamative, citing a prayer from Kierkegaard's *Works of Love*: "How could love be rightly discussed if you were forgotten, O God of love, source of all love in heaven and on earth, you who spared nothing but gave all in love, you who are love . . . you who made manifest what love is, you, our Savior and Redeemer, who gave yourself to save all!"[72]

The salient point is that, for Webster, "all Christian doctrines are functions of the doctrine of the Trinity."[73] Furthermore, when it comes to the doctrine of the Trinity, Webster consistently gives pride of place to the immanent Trinity, God's own perfect triune life: "God's immanent triune perfection is the first and last object of Christian theological reflection and governs all else."[74] There is little wiggle-room here in Webster's first theology. Again, the contrast with Oord could hardly be greater, because, in the words of one reviewer, the immanent Trinity "seems extraneous to [Oord's] main concerns. . . . His system would hang together with no tri-unity at all—just God as one undifferentiated Spirit."[75]

Webster's enthusiasm for the immanent Trinity stems not from an interest in speculative theology but rather from an evangelical concern to preserve the integrity of the God of the Gospel: "An account of the gospel which neglected theological metaphysics would soon falter in its attempts to speak of the God of the gospel."[76]

---

[70] See my "Analytics, Poetics, and the Mission of Dogmatic Discourse," in *The Task of Dogmatics: Explorations in Theological Method*, ed. Oliver D. Crisp and Fred Sanders (Grand Rapids, MI: Zondervan, 2017).
[71] John Webster, "The Fruit of the Spirit: Walk by the Spirit (part 1)," http://www.reformation21.org/featured/the-fruit-of-the-spirit-walk-by-the-spirit-part-1.php (accessed May 10, 2017).
[72] Ibid.
[73] John Webster, *God without Measure: Working Papers in Christian Theology* vol. 1 *God and the Works of God* (London: Bloomsbury T&T Clark, 2016), 128.
[74] Ibid.
[75] Rob L. Staples, "Review of Oord, *The Nature of Love*," *Wesleyan Theological Journal* 42, no. 2 (2011): 267.
[76] John Webster, "It Was the Will of the Lord to Bruise Him: Soteriology and the Doctrine of God," in *God of Salvation: Soteriology in Theological Perspective*, ed. Ivor J. Davidson and Murray A. Rae (Farnham: Ashgate, 2011), 21.

Only a robust doctrine of the Trinity can provide "an identity description of the agent of salvation, upon which a definition of salvation depends."[77] Call it Webster's law of "immanent domain": in order to do justice to the story of salvation, and every other doctrine, we need to be clear about the ontology of the saving agents—Father, Son, and Spirit. The God who comes to save the world (economic Trinity) is able to save only because he has no need of and is perfect independent of the world (immanent Trinity).

God's perfect life in himself constitutes the ground of his self-communication to creation, and it is the triune character of God's perfect life that is "the distinguishing feature of the confession of God's aseity."[78] Here is how Webster paraphrases Jesus's statement in Jn 5:26: "For as the Father has life in himself, so he has granted the Son also to have life in himself": "*God is from himself, and from himself God gives himself.*"[79] The life God has in himself is the relations of Father, Son, and Spirit, and it is precisely in these intra-trinitarian relationships that God lives, and moves, and has his perfect being.

That God has life in himself is crucial for understanding the divine attributes or perfections, including love. Webster refuses to ground his account of divine perfections in either phenomenology or perfect being theology, for each mistakenly attempts to determine the content of the divine predicate first, and only then to apply it to God. Christian dogmatics proceeds contrariwise, giving conceptual expansion to the name of God, which is his enacted identity. We only understand the missions of the Son and Spirit (the economy) in light of the eternal procession of the persons in the Godhead (the immanent Trinity). This inner activity—the infinite underivative movement of God in himself—is "the founding condition for the economy."[80] In himself, God is the mutual love and delight of Father, Son, and Spirit, an eternal communication of the goodness of his own life and light. This is God's essential nature. The form this love takes "is God's inner acts of relation" (i.e., paternity, generation, and spiration).[81] When Webster speaks of God's love, then, it is principally this inner communion of the divine being he has in mind.

Unlike Oord, Webster does not have a set definition of love. Let me therefore propose one on his behalf, keeping in mind his law of immanent domain, that is, the rule that all God's perfections must be referred to God's triune life *in se*: *God's love is his self-communicative activity by which he communicates goodness—ultimately his own light and life—to others for the sake of consummation and communion.*[82]

---

[77] Ibid.
[78] John Webster, "Life in and of Himself: Reflections on God's Aseity," in *Engaging the Doctrine of God: Contemporary Protestant Perspectives*, ed. Bruce L. McCormack (Grand Rapids, MI: Baker Academic, 2008), 113.
[79] Ibid., 114. Emphasis in original.
[80] Webster, *God without Measure*, vol. 1, 86.
[81] Webster, "The Fruit of the Spirit."
[82] Elsewhere I have defined God's love as "God's active disposition to communicate the Father's communion with the Son to others in the Spirit" (Kevin Vanhoozer, "Love of God," in *New Dictionary of Theology: Historical and Systematic*, 2nd ed., ed. Martin Davie, Tim Grass, Stephen R. Holmes et al. (Downers Grove, IL: InterVarsity Press, 2016), 536. Webster defines human love in at least one place: "Love is an active inclination of the self to a known good, an extension of mind, will, and affections to that good, and it generates an aspiration to be in its company, there to find satisfaction" (Webster, "Fruit of the Spirit").

God in himself is love as the eternally active fellowship of Father, Son, and Spirit. This was Carson's first category for thinking about the love of God: the peculiar love of Father for the Son and vice versa. For Webster, this intra-trinitarian love is the source from which all the other senses of love flow: the Trinity is love defined, the incarnation and atonement are love enacted, the salvation of the sinner through the work of the Spirit is love communicated, and the reconciliation of all things in Christ is love consummated.[83] Here is the key implication, to be explored further below: God's love for what is not God (i.e., creation/creatures) is "a turning out of fullness, not out of lack."[84]

One other feature of Webster's law of immanent domain distinguishes his position from Oord's. Where Oord insists that love was God's primary or essential attribute, Webster holds to a more traditional account of divine simplicity, according to which each of God's perfections describes the whole of God's being. In his essay, "The Holiness and Love of God," Webster defines God's holiness as his absolute difference from all else—his set-apartness—and notes that this is also a quality of God's love.[85] We must therefore speak of God's holy love—as well as his wise, powerful, patient, and so on, love—and his loving holiness.

4.2 Essential *plerosis*: Trinity, Christ, and creation

God's perfect life is the sheer positive plentitude of God's triune being: "To speak of God's perfection is to speak of the fullness with which he is and acts as the one he is."[86] Webster thus helps us to see that the love of God, and any other divine perfection, is a matter not of God's essential *kenosis* but essential *plerosis* ("fullness"). From this ground, Webster derives an important corollary: "God's integral perfection does not exclude but rather includes the movement of his perfect being toward creatures in the works of love."[87] Far from being essentially limited in his dealing with creation, as Oord contends, God according to Webster is essentially limitless: "God's boundless immanent life is the ground of his communication of life."[88]

The distinction between divine *kenosis* and *plerosis* brings both the dogmatic fruitfulness of Webster's law of immanent domain and the starkness of his contrast with Oord into sharper focus. For Webster, the *kenosis* of Phil. 2:5-11 is not the revelation of a God who is essentially limited in power; it is rather an assurance that the subject of the history of Jesus is the one through whom all things were created and in whom all things hold together, the second person of the Trinity who has life in himself (Jn 5:26). Even under the form of a servant, says Paul, "the whole fullness [*pleroma*] of deity dwells bodily" in Jesus Christ (Col. 2:9). The incarnation is not the

---

[83] Cf. John W. Mahony: "The Trinity is love defined, the incarnation is the love of the Trinity displayed, and the salvation of the sinner is the love of the Trinity realized" ("Love in the Triune Community?" in *The Love of God*, ed. Christopher Morgan (Wheaton, IL: Crossway, 2016), 97.
[84] Webster, *Confessing God*, 198.
[85] Ibid., 109–30.
[86] Webster, "God's Perfect Life," in *God's Life in Trinity*, ed. Miroslav Volf (Minneapolis, MN: Fortress Press, 2006), 143.
[87] Ibid., 145.
[88] Webster, "Soteriology and the Doctrine of God," 18.

event of God's self-contraction but self-communication, the publication of the radiant form and enactment of the glory God is in himself "in the perfect majesty and beauty of his being."[89]

Webster insists, with the tradition, that God is complete in himself—that God is love—without creation. Neither creation nor the cross constitutes God as love; rather, they are events that establish and accomplish his loving purpose of holy fellowship with creatures.[90] Our species is so self-centered that we easily forget that God *has* a life, quite apart from us, and always has. Father, Son, and Spirit have been sharing light, life, and love eternally. We therefore misunderstand God's love for the world if we fail to respect what Webster calls "the Christian distinction," namely, "the difference between God and creatures which is beyond both reciprocity and dialectic."[91]

Contra Oord, God is not simply the biggest thing around nor has he been creating forever: "The creator is not contained with *ta panta*: he is 'before' (*pro*) them (Col. 1:17)."[92] Webster affirms creation as a gratuitous act, a loving act whereby the Triune God freely, out of the abundance of his sheer generosity, communicates his goodness to the "other" of creation: "Out of his unrestricted goodness, God wills and brings into being objects of love other than himself, conferring life and, in the case of his human creatures, giving a capacity to love."[93] The necessity with which love creates is not the involuntary necessity that Oord thinks follows from God's essentially loving nature, but "purely the necessity of God's own self-determination to be in fellowship with that which is other than himself."[94]

Creation ex nihilo is at once a radical beginning and a commitment to an enduring relation. It is the nature of this relation—the God/world relation of love—that is of particular interest here: "By the work of divine love, finite things come to share in the universal good of being, but only in a finite manner, and only as they stand in relation to the creator God.... This relation *constitutes* creatures."[95] The first thing to note is that God is complete within himself, and neither gains nor loses anything by the existence or nonexistence of his creatures. Webster next makes a point that at first blush sounds paradoxical but on closer inspection proves dogmatically decisive and marks a decisive parting of the ways from Oord: "To deny that God bears a 'real' relation to created things is to characterize the *kind* of relation which he has to creatures."[96]

The way Aquinas makes this point has proven controversial, for he says the relation is "real" (i.e., ontological) on the side of the creature but "conceptual" (i.e., notional) on the side of God. This idea perturbs many who read Scripture as describing a God who

---

[89] Webster, *God without Measure*, vol. 1, 73.
[90] Webster, *Confessing God*, 126.
[91] Webster, *God without Measure*, 90. Webster takes the phrase "the Christian distinction" from Robert Sokolowski, *The God of Faith and Reason* (Notre Dame, IN: University of Notre Dame Press, 1982).
[92] Webster, *God without Measure*, 91.
[93] Webster, "The Fruit of the Spirit." See also John Webster, "Creation out of Nothing," in *Christian Dogmatics: Reformed Theology for the Church Catholic*, ed. Michael Allen and Scott R. Swain (Grand Rapids, MI: Baker Academic, 2016), 126–47, esp. 138.
[94] Webster, *Confessing God*, 198.
[95] Webster, *God without Measure*, vol. 1, 107.
[96] Ibid.

is actively, dialogically, and emotionally involved in human history. It certainly disturbs Oord and other open or "relational" theists. The question is whether a misleading picture of relationality holds moderns captive. Moderns typically have difficulty with Aquinas's comparing God to a stone column, which has no real relation to animals (or persons) who walk around it.[97] Columns do not *care*. Yet Scripture depicts God's relation to creation in caring and *personal* terms—father, husband, and shepherd, to name but a few.

Everything hangs on the concept of a "real relation." Thankfully, Webster wrote an essay on this very point: "*Non Ex Aequo*: God's Relation to Creatures."[98] The Latin means "not from an equality." All created beings have a real relationship to God because they are ordered to God as to their beginning, continuation, and end. If God *had* a "real" relation to the world—a relation that runs in both directions and thus makes the two terms codependent—then he and his creatures would have to compete on the same causal level. In affirming that God has a "mixed" relation with the world ("real" on the side of the creature; a "relation of reason" on the side of God), Webster is retrieving Aquinas, who wants to say that creation depends on the Creator, who does *not* depend on it.[99]

Both Aquinas and Webster do affirm "real relations" in God—relations according to *being* (the way things are) and not simply to *speech* (the way things are talked about). However, the only real relations that constitute God's eternal being are the *ad intra* trinitarian processions intrinsic to God's perfect life. For example, the Father's relationship to the Son is constitutive of his fatherhood in a way that his relation to Abraham is not. Hence the Father and the Son are in a "real relation" (paternity; filiation). The trinitarian processions alone are relations without which God would not be God; hence they are real relations *ad intra*.[100] To be sure, Scripture depicts God interacting with creatures, but these relations are not constitutive of God; they have no bearing on his essential being. Two more examples should make this clear: (1) my knowing the speed of light depends on (i.e., has a real relation to) that external reality, but the speed of light does not depend on my knowing it; (2) the character of Oliver Twist has a real relation to Charles Dickens (who is the ground of Oliver's being), but Dickens has only a logical relation to Oliver (Oliver's existence depends on Dickens's creative authorship but not vice versa). Creation, similarly, depends on God's creative power or "authorship." It is not that notional or logical relations are insignificant, much less fictional; it is rather that they are ontologically non-constitutive and causally asymmetrical.[101]

---

[97] Aquinas appeals to this image in *ST*, 1.13.7.
[98] In Webster, *God without Measure*, vol. 1, 115–26.
[99] See further Matthew R. McWhorter, "Aquinas on God's Relation to the World," *New Blackfriars* 94 (2013): 3–18; and Michael J. Dodds, "Ultimacy and Intimacy: Aquinas on the Relation between God and the World," in *Ordo Sapientiae et Amoris*, ed. C.-J. P. de Oliviera (Fribourg: Editions Universitaires, 1993), 211–27.
[100] See Aquinas, *ST*, 1.28.1-4.
[101] See further Muller, "Real Relations and the Divine," 673–95. See also Brian Davies's suggestion that God's interactions with the world count as "merely Cambridge changes"—that is, an apparent change in the way something can be described (e.g., "the stone column that was on my left is now on my right") when in fact the thing has not changed in itself (*The Thought of Thomas Aquinas*, 77–79).

What does this have to do with God's love for the world? Everything. Webster denies God's "real" relation in order to provide clearer specification to the true nature of the relation. The goal is a properly theological understanding of the God-world relation rather than an extension of a univocal concept of relation learned from observing the created order. God is not one term in a dyad, in a zero-sum metaphysical arena, which is what "mutuality" and "reciprocity" suggest. Webster retrieves Thomas's distinction, denying God's "real relation" to the world, in order to better establish the true nature of God's loving relation to the world. It is precisely because God lacks nothing and needs nothing from the world that he can communicate his own good fullness to it: "God is . . . inexhaustibly alive, stable and entire in himself and so beyond the reach of any agent or act of contestation."[102] There can be no real relation to creation because in God there is "no constitutive relation to that which is not himself."[103] Webster insists that it is only by remembering that God lives and acts out of his own perfect life that we can rightly read Scripture's description of God's dealings with creatures. The one who is present and active in human history is the one whose being is self-subsistent and wholly realized—perfect: "It is precisely because God's relation to creatures is not 'real' that his love is of infinite scope and benevolence. In God, absence of reciprocity is not absence of relation but the ground of limitless relation."[104] It is because God is not in "real relation" to the world that he can love so intimately and impassionedly: "Only because the God who is for us is in himself God, entire without us, is his being for us more than a projection of our corrupt longing for a satisfying divine counterpart."[105] In sum, it is precisely for the love of God that Christian theologians ought to refrain from saying that God is in a "real" relation to the world.

4.3 Providence and the unequalable love of God

Providence is God's love *ad extra*, his outer work of doing good in and to creation: "Providence is that work of divine love for temporal creatures whereby God ordains and executes their fulfillment in fellowship with himself."[106] The doctrine of providence is "a conceptual meditation on the . . . hope that this work of love generates."[107]

Immediately we see a contrast with Oord. Webster will not be forced into reacting to the problem of evil. This way leads to dogmatic disorder, namely, "dominance by questions . . . not derived from the Christian confession."[108] It is not the amount of evil that makes it problematic for providence but rather our refusal to focus on providence rather than evil. This is both a spiritual and argumentative task: "Reconciling providence

---

[102] Webster, *God without Measure*, vol. 1, 120. Aquinas defines the love of God as benevolence, willing of some good to another (*ST*, 1.20.1).
[103] Ibid., 121.
[104] Ibid., 125.
[105] Ibid., 126. See further Thomas Weinandy, *Does God Suffer* (Notre Dame, IN: University of Notre Dame Press, 2000); and Rob Lister, *God Is Impassible and Impassioned: Toward a Theology of Divine Emotion* (Wheaton, IL: Crossway, 2013).
[106] Webster, *God without Measure*, vol. 1, 127.
[107] Ibid.
[108] Ibid., 129.

and horrors is a task within fellowship with God."[109] In dogmatics, Webster insists, *disputatio* (apologetics) is subordinate to *expositio* (conceptual elaboration). In this spirit, Webster describes the content of providence as an account of "how the Father's plan for the fullness of time is set forth in Christ and made actual by the Holy Spirit."[110]

"Because God loves his creatures, he teaches them."[111] It is because God loves us that he does not give us "the silent treatment," but communicates with us through creation, canon, and Christ. We come to know divine providence, and thus to be aware of God's love, as we in faith receive his word and come to perceive his communicative presence and activity. It is faith that allows us to see past the horrors to the whole history of fellowship between the creator and his creatures and, in light of this whole, to see how God is ordering things to our good (Rom. 8:28). Of course, the ultimate good God wills for his beloved creatures is himself. Communion with God is the end for which human beings were created, and the promise of his covenant to create a people for himself.

God's love is his determination to bless his creatures, to communicate something of himself to the end of greater communion with another. Webster can agree with Oord that God is free to decide *how* to love his creatures. Yet Webster notes that general providence (God's love for the world in general) is subordinate to singular providence (God's love for the elect or the church) inasmuch as the church "is the interim realization of the goal of rational creatures, namely fellowship with the creator."[112]

God's love is powerful, bestowing and perfecting life, effectually communicating the good that is God to the church. Is this a "controlling" love that Oord thinks overpowers freedom? Webster defines freedom as "existence in accordance with created nature and toward created ends, not self-authorship or aseity."[113] God's providence moves the creature's will in a way that does not constrain but fulfills the creature's self-determination, namely, by perfecting/restoring the creature's nature. Stated differently, God causes creaturely causality, which, in the case of humans, means freedom.

For what may we hope? There is no index entry for "hope" in Oord's book on providence, probably because his entire project takes his bearings from the problem of evil. In contrast, Webster follows his law of immanent domain and begins with the identity of God as the ground and goal of Christian hope (cf. Rom. 15:13). Hope is the human disposition that corresponds to God's self-determination to achieve his purpose for creation. There is resistance to the divine purpose, but the work of the Son and Spirit has successfully begun to reintegrate creation into the Father's loving purpose. Human history is caught up and encompassed by the divine economy—a loving triune embrace. The object of hope for Webster is God's steadfast love: the self-communicating activity of Father, Son, and Spirit, the Triune God who will not be thwarted in his aim to share his goodness with others for the sake of their perfection. Hope in providence arises from the conviction that the Father's will to fellowship has been fulfilled in Christ. The hope that God's love will ultimately triumph depends not

---

[109] Ibid., 127.
[110] Ibid., 131.
[111] Webster, "The Fruit of the Spirit"
[112] Webster, *God without Measure*, vol. 1, 138.
[113] Ibid., 139.

on a satisfactory answer to the problem of evil. On the contrary, only by holding fast to God's steadfast *sovereign* love "is it possible to developing anything like a responsible Christian theodicy."[114]

5 Conclusion: Essential *kyriosis*

Love is a relation, and God's love for the world is real. Does it not then follow that God's love for the world is a "real" relation? I have sought to clarify what is at stake in this question, and the factors that complicate a clear response, through a comparison of Oord and Webster. What may we now say? Let me suggest three morals and a conclusion.

First, conceptual analysis has an important ministerial role to play in elaborating certain concepts, such as "real relation." *Relation* is a slippery term, not least because there are many kinds of relations: causal, logical, familial, numeric, marital, and so forth, only some of which entail mutuality and reciprocity. After all, master/slave is a relation too. In retrieving certain key distinctions from Aquinas, Webster has also retrieved, as it were, a premodern form of analytic theology.[115]

Second, the subject matter of theology, God and all things in relation to God, requires us to become adept at recognizing different kinds of relations. There is an essential difference between the relations God has in himself and the relations God has with the world. The intra-trinitarian processions are God's perichoretic relations unique to the Godhead. The way creatures relate to God as Creator will be different in at least one respect to all other kinds of relation. The world is not constitutive for the being of God, which is why Webster, following Aquinas, denies the God-world relation is a real (i.e., reciprocal, ontological, constitutive) relation.

Third, though both Oord and Webster describe God's love in terms of self-giving, their respective approaches—essential *kenosis* and essential *plerosis*—differ fundamentally in how they construe God's relation to creation, providence, and the event of Jesus Christ. For Oord, God expresses his love through his causal but ultimately non-effectual (because noncoercive) call for creatures to get with the plan and promote overall well-being. For Webster, God expresses his love through the missions of the Son and Spirit that fulfill the Father's plan for creation to promote the creature's perfection.

I submit that Webster's description of what we might call God's essentially *kyriotic* love is both more biblical than Oord's and more successful in rendering God's love more genuinely real and relational than Oord's kenotic counterpart, even if it is not, strictly speaking, a "real" relation in Thomas's scholastic (i.e., metaphysical) sense.[116] To repeat: the motive in denying that God is in "real" relation with the world is to preserve

---

[114] Webster, *Confessing God*, 205.
[115] For an introduction to the modern variety, see Thomas H. McCall, *An Invitation to Analytic Christian Theology* (Downers Grove, IL: InterVarsity Press, 2015).
[116] I have dealt with God's kyriotic love as an alternative to other kenotic-relational views in my *Remythologizing Theology*, 434–68.

the integrity of God's true relation to the world. The one who creates and redeems is the one who is perfect in himself. God is Father of all, but he is not our metaphysical relative. On the contrary, he is Lord. It is precisely as Lord that God loves, and this means there are no restrictions on his loving presence and activity: "In God, absence of reciprocity is not absence of relation but the ground of limitless relation."[117]

It is out of his limitless love that the Creator binds himself to a fallen creation in taking a covenantal initiative, promising to be with and for the children of Abraham. In Jesus Christ, the covenant lord becomes covenant servant without ceasing to be covenant lord. This lordly love does not simply sympathetically share but sovereignly transforms the beloved's situation. It is a *kyriotic* love because it is self-moved (i.e., free), enduring (i.e., steadfast), and effectual (i.e., determining but not coercive—it's a long story). What God communicates is not merely sympathy (good vibrations), condolences (good thoughts), influence (good intentions), but rather the life and light of Jesus Christ (goodness incarnate). Given the problem of evil, only *kyriotic* love can help. Only by denying God's "real" relation to the world—essential *kenosis*—can we affirm God's love without measure.[118]

---

[117] Webster, *God without Measure*, vol. 1, 124.
[118] I wish to thank Oliver Crisp and the participants in the analytic theology seminar at Fuller Theological Seminar for their interaction with an earlier oral version of this chapter, as well as Ryan Fields and Derek Rishmawy for their comments on an earlier draft.

2

Analogies of Love between God and Creatures: A Response to Kevin Vanhoozer

Thomas Jay Oord

I am honored that Kevin Vanhoozer would reflect on my theology of love and compare it to John Webster's. I respect Vanhoozer's theological acumen and consider him a leading voice in constructive theology today. His chapter offers insights and questions my work, and in this chapter, I am happy to respond. I am also grateful to Jordan Wessling for bringing Vanhoozer's work to my attention and arranging for my rejoinder.

My response divides into two sections. The first addresses Vanhoozer's worries about and objections to my theology of love. I focus on differences he highlights between my views and Webster's, many differences I assume also exist between my views and his own. One of Vanhoozer's central criticisms is methodological. He (rightly) says my work does not show evidence of taking intra-trinitarian—*ad intra*—love as my methodological starting point. In the second section of my response, I consider whether his preferred theological method is compatible with my claims about God and love. Does beginning with the Trinity, I ask, necessarily lead to the particular theology of love that Webster and Vanhoozer endorse? Or can one begin with and accept trinitarian logic and endorse the love theology I proffer?

1 Addressing the questions of love

Vanhoozer does an admirable job summarizing my theology of love. Because he recapitulates my work well, I am able to spend the majority of this section addressing his worries, concerns, and questions. I am grateful for his gift!

1.1 Is God's love relational?

In various portions of his essay, Vanhoozer explores how we might best think of God's relations with creatures. In various publications, I have argued that love between Creator and creation requires give-and-receive relations.[1] Such analogical relations

---

[1] See especially Oord, *The Nature of Love: A Theology* and *The Uncontrolling Love of God*.

are bidirectional; God relates to creatures and creatures relate to God. By contrast, Vanhoozer affirms a Thomistic view, which says that God is logically related to creation but not engaged in relations that involve divine reception. Divine love is unidirectional, on this view. God never receives from creatures in a way that affects God's experience.

My claim that God's love involves give-and-receive relations begins with Scripture. As I read the Bible, I find the God described therein consistently affecting creatures and being affected by them. The God biblical writers describe is passible rather than impassible, to use the classic language. Depending on how creatures act, God might be pleased, angered, saddened, blessed, or something else. Biblical writers even sometimes say God repents—has a change of mind—and makes new plans in light of how creatures act.[2] While God loves steadfastly, creaturely actions affect God and can prompt changes in divine expressions of love.

My experience and observations of creaturely love also incline me to think that God's love involves give-and-receive relations. Love relationships among creatures are more than just logical. Loving creatures are influenced, affected, or "moved" by those they love. I have no good reason to think divine love is different in this respect. Relating to others in giving-and-receiving influence seems a prerequisite for any ongoing activity we consider loving. And this view of love helps me make sense of biblical admonitions, such as the Apostle Paul's instructions to "imitate God, as dearly loved children, and live a life of love" (Eph. 5:1). Bidirectional analogies are important for making sense of the biblical portrayal of God and Christian ethics.

As Vanhoozer knows, important Christian theologians disagree with my view. Many reject the idea that God gives and receives, and they affirm divine impassibility instead. Such theologians sometimes argue that God has logical relations with others but not real, mutually influencing relations. They worry that abandoning impassibility implies that God is unstable and imperfect. These theologians take literally biblical passages that portray God as impassible (unaffected) and immutable (unchanging) but consider as anthropomorphic projections passages that portray God as passible (affected) and mutable (changing).

By contrast, I reconcile these diverse biblical passages by distinguishing between God's relational experience and God's timeless nature. God's experience as the Living Lord of history is characterized by giving and receiving and, therefore, changing relations. God's experience is passible, because love requires a measure of possibility. But God's timeless nature remains unchangingly eternal. Creatures cannot affect or change the immutable divine essence.

On the issue of God's relations with creatures, Vanhoozer admits, "Scripture depicts God interacting with creatures." But he makes the metaphysical assumption that "these relations are not constitutive of God; they have no bearing on his essential being." I agree that such relations do not change God's essence. But I believe such relations influence God's experience of and love for creation. They make a real, relational difference to how God decides to love.

---

[2] Terence E. Fretheim well describes the passible God in the Bible, first in *The Suffering of God: An Old Testament Perspective* (Philadelphia, PA: Fortress, 1984), and then in *God and the World in the Old Testament: A Relational Theology of Creation* (Nashville, TN: Abingdon Press, 2005).

Vanhoozer offers two examples to clarify how God can interact with creatures without such interactions affecting God:

> (1) my knowing the speed of light depends on (i.e., has a real relation to) that external reality, but the speed of light does not depend on my knowing it; (2) the character of Oliver Twist has a real relation to Charles Dickens (who is the ground of Oliver's being), but Dickens has only a logical relation to Oliver (Oliver's existence depends on Dickens's creative authorship but not vice versa).

To my mind, these are powerful examples for why we should *reject* the view that love is unidirectional rather than involving giving and receiving. Neither a person's knowledge of the speed of light nor Oliver Twist's relation to Charles Dickens strikes me as examples of love. In the first example, knowledge of light's speed is not a giving-and-receiving relationship, nor loving. In the second example, an abstract character is not alive and thus cannot engage in give-and-receive love relations. By contrast, I believe a love relationship involves multiple parties being affected. And I think love presupposes that the lover has been influenced by the beloved. In sum, Vanhoozer's examples do not jibe with how it seems likely that God loves others.

Vanhoozer rightly quotes me as believing we should regard love as God's foremost or governing attribute. With John Wesley, I sometimes say God's "reigning" attribute is love. Vanhoozer worries, however, that this approach "departs from the traditional doctrine of divine simplicity, according to which God is the whole of his divine perfections." Vanhoozer claims, "To rank love over the other divine attributes is to suggest that God is made up of different parts or properties."

I share Vanhoozer's disdain for believing God has various parts. I affirm divine simplicity when defined as God not having actual parts. But I claim that love comes *logically* first in God's nature. To say love comes first logically does not require me to think love is one part alongside others. Because God's nature is abstract while God's experience concrete, I can affirm the simplicity of the divine nature. Abstract properties have no parts with ontological status. Conceiving of love as logically first in God helps us make sense of other divine attributes, including how we best understand those attributes in light of love. The property or attribute of love comes first in God.

1.2 What divine love does

Vanhoozer wonders about how I understand God's loving activity. He asks, for instance, what God's love actually *does*. "If it is real," he says, "it should make a difference." I agree with Vanhoozer that love should make a difference. My theology emphasizes that God's love makes an actual difference in creation. God acts in *many* ways to promote well-being. God is the necessary cause in the existence of everything, moment by moment. But I do not think God's action controls others. I often refer to Aristotelian notions of causation when explaining my view. I think God expresses love as efficient, final, or formal causes, for instance. But God never acts as a sufficient cause. That would involve divine control. God always loves, and divine love is uncontrolling.

Vanhoozer's comments remind me of a worry Arthur Holmes once raised. Holmes argued against theologies that say God lovingly persuades but never coerces. To him, the God who persuades "cannot act."[3] Holmes seems not to see the important distinction between (1) acting that affects outcomes and (2) acting that unilaterally determines outcomes. The vast majority of, if not all, actions affect others without controlling. In my view, God's action is also uncontrolling. My theology claims that God always acts, and divine love is action that makes a difference. Creatures or creation more generally cannot prevent God from acting. The outcomes God desires for creation, however, require creaturely response to be generated. Because God's actions are always loving, God never controls others to generate outcomes unilaterally.

To use an example, I acted when asking my fiancée to marry me. Her favorable response, however, was required for the outcome I desired. If I had tried to force, control, or unilaterally determine her, few would call such coercion loving. If she responds positively to me, however, we can say my action made a difference in generating the outcome I wanted. I think divine love is analogous.

Vanhoozer introduces a word in his essay that I do not think describes my view of God's action well. That word is "non-effectual." When summarizing my theology, he says I believe "God thus loves creatures not by strongly causing (i.e., determining) good things, but rather by constantly issuing non-effectual calls, thus weakly causing good things (when they happen)." The word "non-effectual," as Vanhoozer uses it, might sound as though he thinks my view entails that God's actions do not produce any effect. He apparently means by "non-effectual" that I am claiming God's actions do not *necessarily* produce God's desired effect.[4]

To describe my view better, Vanhoozer might rephrase his sentence. The sentence might say "God loves creatures not by controlling events and thereby unilaterally causing good things but rather by constantly calling and empowering creatures, thereby symbiotically causing good things (as creation cooperates)." This alternative statement rightly emphasizes my view that God's actions are causal but not controlling. God's actions in the world require creaturely cooperation to produce the results God wants. God's actions prompt creatures to act in ways to produce some desired effect, but they do not necessarily produce such an effect.

In summarizing my view, Vanhoozer says "strong" divine action is "determining." This implies that weak divine action involves lack of control, in the sense of not producing the desired effect necessarily. It seems that Vanhoozer believes controlling others to produce desired outcomes is the "stronger" form of power. I once believed this. But as I have argued in various publications, I now believe God's almighty power is uncontrolling love.[5]

Let me conclude this section with a few brief words about God's being. Like most theologians, I think that God is incorporeal. God is spirit (Jn 4:24). I deny that God has a localized, physical, divine body with which God exerts an impact. I think the biblical

---

[3] Arthur F. Holmes, "Why God Cannot Act," in *Process Theology*, ed. Ronald Nash (Grand Rapids, MI: Baker, 1987).

[4] I am grateful to Kevin Vanhoozer for responding to a first draft of this chapter and clarifying what he means by "effectual." I tried to incorporate his thoughts here.

[5] See my books, *Defining Love*; *The Nature of Love: A Theology*; and *The Uncontrolling Love of God*.

notions of God as *ruach* and *pneuma* are important for understanding why God fails to prevent genuine evil. While in some instances we use our bodies to prevent evil, God as spirit has no localized divine body to use in this way. As spirit, God exerts efficient causation of the sort we think metaphysically analogous to other causal occurrences in the world. But efficient causation does not mean sufficient causation. One view of the human mind-body relationship helps as an analogy. Just as our minds exert efficient causal influence upon our bodies without entirely determining them, so God as spirit exerts causal influence upon creatures without entirely determining them. God acts causally without controlling others.[6]

1.3 Special divine action

Vanhoozer concludes the substantive portion of his review by looking at miracles. He wonders how I distinguish between God's special actions from God's constant love for all creation. After rightly noting my disdain for the language of "intervention," Vanhoozer says, "'special action' must be something other than intervention (though I know not what)." I understand this puzzlement. I did not explain special divine action in significant length in the material Vanhoozer read. But I did offer paragraphs on the subject in *The Uncontrolling Love of God*. Below I quote a few of them to explain what I mean by God's "special action":

> The special divine action that makes miracles possible occurs when God provides new possibilities, forms, structures, or ways of being to creatures. These gifts for the miraculous may reflect dramatic or remarkable ways of existing should they be embodied or incorporated. The possible ways that creatures act and possible situations that might emerge are prospects God gives for new and sometimes awe-inspiring ways of being in the world. Special divine action involves God giving new forms of existence to which creatures or creation might conform.

Miracles are possible when God offers good and unusual forms of existence.

> The novel opportunities and new ways of existing that God provides are context and creature appropriate. God takes into account the relevant ways creatures have acted in the past and might act in the future. God takes into account the past actions of other creatures and entities pertinent to the person or place. In light of the past and present, God lovingly invites creatures and creation to cooperate to enact a future in which well-being is established in surprising and positive ways. When creatures respond well to this special divine activity, miracles occur.
>
> God's self-giving love takes a variety of forms. These forms make available redemption, release from oppression, fresh beginnings, healings, transformation, resurrections, exorcisms, rescues and more. Because the context warrants

---

[6] For more on God acting as a spirit, see my essay, "The Divine Spirit as Causal and Personal," *Zygon* 48, no. 2 (2013): 466–77.

them, new forms of existing, new possibilities for acting or new avenues for transformation become the basis for a new event in relation to creation. God sometimes desires well-being through diverse forms and multifarious dimensions.

Because God steadfastly loves all creation, God is not able to present forms of existence that would be unloving. God's steadfast love cannot coerce some elements of creation when offering ways of existing or dramatic changes to others. Despite this limitation, the possibilities God can present to creation may surprise us and inspire joy. They may be unusual and good in ways that exceed our expectations.[7]

Special divine action as I conceive it does not involve extra effort on God's part. Nor does it mean God occasionally controls. And it does not involve intervention, in the sense of God occasionally interjecting among creaturely causes while otherwise being uninvolved. As I conceive it, special divine action involves God introducing novel and often-surprising possibilities to creatures or inanimate creation. In contrast to the nonrelational God of deism or the Thomistic God who does not engage in bidirectional, give-and-receive relations with creatures, the God I envision responds to creatures by offering new possibilities appropriate (though sometimes unexpected) for the situation at hand. Something new and unexpected can occur—a miracle!—due to special divine action in relation to creation.

Introducing novel possibilities involves more than simply "suggesting." God exerts efficient causation when introducing such possibilities. God is actually present to creation and makes a difference. But this causal difference, as I have said often already, never involves complete control. Like a good parent who is actually present to and instrumental in a child's life without being controlling, so God is actually present to and instrumental in creation without being controlling.

1.4 Nature miracles

Vanhoozer mentions two test cases in his discussion of special divine action. The first fits in the category biblical scholars often call "nature miracles." Before I address it, let me note that the majority of miracles mentioned in the Bible or that occur today pertain to healings, exorcisms, and personal transformation. These miracles involve persons or organisms rather than inanimate objects.

My proposal that God acts miraculously through uncontrolling love accounts well for the person and organism miracles we find in the Bible and witness today. These miracles either explicitly mention creaturely cooperation or we can easily imagine such cooperation playing a role. My proposal has more difficulty explaining nature miracles. Nature miracles involve inanimate objects, and I do not think inanimate objects have the capacity for intentional response. To account for God's uncontrolling love in nature miracles, therefore, I explore in *The Uncontrolling Love of God* quantum and chaos theories. Vanhoozer correctly summarizes my

---

[7] Oord, *The Uncontrolling Love of God*, 199–200.

view that prominent theories in physics could provide an explanation for the creaturely component in the Red Sea miracle. Such theories compliment my view that when doing nature miracles, God acts in relation to inanimate creation without controlling it.

After summarizing my view of nature miracles, however, Vanhoozer says, "Oord fails to deal with the episode where Jesus works a miracle that elicits the astonished response, 'Who is this, that even the wind and sea obey him?' (Mark 4:41)." Vanhoozer is right that I had yet to address this biblical statement. Interestingly, the straightforward reading of this exclamation in Mark leads one to regard the wind and sea anthropomorphically. The language of the text suggests that wind and sea act like personal entities capable of choosing to obey Jesus (or perhaps not). If wind and sea are capable of obedient responses, my view that miracles require creation to cooperate with God fits this story well.

Many Christians have read into the biblical text, however, the idea that creatures can do no other than obey God. But I think differently. Uncontrolling love can be disobeyed, as we know so well from our own experiences. I often ask my daughters to obey me, for instance, but they refuse. Saying someone obeyed God need not be construed to mean the person had no choice. Such construal would make biblical references to creaturely disobedience unintelligible. If we move against a straightforward reading of the text and instead think of wind and sea as inanimate objects, however, we will need theories in physics to account for God's powerful but uncontrolling activity. As I admit above, accounting for miracles among inanimate systems is more difficult. But I think it is possible, as I have also mentioned above.

The more important biblical point is this: there is nothing explicit in Scripture saying God's miraculous activity involves control over others, even over inanimate creation. Christians have typically read the biblical miracle stories through perspectives shaped by metaphysical assumptions about divine power not explicitly supported by the text. But I know of nothing in Scripture that explicitly says God entirely controlled creatures or inanimate creation.[8]

1.5 God unilaterally raised Jesus?

The second test case Vanhoozer mentions is the resurrection of Jesus. I regard this miracle, so central to Christian faith, as easier to understand in light of God's uncontrolling love than the miracles involving inanimate objects. The resurrection involved a person and various organisms making up the person's body. Vanhoozer deftly describes my view, which entails God's actual resurrection of Jesus. He rightly summarizes me as believing this resurrection includes cooperation from Jesus's

---

[8] The text most often cited as describing unilaterally determinative divine power—coercion—refers to God hardening Pharaoh's heart. But this passage does not explicitly say God controlled Pharaoh. Besides, other biblical passages say Pharaoh hardened his own heart. It appears that translators have assumed divine coercion when choosing words like "hardened" to describe God's activity in relation to Pharaoh. But other English words are also viable translations, and these do not have the connotations of coercion that "hardening" can have. On these issues, see Terence Fretheim, *Exodus: Interpretation* (Philadelphia, PA: Westminster/John Knox, 2010).

mind/soul and Jesus's bodily members. Vanhoozer wonders, however, whether my explanation does justice to the idea that, as biblical writers sometimes put it, "God raised Jesus from the dead."

I think it does. If biblical writers had said, "God unilaterally raised Jesus from the dead," my view would be harder to defend biblically. But in various Scripture stories, we can easily imagine creaturely activity even though biblical writers only mention God's action. In other stories—even miracles stories—biblical writers do not mention divine action at all (Acts 3:1-10, 14:8-10, etc.), but we might think God was still active. Most Christians have assumed that at least God's providential action played a role in those stories. In sum, just because a text mentions only one cause (e.g., God), we need not think other causes are absent.

In February 2016, I was thinking about how we often mention only one cause when explaining an outcome. "Tom Brady won the Super Bowl," I heard over and again. "Brady Brings another Super Bowl Trophy to New England," said one headline. Both of these statements are true. But when reading them, we might wrongly think Tom Brady was the only cause in the Patriots' win. Those who watched the game know this is not true. It may be true that the Patriots would have lost the Super Bowl had they relied on some other quarterback. Brady may have been a necessary cause in the victory. He may even have been the primary cause. But he was not the unilateral cause.

We can use this causal analogy in relation to divine action. Many Christians think God at least sometimes determines outcomes unilaterally, being the only cause at play. Especially when they think about miracles, these Christians assume God exerts unilaterally determining power. Consequently, they fail to notice statements in the miracle narratives that point to creaturely factors or cooperation. In a high percentage of his miracles, for instance, Jesus refers to the importance of the (cooperative) faith of those healed. And Jesus blames the lack of faith (noncooperation) on why he sometimes *cannot* do miracles (Mt. 13:58; Mk 6:2-5).

When the biblical text does not explicitly mention creaturely causes, many Christians assume God acted alone to generate some outcome. Vanhoozer makes this assumption, for instance, when he rightly notes that biblical writers say God raised Jesus from the dead. Such metaphysical assumptions about God's power prompt many Christians to think miracles are examples of divine control.

Let me reiterate what I wrote above: I know of no biblical text that *explicitly* says God exerts unilaterally determinative power.[9] I know of no biblical passage that *explicitly* says God controlled creatures. I know of no miracle story that *explicitly* says God acted alone and no other causes were active. I believe the overall biblical witness, the logic of love, the problem of evil, and other reasons make it more plausible to think God does *not* have controlling capacities. In other words, it makes most sense to me to believe God *never* controls creatures. Christians can make better sense of God and life if they embrace the view that God's self-giving, others-empowering, and almighty love is inherently uncontrolling.

---

[9] See previous footnote about Pharaoh.

1.6 Five questions

Vanhoozer asks five questions in his chapter. I list them below and offer brief answers.

(1) *How does Oord reconcile his definition of love as intentional action with his insistence that God necessarily loves everyone, everywhere, all the time?*
Answer: I affirm that God can love both intentionally and necessarily. I see no conflict in affirming both. In my view, God necessarily loves, but God freely chooses various ways to love. Because love comes logically first in God's nature and God "cannot deny himself" (2 Tim. 2:13), God must love. God is not free to do otherwise. But God *is* free when deciding *how* to love. The how of love is contingent, not necessary.

I embrace the essentialist tradition when it comes to believing God cannot deny God's own nature. But because I believe God faces an open and yet to be determined future, I also embrace voluntarist claims about God's free choices in choosing how to love. God freely acts in various ways when anticipating what may occur in the future.

As an analogy, let us assume that my human nature leads me necessarily to act humanly. I can necessarily act as a human and still intentionally choose to type this sentence instead of another. I am free in this sense. In fact, I am free to type a wide variety of sentences, despite not being free to be other than human. In this way, necessity in nature and free intentional action coexist. We can necessarily be human and yet free to act variously as humans. Analogously, God can necessarily love everyone and yet freely and intentionally choose how to love moment by moment.

(2) *Does Oord truly preserve the Creator/creature distinction, or is God on the same metaphysical level with the rest of created reality? If the call to love that God gives each creature is in one sense "no different from the causal influence that other creatures exert," then doesn't God exist on the same plane of being as everything else?*
Answer: At the start of his chapter, Vanhoozer provides a teaser about the worries he voices in this question and that emerge later in his chapter. He worries that my theology might be a Feuerbachian projection. Vanhoozer offers theological realism as an alternative to anthropomorphic hubris, a position that says we can be wrong in our descriptions of God's love. I join Vanhoozer in being a realist in this sense. I do not think we can ever grasp divine love fully or define it perfectly. We see through a glass darkly.

I also believe, however, that we should seek to know something of the God whom we can never fully know. I think we should try to grasp divine love as best we can and define it as well as possible. In this, I steer clear of both absolute apophatism and thoroughgoing anthropomorphism. To make sense of God's love and actions, I think we should draw bidirectional analogies between Creator and creatures. Without them, I think we fail to do justice to the biblical witness and fail to understand well what it means to be made in the image of God. We can embrace such bidirectional analogies without considering God to be on the same metaphysical level or plane as creatures. Creator and creatures differ in some respects but also share some similarities. I will address this more in the second half of this chapter.

(3) *Does Oord derive his definition of love from the event of Jesus Christ or from somewhere else?*

Answer: Vanhoozer asks this question as an either/or choice. For me, the answer is both/and. I accept the revelation of God's love found in Jesus and the revelation of God in creation more generally. As I see it, the clearest expression of love comes in Jesus, and therefore he becomes crucial to defining love well. But I am also confident that my views of love have been shaped by the broader biblical witness, the Christian community, and the revelation of God in creation more generally.

Because God is omnipresent and self-revealing to all creation, those who know nothing of Jesus can accept my definition of love. In fact, adherents of other religious traditions affirm my definition. Those involved in other religions may find resonance between my views of love and what they find about love in their own texts and communities, thanks to God's prevenient grace expressed throughout all creation.[10]

(4) *In "solving" the problem of evil by stipulating God's nature as uncontrolling love, does Oord render insoluble the equally important question, "What may we hope?" Oord stresses the importance of human participation in what he calls "participatory eschatology": "God's kenotic love invites creatures to participate in securing victory." But why think that the entropic universe, much less rebellious children, will come around to God's way at the end of time? Does not this solution to the problem of evil render evil metaphysically unavoidable and necessary?*

Answer: There are several questions here. All of them point to eschatological concerns. Answering them well requires at least a book.[11] But I will offer a few brief responses that I hope provide light.

My theology of love's eschatological vision does not support the kind of universalism that some theologians desire. Although it supports the *hope* that all creation, in the end, will cooperate with God, it does not support theories that require divine coercion for redemption. My participatory eschatology provides some guarantees. It guarantees that God never gives up seeking to save the lost. It guarantees that God's love is always uncontrolling. God never uses coercion but always calls creatures to say "yes" to abundant life. This inviting, empowering, but uncontrolling love is expressed both in this life and the next. God's wooing never ceases.

My eschatology also guarantees that those who cooperate with God in this life and the next enjoy abundant life. It supports the hope that cooperators enjoy untold bliss in the afterlife. It cannot guarantee that everyone will enjoy this bliss, because it says God never forces the good life on others. God respects the freedom of rebellious children who continue to reject salvation.

In sum, my eschatology rejects unilaterally secured universalism. But it also rejects the view that God gives up loving creatures and offering eternal life. My vision provides genuine hope for abundant life here and now and eternal bliss there and then for those who cooperate with God's love.

---

[10] As just one example, see Rabbi Bradley Artson's work on love, which draws from my definition, in *God of Becoming and Relationship* (Nashville, TN: Jewish Lights, 2016).

[11] See especially *The Nature of Love: A Theology*, chap. 5.

(5) If Oord is right, is the God who is uncontrolling love more deserving of our worship or sympathy?
Answer: The God of uncontrolling love is worthy of our worship. I worship this God unreservedly and wholeheartedly. Doing so brings me great joy! I have spent significant time thinking about what vision of God provokes my worship. I have come to think that it is impossible for me to worship a God who could prevent genuine evil but fails to do so. I do not unequivocally respect humans who fail to prevent evil when their doing so was possible. Likewise, I cannot unequivocally worship a God capable of preventing genuine evil but who fails to do so. I may dread this God. But I could not unreservedly love and worship such a being. As I see it, the God who can control is unworthy of my worship.

Vanhoozer's chapter mentions pity as a possible response to my vision of God, and this reminds me of a recent conversation. I was explaining to a fellow theologian that the uncontrolling God cannot prevent genuine evil by acting alone. My friend responded that he prefers a God who can control. He smirked and said, "You know, Tom, your God is just doing the best He can." I thought about his remark and responded, "Your God could be doing *a whole lot* more. But He apparently doesn't care enough to do so!"

I mention this conversation, because it illustrates how love is my fundamental theological intuition. When I think about a God worthy of worship, I find far more winsome the vision of a God who consistently loves but cannot control than a God who can control but loves inconsistently by causing or allowing evil. Some claim the God they affirm both controls and loves consistently. In light of evil, they typically say it is a mystery how God does both. This measure of mystery, however, detracts from my worship. I am unable to worship a God who cannot be understood to such a degree. It is difficult for me to imagine why one would feel motivated to worship a God so incomprehensible.

2 My theology of love coheres with trinitarian theological methodology

In various segments of his chapter, Vanhoozer criticizes the method I use for constructing my theology of love. He rightly notes that interdisciplinary work— theology, philosophy, and science—shapes my constructive proposals. By contrast, he argues that a proper theological method begins with love as expressed in Godself—*ad intra*—rather than God's love for creation. "A well-ordered Christian dogmatics first treats God in relation to himself," as Vanhoozer puts it, "and only then God in relation to creatures."

I suspect some readers will sympathize with Vanhoozer on this matter. Others will find my methodology more appealing. I am guessing Vanhoozer cares at least some about how interdisciplinary research affects theology. I care about trinitarian thinking. I suspect we differ on emphasis and order. In my view, all theological construction involves speculation, no matter one's method. As I see it, claims about what transpires within the Trinity are especially speculative. We know very little about the inner trinitarian workings. Such knowledge comes from the words of Jesus, and these words were written by humans not privy to intra-trinitarian intimations. In my view, we have a firmer base of knowledge about love from God's action toward creation and from creaturely love in response. We have more evidence for the ways of the economic Trinity, in other words, than the immanent. Of course, there is plenty of speculation in any method. But I think observations about life are less speculative than speculation about what transpires within the Trinity. We might put it this way: we have some idea of God's *ad intra* love because of the revelation of God's *ad extra* love. Vanhoozer seems to reverse this emphasis.

But we might ask: Could we begin with Vanhoozer/Webster's preferred method and come to the basic ideas in my theology of love? To put it differently: Could we start with the Trinity and still affirm my theological proposals? I think so. If I am right, beginning *ad intra* does not require one to embrace the theology of Aquinas and Webster rather than my theology of love.

For instance, we could begin with claims about God's inner trinitarian love life but also say God has real, give-and-receive relations with the world. We might say Jesus's own give-and-receiving relationship reveals God's give-and-receive relationships with the world. Those who wish to do theology from a decidedly Christological foundation will see the advantage of this approach. And it begins *ad intra*.

We could also begin *ad intra* and say God is necessarily related to the world. One could say God necessarily relates in Godself, in other words, and necessarily relates to creation. There is no logical contradiction in affirming both necessities. In fact, it is hard to imagine a more thoroughgoing relational theology that the one offered by this doubly necessary relatedness! These points and some to follow tell us that one's methodological starting point is not the essential issue of difference between my theology and those Vanhoozer explores. One could begin *ad intra* or *ad extra* and yet affirm the theology of love I propose. At issue are various theological claims and their metaphysical implications.

2.1 *Kenosis* and *plerosis*

In his able summary of my views, Vanhoozer rightly notes my use of Phil. 2:5-11. I use it as a touchstone for my essential *kenosis* theology of love. I refer to this influential passage, of course, because the word "*kenosis*" is present therein. Theologians rightly focus on this verdant text when considering the love of God revealed in Jesus Christ. Vanhoozer seems to think, however, that I believe the Philippians passage inevitably leads to beliefs about God's necessary limitations or relations to the world. I do not believe this. My claims about God's power and relations involve metaphysical assumptions not explicit in the Philippians text. But it is important to note that claims about God's power being voluntarily self-limited or God being contingently related to creation also rest on metaphysical assumptions not explicit in the text. Scripture alone cannot adjudicate these matters. As I see it, we should ask whether God's *kenosis*—self-giving, others-empowering love—is necessary or contingent in light of many issues, not least the problem of evil.

Vanhoozer (wrongly) says that I interpret "*kenosis* not as a verb that signals a covenantal initiative... but as a noun that pictures the God/world relation as permanent, essential, and metaphysical." I do think *kenosis* is a verb. But God can necessarily act (verb) in particular ways, because love comes logically first in God's nature (see my comments in the first half of this chapter). Vanhoozer reveals his own metaphysical assumptions, which are not explicit in the Philippians passage nor, I would argue, explicit elsewhere in the Bible. He assumes God's covenants with creation are entirely voluntary. In my view, the God who necessarily relates to creation necessarily engages in covenant but freely chooses the forms of this loving engagement. When it comes to the necessarily existing and essentially loving God, covenants with creatures can be necessary expressions of divine love. The specifics of the covenants can be freely chosen while the covenants themselves can be seen as necessary expressions of God's loving nature.

In sum, Philippians and other biblical passages provide grounds to speculate that God necessarily loves others, is necessarily related to creatures, and is necessarily uncontrolling. I find such speculation appropriate and helpful, given a host of theological concerns. But the Bible neither unequivocally supports my metaphysical claims nor unequivocally supports Vanhoozer's (or Webster's or Aquinas's).

2.2 Holy love

I partly agree with Vanhoozer's claims about the meaning of love. He offers a definition on behalf of Webster: "God's love is his self-communicative activity by which he communicates goodness—ultimately his own light and life—to others for the sake of consummation and communion." I might quibble a bit with this—for example, where is the claim that says God's love promotes goodness or well-being?—but I mostly like it.

What I find most interesting about Vanhoozer's definition is the failure to reference creaturely love. Vanhoozer says he wants to give a love definition, but he mentions only God's actions. Does he believe that creatures love? Or does he affirm a theological determinism that amounts to believing so-called creaturely love is really God's love? Or does Vanhoozer think divine love is *entirely* different from creaturely love such that there can be no unifying definition?

Vanhoozer refers to "holy love" as Webster's way to talk about God being different from creatures. I think our Creator differs from creatures in many ways, of course, and I understand the practice of using "holy" to mark differences. I am fine using "holy" to speak of God's "set-apartness," so long as doing so does not make God different in *all* respects from creatures. Absolute apophatism leads to absolute mystery.

In my own work, however, I shy away from the phrase "holy love." I do so, because I think love always promotes value/good/well-being and all love has its source in God. Consequently, I think all love (properly defined) is holy. There is no such thing as "unholy love." In my view, the phrase "holy love" is like "divine God." It is redundant.

Vanhoozer's main point in offering a definition, however, seems to be to emphasize the view that God loves out of fullness rather than lack. I agree with this. I do not define *kenosis* in terms of divine lack. I have no problem saying divine *kenosis* flows from divine *plerosis*. We can affirm this whether we start our theological method with the Trinity or not. God can love out of fullness and yet desire loving relationship with creatures.

Vanhoozer uses Webster to criticize my view of the God-world relation. He believes God's relation with creation is "free," in the sense that God is not essentially related to creation. By contrast, I reject the idea that God is free from creation in all respects. Let me mention one reason for my rejecting this view: If God does not necessarily love creatures, this means God's love for creatures is contingent. To love someone contingently means one may or may not love that person. It is not necessary that one loves that person. In this case, the God who contingently loves may or may not love us. But if God's love for creation is contingent in this sense, God can stop loving creatures. And God may not love some creatures. God's love may be inconsistent. We have no metaphysical grounds to say that God has always loved creation in the past or that God will always love creation in the future. God may love us only on Tuesdays, for all we know!

Vanhoozer and others may counter this problem of contingent divine love by saying we can trust God to love creation because God is love or God loves necessarily within the Trinity. But this "trusting" based on God being love or necessarily loving in Trinity seems to imply that God *does* essentially love creation. And these are metaphysical claims. If God's necessary love within Godself is the basis for God's love for us, we have grounds to speculate that God also necessarily loves creatures. And if God's necessary love for others in the Trinity is the basis for God's love for us, we have grounds to speculate that God also necessarily loves creatures. These two circuitous ways of affirming God's necessary love for creatures works for me. They are not as direct as I would prefer. But they overcome the worry that God might love us only on Tuesdays, because they make God's love for creation necessary. And, by the way, they offer another example of how one might begin with God's life *ad intra* and come to key ideas in my theology of love.

2.3 The problem of evil

I conclude this response to Vanhoozer with another statement about *ad intra* theological method. Not only can one affirm my claims about divine love and relations when starting with the Trinity; one can affirm my claims about God's power when starting with the Trinity. We can rightly speculate that trinitarian members express uncontrolling power first among themselves and then toward creation. This claim—based as it is on uncontrolling love—goes a long way toward solving the problem of evil.

As I see it, a major deficit in Vanhoozer's (and Webster's) theology is an unwillingness to rethink God's power in light of evil. To illustrate my criticism, I quote a few paragraphs from Vanhoozer:

> Immediately we see a contrast with Oord. Webster will not be forced into reacting to the problem of evil. This way leads to dogmatic disorder, namely, "dominance

by questions . . . not derived from the Christian confession." It is not the amount of evil that makes it problematic for providence but rather our refusal to focus on providence rather than evil. This is both a spiritual and argumentative task: "Reconciling providence and horrors is a task within fellowship with God." In dogmatics, Webster insists, *disputatio* (apologetics) is subordinate to *expositio* (conceptual elaboration). In this spirit, Webster describes the content of providence as an account of "how the Father's plan for the fullness of time is set forth in Christ and made actual by the Holy Spirit."

"Because God loves his creatures, he teaches them." It is because God loves us that he does not give us "the silent treatment," but communicates with us through creation, canon, and Christ. We come to know divine providence, and thus to be aware of God's love, as we in faith receive his word and come to perceive his communicative presence and activity. It is faith that allows us to see past the horrors to the whole history of fellowship between the creator and his creatures and, in light of this whole, to see how God is ordering things to our good (Rom. 8:28). Of course, the ultimate good God wills for his beloved creatures is himself. Communion with God is the end for human beings were created, and the promise of his covenant to create a people for himself.

These paragraphs point to differences—methodological, apologetic, and theological—between Vanhoozer/Webster and me. But in particular, I find it troubling that, as Vanhoozer puts it, "Webster won't be forced into reacting to the problem of evil." I am also troubled that addressing evil might lead to being dominated by questions "not derived from the Christian confession."

These statements suggest that Webster/Vanhoozer think we should not be particularly concerned with the number one reason atheists say they cannot believe in God! And to Christians puzzled by evil, Webster/Vanhoozer seems to be saying that because the creeds do not offer a solution, Christians should not be overly concerned with the puzzle. We are to "see past the horrors," says Vanhoozer, and simply have faith that God will bring about ultimate good. I agree with Vanhoozer and Webster that Christians need faith. I share Vanhoozer's hope for God's ultimate victory for good. I believe God desires communion and fellowship. And I think God communicates with creation. But I disagree with Vanhoozer and Webster on the importance of allowing theodicy a major role in theological construction.

For the sake of witness both outside Christian faith and to fellow believers, Christians should rethink the traditional view of God's power. They should do so, in part, because of the problem of evil. In my view, Christians must face evil rather than looking past it. We must place the problem of evil among the primary questions of faith, using it to lead us toward plausible views of God's love, power, and relatedness. When it comes to solving the problem of evil, we need more than insights from past theologians and venerable creeds. They alone cannot give a winsome account today for the hope that lies within us. Because the problem of evil affects our view of God's love and power, failing to consider it a primary question leads to our peril.

3 Conclusion

I again thank Kevin Vanhoozer for taking my ideas seriously and doing an admirable job of describing them. We think about many issues differently. We both seek through a glass darkly. I hope that my responses have shed light on my own views. And I trust that this theological exercise might prove beneficial in some way to the reader and bring praise to God!

3
Divine Love and Personality*

Michael C. Rea

My goal in this chapter is to examine the nature and scope of divine love with an eye to addressing the problem of divine hiddenness. It will emerge along the way that taking seriously the idea that God has a personality provides reason to doubt some key assumptions about divine love that drive the hiddenness problem.

The problem of divine hiddenness is typically expressed by way of something like the following argument, due to J. L. Schellenberg:

(S1) If a perfectly loving God exists, then there exists a God who is always open to a personal relationship with any finite person.
(S2) If there exists a God who is always open to a personal relationship with any finite person, then no finite person is ever nonresistantly in a state of nonbelief in relation to the proposition that God exists.
(S3) If a perfectly loving God exists, then no finite person is ever nonresistantly in a state of nonbelief in relation to the proposition that God exists (from 1 and 2).
(S4) Some finite persons are or have been nonresistantly in a state of nonbelief in relation to the proposition that God exists.
(S5) No perfectly loving God exists (from 3 and 4).
(S6) If no perfectly loving God exists, then God does not exist.
(S7) God does not exist (from 5 and 6).

---

* Earlier versions of this chapter were presented or discussed in reading groups at Fuller Theological Seminary, the University of Notre Dame, and Baylor University. I am grateful to the attendees on those occasions for helpful discussion. I would also like to thank the following people for their comments on drafts of various portions of the chapter, some of which came in the context of the presentations and reading groups just mentioned, others of which came independently: Karl Ameriks, Robert Audi, Max Baker-Hytch, Matt Benton, Rebecca Chan, Nevin Climenhaga, Dustin Crummett, Kate Finley, Andrew Helms, Jack Himelright, Liz Jackson, Pat Kain, John Keller, Lorraine Keller, Chris Menzel, Joe Milburn, Andrew Moon, Sam Newlands, Michelle Panchuk, Caroline Paddock, Jeff Snapper, and three anonymous readers for Oxford University Press. I owe a special debt of thanks to Michelle Panchuk for extensive conversations about the topic of this chapter, and to Charity Anderson, Michael Bergman, Jeff Brower, Sarah Coakley, Oliver Crisp, Terence Cuneo, Trent Dougherty, Amber Griffioen, Daniel Howard-Snyder, Hud Hudson, Cristian Mihut, Kathryn Pogin, and Meghan Sullivan, each of whom participated in one of two workshops that were convened to discuss this and other material in the book from which this chapter has been drawn.

There is a lot to say about each of these premises. My own solution to the problem, developed at length in the book from which this chapter is drawn (*The Hiddenness of God*), focuses on S1.

In the literature, support for S1 (and relevantly similar premises) depends explicitly or implicitly on the following claim:

(DL1) Divine love is an idealized version of some important kind of human love.

In the chapter of *The Hiddenness of God* that precedes the one from which this chapter is drawn, I argue that the doctrine of divine transcendence undercuts our justification for believing DL1. In this chapter, I argue that even if we set aside the doctrine of divine transcendence, we still have good reason to reject DL1. I do not believe that this by itself affords a complete solution to the hiddenness problem—it leaves some important questions lingering, which I will mention but not discuss in detail at the end of the chapter.[1]

1

Love comes in many different varieties—romantic, erotic, filial, parental, and so on. Let us focus our attention on the best kinds, the purest and most noble versions of love, the ones that are the most plausible candidates for being identified with divine love. Parental love is surely one candidate; perhaps spousal love, or the love that obtains between the closest of friends, will be good ones as well. Perhaps the very best kind of human love is some amalgam of these, and perhaps that one will be the best candidate of all. In any case, let it be understood that when I talk without qualification about "love," "human love," or "ideal love," the kinds of love I have in view are these "best" kinds, and, in particular, whichever among them is most apt to be identified, in its ideal form, with divine love.

There is a great deal of controversy about what exactly is involved in love. Despite the controversy, however, there are at least two points of widespread general agreement, and affirming these is all that I will need to move forward with the argument of this chapter. First, it is widely held that at least one of the following two desires belongs to the very essence of love: desire for *the good* of the beloved, and desire for *union* with the beloved.[2] That is to say, one does not count as displaying love toward someone unless one has for that person at least one of the two desires just mentioned.

One might doubt this claim if one's attention is focused on kinds of love—erotic love, for example—that are not likely candidates for being identified with divine love.

---

[1] I address those questions in detail in chapters 6–9 of Michael C. Rea, *The Hiddenness of God* (Oxford: Oxford University Press, 2018).

[2] See, for example, Harry G. Frankfurt, *The Reasons of Love* (Princeton, NJ: Princeton University Press, 2004); Mark Murphy, *God's Own Ethics: Norms of Divine Agency and the Argument from Evil* (Oxford: Oxford University Press, 2017); and Eleonore Stump, "The Non-Aristotelian Character of Aquinas's Ethics: Aquinas and the Passions," *Faith and Philosophy* 28 (2011): 29–43.

Or one might doubt it if one thinks that love has no well-defined essence.[3] But neither of these two reasons for doubting is pertinent for the purposes of this chapter. The first is irrelevant because our focus here is on kinds of love that *are* candidates for being identified with divine love. The second I am setting aside for the sake of argument because affirming it would only cast further doubt on the soundness of the hiddenness problem. The expectations that drive that problem are predicated on the assumption that God desires union with us, desires our good, or both.[4] If this assumption were false, the key premise in the hiddenness argument (S1) would be much harder to motivate.

This brings us to the second point of widespread agreement, namely, that divine love includes not just one but *both* of these desires: God desires union with us, *and* God desires our good. The idea that God desires our good is central to the tradition. The idea that God desires—indeed, longs for—unitive relationship with human beings is also prevalent, especially in contemporary evangelicalism (which I think has, for sociological reasons, had a rather significant impact on the literature on the hiddenness problem). For example, in their best-selling devotional guide *Experiencing God*, Henry T. and Richard Blackaby write:

> God created you for a love relationship with Him. He yearns for you to love Him and respond to His immeasurable love for you. God's nature is perfect, holy, total love. He will never relate to you in any other way although you may not always understand His actions.[5]

The idea is also to be found in the work of process theologians and some who have been influenced by them.[6] This is not to say that the idea is a twentieth-century invention—Eleonore Stump attributes it to St. Thomas Aquinas, for example[7]—but it has certainly been prevalent in the twentieth and twenty-first centuries.[8]

One might worry that attributing desires to God is problematic on the traditional assumption that God is impassible. One might also worry that attributing desire for union with creatures to God portrays God as objectionably dependent upon creatures,

---

[3] Carrie Ichikawa Jenkins, "What Is Love? An Incomplete Map of the Metaphysics," *Journal of the American Philosophical Association* 1 (2015): 349–64, affirms this about romantic love. On her view, romantic love is a functional kind, and is present wherever one person x is prompted "to a sufficient degree, to engage in sufficiently many things on [some] list" of defining characteristics with respect to another person y (p. 360). One might say something similar about other kinds of love.

[4] As I note in *The Hiddenness of God*, Schellenberg's defenses of the claim that a perfectly loving God would not permit reasonable nonbelief to occur trade explicitly on the assumption that perfect love includes a desire for what is best for the beloved, and that perfect love includes a desire to "come close" and "share [one's] life"—in other words, to enjoy a kind of union—with the beloved.

[5] Richard Blackaby and Henry T. Blackaby, *Experiencing God*. Revised and expanded (Nashville, TN: B&H Publishing Group, 2014), 11.

[6] Cf. Oord, *The Nature of Love: A Theology*; and John Sanders, *The God Who Risks: A Theology of Providence* (Downers Grove, IL: InterVarsity Press, 1998), 87–88, 175–81.

[7] Eleonore Stump, *Wandering in Darkness: Narrative and the Problem of Suffering* (Oxford: Oxford Univeristy Press, 2010), Ch. 5.

[8] For a very helpful survey and discussion of different views of divine love in the tradition, see John Peckham, *The Concept of Divine Love in the Context of the God-World Relationship* (New York: Peter Lang, 2015); and *The Love of God*.

suggesting that God needs something from us in order to be fully content.[9] But the idea that God *wills* our good is prevalent in the tradition, as is the idea that God wills union with us; and the fact that God wills something seems sufficient for at least the analogical attribution of desire for it to God. So I think that these concerns can also safely be set aside.

For purposes here, then, I will affirm both of the two widely agreed upon claims that I have just identified—that God desires union with human beings and desires their good, and that human love would, in its idealized form, *have to* include at least one of the two desires. If God loves us at all and these claims are not true, then solving the hiddenness problem is easy; for, in that case, one of two conclusions would follow. Either divine love is radically different from human love in its idealized form (a claim I hope to establish by other means in this chapter) or those working on divine hiddenness over the past quarter century have been importantly mistaken about what ideal human love might look like (a claim I reject, but whose truth would cast serious doubt on the premises that drive the hiddenness problem).

What I now want to show is that *perfect love*, or *divine love*, cannot plausibly be identified with idealized human love. In a somewhat misleading slogan: perfect love is not the same as love perfected. By *divine love*, I mean whatever kind of love a perfect being might have for another person or group of persons. Since any instance of divine love will be in accord with God's absolute perfection, any instance of divine love will also appropriately be described as a case of *perfect love*. *Ideal*, or *idealized*, love is the kind of love that one person would have for another person or group if she were to have for that person or group an idealized version of one of the best kinds of human love. We shall see that there are strong reasons for thinking that a perfect being *would not* have this latter kind of love for human beings (either individually or as a group). The upshot, then, will be that there is strong reason to doubt that divine love is equivalent to ideal love.

2

Let me begin by explaining what it means, in general, to have an attribute in an ideal way. Some attributes are primitive; they cannot be analyzed into simpler component ones. If *existence* is an attribute, it is plausibly like this. Maybe *concreteness* and *abstractness* are like this as well. In the case of traits like these, it is hard to say exactly what we mean when we speak of their idealization; but usually, if it is meaningful at all, it involves at least (and maybe no more than) the removal of all relevant limitations. So, for example, the idealization of existence is (plausibly) just necessary existence, since one way for something's existence to be limited is for it to be temporary or otherwise contingent. Or, if there are modes of existence corresponding to the most general kinds of things, then the idealization of (generic) existence might involve the removal of all limitations that would be imposed under any particular mode of existence.

For complex attributes, idealization will likewise involve the removal of relevant limitations. But it will also involve idealization of component properties. So, for

---

[9] Cf. Anders Nygren, *Agape and Eros* (New York: Harper & Row, 1969).

example, if being human is analyzed as being a rational animal, the ideal human would be ideal with respect to rationality and ideal with respect to animality (whatever exactly that would mean). Perhaps obviously, the idealization of a property—simple or complex—will involve *only* the removal of limitations that are consistent with still having the trait. So an ideal human will *not* be an ideal being, and vice versa, since (I assume) no human being is omnipresent in space-time.[10]

Consider, then, the idealization of love, understood as including desire for the good of the beloved or desire for union with the beloved. In light of what has just been said, a person who loves an individual or group of individuals in an ideal way would be unlimited in her desire for union with her beloved, unlimited in her desire for the good of her beloved, or both. But now consider what it would mean to be unlimited in these ways. One who limitlessly desires the good for an individual or group would desire their good in a way that eclipses in priority and strength any desires focused on anyone or anything apart from that individual or group, including desire for one's own good. Likewise for someone who limitlessly desires union with their beloved.

So, for example, imagine two parents, one of whom desires the good of her children to some particular degree, and the other of whom desires the good of her children ever so slightly more. Perhaps the second parent is slightly less focused on her own good; perhaps she is slightly less focused on the good of others. Clearly, whatever else we might say about the virtues and vices of these two parents, it is the second parent who (for better or worse) comes closer to the least limited, most idealized form of *desire for the good of her children*. Likewise if the desire in question were desire for union.

In reflecting on this example, one might already find reason to doubt that what I am calling *ideal* love could sensibly be identified with *perfect* love. One might also think that it is not aptly called "ideal" love. Mark Murphy, en route to defending conclusions similar to those I will be defending here, raises the same concern. As he puts it, "Our ordinary conception of being excellently loving involves appropriateness conditions, so that the extent to which one is motivated toward the good of another and seeks union with that other is fitting to the relationship between them."[11] I agree, and will say more about this as the chapter unfolds. But

---

[10] Close attention to this fact reveals some thorny problems with the method of perfect-being theology. On this, see Jeff Speaks, *The Greatest Possible Being* (Oxford: Oxford University Press, 2018). It also stands in prima facie conflict with the doctrine of the incarnation, since one wants to say that, as God, the incarnate Christ is an ideal *being* and, as a man, he is an ideal human being. This concern, however, can be addressed by noting that the ideal *being*, according to Christian doctrine, is the Triune God, with whom the incarnate Christ is not strictly identical. For further explication of my views on the Trinity and incarnation, see Michael C. Rea, "The Trinity," in *The Oxford Handbook of Philosophical Theology* (Oxford: Oxford University Press, 2009); and "Hylomorphism and the Incarnation," in *The Metaphysics of the Incarnation*, ed. Anna Marmodoro and Jonathan Hill (Oxford: Oxford University Press, 2011).

[11] Murphy, *God's Own Ethics*, 36. I said that Murphy defends conclusions *similar* to those I will be reaching here. (See also Murphy, "Toward God's Own Ethics," in *Challenges to Religious and Moral Belief*, ed. Michael Bergmann and Patrick Kain [Oxford: Oxford University Press, 2014], 154–71.) At first glance one might think that he is defending the *same* conclusions. In particular, he argues that God would neither be maximally devoted to the pursuit of human welfare nor maximally

for now, let us hold this objection in abeyance and suppose that, at least for God, it is *not* obvious that excellence in loving would diverge from what I am calling ideal love; and let us entirely set aside, because they are wholly insubstantial, any objections to the label, "ideal."[12]

In addition to wondering whether ideal love would be a good thing, one might also wonder whether it is even possible. There are at least two reasons why one might think it is not.

First, desire for union with someone and desire for their good can conflict. There are limits on how much interpersonal union human beings can endure, and from whom, and under what circumstances. So one person's limitless desire for someone else's good might well conflict with or force limits upon her desire for union with them, and vice versa. Perhaps this is how it would be with God's desires toward us. If so, then it follows immediately that if God is a perfect lover, God would not, indeed could not, love anyone in a way that is ideal with respect to both desires.

It is not obvious to me that a *perfect* being's unbounded pursuit of union with some individual or group would inevitably conflict with pursuit of their good; but I think this possibility should not be ruled out by a characterization of ideal love. So let me qualify the characterization of ideal love as follows: ideal desire for the good of a person or group and ideal desire for union with them, is as I have already characterized them; but ideal *love* that includes both desires will hold and pursue the two desires in balance with one another. To put it in other words: if someone ideally desires the good for a person or group, then that desire is motivationally predominant for her, and likewise for ideal desire for union; but ideal *love* that includes both desires

---

devoted to the pursuit of union with human beings. Superficially, this is *exactly* the conclusion I will be reaching. So why not just help myself to Murphy's arguments and move on?

The answer, in short, is that Murphy and I differ in our concept of *maximal love*. Murphy's goal is to show that one cannot reason from the belief that God is perfect to the conclusion that God is *loving*. He thinks that scripture provides reason to believe that God is loving, but he denies that *love* is included in the concept of perfection. His reason for denying this is that, on his view, perfections—attributes included in the concept of perfection—have intrinsic maxima, whereas love does not. The intrinsic maximum for a property is "a point beyond which one cannot more valuably realize that property, either because the property cannot be realized more fully, or if it can be realized more fully, its realization would not be more valuable" (p. 35). But, he argues, pursuit of human welfare and pursuit of union do not have intrinsic maxima; so neither does love. It is in *just this sense*, for Murphy, that God fails to be maximally devoted either to our good or to the pursuit of union with us.

As I am conceiving of it, however, *maximal* devotion does not require that there be an upper limit on the realization of the devotion in question. Rather, it requires only that *nothing else is of equal or higher priority*—the maximally devoted person is not disposed to sacrifice the object of devotion for the sake of any other object or goal. Murphy does not seem interested in ruling out the possibility that God is, *in this sense*, maximally devoted to our good or to pursuing union with us. His concern lies elsewhere. Thus, his arguments do not establish the conclusion I aim to establish.

[12] Objections to the label are insubstantial because the label is not meant to convey a *view* about excellence in loving. The kind of love I have in mind needs *some* label to facilitate discussion, and "ideal" is reasonably well motivated. But we could easily change the label without affecting the substance of the discussion. The first objection, that my conclusion is already obvious, I hold in abeyance because I think that it is not antecedently obvious that excellence in loving diverges from what I am calling ideal love, even if that conclusion starts to seem obvious as the discussion goes on. As shall emerge over the course of the chapter, many seem to identify perfect love with ideal love as I have characterized it here.

will accord motivational predominance not to either desire on its own, but to the pair, in balance.[13]

Second, one might worry that ideal love toward *everyone* is impossible because ideal desire for the *good* for everyone would be precluded by conflicts between what is in various people's best interest. Jeffrey Jordan, for example, maintains that God loves everyone with equal intensity only if God equally "identifies" with each person's interests, or equally takes each person's interests as God's own; and he goes on to argue that this, together with the obvious fact that people's interests often conflict with one another, implies that God does not love everyone with equal intensity. On the assumption that limitlessly desiring the good for someone implies identifying with their interests in the relevant sense, Jordan's conclusion also implies that it is impossible for God to desire, in an unlimited way, the good for two individuals whose interests conflict.[14]

Jordan's argument is vulnerable to plausible criticism on at least two points: first, it is unclear that love for a person requires identifying with their interests; second, it is unclear that God cannot maximally identify with the interests of two individuals whose interests conflict.[15] But even if his argument is correct, his conclusion remains consistent with the thesis that a perfect being would love *some* human beings—indeed, might love *very many* of them—in an ideal way. His conclusion is also consistent with the claim that a perfect being would love human beings *collectively*, even if not individually, in an ideal way; for all that would be required for this would be a limitless desire for the good of humanity (which would sidestep the worry raised by human beings whose interests conflict) together with a limitless desire for union with all of humanity.

My own view, by contrast, is that a perfect being would love *no* particular human being in an ideal way; nor would God love human beings collectively in an ideal way. Furthermore, unlike Jordan's argument, mine depends on no controversial theses about the necessity of God identifying with someone else's interests. So I will set aside the dispute between Jordan and his critics, and I will simply stipulate that, considerations of goodness and rationality aside, it is at least possible for an otherwise perfect being to love human beings ideally—to be maximally oriented toward them, according motivational predominance both to the desire for union with them (individually or collectively) and to the desire for their good, or to the pair in balance with one another if they happen to conflict.

---

[13] I thank Robert Audi for the suggestion to understand the idealization of the desires of love in terms of motivational predominance. If a definition of motivational predominance is wanted, I tentatively offer the following: a desire d is motivationally predominant for a person $s =_{df} d$ provides s with a reason to act with the aim of fulfilling the desire, and s has no reason of equal or greater strength not to act with the aim of fulfilling d. Note that this definition allows for multiple non-competing desires to have motivational predominance for a person; but it does not allow for competing desires to be motivationally predominant, except in the case where they are held in balance with one another as components of a larger desire.

[14] See Jeff Jordan, "The Topography of Divine Love," *Faith and Philosophy* 29, no. 1 (2012): 53–69.

[15] Ross Parker, "Deep and Wide: A Response to Jeff Jordan on Divine Love," *Faith and Philosophy* 30 (2013): 444–61. Thomas Talbott, "The Topography of Divine Love: A Response to Jeff Jordan," *Faith and Philosophy* 30 (2013): 302–16, raises additional objections, one of which is that there are no genuine conflicts of interest in a theistic universe. This objection is relevant to my own argument, so I will deal with it later. Jordan's own reply is in "The Topography of Divine Love: A Reply to Thomas Talbott," *Faith and Philosophy* 32 (2015): 182–87.

3

I turn now to my argument for the conclusion that divine love is not ideal love. I will start by challenging the idea that a perfect being might ideally desire the good for human beings.

Jordan Wessling uses the term "supreme love" to describe this kind of devotion: "When God has supreme love for a person, He desires her highest good, and His character generates no contradictory desire of equal or greater strength; God therefore does all that is morally permissible and metaphysically possible to fulfill this desire."[16] Wessling himself affirms that God has supreme love for every human being, and he furthermore acknowledges (by way of trying to explain why it makes sense to *argue* for that claim, as he does in his paper) that the view is "widely assumed" among contemporary philosophers of religion.

If this view is correct—if God does have supreme love for everyone—then God is something like what Susan Wolf would call a *(loving) moral saint*, someone who is maximally committed to improving the welfare of other people or of society as a whole, to the exclusion of the promotion of her own interests or welfare and even to the exclusion of the promotion of other competing goods.[17] However, Wolf argues persuasively that moral sainthood as she conceives of it is not a state toward which it would be at all rational, good, or desirable for a human being to strive. For similar reasons, so I shall argue, neither would it be rational, good, or desirable for a perfect being to strive for moral sainthood so conceived.[18] Thus a perfect being would not love any human being, or group of human beings, in an ideal way.

At the heart of Wolf's argument is the idea that it is genuinely good to cultivate and embrace love for goods other than the well-being of others, and to love these goods for their own sake or for what one personally gets out of them, rather than simply for what they contribute to the well-being of others. Examples include love for art, natural beauty, good food, sport and leisure, and the like. It is also good, she thinks, to devote resources—even resources that could have instead been used to safeguard or promote the well-being of others—to nurturing these loves, and to developing one's own personal talents, interests, and projects. By virtue of their inherent limitations, however, human beings cannot do these things while at the same time dedicating themselves to promoting as much good as possible for others. For people who must make choices between goods to love and projects in which to invest, the good life will involve making trade-offs between promoting the welfare of others and promoting one's own personal interests. So, on the assumption that we rationally ought to strive for a good life, we ought not to strive for moral sainthood.

---

[16] Jordan Wessling, "The Scope of God's Supreme Love," *Philosophia Christi* 14 (2012): 338.
[17] Susan Wolf, "Moral Saints," *Journal of Philosophy* 79/8 (1982): 419–39.
[18] Some who resist Wolf's conclusion that sainthood is not an ideal worth striving for have been inclined to challenge her *characterization* of sainthood. (See, for example, Robert Merrihew Adams, "Saints," *Journal of Philosophy* 81 (1984): 392–401.) I think that there is merit to these objections, but for purposes here, I want to stick with Wolf's understanding of sainthood, just for the sake of convenience. The question here, after all, is whether it makes sense to suppose that God would manifest the sort of devotion to human good that Wolf associates with the term "moral saint," and to answer that question, it does not really matter whether she is correct in making that association.

Might it be the case that moral duty requires us to sacrifice a "good life" for the sake of devotion to the well-being of others? No; for, in that case, what I am calling a *good life* would not genuinely be good, and it would be (contrary to what Wolf argues) rational and good to strive for moral sainthood after all. In other words, the very intuitions that tell us that it is good to pursue goods besides the well-being of others also tell us that we should not be pursuing moral sainthood.

But what about God, who is unlimited in resources and cognitive capacity? Wolf's arguments have not, to my knowledge, been cited as providing reasons for thinking that God would not be maximally devoted to the promotion of human welfare; and I think that the reason has mainly to do with divine omnipotence. One of the most widespread, even if generally unspoken, assumptions underlying the literature on the problem of evil and the problem of divine hiddenness is that, because God is all powerful, God faces no interesting or morally relevant choices between the promotion of God's own interests, projects, and so on (whatever they might be) and the promotion of human well-being. For this reason, people have tended to think that God is justified in permitting evil, suffering, and divine hiddenness only if those things serve human goods—only if, in other words, God's permission of those things is consistent with God's being maximally devoted to the promotion of human welfare.

As I see it, however, part of what it is for God to be genuinely and perfectly personal is for God to be someone with interests and desires distinct from and not necessarily oriented around those of others, projects that further those interests and desires, and a personality that is at least partly expressive of them. With regard to human beings, Wolf observes that "[the pursuit of moral sainthood] seems to require either the lack or denial of the existence of an identifiable, personal self."[19] To my mind, this is true regardless of whether the "self" in question is human or divine.

It is not that having distinct interests, projects that further those interests, and a personality expressive of them are necessary conditions on personhood. Rather, the idea is that these things comprise a central aspect of who one is, and lacking them is a deficiency that somehow diminishes one's personhood. If this is right, then the view that God is maximally devoted to human welfare is inconsistent with the idea that God is genuinely and perfectly personal: it implies that either God is perfect but not really or fully personal, or God is personal but importantly deficient as a person.

If the writings of contemporary philosophers of religion are any guide, many will be content with a concept of God as somehow less than perfectly personal. Although God is typically characterized as a being with personal attributes—knowledge, love, power, and so on—it is also fairly typical to find God talked about in ways that make sense only on the supposition that God is little more than a kind of machine whose programming requires it to entertain and affirm as many truths as possible while at the same time causing, allowing, or preventing worldly events in such a way as to maximize various kinds of moral and nonmoral goods. Of course, nobody explicitly *says* that this is how they think of God; but (so I say, anyway) it is hard to read much contemporary philosophy of religion without getting the sense that this is in fact the picture that underlies much of it.

---

[19] Wolf, "Moral Saints," 424.

In contrast to this, the Christian scriptures seem to encourage us to take very seriously the idea that God is personal and, indeed, that God has a unique personality that is at least partly expressive of God's own purely *self-regarding* interests and desires. For example, the God of the Old Testament is predominantly portrayed as a God of *covenant*, which requires robust personhood;[20] and one might think that part of why it is important that God enter into covenants with human beings is precisely that (as is typical with parties to a covenant) divine goods do not perfectly coincide with human goods, and God is interested in promoting the latter in balance with rather than to the exclusion of the former. We are told that God's ways are not our ways, that God's thoughts are not our thoughts (Isa. 55:8); and we are often reminded (and, frankly, put off by the fact) that God is interested in maximizing God's own glory (whatever exactly that means) and often in ways that seem to conflict with human interests. The scriptures do insist that God loves human beings; but the overall biblical portrait of God is one of a personal being with a unique and beautiful personality who has, in addition to an overwhelming interest in the good of human beings, a strong interest in living out the divine personality for its own sake.

Admittedly, it is at least possible that God's interest in living out God's own personality and in promoting non-anthropocentric goods would never conflict with promotion of the good for all human beings. The possibility seems remote, and I see no reason for thinking that matters have in fact turned out this way. But one might object that, so long as the possibility is there, my claim that ideal love for everyone is *inconsistent* with genuine personality is shipwrecked. For it looks as if a personal being *can* also succeed in promoting everyone else's good.

But *maximal* devotion to something is not just a matter of pursuing it when it poses no conflicts with other things one values; it is, rather, a disposition to promote that thing *regardless* of whether it conflicts with other goods one might wish to promote. So a being who is disposed to promote human welfare *only* in the eventuality that doing so does not conflict with the promotion of his or her own good falls well short of moral sainthood. Such a being is, at best, what we might call an *opportunistic saint*. Opportunistic sainthood is not supreme love, even if it superficially satisfies Wessling's characterization, since we can easily imagine a being whose love for human beings is more intensely focused upon them. So if God is merely an opportunistic saint, then God is not ideally loving toward anyone.

Consider the case, then, where God does face genuine choices between the promotion of purely human goods and the promotion of conflicting divine goods. In that case, moral sainthood would be no more rational, good, or desirable for God to pursue than for human beings to pursue. In fact, there is every reason to think that it would be irrational, bad, and undesirable for God to pursue it. For when the promotion of human goods conflicts with the promotion of divine goods—the living out of God's unique and maximally beautiful personality, the promotion of God's

---

[20] Cf. Stephen A. Geller, "The God of the Covenant," in *One God or Many? Concepts of Divinity in the Ancient World*, ed. Barbara Neveling Porter (Chebeague, ME: CDL Press, 2000), 273–319; and Rea, *The Hiddenness of God*, chap. 3.

other, non-anthropocentric projects, and so on—there is no more reason to think that the promotion of human goods should take priority than there is for thinking that the promotion of mosquito goods should take priority over the promotion of human goods. So even if God has all the power and resources necessary to be maximally devoted to promoting the good for God's beloved, if God is *perfect* God will not be so devoted because to be so would involve a failure of rationality.

Just as there is reason to doubt that God would desire in an unlimited way the good for God's beloved, so too there is reason to doubt that God would desire in an unlimited way union with every individual beloved by God. This for two reasons.

First, it is at best unclear that we, or our personal autonomy, could survive God's *acting* on an unlimited desire for union with us. Imagine being the child of a parent, or the spouse of a man or woman, who came as close as humanly possible to an unlimited desire for union. Being the object of such desire can hardly be said to be an unmitigated good. Can we really be sure that matters would be any different if the parent or spouse in question were God?

Here we must recall again Mark Murphy's observation that what I am calling *ideal* love does not neatly map onto our concept of *excellence* in love. Perhaps there is something about God that would allow us to endure being the object of an unlimited *divine* desire for union. But, again, whether that is so is at best unclear. If we could not endure God's acting on an unlimited desire for union with us, then God would know this and, being perfectly rational, would not have such a desire in the first place. A perfectly rational and omniscient being would have a desire for union that is limited in accord with the amount of union that we could actually endure and enjoy.

In making this argument, have I perhaps misconstrued the notion of "unlimited desire"? One might object that *unlimited desire for union* is not the same as *desire for unlimited union*. Granted, we could not endure unlimited union, and so God would not desire this; but why not think that God's *desire for appropriately limited union* might itself be *unlimited*—presumably in its intensity or in the ardor with which God is disposed to pursue it? One response might be to say that this too is a sort of desire that we could not endure. This way of thinking attributes to God what sounds like an absurdly and unsettlingly fanatical devotion to union with us. One wants divine love, to be sure; but few want to be the object of unlimitedly intense focus and longing on the part of another person.

But suppose we can endure God's unlimitedly desiring (appropriately limited) union with us. Still, there is a second reason to doubt that God would desire us in this way: namely, it is doubtful that human beings individually or together are fitting objects for an unlimited desire for union. In human relationships, we readily acknowledge that some individuals are more fitting objects for unitive desire, or certain degrees of that desire, than others. One should not, for example, desire union (even "appropriately limited" union) with one's cat to the same degree that one would desire union with a human spouse, sibling, or close friend. Even if one were capable of achieving some kind of personal union with a cat, and even if one had the capacity to pursue this in an intense way without sacrificing any aspect of one's pursuit of union with other human beings, the cat simply is not the right sort of object for that degree of unitive desire. The reason for this has to do with the limits on the kind of union that one can have with a cat, as compared with the kind of union one can have with other sentient creatures. Personal union with other human beings is better—instrumentally and for its own sake—than whatever kind of union one can have with a cat; and a rational pattern of desire structure would reflect this fact.

For the same reason, human beings seem not to be appropriate objects for an unlimited divine desire for union. Surely God loves creatures other than human beings—cats and dolphins, for example. But presumably God desires union with such creatures to a lesser degree than God desires union with us; for the kind of union God can have with us is better than the kind of union God can have with them, and God's perfectly rational desire structure will reflect this difference in value. Likewise, however, the kind of union God can have with us is inferior to the kind of union God could have with more Godlike beings; and a perfectly rational desire structure would reflect this fact as well.

Are there more Godlike beings than us? Even if there are not, my point here still stands. Just as the last human being on earth *still* should not have *unlimited* desire for union with members of the "next best" species, so too a perfectly rational deity would not have unlimited desire for union with us simply because we happen to be the best objects available. But, in fact, the Christian doctrine of the Trinity guarantees that, for each member of the Trinity, there *are* more Godlike beings with whom that person can have a unitive relationship. Union with another member of the Trinity will be the best of all possible kinds of union; and so it is that to which each member of the Trinity will direct his or her unlimited unitive desires.

I have now argued that God would have neither an unlimited desire for our good nor an unlimited desire for union with us. I take it as evident that exactly the same reasoning, if sound, will show that, if it turns out that divine love includes both desires and the two desires can conflict with one another, God would not accord motivational predominance to that *pair* of desires. Thus, I take myself to have shown that a perfect being would not be an ideal lover of human beings, and this because maximizing either of the desires of love, or both in balance with one another, toward human beings would be neither good nor rational for a perfect being.

For those who have lingering doubts, perhaps the following consideration will serve to drive the argument home. Unlimited desire for union (even unlimited desire for *appropriately limited* union) with someone or some group, unlimited desire for their good, or unlimited love for them that includes both of these desires held in balance with one another would amount to a kind of worship. The Christian tradition has *never* maintained that human beings are appropriate objects of worship. It has never maintained that desire for the good of *any* creature, or desire for union with them, or both desires held in balance with one another are appropriately accorded motivational predominance. By contrast, it has *always* held that God is the only appropriate object of worship, and that desire for union with God, for divine goods, and for the furtherance of divine projects are precisely the sorts of desires that deserve to be accorded motivational predominance. So to suppose that God has a fundamentally different desire structure—one that locates human beings and their good at the center of all things—is, at best, absurd from a Christian point of view; and, at worst, it is blasphemous.

4

If the conclusion that I have just defended is correct, then there is no incoherence in supposing that God loves human beings perfectly but nevertheless permits divine hiddenness or various other things that cause human pain and suffering for reasons that have nothing to do with the promotion of human goods. Perhaps such things are permitted instead for the realization of legitimate and worthwhile divine goods, or perhaps other goods wholly beyond our ken.

One might try to resist my conclusion by adapting a thought experiment from Jordan Wessling. As I mentioned earlier, Wessling thinks that God would manifest supreme love toward everyone. He offers two positive considerations in support of this claim. First, following a suggestion of Thomas Talbott, he says:

> Maximal love, like God's other great-making properties when directed at creation, must be of universal scope and uppermost quality. Just as God's perfect knowledge ensures that he knows all true propositions infallibly, God's maximal love entails that He loves all created persons supremely.[21]

This consideration I take myself already to have addressed in section 3: understanding divine love in the way that Talbott recommends leads to conflicts between divine love and divine goodness and rationality. Wessling's second consideration is a thought experiment. He invites us to consider two deities, Zeus and Thor, who differ in just the following way: whereas Thor supremely loves everyone but the Athenians, Zeus supremely loves absolutely everyone. Wessling then asks who, of the two, is the more perfect lover? Clearly, he thinks, it is Zeus.[22]

I think that Wessling is right to think that, as the two deities are described here, Zeus is a more perfect lover *of humanity* than Thor; but I do not think that this thought experiment shows that Zeus more closely approximates *absolute* perfection in love. Whatever else one says about perfect love, one at least ought to say this: perfect love *might* be manifested by a perfect being. But supreme love as Wessling conceives of it is pretty much the same as what I have been calling *ideal* love; and I have been arguing throughout this chapter that a perfect being would not love *anyone* in an ideal way. Wessling's thought experiment does not challenge any premise of that argument; and so I see no reason to think that it counts against my conclusions.

I must admit, however, that I find my own conclusions discomforting. I have, as the saying goes, followed my arguments where they lead; and the view at which I have arrived seems to me to be the one that best fits the relevant data (scripture, intuition, empirical fact). But at the same time I *want* God to be maximally oriented toward the promotion of my good, and I want God to have at least a very strong desire for union with me. I do not want to hear that God might balance my interests against God's own; and I am positively disturbed to think that my own interests might well lose out in the balance. God is supposed to be my heavenly parent, after all; and at the heart of

---

[21] Wessling, "The Scope of God's Supreme Love," 344.
[22] Cf. Ibid.

all my own twenty-first-century parental guilt is the impossible idea that parents are supposed to sacrifice absolutely everything to promote the well-being of their children. And so God must do for me.

But my discomfort at hearing that God might prioritize divine interests over my own comes from exactly the same source as the discomfort I would feel if my wife or one of my parents were to say, "I'm sorry, but your interests and mine conflict on this occasion, and today my own interests are going to win out." Those are hard words to hear, and for that reason people do not often say them to one another. In the face of them, one wants to complain that one is being treated hardly, loved poorly. But such decisions are taken all the time in healthy loving relationships, and if people did not make such choices, their relationships would soon become unhealthy. The source of complaint—at least against the *abstract* claim that sometimes the other person's interests will take precedence over one's own—is ultimately selfishness. For, again, moral sainthood is neither a good nor a rational ideal, and so we have no right to demand it of anyone.

Moreover, it is worth pointing out here, precisely against the backdrop of the conclusions reached thus far, what an incredible and comforting surprise it is to learn from scripture (assuming the Christian scriptures are a source of genuine information about God's love for and dispositions toward human beings) just how *much* God loves us.[23] At the same time that the conclusions of this chapter disappoint our deeply self-oriented hopes and expectations for God, so too they dramatically underscore the beautifully comforting exclamation from the epistle of St. John: "Behold what manner of love the Father has bestowed on us, that we should be called children of God!"[24]

The gospels and the New Testament epistles tell us that, although we had no right to this—no moral claim upon God such that perfect goodness would demand this—God loved us enough to become incarnate and to die on a cross for the sake of our salvation. Whatever exactly we make, philosophically speaking, of the doctrine of the atonement, the fact that God would make that sort of sacrifice on our behalf in the absence of some obligation to do so is, in light of the conclusions of this chapter, absolutely stunning. So likewise is the claim, in the epistle to the Romans, that God causes all things to work together for the good of those who love and are called by God. Nothing in the argument of this chapter (or the book as a whole) is intended to negate this important scriptural claim.

Indeed, I want to go a step further and say that I intend my account to be consistent with the view (which I affirm, in no small part because it is plausibly implied by Rom. 8:28) that part of what is involved in God's loving us is a disposition to satisfy a constraint that Marilyn McCord Adams insists must be part of any successful theodicy: namely, that God arranges for the sufferings God permits in our lives, and for the horrendous evils[25] in which we participate either as perpetrators or victims, to

---

[23] Although I do assume that scripture is a source of information about God and God's character, I do not take it to be a wholly unproblematic source. On this, see Rea, *The Hiddenness of God*, chap. 4.

[24] 1 Jn 3:1, NKJV. Copyright ©1982 by Thomas Nelson. Used by permission. All rights reserved.

[25] Adams characterizes horrendous evils as "evils the participation in which (that is, the doing or suffering of which) constitutes prima facie reason to doubt whether the participant's life could (given their inclusion in it) be a great good to him/her on the whole." See Marilyn McCord Adams, "Horrendous Evils and the Goodness of God," in *The Problem of Evil*, ed. Marilyn McCord Adams and Robert Merrihew Adams (Oxford: Oxford University Press, 1990), 26.

be *defeated* within the context of our lives. Defeating something bad is not the same as compensating a person for it, or seeing to it that its badness is outweighed. It is, rather, a matter of the bad thing's being "included in some good enough whole to which it bears a relation of organic (rather than merely additive) unity"; and an instance of evil or suffering is defeated *within the context of someone's life* if their life "is a good whole to which [that instance of evil or suffering] bears the relevant organic unity."[26]

So, on the one hand, I affirm that God is not maximally devoted to our good, and may sometimes allow our proximate good to be sacrificed; and I deny that we have any guarantee that these sacrifices will be allowed *for the sake of* our ultimate good rather than for the sake of other and perhaps non-anthropocentric goods. But, on the other hand, I also affirm that it is part of divine love as revealed in scripture that God will, in any case, work good *for us* out of the evil and suffering in our lives, defeating their badness and guaranteeing that even lives marked by horrendous evil will be great goods, on the whole, to those who have them.[27]

At this juncture, however, one might want to ask what other projects God might have and love so much that God would sometimes prioritize them above promoting our good and pursuing union with us.[28] What sort of personality might God have such that God's pursuing union with us or promoting our good might conflict with God's living out that personality in the way that God wants to?

So a mosquito might ask about us and our projects and personalities. Tempting though it may be to ask such questions, we cannot possibly hope to find defensible answers. *Maybe* one of God's projects involves interacting with humans on certain terms that suit God's personality better than other, more humanly desirable modes of interaction. *Maybe* one of God's projects involves bringing us into a certain kind of relationship with God, or accomplishing certain earthly goals with creation.[29] *Maybe*

---

[26] Adams, "Horrendous Evils," 28.

[27] Thanks to Caroline Paddock for urging me to be explicit about the points in this paragraph and the one preceding it.

[28] J.L. Schellenberg, *The Wisdom to Doubt: A Justification of Religious Skepticism* (Ithaca, NY: Cornell University Press, 2007), 200, seems to dismiss "the whole idea of God pursuing external, perhaps unknown goods for the good of creatures" out of hand on the grounds that God is the good, and so nothing "could provide for a total state of affairs as good as one in which only God exists apart from a creation in every corpuscle aflame with the presence of God." If sound, the same reasoning would justify dismissing the idea of God pursuing unknown goods *not* for the sake of promoting the good of creatures, too. But I do not share the intuitions on which Schellenberg's claims in this passage seem to rest. Moreover, the biblical creation accounts in Genesis 1 and 2 seem to speak against his reasoning. God is depicted as creating all manner of different things, declaring them to be good; but, between creating the first human being and the second one, God declares that it is *not* good for the first one to be alone, thus leading God to create a second human being. None of this makes any sense, however, on the supposition that there are no further goods to be gained once one has a creation whose every corpuscle is aflame with the presence of God. Moreover, contrary to what is argued on pp. 198–201 of Schellenberg's book, I see no support whatsoever coming from *these* ideas to the conclusion that God "would make conscious awareness of the Divine available to every finite personal creature" (p. 200). For there are many ways in which a creature, even a conscious one, might be "aflame with the presence of God" without being consciously aware of God's presence as such.

[29] Some commentators on the book of *Job* read the divine speeches as emphasizing that human beings are not the focal point of creation. See, for example, Kathryn Schifferdecker, *Out of the Whirlwind: Creation Theology in the Book of Job* (Cambridge, MA: Harvard University Press, 2008), chap. 2 and p. 106.

these or similar projects inherently involve some degree of divine hiddenness. Or maybe not. This is precisely the corner of the space of possible goods about which we can most expect to be in the dark.

Then again, perhaps we can just see that there *could not* be other divine loves or projects that conflict with the promotion of human goods. I see two ways of pressing this objection:

One is to suggest that this idea conflicts with God's "psychological aseity."[30] Psychological aseity is the attribute of God whereby God has intrinsically all of the resources necessary and sufficient for being maximally content. Wessling appeals to psychological aseity in order to rebut the claim that God's *creative activity* is fundamentally motivated by self-glorification. I do not affirm that claim, so much of what Wessling says in response to the objection he is concerned to address will not apply to me and my views. But his remarks can be adapted to address claims that I do affirm, and that I appeal to in order to support my conclusions. In particular, Wessling might argue as follows. Psychological aseity guarantees that God has no *self-interest* in the success of projects or the promotion of goods extrinsic to the Godhead. So the idea that God has a *personality* partly characterized by non-anthropocentric loves and interests suggests either that God lacks psychological aseity or that God somehow *disinterestedly* promotes goods that might compete with the good of human beings. Both claims might seem problematic.

I have to admit that I am not particularly motivated to save psychological aseity as Wessling understands it.[31] But suppose I were so motivated. In that case, what I would want to argue—and what, in fact, I am inclined to argue in any case—is that whatever resources we have for making sense of the claim that God *disinterestedly* desires to promote the good for human beings, to pursue their salvation, and to allow them into unitive relationships with God can just as easily be marshaled to make sense of the claim that God disinterestedly desires to promote *other* conflicting goods, or to live out the divine personality in a way that happens to include some measure of divine hiddenness. In short, I see no reason to doubt that pretty much everything I have said so far can be recast in such a way as to avoid the suggestion that God derives any contentment from the goods, whatever they are, with which human interests are in competition.

The second way of pursuing the objection that human interests cannot plausibly compete with non-anthropocentric divine interests is to appeal to Thomas Talbott's argument for the conclusion that, in a universe governed by God, there can be no genuine conflicts of interest *at all*. Talbott acknowledges that there may well be conflicts between two people's *perceived* interests; but, he says, it "is by no means obvious that

---

[30] Wessling, "The Scope of God's Supreme Love," 345ff. Cf. also James Beilby, "Divine Aseity, Divine Freedom: A Conceptual Problem for Edwardsian-Calvinism," *Journal of the Evangelical Theological Society* 47 (2004): 649ff.

[31] Nor would appeal to psychological aseity help the proponent of the Schellenberg problem. That problem is built on the idea that a perfectly loving God would desire relationships with human beings. Could that desire be a disinterested one? I doubt it, for it is hard to make sense of a disinterested desire *for a relationship* with someone. It seems to me that part of what it is to desire a relationship with someone is to take some sort of special interest in them.

the best interest of one person could ever conflict with that of another."[32] This is partly because it is hard to imagine goods the promotion of which would conflict with someone's *best* interests. But it is also because, as he puts it, "love creates a common set of real interests" since, if X loves Y, then what is in Y's best interests is also in X's interest. So likewise, one might think, with God: if God *were* to love us maximally, our best interests would coincide with God's; hence, maximal devotion on God's part to the pursuit of our best interests would perfectly coincide with maximal devotion to the pursuit of God's own interests.

I do not find Talbott's defense of the claim that our interests cannot possibly conflict with God's at all plausible.[33] But rather than rest weight on my objection to that defense (which can be found in note 33) I want simply to note that embracing Talbott's views will be of no help to proponents of the hiddenness argument. Suppose Talbott is right in thinking that if God were to love us maximally, then our best interests coincide with God's. Then one of three conclusions will follow: (a) God does not love us; (b) God does not always do what is in God's own best interests; or (c) sometimes, despite all appearances to the contrary, it is in *our* best interests for divine hiddenness to occur in the ways that it does, and to produce the various negative effects that it does. This is, in effect, a crude restatement of the hiddenness problem, but Talbott's thesis about how love creates a common set of interests changes the dialectic in a significant way. For there are plenty of real and imaginable scenarios where the best interests of lovers seem to conflict; and Talbott's principle, if true, guarantees that all of these—regardless of how much evidence each party might have for thinking there is a genuine conflict, and regardless of how strongly each party might believe that the conflict is genuine—are scenarios in which at least one person is mistaken about what is in their best interests. In light of this, it seems that we should be deeply skeptical about what is in our own best interests, and this opens the door to solving the hiddenness problem by embracing option (c). I do not myself advocate that option, of course, but I do not see how those who agree with Talbott about the necessary coincidence of the best interests of lovers can justify dismissing it.

One might also be tempted to demand an answer to the question of just how far from the *idealization* of love (as characterized above) someone's behavior can depart and still count as love. For, after all, divine hiddenness causes great anguish in some, and the range of other evils permitted by God is absolutely horrendous. Grant that God might sometimes prioritize God's own interests over ours; grant that divine love will not be exactly like human love. Still, there have to be *some* boundaries on what sort of behavior can plausibly count as loving; and one might well object that

---

[32] Talbott, "The Topography of Divine Love: A Response to Jeff Jordan," 313.
[33] Suppose romantic partners X and Y are each at the same time offered once-in-a-lifetime career-advancing opportunities on opposite sides of the globe; and suppose it is true of each of them (and each knows this truth about themselves) that they will flourish as persons only if they are accompanied by the other and are not embittered by the sacrifice of a once-in-a-lifetime career-advancing opportunity. The story can be fleshed out in different ways, but it seems clear that, on one way of fleshing it out, what is in X's best interests is for Y to come to terms with making the sacrifice, and what is in Y's best interests is for X to come to terms with making the sacrifice. If Talbott's principle about love is correct, however, it follows from this that it is in each one's best interests to sacrifice *their own* opportunity. This seems highly counterintuitive at best, incoherent at worst.

permitting wars and genocides, beatings and molestations, paranoid delusions and crippling depression, all manner of violent and degenerative illnesses, not to mention earthquakes and fires and tornadoes and tsunamis is, after all is said and done, rather a distant departure from what we normally think that a person can willingly permit to be done to someone she claims to love.

I think it is true that there are boundaries on what sort of behavior can plausibly count as loving; but *identifying* the boundaries requires a level of knowledge about the range of possible reasons for divine action that I do not think we possess. It is, I think, quite reasonable to think that at least some of the behavior of an omniscient deity might be aimed at securing goods well beyond our ken. This is not to say that we can identify *no* boundaries on what sort of behavior could possibly be consistent with divine love. But I think that our grasp of the range of possible goods and evils and relations among them is insufficient for us to be warranted in thinking of any *actual* evil that it falls outside the bounds of what is consistent with divine love.[34]

Where does that leave us, then, with respect to the question whether divine behavior toward human beings deserves to be called loving? More pertinently, where does that leave us with respect to the question whether divine hiddenness should be taken as evidence that God (if God exists at all) is *not* loving toward human beings, even in an analogical way? If we cannot answer these questions by asking whether God's behavior satisfies some identifiable set of necessary conditions on love, then how *do* we answer them? In the remainder of this chapter, I try to answer that question.

5

On the assumption that God exists and that the Christian scriptures provide reliable testimony about the character and behavior of God, answering the question whether divine behavior deserves to be called loving might seem relatively straightforward. The texts of scripture report that God enters into and faithfully keeps covenants, blesses creatures in various ways, harbors attitudes toward creatures that we normally think of as loving, manifests excessive kindness and mercy to creatures, and so on. We are given parent analogies and told that God *is* love. What more could we ask?

The trouble, of course, is that both scripture and experience also deliver up evidence that seems to undercut the portrayal of God as loving. God enters into and faithfully keeps covenants, but God is also portrayed as commanding genocide. God manifests excessive kindness and mercy to human beings, but hands Job over to be

---

[34] For defense of this claim, see Michael Bergmann, "Skeptical Theism and the Problem of Evil," in *The Oxford Handbook of Philosophical Theology*, ed. Thomas P. Flint and Michael C. Rea (Oxford: Oxford University Press, 2008), 374–99; Michael Bergmann, "Commonsense Skeptical Theism," in *Reason, Metaphysics, and Mind: New Essays on the Philosophy of Alvin Plantinga*, ed. Kelly James Clark and Michael Rea (New York: Oxford University Press, 2012), 9–30; Daniel Howard-Snyder, "Epistemic Humility, Arguments from Evil, and Moral Skepticism," *Oxford Studies in Metaphysics* 2 (2009): 16–57; and Michael C. Rea, "Skeptical Theism and the 'Too-Much-Skepticism' Objection," in *The Blackwell Companion to the Problem of Evil*, ed. Justin P. McBrayer and Daniel Howard-Snyder (UK: Wiley & Sons, 2013), 482–506.

tormented by the accuser and allows Israel to be ravaged by her enemies. God is silent in the face of human suffering, apparently hard to find even when ardently sought, and apparently wholly unknown to substantial segments of the human population. How is it that God is aptly described as loving *even in the face of* such undercutting evidence? How is it that God is loving toward those who are suffering and toward those who are experiencing in various different ways the hiddenness of God? How is it that these people are able to participate in a positively meaningful relationship with God just by trying?

Asking these questions might seem equivalent to asking for an answer to the problem of evil, a theodicy, an answer to the question of how a perfect being could be justified in allowing people to suffer in the ways that human beings do. But in fact they are not equivalent. At the end of the previous section, I appealed to the gap between our grasp of the range of possible goods, evils and relations among them, and God's grasp of the same to defend a broad skepticism about claims to the effect that the occurrence of some particular bad event is inconsistent with divine love. This is a version of the so-called *skeptical theist* response to the problem of evil, which is, on its own, a *complete* response to that problem. But even if one solves the problem of evil by adopting skeptical theism, the question might still arise as to how it could possibly be *apt* to characterize a God who permits (say) the holocaust as loving toward the victims of the holocaust. Skeptical theism blocks the inference to the conclusion that God is not perfectly good or perfectly loving; it even blocks the inference to the conclusion that God is not perfectly loving toward those particular victims. But it does not tell us why we should not at least be in doubt about the excellence of God's love toward those victims.

The same is true in the case of divine hiddenness. Let us stipulate, for present purposes, that all divine behavior, including all that relates to divine hiddenness, is *justified*. God has perfectly good unknown (and perhaps unknowable) reasons for permitting creaturely suffering; God also has perfectly good reasons for allowing or causing the phenomena associated with divine hiddenness. Given this stipulation, God's perfect goodness is beyond question. On the plausible assumption that an imperfect lover—that is, a being who manages to love, but does so imperfectly—is also imperfect as regards goodness, God's perfect lovingness is beyond question too.

Still, we might well wonder how God's relationship with individual human beings—particularly those who suffer and those who experience God's hiddenness— is *aptly described* as loving. We might wonder what *signs* of divine love there are in the relationship. These are the "lingering questions" that I mentioned at the outset of this chapter—the questions that must be answered in order to make my solution to the hiddenness problem *satisfying*. The reason these questions linger is that there is distance between divine love and even the best human love, such that (as we have seen) it is not given *a priori* that a *perfectly loving being* will love all human beings equally or even at all. That God loves *us* is an article of faith, not philosophy; a dogma of revealed theology rather than natural theology. And so we must ask what it is about God's relationship to such human beings that lets us hang on to the positive analogies traditionally used to characterize divine love and to resist more negative ones. This question I take up in detail in the second half of *The Hiddenness of God*.

4

The Hidden Love of God and the Imaging Defense

Sameer Yadav

1 What *must* a loving God do?

When we look out at the world, what must we expect to find if it is truly the case that a perfectly loving God exists? J. L. Schellenberg has argued that, at a bare minimum, we should expect that such a God would ensure that everyone who is capable of and open to embarking on a personal relationship with God would believe that God exists.[1] The thought expressed here is that openness to a personal relationship with the beloved belongs to the very nature of a loving being.[2] Furthermore, it is impossible to be truly open to a personal relationship with the beloved if the lover is unwilling for the beloved to believe that the lover even exists. Thus, by definition, if God is to be loving, God must be willing for all of his human creatures, which are capable and nonresistant to the belief in God's existence, to believe that God is in fact there.[3] Moreover, because it belongs to the very idea of divine perfection that God also has perfect knowledge and power, God's perfect love would thus not only be necessarily *willing* to prevent nonresistant nonbelief in God's existence but also be *able* to prevent such unbelief.[4] If this form of thinking is correct, then it logically follows—just in virtue of an analysis of what it would mean for there to be a perfectly loving God—that there must be no such thing as humans who are open to forming personal relationships with God, but who fail to believe the proposition that God exists. Perfect love would motivate God

---

[1] I will be drawing principally from two of Schellenberg's most recent publications explicating and defending the argument from hiddenness. The first is *The Hiddenness Argument: Philosophy's New Challenge to Belief in God* (New York: Oxford University Press, 2015) and the second is an essay entitled "Divine Hiddenness and Human Philosophy," in *Hidden Divinity and Religious Belief: New Perspectives*, ed. Adam Green and Eleonore Stump (New York: Cambridge University Press, 2015), 13–32. Although a more popular recounting, *The Hiddenness Argument* has the virtue of displaying very clearly the logical structure of Schellenberg's argument and his primary strategies for supporting its premises. "Divine Hiddenness and Human Philosophy," on the other hand, provides a more detailed clarification of the argument in the face of the interpretations and objections put forward by his most influential critics.
[2] Schellenberg, *The Hiddenness Argument*, 38–51.
[3] Ibid., 52–53.
[4] Ibid., 45, 57.

to prevent such failures of belief in humans nonresistant to personal relationships with God, and perfect knowledge and power would enable God to ensure that no such failures of belief occur.[5]

If a perfectly loving God exists, then, necessarily, belief in God's existence is evident to anyone cognitively capable and reasonably open to recognizing it. But, Schellenberg observes, that is not what we find when we look at the world. Instead, we find many instances of human beings who are not (or were not) resistant to forming the belief that God exists, but who nevertheless are (or were) unable to believe that God exists or that he is open to a relationship with them. Some such people would very much *like* to believe that God exists and desires a relationship with them, but simply cannot genuinely and honestly come to form that belief.[6] God remains hidden to them. Others in human history—including our earliest ancestors in human prehistory—have lacked the requisite cultural and religious infrastructure, training, or background to so much as conceive of the existence of a personal and perfect divine being who desires relationship with them. Such people would not have even had the wherewithal to desire relationship with God or recognize God as hidden. Having literally no conception of a perfectly loving divine being, they therefore could not have knowingly resisted an open relationship with that being. Still, we can assume that many such people, if they could have formed the relevant conception of God, would have desired relationship with God. But these facts of divine hiddenness violate what we must expect to find if there really were such a thing as a perfectly loving God. Given the existence of divine hiddenness, we are logically forced to conclude that such a God does not exist.[7] But if God is supposed to be *essentially* loving, then the nonexistence of a loving God entails simply that there is no God.[8]

In putting forth this atheistic argument from the hiddenness of God's existence,[9] Schellenberg is careful to distinguish it from the atheistic argument from evil. The problem of divine hiddenness, he notes, is not merely a version of the problem of evil, since it does not require us to think of God's hiddenness as *bad*.[10] The phenomenon of nonresistant nonbelief in God's existence is not cited as a barrier to belief in God because it is an evil that God ought to prevent. Rather, the phenomenon of nonresistant nonbelief is a barrier to belief in God because its existence is logically incompatible with a divine attribute—love—that God is supposed to have essentially. Moreover, it is precisely divine love, and not divine goodness or power or knowledge that generates the problem. Whereas divine goodness or benevolence, for example, aims at the well-being of others, divine love is aimed at a mutual conscious awareness of others in personal interactive relationship with them.[11] In other words, the demands of divine love include not merely a pursuit of our highest good, but also a divine pursuit of

---

[5] Ibid., 56–73.
[6] Ibid., 74–86.
[7] Ibid., 86–88.
[8] Ibid., 102–03.
[9] For a more formal presentation with numbered premises and the conclusions that follow from them, see ibid., 103; and Schellenberg, "Divine Hiddenness and Human Philosophy," 24–25.
[10] Schellenberg, *The Hiddenness Argument*, 28–31.
[11] Ibid., 38.

fellowship or communion with us, and it is that demand that Schellenberg takes to be logically or conceptually inconsistent with nonresistant nonbelief.

Despite the fact that Schellenberg's argument is distinct from the traditional problem of evil, it nevertheless bears a striking structural resemblance to the deductive formulation of that problem.[12] Both purport to be deductive arguments to the conclusion that God does not exist. Both are predicated on a conceptual analysis of divine attributes combined with an empirical premise that is taken to be logically inconsistent with that analysis. Both, that is, take the following form:

(1) If God exists, God is essentially F
(2) If God is essentially F then, necessarily, P
(3) Not-P
(4) Therefore, God is not essentially F (from 2 & 3)
(5) Therefore, God does not exist (from 1 & 4)

Premise 1 specifies some essential attribute(s) F of God. In the problem of evil F is divine goodness, power, and knowledge, whereas in the problem of hiddenness F is divine love. The second premise is a conceptual analysis of F, which claims that there is some empirical fact P that is *entailed by* F, some state of affairs that *necessarily follows from* F. As Alvin Plantinga shows in *God Freedom and Evil*, the classical formulation of the problem is only made fully deductive once this premise is made explicit.[13] Once it is made explicit, the deductive or "logical" problem of evil can be seen to claim that if God is essentially perfect in knowledge, power, and goodness, then, necessarily, evil would not exist. On Schellenberg's argument, this premise is explicitly spelled out, but in terms of the claim that perfect love is necessarily open to personal relationship and that openness to personal relationship necessarily precludes nonresistant nonbelief. Thus, Schellenberg's claim is that if God is essentially perfect in love, then, necessarily, nonresistant nonbelievers would not exist.

It is only once we get to premise 3 that we have moved out of conceptual analysis of what would necessarily follow if God were F and into the empirical territory of what is in fact the case. In the logical problem of evil, the empirical claim not-P in premise 3 is that it is not the case that no evil exists (i.e., evil exists), whereas for Schellenberg, the premise not-P is that it is not the case that there is no nonresistant nonbelief (i.e., there are nonresistant nonbelievers). But if God having the relevant essential attribute *necessarily* requires there is no evil or there is no nonresistant nonbelief (premise 2), then finding some evil or some nonresistant nonbelievers logically entails the conclusion 4, that God does not have an essential or defining attribute F; on the problem of evil this means that God does not have perfect knowledge, power, and goodness, whereas on the problem of hiddenness the entailment is that God is not perfectly loving. But since

---

[12] Michael Rea and Michael Murray also point out the parity of Schellenberg's current argument with the logical problem of evil. See Michael J. Murray and Michael C. Rea, *An Introduction to the Philosophy of Religion* (New York: Cambridge University Press, 2008), 182.

[13] Alvin Plantinga, *God, Freedom and Evil* (Grand Rapids, MI: Eerdmans, 1977), 12–23.

(according to premise 1) these are essential attributes of God, God lacking the relevant property logically entails the stronger conclusion in 5, that God does not exist.[14]

The deductive validity of the argument therefore depends on the inconsistency of that empirical claim with a necessary truth about God given in premise 2. Schellenberg appears to recognize this fact in his most recent formulation of the problem in *The Hiddenness Argument.* There he says that from the premise that "a loving God *would not* permit nonresistant nonbelief, it deductively follows that there are no goods, known or unknown, such that for their sake God *might* do so."[15] A charitable reading requires us to suppose that what Schellenberg means is not that a loving God merely *would not* permit nonresistant nonbelief, but that he *could not*. If permitting nonresistant nonbelief were something God merely would not do, as a matter of what we have reason to believe God is disposed or inclined to do, given some things we take ourselves to know about God, then we might be able to come up with some further considerations about God or some possible scenarios in which we *could* imagine God in fact permitting nonresistant nonbelief for some reason that does not impugn God's perfect love. Even if it is unlikely for God to permit it, maybe he could—just as we might say that Mother Theresa would not eat a baby, but she could. There is a possible world in which she *does*, but it is just an extremely remote possible world.

If Schellenberg similarly has in mind, not that God remaining hidden from nonresistant nonbelievers is a conceptual or logical impossibility, but rather that what we can know of God makes the likelihood of remaining hidden vanishingly small, then premise 2 in the above argument would have to be revised. Instead of affirming the impossibility of nonresistant nonbelief, it would have to say, "If God is essentially loving, then *possibly* there is no non-resistant non-belief" or "If God is essentially loving, then there is *likely* no non-resistant non-belief." But on any such revision we would no longer have a deductively valid argument. Even if an essentially loving God permits something unlikely, given what we know or can know about divine love, it does not follow that God is not essentially loving or that God does not exist. We should therefore suppose that Schellenberg instead wants us to read premise 2 with the full force of conceptual, logical, or metaphysical necessity in place.[16] If God is essentially loving, then nonresistant nonbelief is *impossible*.

Making explicit this formal parallel between the logical problem of evil and Schellenberg's logical problem of divine hiddenness provides a helpful way of identifying

---

[14] Cf. Schellenberg, *The Hiddenness Argument*, 103; and "Divine Hiddenness," 25. Michael Rea has pointed out to me in private correspondence that, although the argument as Schellenberg currently defends it takes the form of the deductive problem of evil, his earlier formulation in *Divine Hiddenness and Human Reason* (Ithaca, NY: Cornell University Press, 1993) claims that the problem of hiddenness is a "special instance of the *empirical* problem of evil" (p. 9, emphasis in original). There Schellenberg appeals to the fact identified by the empirical premise—that nonresistant nonbelievers exist—as a phenomenon that is both an evil and one that gives us sufficient reason to suppose that God probably does not exist. This formulation of the problem more nearly approximates an *evidential* problem of hiddenness. However, there is also an *existential* problem of hiddenness consisting in God's permitting us to undergo a subjective condition that is bad for our relationship with God. This chapter does not seek to address the evidential or existential problems, but in subsequent work I will aim to extend the defense I outline here to address them as well.

[15] Schellenberg, *The Hiddenness Argument*, 111.

[16] It will not much matter for the purposes of my argument what sort of necessity is involved here, only that the state of affairs I posit as a defense can be plausibly regarded as possible in the corresponding sense.

the appropriate strategy for responding to the argument. The parallel should call to mind the strategy for undermining the logical problem of evil made famous by Plantinga's treatment of it in *God, Freedom and Evil*. Plantinga pointed out that in order to show that premise 2 is false, and thus that the deductive argument fails, all we need to do is undermine its strong modal claim that P is a *necessary* consequence of God's being essentially F. To do that, it is sufficient to adduce a scenario on which P is *possible* for a God who is essentially F, however remote the possibility might be. Provided that the imagined scenario includes a plausibly coherent possibility that P, we will have a defeater for the claim of premise 2 that P is impossible. Thus, with respect to the logical problem of evil, premise 2 would require that if God is essentially perfectly wise, powerful, and good, then necessarily, no evil exists. But since this entails that there is no possible reason that a God who is essentially perfectly wise, powerful, and good might permit any evil, showing that it is false is as simple as offering a counterexample—a plausibly coherent scenario in which an essentially perfectly wise, powerful, and good God possesses a sufficient reason to permit an instance of evil. Plantinga suggests that a divine interest in human free will is one possible such reason. He is careful to identify this scenario as supplying us with a "defense" rather than a "theodicy" because he does not purport to show that the divine interest in promoting human free will is the *actual* reason a perfectly wise, powerful, and good God in fact permits evil, or even a *likely* reason that God permits evil. He only purports to show that it is a possible reason.[17] But if it is so much as possible, then premise 2 of the deductive argument from evil is false and the argument fails.[18]

Given the formal parity between the logical problem of evil and Schellenberg's problem of hiddenness, a Plantingian defense should likewise be sufficient to undercut Schellenberg's argument. If we can cite a merely possible scenario in which God remains in the relevant sense essentially perfectly loving while nevertheless failing to ensure, for every nonresistant finite person S capable of personal relationship with God, that S believes the proposition that God exists, then premise 2 comes out false and the atheistic conclusion does not follow. Moreover, as was the case with respect to the logical problem of evil, the relevant counterexample need not mark out any actual state of affairs, only a possible one. Many, perhaps most, of the proposed responses to Schellenberg that theists have formulated can be plausibly interpreted as Plantingian defenses.[19] We can read them as possible counterexamples to Schellenberg's claim

---

[17] Plantinga, *God, Freedom and Evil*, 28–29.
[18] Or, at any rate, it is defused by shifting the burden of proof back onto the atheist to demonstrate that there is something about God's being essentially F that entails the impossibility of P despite the counterexample offered by the Plantingian Defender.
[19] Thus, for example, while the contributors of *Divine Hiddenness: New Essays*, ed. Daniel Howard-Synder and Paul K. Moser (New York: Cambridge University Press, 2001) take themselves to be responding primarily to an evidential rather than logical problem, they all offer some defense of the *compatibility* of divine love with the existence of nonresistant nonbelief. Michael Murray offers a freewill defense (p. 63), while Laura Garcia (p. 95), William Wainwright (p. 115), and Paul Moser (p. 145) all hold that hiddenness is compatible with an essentially loving God's general plan for the world. In reckoning with Schellenberg's explicit argument for the incompatibility of divine love with the existence of nonresistant nonbelief, many of the contributors to the more recent *Hidden Divinity and Religious Belief* (e.g., Moser, Howard-Snyder, and Green) likewise attempt to adduce some plausible scenario in which perfect divine love possibly coexists with nonresistant nonbelief.

that a perfectly loving God must not permit nonresistant nonbelief, which purport to offer scenarios on which a perfectly loving God could possibly permit nonresistant nonbelief. My aim in this chapter is to add another Plantingian defense onto the heap, but one of a different sort than is typically given.

2 What *might* a loving God do?

Recall that the argument from hiddenness specifies premises 1 and 2 of the argument schema above in the following way, which I will call H1 and H2:

H1: If God exists, then God is essentially perfectly loving.
H2: If God is essentially perfectly loving, then, necessarily nonresistant nonbelief does not exist.

We saw that the kind of necessity involved in H2 is supposed to be a conceptual, logical, or metaphysical necessity, derived from the very meaning of being essentially perfectly loving. So on what analysis of "perfectly loving" can Schellenberg claim that perfect love excludes the existence of nonresistant nonbelief in the lover? Schellenberg derives this analysis by looking, first, at what he supposes love must involve, and then, adding to this his analysis, what *perfect* love must involve. He holds the following three claims L1–L3 about the nature of love relationships between any lover S1 and a beloved S2:

L1: S1 loves S2 only if, when morally and metaphysically possible, S1 is open to a personal relationship with S2, where a personal relationship involves valuing, desiring, and seeking mutual conscious reciprocal interaction between S1 and S2.[20]

L2: S1 is open to a personal relationship with S2 only if S1 does whatever is morally and metaphysically permissible to ensure that where S2 is capable of a personal relationship with S1 and not resistant to it, S2 stands in a state of belief in relation to the proposition that S1 exists.[21]

---

[20] Schellenberg claims that love requires a minimal kind of valuing, desiring, and seeking to pursue personal relationship and further claims that such seeking "normally requires openness" ("Divine Hiddenness and Human Philosophy," 20). In the case of human love, he acknowledges "possible and generally unusual circumstances in which a lover may lack the resources to accommodate the possible *consequences* of openness, that is, to make them consistent with the flourishing of all relevant parties and of any relationship that may exist or come to exist between them. But since God is not such a lover, we may ignore this qualification hereafter" (ibid.; cf. also 29–30; and *The Hiddenness Argument*, 49–50). I have accounted for Schellenberg's qualification of the relatively limited resources of human lovers by simply building it into his general analysis of love as constrained by moral and metaphysical resources of the lover. Thus, for human lovers, in some cases it is morally or metaphysically impossible to remain open to relationship with the beloved despite valuing, desiring, and seeking to cultivate personal relationship.

[21] His strategy for securing this analysis is to defend the claim that a lover's failure to do what is morally or metaphysically possible to ensure that a beloved believe that the lover exists necessarily belongs to the definition of being "not open" to personal relationship. See "Divine Hiddenness and Human Philosophy," 23, 27; and *The Hiddenness Argument*, 57.

It follows from this analysis of love that

> L3: S1 loves S2 only if S1 does whatever is morally and metaphysically permissible to ensure that where S2 is capable of a personal relationship with S1 and not resistant to it, S2 stands in a state of belief in relation to the proposition that S1 exists.

On Schellenberg's analysis of what it means for God to be an essentially *perfect* lover, God must love every finite person.[22] Since a perfect God must be a lover of every finite human person, it follows on the above analysis of love that God satisfies L3 and does whatever is metaphysically possible and morally permissible to ensure that every finite person capable of entering into a relationship with God and not resistant to God actually believes the proposition that God exists. But ensuring the beloved's belief in God's existence is both metaphysically possible and morally permissible for a being with perfect knowledge and power such as theists think God is. It necessarily follows, therefore, that a being of that sort, who is also essentially perfect in love, would ensure that every finite being stands in a state of belief in relation to the proposition that God exists.

From the above analysis of what constitutes a perfectly loving God, it does not merely follow that, if such a being exists, there *are* no such things as nonresistant nonbelievers in God's existence. Rather, what follows is the stronger claim that there could *not possibly be* any nonresistant nonbelievers in God's existence, which is the claim we find as the second premise of the argument in H2. If God could *possibly* love someone without being open to relationship with that person (contra L1), or if God could be open to relationship with a beloved without doing whatever is morally or metaphysically permissible to ensure that the beloved believes in God's existence (contra L2), then there might well be nonresistant nonbelievers who are nevertheless loved by God, and H2 comes out false. So the necessity expressed in H2 derives from the claim that L1 and L2—and consequently L3—are necessary conditions for a love relationship. It is this necessity of love's demands that Schellenberg applies to God as an essentially perfect lover in order to secure the necessity of H2—such that God being a perfect lover with a universal scope, sufficient motive, and infinite resources necessitates that all nonresistant humans necessarily come to believe in God's existence and openness to them.

We can therefore undermine H2 by undermining either L1 or L2 (or both) as necessary conditions for a loving relationship, and we can do that by offering a Plantingian possible counterexample to either L1 or L2 (or both). If we can adduce any merely possible instance in which love—even perfect love—might coherently be thought to coexist with a closure to personal relationship or without the lover necessarily having to ensure that the beloved believes in that lover's existence, then L3 would not necessarily follow. But if L3 does not necessarily follow, then H2 would lose the force of necessity as well, and Schellenberg's argument would fail in just the same

---

[22] *The Hiddenness Argument*, 40.

way that the logical problem of evil does. Accordingly, many Plantingian Defenders have pursued the route of finding plausibly coherent counterexamples to L1 or L2.

The Plantingian counterexamples currently offered in the literature on hiddenness tend to be grounded in a resemblance between God's love for us and our love for one another. "Perhaps," Schellenberg supposes, "someone will suggest that God could be perfectly loving without perpetual openness to relationship if what it is for *God* to be loving is very different from what it is for *us* to be loving. Why should we think that ultimate love would be at all like our love?"[23] Rather than contemplating the prospects for this line of reply, Schellenberg simply dismisses the suggestion as a kind of special pleading:

> The short answer is that it had better be, since otherwise we have no business using that word to refer to it! A somewhat longer one [would say that w]hat it would *feel like* (to put it crudely) to be God loving, and more generally *what would happen* in God—this might indeed by very different from what we find in any finite human case. But what it *means* to be loving is determined by facts about human language, which link it to giving and sharing relationship. The concept of love is our concept. . . . If so then of course what I've said applies [to God's love as well as ours]. . . . If not, then . . . who knows what someone who makes that suggestion [i.e., that God is loving] is talking about?[24]

Likewise, with the notable recent exception of Michael Rea (on which, more in a moment), Plantingian Defenders have granted this parity between divine and human love. They therefore begin by considering scenarios of human love relationships where it seems possible for love to remain non-defective while permitting the beloved's nonresistant nonbelief in the lover's existence. Such instances of hidden human love are then applied to the case of hidden divine love in order to undermine the inference in H2. Thus, for example, just as there are some possible scenarios involving a human beloved and a human lover on which it would be better for the beloved if the knowledge of the lover's existence and openness were hidden, so too there are possible scenarios on which it would be better for us if a divine lover withheld knowledge of God's existence and openness from us.

Defenses that depend on some essential resemblance between the kind of love relationship with us to which God is open and the kind of love relationships to which humans might be open with one another are what we might call *anthropological defenses*. They are grounded precisely in those features of divine-human love relations that we can likewise adduce from human-human love relations. So, to cite one influential example, Daniel Howard-Snyder has suggested that, just like human love relationships can sometimes include short-term expressions of closure to personal relationship (thus undermining the necessity of L1 in an analysis of love), so can God's relationship to us.[25]

---

[23] Ibid., 48.
[24] Ibid., 49.
[25] See Daniel Howard-Snyder, "Divine Openness and Creaturely Nonresistant Nonbelief," in *Hidden Divinity and Religious Belief*, ed. Adam Green and Eleonore Stump (New York: Cambridge University Press, 2015), 126–38.

Schellenberg's reply to this sort of strategy has been to remind us that where it is God who is doing the loving, we have to consider what the *perfect love of an ultimate creator* would require us to expect from God, and accordingly we should suppose that if a perfectly loving God had the choice of creating finite persons to whom God could remain open and for whom God could ensure nonresistant belief in his existence and if the interests of a loving relationship were better served by doing so, then a perfectly loving God would necessarily do so.[26] In response, the Plantingian Defender might then try to double down on the idea that in the human case we are applying to God, the love relationship could not be improved, perhaps because in creating, God could not or would not set things up to improve the situation or because we can find cases of human love to apply to God in which securing the beloved's belief in the lover's existence would not necessarily be a better or more perfect way to initiate the personal relationship in question.[27]

Another example of an anthropological Plantingian defense is Michael Rea's recent argument that perfect love cannot be identified with any maximal or idealized version of human love.[28] On Rea's view, perfect love would still require the appropriate balancing of another's interests with one's own, and sometimes being a perfect lover requires that we close ourselves to seeking personal relationship with others for the sake of preserving our own personhood. Appropriating an influential argument of Susan Wolf, Rea claims that if "moral sainthood" always demands the sacrifice of one's own interests for the sake of another, then moral saints are not perfect agents, whether they are human or divine.[29] The love of a perfect agent, therefore, would only seek to be open to relationship with nonresistant nonbelievers if this did not require the sacrifice of that agent's own interests. But it is at least possible that in some cases there are conflicts between God's pursuit of God's own projects or interests and remaining open to some nonresistant nonbelievers. Therefore, as a perfect agent, God possibly prefers to preserve God's own personhood by remaining closed to relationship with such persons.[30] If so, then L1 is false. Notice, though, that like Howard-Snyder, Rea derives his counterexample by appealing to possible requirements on the preservation of personhood derived from the human case and applied to the divine case. The love

---

[26] Schellenberg, *The Hiddenness Argument*, 45–48; "Divine Hiddenness and Human Philosophy," 29–30.
[27] Howard-Snyder pursues responses along these lines in "Divine Openness and Creaturely Nonresistant Nonbelief," 134–36.
[28] See Rea, "Divine Love and Personality," chap. 5 of *Divine Hiddenness* (Oxford University Press, forthcoming). Subsequent references are to a prepublication draft, 1–33.
[29] Susan Wolf, "Moral Saints," *Journal of Philosophy* 79/8 (August, 1982): 419–39; Rea, "Divine Love and Personality," 11–18.
[30] "It is not that having distinct interests, projects that further those interests, and a personality expressive of them are necessary conditions on personhood. Rather, the idea is that these things comprise a central aspect of who one is, and lacking them is a deficiency that somehow diminishes one's personhood. If this is right, then the view that God is maximally devoted to human welfare is inconsistent with the idea that God is genuinely and perfectly personal: it implies that either God is perfect but not really or fully personal, or God is personal but importantly deficient as a person" (Rea, "Divine Love and Personhood," 13–14).

of perfect human persons can possibly permit closure to personal relationship, and so too might perfect divine personhood.[31]

We can imagine Schellenberg responding by claiming that the morally permissible conflicts of interest between divine and human persons are constrained by what we owe to one another. Perfect parental love may permit, say, refusing to satisfy my child's interests and well-being when, upon my return from a stressful day at the office, I need to rest for a moment alone before commencing to play with her. But given that I have adequate resources and opportunity, and in the absence of any discernible benefit she might derive, there are no interests of mine that could morally justify my refusing to feed her to the point of her starvation. Similarly, given the asymmetry of power and dependence between God and God's creatures, and the divine choice whether to create any finite beings whose good requires relationship with God or not, it seems as if we have better reason than not to regard it as a morally irresponsible defect of a loving God to neglect the basic good of God's creatures for the sake of other divine interests, known or unknown.[32] And likewise, I am sure that there are strategies that are open to Rea to reply.

But surprisingly few Plantingian Defenders have attempted to show that L1 or L2 fail, not on the basis of what a perfectly loving divine person might have in

---

[31] Thus, while Rea attempts to differentiate divine love from human love, the difference turns out to be in respect of the *idealization* of human love, rather than an explication of any difference in the *kind* of love God exhibits from the sort humans exhibit. Instead, Rea's defense appeals to self-preservation in one's projects and interests as a common constraint on both perfect human and perfect divine personhood. As per Wolf, moral sainthood "seems to require either the lack or denial of the existence of an identifiable personal self" (Wolf, "Moral Saints," 424), and this is true, Rea supposes, "regardless of whether the 'self' in question is human or divine" (Rea, "Divine Love and Personality," 13).

[32] I owe this line of criticism to Jordan Wessling. See his "Michael Rea on Love and Divine Personality," http://analytictheology.fuller.edu/michael-rea-love-divine-personality/ (February 2, 2017). Wessling asks us to "consider a relevantly analogous case were a human accumulates twenty cats, knowing full well that he cannot care for them. We would fault him not for occasionally choosing his own interests over the cats but for taking them into his care when he knows he hasn't the resources to meet their most basic needs. Such a person hardly loves the cats. . . . Yet here we are, in a world filled with people who seek God with no response. Doesn't this provide *some* evidence against the existence of a loving God? It's difficult to confidently answer 'no.'"

The stronger response available to Schellenberg is just that the problem of moral sainthood in the context of moral obligations to dependents necessarily demands one's failure to meet one's moral obligations to *both* oneself *and* to one's dependents. Avoiding the introduction of a deficiency in one's personhood in such situations requires settling the dilemma by preferring to satisfy one's obligation to oneself over one's obligation to one's dependent. But, ex hypothesi, God is not merely perfect in personhood but also an essentially *morally perfect* person. For a person such as that, a failure to meet a genuine moral obligation (even an exculpating failure) is by definition impossible. God must therefore refuse to create a world in which God is required to morally fail to meet God's obligations to finite persons, even if doing so has the exculpating justification that it is for the sake of preserving divine personhood. If an essentially morally perfect God who is also perfectly loving exists, there should be no such thing as dependents to whom God fails to meet God's moral obligations, and this includes God's obligations to remain open to those nonresistant nonbelievers that God creates as objects of divine love. If a perfectly moral and loving God chooses to create a world, it must therefore be one without a conflict of interest between God's obligations to Godself and those created for divine love. Creating a world in which no such conflict arises would not thereby make God a merely "opportunistic" saint (contra Rea, "Divine Love and Personhood," 15), because given the moral perfection of the divine nature there would simply be no alternative worlds open to God to create. Nor is this to beg the question against the notion of perfect love, but rather to point out that for any person who is *both* morally perfect and perfectly loving (such as God), that person's moral perfection constrains the ability to express perfect love.

common with any instances of human loving persons, but rather on the basis of what *differentiates* divine personal love from human personal love. This would be to give a properly *theological* Plantingian defense rather than an anthropological one. A theological Plantingian defense aims to adduce a possible scenario that undercuts the alleged necessity about love claimed by L1 or L2, but the grounds for the relevant counterexample are not derived by generalizing from the case of human personal relationships and applying what we find there to the divine case. Instead, I will grant that it might well be the case with respect to human love that such love necessitates openness to personal relationship with the beloved and, further, that such an openness necessitates that the lover ensures that the beloved believes in the lover's existence.

My claim, however, is that things stand differently in the case of divine love. While I will grant L1 with respect to God, that perfect love necessarily requires some kind of expression of openness to personal relationship, I shall deny L2 only in the divine case. Whereas a perfected form of loving relationship that humans enjoy with one another might necessitate that the lover always ensures that the beloved believes in the lover's existence whenever morally or metaphysically permissible, the perfected form of loving relationship that God enjoys with humans does not require this. It is at least possible that there is a unique kind of personal relationship that can only be initiated and sustained with humans by God *qua* God, wherein God's openness to personal relationship with humans is precisely an openness to this unique sort of personal relationship. Further, it is possible that nonresistant nonbelievers in the proposition that God exists can make a start on this kind of personal relationship with God just as well (or, in some cases, perhaps better) than can nonresistant believers in God's existence. If we can describe a scenario on which this is merely possible then we would have a properly theological rather than an anthropological Plantingian defense sufficient to undercut the hiddenness argument.

So what type of personal relationship might God uniquely intend for humans, the best kind of initiation into which would not necessarily require their belief in God's existence? On at least one possible way of articulating a Christian conception of God's relationship to humanity, given in Gen. 1:26, God creates humanity for the intended purpose of *imaging* God. In the remainder of the chapter, therefore, I will spell out divine image-bearing as a distinctively divine form of loving relationship that forms the paradigm of the conscious reciprocal interactive relationship between God and humans. I will argue that this kind of divine-human love relationship is distinct from human relationships of friendship, spousal love, or parenthood and that God's manifesting openness to the personal imaging relationship is compatible with permitting the beloved's nonresistant nonbelief in God's existence, whether or not nonresistant nonbelief turns out to be compatible with any perfected version of those human love relationships.

3 Divine love as imaging

On one reading of the possible world depicted in the Genesis account, God makes the whole of the created order and acts as a beneficent ruler over the creaturely domain.³³ God makes the human creature to *resemble* or *mirror* God's beneficent rule over the created order.³⁴ In other words, to have a human nature is to be the sort of thing that God intends to be in some respect like God in cultivating, nurturing, caring for, and delighting in creation. But humans are still creatures, they are not just little versions of God but rather creaturely resemblances of God *qua* providential ruler.³⁵ It is for this reason that God makes humans to exist as a society, because mirroring God's providential care for creation confronts creatures with a coordination problem that God does not face.³⁶ It is also for this reason that God endows humans with capacities for rational, moral, and social growth, because these are necessary capacities for resembling God within creaturely limits. So, at a minimum, God's relationship to humanity is intended as a relationship of inviting something creaturely to resemble something divine. Imaging in this sense therefore exhibits both a kind of symmetric relationship to God and a kind of asymmetric relationship to God. It is symmetrical insofar as humans are persons who, like God, are constituted as minds and wills and who, like God, are capable of employing mind and will to serve the best interests of creation.³⁷ But it is asymmetrical insofar as human persons are also creatures who depend upon divine judgment to care for creation as God cares for it, and insofar as humans are creatures alongside the rest of creation, receiving divine care as well as channeling it.³⁸

---

33 Commenting on Genesis 1's opening line, "In the beginning God created the heavens and the earth" (1:1, Revised Standard Version. All subsequent biblical translations are taken from the RSV), Bill Arnold notes, "There can be no victory enthronement motif because God's victory was never in doubt; rather God has never *not* been enthroned … he has simply never been *less than* sovereign." See *Genesis: New Cambridge Bible Commentary* (New York: Cambridge University Press, 2009), 32.

34 "Let us make man [sic] in our image, after our likeness; and let them have dominion over the fish of the sea, and over the birds of the air, and over the cattle, and over all the earth, and over every creeping thing that creeps upon the earth. So God created man [sic] in his own image, in the image of God he created him; male and female he created them" (Gen. 1:26-27).

35 Arnold again remarks, "The image of God is about the exercise of rulership in the world. While it may be objected that an entire species of humans cannot stand in God's place as an individual kind, it seems likely that the office of God's representative has been 'democratized' in 1:26-27" (Arnold, *Genesis*, 45).

36 A "democratized" human rule that approximates God's care over the whole of the human domain requires localization at the site of that rule, and this is why the Genesis narrative issues the command to "be fruitful and multiply, and fill the earth" (1:28) before issuing the command to "subdue" and "exercise dominion" over it.

37 Thus, the depiction of the human as not merely formed from "the dust of the ground" but also as having the "breath" of divine life breathed into him (Gen. 2:7). God is represented as equipping humans for their vocation of mediating God's own rule through granting and guiding powers of mind and will that approximate those exhibited by God in creation. Thus, just as God spoke the world into being, God commands Adam to speak the names of the animals, and "whatever the man called every living creature, that was its name" (2:19).

38 The Genesis narrative displays the symmetry of human fellowship with divine rule in naming the animals as a kind of cooperation of God's creative act of speaking and in keeping and tilling the garden on God's behalf (2:14, 19). It displays the asymmetry of human dependence on God in the requirement God imposes on Adam to refrain from eating of the tree of the knowledge of good and evil in the center of the garden (2:17). The significance of the prohibition seems to be that the power of creaturely governance God shares with humans cannot be exercised according to judgments about good and evil derived autonomously from God, but must rather be exercised with recognition that such judgments can come from God alone. See Arnold, *Genesis*, 59.

So humans are divine images whose highest good is to so resemble the divine mind and will within their creaturely limits, and to do so well rather than badly. The principal way in which God engages humans to cultivate this resemblance relation is by way of the goodness and beauty of creation itself.[39] As many theologians of the early Christian church taught the significance of the creation account, the inherent value of the world is presented to humans as manifestations of God's presence to us,[40] and such manifestations are given to us for our cultivation of divine image-bearing. When we respond appropriately to the manifestations of God's goodness and beauty in creation, we thereby partner with God in the formation of our minds and wills to achieve greater resemblance to God.[41] In doing that, moreover, humans enjoy a kind of communion with God, a kind of intimate sharing in the divine mind and will, so that we may come to find God uniquely formed within our own individual personhood.[42]

Does divine imaging count as a loving personal relationship? It seems to me that by Schellenberg's lights it counts as a personal relationship, insofar as it counts as a conscious and reciprocal relationship between a divine and a human agent, and it counts as a love relationship insofar as it is one that God "values for its own sake."[43] Moreover, we can see that it is a relationship in which God values each individual person for their own sake, since each individual's mode of bearing the divine image is the unique way of manifesting that person's humanity.[44] It also counts as a kind

---

[39] This way of reading the significance of God's self-reflection in the act of creation is a pervasive feature of the early Christian theological tradition. For example, consider the fourth-century church father Gregory of Nyssa, expanding on his brother Basil of Caesarea's commentary on *Genesis* in "On the Making of Man," trans. Henry Austin Wilson, in *Nicene and Post-Nicene Fathers*, ed. Philip Schaff and Henry Wace, vol. 5, second series (Peabody, MA: Hendrickson, 1994), 398: "For since the most beautiful and supreme good of all is the Divinity Itself, to which incline all things that have a tendency towards what is beautiful and good, we therefore say that the mind, as being in the image of the most beautiful, itself also remains in beauty and goodness so long as it partakes as far as is possible in its likeness to the archetype."

[40] Again, Gregory of Nyssa, in "The Second Book against Enoumius (Translation)," trans. Stuart George Hall, in *Gregory of Nyssa: Contra Eunomium II*, ed. Lenka Karfíková, Scot Douglass, and Johannes Zachhuber (Leiden: Brill, 2004), Book II, §§222–24: "And because as the Apostle says, 'His eternal power and divinity is seen, perceived from the creation of the world,' therefore the whole creation, and above all the ordered display in the heavens, by the skill revealed in generated things demonstrates the wisdom of their Maker. What he seems to me to want to explain to us is the evidence of visible realities that what exists has been wisely and skillfully prepared and abides forever by the power of the Governor of the universe. The very heavens themselves, he says, by displaying the wisdom of their Maker, all but utter sound as they cry out and proclaim the wisdom of their Designer, though without sound. One may hear them instructing us as if in speech, 'As you look to us, you men, to the beauty and the greatness in us, and to this perpetually revolving movement, the orderly and harmonious motion, I always in the same paths and invariable, contemplate the one who presides over our design, and through the visible beauty let your mind rise to the original and invisible Beauty. For nothing in us is ungoverned or self-moving or self-sufficient, but every visible thing about us, every perceptible thing, depends upon the sublime and ineffable Power'" (107–08).

[41] For a more careful defense of the coherence of this idea, see the account I offer, which is also an attempt to retrieve and contemporize the picture I find articulated in Gregory of Nyssa, in Chapter 9 of Sameer Yadav, *The Problem of Perception and the Perception of God* (Minneapolis, MN: Fortress Press, 2015), 394–432.

[42] See Yadav, *Problem of Perception*, 449.

[43] Schellenberg, "Divine Hiddenness and Human Philosophy," 19.

[44] That is, goodness and beauty responsiveness can be both objective and person-dependent. See Yadav, *Problem of Perception*, 424–26.

of love relationship according to a traditional analysis on which love involves both union with the beloved and the pursuit of the interests or highest goods of the beloved for its own sake.[45] Imaging in this sense thus exhibits a loving personal relationship of love when instantiated by God toward humanity. However, it does not similarly count as an instance of love when instantiated by humans in their relationships with one another. When we attempt to reproduce our own image in one another as such, it does not count as seeking one another's highest good, nor as valuing another for her own sake. God is the only one whose mode of agency merits being reproduced in the human person.[46] Imaging is therefore a uniquely loving personal relationship that is instantiated in God's love for us. It is only instantiated in our love for one another insofar as humans can become divine means or vehicles for forming us into the divine image.[47]

The relevant question for Schellenberg's argument on this picture is whether it is possible for God to be open to being imaged in a nonresistant nonbeliever. In order to be perfectly loving, does God's openness to imaging the divine self in the human person necessarily require God to ensure that the beloved believes that God exists? Howard-Snyder observes that it is possible to be aware of a thing *de re* (i.e., to register its presence) without knowing or even believing that you are aware of it *de dicto* (i.e., without being able to conceptually or propositionally identify that which is present to you): "You can be aware of Jimmy Carter without being aware that Jimmy Carter is the one you are looking at."[48] Similarly, it is possible for humans to be aware of God's presence and agency within creation that calls to us to resemble God in mind and will, without being aware *that* the various manifestations of goodness and beauty in creation are God's call to you. As William Wainwright puts it,

> If I don't believe that God exists, I can't respond to God *under that description*. It doesn't follow that I can't respond *to God*. In the *Symposium,* Plato argues that our response to goods is (or can be) a response to *the* Good. According to traditional Christianity, however, *God* is the Good.[49]

---

[45] See Rea's summary of divine love as willing union with us and desiring our good ("Divine Love and Personality," 5).

[46] As Jesus puts it in Mk 10:18: "Why do you call me good? No one is good but God alone." See also Augustine, "The Nature of the Good (*De Natura Boni*)," in *Augustine: Earlier Writings*, ed. and trans. J. H. S. Burleigh (London: Westminster John Knox Press, 1953), 326–48.

[47] Expressions of human love for one another are thus instances of the love of God "shed abroad in our hearts" (Rom. 5:5).

[48] Howard-Snyder, "Divine Openness and Creaturely Nonresistant Nonbelief," 138. See also Trent Dougherty and Ted Poston, "Divine Hiddenness and the Nature of Belief," *Religious Studies* 43/2 (2007): 183–98, 185.

[49] W. Wainwright, "Jonathan Edwards and the Hiddenness of God," in *Divine Hiddenness: New Essays*, ed. Daniel Howard-Synder and Paul K. Moser (New York: Cambridge University Press, 2001), 113. There is no one way to defend a Platonistic conception of creaturely sharing in divine goodness of the sort Wainwright here attributes to Edwards. For that conception is not itself a substantive metaphysical thesis but rather the consequence of some such thesis. For various different ways of spelling out and defending a metaphysics of value that can accommodate the relevant kind of sharing in divine goodness, see, for example, Robert Adams, *Finite and Infinite Goods* (New York: Oxford University Press, 1999); Mark Murphy, *God and Moral Law: On the Theistic Explanation of Morality* (New York: Oxford University Press, 2011); and Yadav, *Problem of Perception*, 393–456.

Moreover, it is possible to consciously recognize oneself as engaged in moral or spiritual formation without recognizing that one is consciously engaged in a reciprocal relationship with God. There can be what Wainwright calls an "extensional equivalence" in the conduct and intentions of one's responsiveness to the manifestations of divine goodness and beauty in the world.[50] In the early Christian commentary tradition, Proverbs, Ecclesiastes, and the Song of Solomon were read successively as a training manual to move us from a merely *de re* acquaintance with God via creaturely gifts to a *de dicto* recognition that it is indeed nothing in creation per se, but only God who is being formed in our souls by way of our engagements with creation, thus initiating a more mature pursuit of intentional relationship with God that is both *de re* and *de dicto*.[51] If it is possible that a perfectly loving God can be open to the personal relationship of imaging by way of ensuring for his beloved a merely *de re* awareness of his existence, then L2, and hence H2, would be false.

So, on this picture, it is at least possible for God to be open to personal relationship with every human without ensuring their belief that God exists. But we might still consider the idea that it would be *better* if there were no nonresistant nonbelievers. This is just how Schellenberg responds to Plantingian defenses about the possibility of divine closure or divine tolerance of nonresistant nonbelief. He suggests that since God is the one who set up the world in the first place, a loving God who aims at relationship with his human creatures could choose to set it up with no nonresistant nonbelievers in the proposition that God exists—that is, such that God's openness to personal relationship ensures that no one ever lacks both *de dicto* and *de re* awareness of God.[52] Alternatively, a perfectly loving God could allow for merely *de re* awareness of God's existence but set things up such that there are no nonresistant nonbelievers whose *de re* awareness fails to develop into a *de dicto* awareness of God's existence. The idea is that since any loving relationship is clearly better served by having both a *de dicto* and a *de re* awareness of the lover than by having a merely *de re* awareness, God could not create a world that includes for some people a merely *de re* awareness and still remain a perfect lover.[53] In that case, divine love manifest as imaging would not prove any exception to L2.

But we can question the idea that God's desire for an imaging relationship with humans is better served by making a world without any merely *de re* awareness of God. Suppose, for example, that every possible world in which God creates free humans involves a Fall from God's original intention of imaging Godself in humanity.[54] Suppose, further, that the Fall in question damages human minds and wills in such a way that *de dicto* awareness of God adds nothing to their capacity or inclination to embark upon a personal relationship of divine image-bearing with God. That is, a *de dicto*

---

[50] Wainwright, "Jonathan Edwards and the Hiddenness of God," 114.
[51] See Martin Laird, "Under Solomon's Tutelage: The Education of Desire in the *Homilies on the Song of Songs*," *Modern Theology* 18, no. 4 (October 2002): 507–25.
[52] Schellenberg, *The Hiddenness Argument*, 45–46.
[53] The idea is that God should be able to achieve within a relationship characterized by *de dicto* belief in God anything that could be achieved with a merely *de re* awareness of God. See Schellenberg, "Divine Hiddenness and Human Philosophy," 29.
[54] See, for example, chapter 7 of Plantinga, *God Freedom and Evil*, on "transworld depravity," 49–53.

awareness might prove an obstacle for the fallen person's motivation to move from mere nonresistance to a reciprocal openness to the God who desires relationship with that fallen person. It might be, for example that, *post-lapsum*, one must first become seduced by the enjoyment of a merely *de re* encounter with divine self-manifestation under a non-divine guise. That encounter could be better suited to priming the beloved with an appropriate kind and degree of asymmetric dependence upon God that would enable her to form a proper *de dicto* belief in God—one that is most conducive to a more intentional pursuit of symmetric relationship to God as image-bearer. That is, it might be that an anonymous *de re* personal acquaintance primes one for intimate *de dicto* personal acquaintance.[55] If that is a possible state of affairs, then it might be that God's perfect love for humanity is not any better served by a universal *de dicto* belief in God's existence. It still may well be the case that ensuring belief in the lover's existence is a preferable situation in various other kinds of personal relationships, like filial love, spousal love, or parental love. But that is not necessarily true of the imaging relation, and on a sufficiently well-worked out theology of God's relationship to humanity we can see how L2's *de dicto* requirement for openness to personal relationship might be false. It would therefore appear that L2 is possibly false in the divine case, and at best merely possibly true. But then we have to emend H2 to read, "If God is perfectly loving then, possibly, God ensures that there are no non-resistant non-believers." But clearly, without the force of necessity in place, the empirical premise 3 fails to contradict anything we *must* expect of divine love, and the conclusion that a perfectly loving God does not exist does not follow.

However, the above reply would only be sufficient to defeat L2, and thus provide a Plantingian defense against H2 if a perfectly loving God would not *also* desire other, non-imaging forms of personal relationship that *would* benefit from there being nonresistant nonbelief in God's existence *de dicto*. So Schellenberg might concede that God is open to the uniquely divine loving relationship of imaging but hold that a perfectly loving God must *also* be open to, say, the divine analogue of human filial, spousal, or parental love, where these analogues must satisfy L2. After all, the very same scriptural witness that leads us to develop the image-bearing possibility also supposes that God wishes to befriend us,[56] that God is a jealous lover,[57] that God is our heavenly parent.[58] I do not think that is a promising line to take, for at least two reasons. First, there is no reason to suppose that a perfectly loving God is under any obligation to love creatures in every way it is possible to love creatures, only that God intends some sort of loving personal relationship with them. Second, on the picture I have been presenting, God's desire for union with us and for our highest good are suited to our nature, the kind of things we are, as (ex hypothesi) divine image-bearers.

---

[55] This is something like the point Howard-Synder makes, but with the crucial difference that "intimate *de dicto* personal acquaintance" is for me cashed out in terms of a conceptual or propositional knowledge of God's imaging in one's person, not in terms of the kind of intimacy characteristic of human relations of parental, filial, or spousal love.

[56] Abraham, we are told, "was called the friend of God" (Jas 2:23).

[57] "I will betroth you to me forever; I will betroth you to me in righteousness and in justice, in steadfast love, and in mercy" (Hos. 2:19).

[58] "Have we not all one Father? Has not God created us?" (Mal. 2:10) and "Father of the fatherless and protector of widows is God in his holy habitation" (Ps. 68:5).

Accordingly, we can hold that it is possible that the personal relationship God desires for us is not filial, spousal, or parental love, but only imaging love.

Still, this may not be a terribly satisfying line to take for those espousing the very Abrahamic faiths from which an imaging defense derives. As a proponent of the scriptural witness in question, I think a further reply is available, according to which these other forms of love are not to be taken literally, but precisely as metaphors for the imaging relation. Speaking particularly about the Hebrew Bible or Christian Old Testament, when Scripture uses filial and spousal language to describe God's love for us, it intends to display the symmetric relation between God and us as creaturely resemblances of God who thereby enjoy a kind of fellowship, joint attention and vocation, and intimate co-naturality with God.[59] When Scripture uses parental language to describe God's love for us, it intends to display the asymmetric relationship of dependence upon God that belongs to our bearing the divine image.[60] So in conveying the divine desire for filial, spousal, and parental union with us, God is conveying different dimensions of the same divine desire for being imaged in us.

We might go further and say that interhuman relationships of filial, spousal, and parental love are not only means of achieving the creaturely solidarity and cooperation required to care for God's creation in resemblance to God. They are in fact creaturely ways of imaging the image-bearing relation. The Platonists thought that when we desire sexual union with a lover, for example, we are just mistaking the immaterial beauty we perceive for its material instantiation, and therefore trying to unite with it in the wrong way.[61] But maybe the picture is rather that when we engage in any kind of loving human relationship, we are engaged in a creaturely analogue of God's own free desire to be reproduced in another. More radically, perhaps one way that Christians should interpret the significance of God's incarnation as Jesus of Nazareth is to regard him as a creaturely analogue of a free divine desire that we be reproduced in God's image.

4 Conclusion

The suggestion that it is possible to construe God's love for us strictly as a sui generis relation of imaging divine goodness and beauty within us raises important questions about its existential and theological viability. But while important, those concerns are immaterial to the primary thesis I have advanced here, which is just that it is

---

[59] Thus, in passages concerned with God as friend or jealous lover, the context reveals that what is at stake is covenantal commitment to the peculiar sort of partnership with God's people in which they display God's justice, mercy, faithfulness and love in care for one another, their fellow creatures, and the environment.

[60] Thus, in passages concerned with God as parent, the context reveals that what is at stake is human dependence upon divine judgment regarding the parameters of proper responsiveness to the divine call to goodness and beauty, which is mediated in the world.

[61] This is the Platonic insight that we found Wainwright observing above from the *Symposium*. But whereas the Platonic picture did not characterize the manifestations of the Good and our engagements with it as *personal*, the particular Christian development of the Platonic picture did. A theology of divine image-bearing of the sort I have adumbrated here was precisely the result of that development.

conceptually, logically, and metaphysically possible that perfect divine love for humanity is the kind of love expressed by the relation of divine image-bearing. If that is so, then there might well be nonresistant nonbelievers to whom God stands in perfect loving relations in God's openness to being imaged in them, whether or not they stand in a state of belief with respect to the proposition that God exists, and Schellenberg's deductive argument from hiddenness fails for lack of support of H2. One of the benefits of taking this theological route for a Plantingian defense, as opposed to the anthropological route pursued by, for example, Howard-Snyder's or Rea's analogies of human closure to relationship, is that it offers a principled way of appealing to sameness and difference in comparing human agency and personhood to divine agency and personhood.

On the one hand, we ought to expect that God's agency and personhood transcends the sorts of agency and personhood humans value in our relationships to one another, while on the other hand we ought to expect that God's agency and personhood is in some way immanent to what we value in our relationships to one another. The imaging relation satisfies both of these intuitions at once.[62] Further, creating space for this distinctively theological defense against the problem of hiddenness has the unexpected consequence of supplying us with possible reasons to prefer some theisms over others. Those of us who understand divine love in terms of imaging can wield Schellenberg's argument against those theists who characterize divine love strictly in terms of human love. We can use it to argue that if a perfectly loving God exists, either that perfectly loving God has made us in the divine image, or else God does not exist for just the reasons Schellenberg adduces precisely by relying on an anthropologically grounded analysis of divine love.[63]

---

[62] My worry about Rea's approach in *Divine Hiddenness*, on the other hand, is precisely that it seems to me to satisfy at most one of these intuitions. For, in his "two pronged" approach, he first argues in chapter 4 ("Divine Transcendence") for the thesis that divine love might transcend human love and as a result might not be identifiable in terms of our filial, parental, or spousal frameworks for thinking about love. But it seems to me that this functions as a purely negative gesture, without any substantial picture of what it might therefore mean for God to have a personally loving relationship with humans. Then, in chapter 5 ("Divine Love and Personality"), he offers his anthropological defense against moral sainthood as an *alternative* to his development of the transcendence intuition, for those who would prefer to bracket the consideration of God's love as categorically different from ours. The imaging defense, on the other hand, specifies both the difference and the sameness that we should expect from the notion of a transcendent *and* personally loving God.

[63] In other words, the replies that I have offered on behalf of Schellenberg against, for example, Howard-Snyder or Rea can also be wielded by the Theological Plantingian Defender who advocates an imaging defense against all manner of Anthropological Plantingian Defenders.

5

The Limits of Divine Love

Jeff Jordan

Compared with classical paganism, one of the innovations of the early Christian church was the proclamation that God loved humans.[1] The deities of classical paganism might love this human or that, but a love of all humans was not characteristic of those enshrined within the pantheon of Olympus. According to Christian teaching, however, God's love flows beyond the boundaries of ethnicity, tribe, and place, to the Gentile as well as the Jew. In short, God loves every human. No human deserves God's love, as God loves without regard to merit by freely loving all. Indeed, according to the Christian gospel, God's love is self-giving and sacrificial as exemplified by the death of Christ. As John, the fourth evangelist, famously put it, "God so loved the world that he gave his only begotten son."

If God is perfect, as Christians believe, what follows for the Christian view of divine love? Does God love perfectly? What would loving perfectly consist in? Are there limits to a perfect love? In what follows, we will seek to answer these questions not via scripture or church tradition but by way of philosophical reasoning, although our navigational North Star will be the Christian proclamation that God loves every human. The universality of God's love will guide our philosophical exploration into the nature and limits of divine love as outlined in three models of divine love. Surprisingly, as we will see, our assessment of the three models will have important consequences for two prominent and much discussed arguments for atheism: the argument from divine hiddenness and the evidential argument from evil.

1 What is a perfect love?

As we explore the idea of divine love from a Christian perspective, we should initially ask about the nature of love itself. While one may love a sports team, a country, or a

---

[1] Larry Hurtado, *Why on Earth Did Anyone Become a Christian in the First Three Centuries?* (Milwaukee, WI: Marquette University Press, 2016), 124–26.

book, what is it to love a person? Thomas Aquinas (1225–74), one of the great thinkers of the Christian tradition, understood love as a uniting and binding force:

> To love a person is to wish that person good. Hence, inasmuch as we love ourselves, we wish ourselves good; and so far as possible, union with the good.... And by the fact that anyone loves another, he wills good to that other. Thus he puts the other, as it were, in the place of himself; and regards the good done to him as done to himself. So far love is a binding force, since it aggregates another to ourselves, and refers his good to our own.[2]

Listening to Aquinas, we will take love as involving a lover willing or desiring good for her beloved. What is it to desire good for another? Foregoing a Thomistic exegesis, we will understand a lover desiring good for his beloved as the lover having a disinterested or selfless concern for the beloved. A selfless concern we may understand in contemporary terms as desiring that the interests of one's beloved are advanced, not for one's own sake, but for the sake of the beloved. Indeed, we should think of this as not just desiring that those interests are advanced but also seeking to advance those interests when feasible. A selfless concern for another implies that the other's good provides the lover with a reason to promote or advance that good.[3] Lovers have a reason to advance or promote the interests of their beloveds. Of course, since lovers desire good for their beloveds, love does not require promoting or advancing interests that are harmful, destructive, or immoral. Could one love another yet lack any concern for person? Clearly not. Could one have concern for another in a self-interested or even selfish way? Yes, one could. But if one is concerned for another only insofar as that impacts oneself then, clearly, one has no deep love for that person as no one can love another deeply while having only a selfish concern for that person. Could one have concern for another and yet not desire that any of that person's interests be advanced? It is hard to see how, since it makes little sense to say that one desires good for Jones, and yet has no reason to seek that good for Jones, or does not care if any of Jones' interests obtain.

When applied to God loving all humans, this understanding of love as a lover selflessly willing and seeking good for her beloved is what we might call benevolence. While benevolence is a kind of love, it is not a deep love. There are deep loves and there are shallow ones, as love comes in degrees. A love deeper than benevolence involves more than willing and seeking the good for those one deeply loves.

---

[2] *Summa Theologica*, Iiae, Q 20, A. 1. See also, *Summa Theologica*, Iiae, Q. 20, A.3.
[3] Does love involve willing good for one's beloved, or does it involve willing what is best for one's beloved? As the latter involves a maximal concern for one's beloved, it may seem the appropriate condition. Yet it may be that what is best for a person is such that only one could receive what is best, while two or more may receive what is good but in a quantity less than maximal. Being the sole object of her parents' attention and resources may be best for a particular child, but that is not something that two or more children of any two parents may share. Imagine that a parent has two children, one very gifted, while the other is in need of special remedial services. Either the parent can move to a location providing better social services that would benefit the child needing special remedial services or the parent can move to a location offering uncommon but superior educational programs for the gifted. It is one or the other, but not both.

Since benevolence is not enough, what more is there to a deep love? Turning again to Aquinas, we see that Aquinas thought that love involved a desire for union with the beloved. Lovers desire an intimacy or closeness of company, care, and purpose with their beloveds. Aquinas says that the lover puts the beloved "in the place of himself." How should we understand putting one's beloved in place of oneself? We might understand this in contemporary terms, in part: the lover takes the interests of her beloved as her own, or identifies with those interests. An interest is something the person cares about, or should care about. A lover, then, adopts the interests of his beloveds. Adopting the interests of one's beloved is a way of effecting a union with one's beloved. Of course, since it is possible to care little or nothing about one's own interests, identifying with the beloved's interests involves not just adopting those interests, but caring about them as well. If you love someone and you know that she cares about something, then her caring gives you a reason to care about that thing also. Love involves a union or sharing of interests and caring involves bringing about what one cares about, or at least, seeking to do so. Identifying with an interest, then, we might understand as caring about what one's beloved cares about because the beloved cares about it, or should care about it, and seeking to advance those interests whenever feasible. Different persons, of course, have different interests some of which are incompatible. Two interests are incompatible just in case bringing about one requires that the other is not brought about.[4] Could one love another without caring about what that other cares about? Perhaps. However, if one loved another but cared little about what the beloved cared about, then, clearly, one has no deep love for the person, as a deep love involves caring about what one's beloved cares about, or should care about.

Of course, identity with the beloved's interests is not indiscriminate, as a lover identifies with nothing incompatible with her beloved's well-being. Lovers desire good for their beloveds, so love does not require identifying with interests harmful, destructive, or immoral. There may also be great goods the achievement of which requires not identifying with interests that are otherwise unobjectionable. We have seen that love comes in degrees and, arguably, the deeper one loves another, the greater the concern one has for the person and, correlatively, the more interests of the beloved that one takes as his own. Identification and concern provide a twofold proportional measure for the depth or intensity of love, as identification and concern increase, so too does the depth or degree of love.[5] A deep love implies a great concern for the beloved and an extensive identification with the beloved's interests. A maximal love we will understand as a love that is deep as possible.

Not all of one's interests are equal. Some interests are a person's best interests. A best interest is what a person should care about, whether or not she knows those are her best interests and whether she even cares about those interests. Best interests are those one would acknowledge if one were fully rational and fully informed. Being

---

[4] More precisely: for any two interests R and R*, R and R* are incompatible just in case in any possible world in which R obtains, R* does not; and any possible world in which R* obtains, R does not.

[5] One might wonder how humans can love God if identifying with the interests of the beloved is required for love. That is, how could a human know the interests of the divine? One answer to this question reminds us of the importance of scripture or revelation, or divine self-disclosure. Arguably, one way a human could learn of divine interests is via a self-disclosure by the divine.

healthy is a common best interest.[6] There are other interests had by persons that are not their best interests as full information and full rationality would not necessitate their acknowledgment. A person might care that the Phillies win even though that interest is not among one's best interests. These less than the best interests we might call a person's mere interests. Mere interests are real interests but are not among one's best interests. People have then mere interests and best interests.

Is equality a necessary companion to universality? That is, given God's love for all, must God love each person to the same deep degree? Should we take a perfect love as characterized by a maximal concern and identification with all and for all? If we do understand a perfect love this way, then, a perfect divine love entails divine impartiality—God would deeply love every human to the deepest degree possible. A perfect love, with this understanding, would be an impartial love in which God loves every human to the deepest degree possible.[7] This is our first model of divine love. According to this model, God loves every human to the maximal degree possible.[8] We will call this the "Maximality" model. Divine love is universal, equal, impartial, and as deep as possible, according to the Maximality model.[9]

The thought that God's love is maximal is natural. Listening again to Thomas Aquinas, however, we hear a dissenting voice as Aquinas held that God "loves some things more than others. For since God's love is the cause of goodness in things ... no one thing would be better than another, if God did not will greater good for one than for another."[10] Indeed, according to Aquinas, "God's loving one thing more than another is nothing else than His willing for that thing a greater good."[11] Aquinas's argument, concisely put, is that some things are better than other things, with the difference in value due to God. God's willing some things a greater good implies, according to Aquinas, that God loves those things more. The idea that God's love is maximal, then, is false if Aquinas is correct. Aquinas's view suggests that a perfect divine love varies,

---

[6] Is there a ranking even among a person's best interests? Can a person's best interests differ from that of another person? Can best interests change, or is the list of one's best interests invariant across one's life?

[7] It is a common claim of Christians that God is perfectly good, and by that, they mean not just that God loves, but that God is morally just. A perfect love, then, would require calibration to a degree compatible with other properties essential to divine perfection.

[8] Some philosophers distinguish between the supreme degree of love and an optimal degree of love. The latter is that deepest degree relative to all other loves one might have, or that deepest degree of love appropriate for what is loved. The former means to love as deeply as possible in an absolute sense. The first model we explore (the Maximality model) takes maximal degree in the absolute sense. The second model we explore (the Equality model) assumes the relative or optimal sense of the divine love.

[9] Marilyn McCord Adams arguably employs the Maximality model in her book, *Horrendous Evils and the Goodness of God* (Ithaca, NY: Cornell University Press, 1999), 29–31. As does Thomas Talbott in his book, *The Inescapable Love of God*, 2nd ed. (Eugene, OR: Cascade Books, 2014). See also his "The Topography of Divine Love: A Response to Jeff Jordan," 302–16.

[10] *Summa Theologica*, Iiae, Q. 20, A.3. Centuries before Thomas, Paul held that God loved some humans more than others. See his *Epistle to the Romans*, chap. 9. Indeed, Paul's use of the text from *Malachi* may suggest that God's love is not universal. I ignore that complication here.

[11] *Summa Theologica*, Iiae, Q. 20, A.4. It is clear in this fourth article, and in the third, that Aquinas is arguing that God can love one human more than he loves another.

as God loves some humans more than he loves others.[12] This embrace of partiality is startling as it runs counter to our contemporary egalitarian sentiments. So, we need to ask, is a perfect love a maximal love?

2 Why a perfect love is not a maximal love

A maximal divine love would be impartially extended to all and as intense or as deep as possible. Is a maximal love possible? Consider a comment by J. S. Mill (1806–73) about human differences:

> Human beings are not like sheep; and even sheep are not undistinguishably alike. A man cannot get a coat or a pair of boots to fit him, unless they are either made to his measure, or he has a whole warehouseful to choose from: and is it easier to fit him with a life than with a coat, or are human beings more like one another in their whole physical and spiritual conformation than in the shape of their feet?[13]

Different people have different interests; and since love has as a necessary constituent identifying with the interests of those one loves, there will be an in-principle obstacle to maximally loving all people, as no rational agent can identify with, or take as his own, interests known to be incompatible. This incompatibility is not just a practical matter, or a matter of limited resources. So, if God were to love humans, and thereby identify with their interests, then even God could not identify with known incompatible interests. In other words, even God cannot love or befriend every human in the deepest way. For example, consider the biblical story of Moses and the Pharaoh. The interests of Moses and Pharaoh were not just different but incompatible, as one sought the liberty of the Israelites, while the other sought to retain them in slavery. The Exodus story makes clear that God identified with the interests of Moses and not with those of Pharaoh. Consider another example. In the first chapter of Acts, the eleven remaining disciples of Jesus sought divine guidance which of two candidates should replace Judas as the twelfth disciple. Casting lots as a way of discerning the divine will, Matthias became the twelfth. Both candidates, Matthias and Justus, very likely cared deeply for the position, but only one could assume it. Any zero-sum situation in which the winning of some requires that others lose, involving outcomes that people care about, will generate an incompatibility between interests.

Might the distinction between best interests and mere interests provide a way to evade this result? Best interests are those interests that a person should care about, whether or not she knows they are her best interests, and whether she even in fact cares about those interests. Should we hold that the same best interests are common to all

---

[12] Aquinas's view, however, implies that God's love is proportional to the degree of goodness of the beloved. This proportional bestowing of love does not fit well with the idea that God's love is without regard to merit or desert, as it is freely given.
[13] See chapter III, "Of Individuality, As One the Elements of Well-being" in Mill's 1859 book, *On Liberty*.

humans? It is far from clear that we should hold that the best interests of each are the best interests of all. While first-person reports are fallible, they do count significantly, and it would be easy to come up with examples of persons reporting what they take to be their best interests, that are also incompatible. For example, a devout Muslim might report caring most that the entire world is Dar-al-Islam. While a committed Christian might say her greatest care is the divine will be done on earth as it is in heaven. A convinced naturalist might say the extinction of all supernatural views. It would be surprising to many Muslims, Christians, and Richard Dawkins, if these three interests were compatible. Let us waive this concern, however, and suppose that everyone shares the same best interests. Might a maximal love require only an identification with best interests and not just mere interests? The point of invoking this distinction is to pare the stock of relevant interests persons have down to a compatible few. Yet, even with the distinction between best interests and mere interests in hand we find an obstacle still, as whatever compatibility this paring provides is achieved at the loss of plausibility. If God loves individuals as regards their particularity and singularity, and not just as bearers of universal features, then advancing or identifying with a thinned set of best interests found among all hardly seems a sufficient fit, as neither our beloveds nor their cares are fungible. To treat something or someone as a fungible is to treat it as interchangeable with another. When you are hungry for a banana, any ripe one will do. Bananas are fungible. The love you have for your children, however, does not permit you to consider them interchangeable with other children, no matter how vexing they might be. If divine love relevantly resembles the love characteristic of the best of human parenting, then simply meeting only those interests of a beloved child interchangeable with those of any other child falls short of the mark. Human parenting at its best involves not just caring about the child's best interests, but also caring about the child's mere interests. It would be a severe father who tells his children, "I care nothing about what you care about, as I care only about your best interests." We would expect, then, like a loving human parent seeking to advance not only the best interests of a beloved child but also the child's mere interests, God would seek the same. A deep love, in short, does not treat its beloved as a fungible. A deep love cannot be concerned only with its beloved's best interests.

One might object that perhaps we could treat the interests of others as fungible while at the same time not treating those individuals as fungibles, so perhaps God can love maximally even if God cannot identify with incompatible interests. Could God, for instance, love individuals as regards their particularity, while identifying only with those interests common to all persons? Not if we understand love as, in part, identifying with the beloved's interests. No one could identify only with those interests of Jones common to all others and yet love Jones as a particular individual. One could of course deny that love implies an identification by the lover with any interests unique to her beloved, as one could love another without knowing the particulars of the beloved: "I love my baby" a newly pregnant woman might truthfully say, even though the pregnancy is but a month along.

Even if it is true that one could love without identifying with interests peculiar to one's beloved, it is clear that one could not deeply love without knowing and identifying with her interests, as a deep love implies an uncommon intimacy between lover and beloved. In short, love involves identifying with the beloved's mere interests and not just with the beloved's best interests only, even though one's best interests are of greater import than one's mere interests. It is important to note that love focusing, at least in part, on the particularity and singularity of individuals explains why a universal and impartial love, with no variance, cannot be the deepest kind of love. The deepest love involves a kind of exclusivity and does not devalue the beloved by treating her, in effect, as a fungible.

One might seek to circumvent the foregoing by asserting that humans surely identify fully with their own interests; yet some of an individual's interests require a trade-off in light of the individual's inability to realize them all, or realize them fully, in the actual world. So, even if God could not realize everyone's interests, it does not follow that God cannot identify with everyone's interests. Just as a human cannot fully realize all of her interests and yet she can fully identify with all of them, so too with God. At least, so one might object.

This objection, however, equivocates on the idea of fully identifying with an interest. In one sense, it is true humans fully identify with each of their own interests, since those are their interests and not someone else's. That sense however is hardly relevant. In the relevant sense, it is not true that every human fully identifies with each of his or her best interests, let alone with all of their interests. One should care about one's health, for instance, but there are smokers. Given the wide phenomena of self-destructive actions and self-hatred, it is clear enough that many humans do not fully identify with each of their interests.

A variant of this objection would hold that one could fully identify, in the relevant sense, with each of several conflicting interests. For example, one could fully identify with the interests of being a conscientious scholar, and of being a loving parent; but there are times when those interests conflict. Even so, one might argue, deciding on this occasion to play with one's children rather than reading a philosophy paper does not mean that one no longer fully identifies with both interests. And if that is so, then God's inability to realize everyone's interests seems no more a challenge to God's ability to fully identify with everyone's interests than the fact that a human cannot concurrently realize all of her interests and yet she can fully identify with all of them; or again, so one might object.

The problem with this objection is that it mistakes not being able to realize interests on certain occasions, with those interests being incompatible. The failure to realize certain interests on this occasion or that may be due to practical limitations such as insufficient time or resources or knowledge and not due to a logical limit. Practical limitations, however, do not generate logical incompatibilities. Recall that two interests are incompatible just in case attempts to bring about one impede bringing about the other. It is clear enough that realizing the interest of being a loving parent does not require that one not be a conscientious scholar.

Can a rational agent knowingly identify with incompatible interests? Persons can have unachievable ideals, so why not incompatible interests? Recall that identifying with an interest provides a reason to advance that interest. It would be an odd notion of "rational" if it tolerated one adopting, knowingly, incompatible reasons for one's actions—knowingly making it the case that one has reasons to advance α, and reasons to impede α. Indeed, odd also that one knowingly adopts a set of interests that one knows cannot obtain. While there may be a place for unachievable ideals, adopting known incompatible interests would involve knowingly adopting reasons to advance something, while also knowingly adopting reasons to frustrate that advancement. That sort of self-sabotage seems far from rational.

With the foregoing, we have good reason to reject the view that God maximally loves every human, as no one in-principle can fully identify with every human's interests. Our first model of divine love—God's love is maximal and impartial and universal—is therefore flawed. Is the failure of the Maximality model sufficient to justify embracing Thomas's view that the divine love is variable? Perhaps not, as a second model of God's love is possible.[14]

3 Why a perfect love is not an equal love

Perhaps instead of seeing God's love as maximal, we might take God's love as universal in scope and uniform in intensity with no variation, but less than maximal. That is, God loves everyone to the same degree, but that degree is less than maximal. If God's love is less than maximal, the problem of identifying with incompatible interests does not arise. With this understanding, a perfect love is an equal love. God equally loves every human, but loves no human in the deepest or maximal way. This is our second model of divine love: God loves all humans equally and significantly, but none maximally. While not maximal, God's love, one might say, is optimal. We might call this the "Equality" model.[15]

Here's an illustration of the Equality model that shows that the Equality model avoids the fungibility problem that plagued the Maximality model: let the integers, 1–8, represent interests had by humans; with 1 and 2 representing best interests shared by all, and any integer above two representing an interest unique to an individual.

---

[14] Another objection: it is far from obvious that every possible world is a world in which the interests of persons conflict; and perhaps this world is a world in which the interests of persons do not conflict. If this were such a world, then it would be a world in which God could maximally love all.
There is, however, strong reason to reject this objection. Consider this argument:
(1) For any possible world W, such that problems of justice arise in W, there are at least two parties which have conflicting interests in W. And,
(2) this is a world in which problems of justice arise. So,
(3) this is a world in which at least two parties have conflicting interests.

The premises of this argument seem beyond reasonable dispute, and if the argument is sound then this latest objection fails. Of course, one might wonder why a perfect being would bring about a world in which problems of justice arise: why is premise (2) true if this is a world brought about by God? One reason, stated all too quickly, is that a world in which real love is possible—where a lover takes as his own the interests of his beloved even when those interest are different or costly to identify with, or even incompatible with his own—will be a world in which problems of justice arise. A world with the possibility of real love will also be a world in which problems of justice arise.

[15] Nicholas Wolterstorff attempts to ground human rights on the idea of an equal divine love of every human. See his *Justice: Rights and Wrong* (Princeton, NJ: Princeton University Press, 2008), 323–41. See also the similar project attempted by Michael Perry in his *Toward a Theory of Human Rights* (New York: Cambridge University Press, 2007), 7–13.

Finally, let any odd prime represent an interest incompatible with some interest had by another. Suppose there are three individuals, X, Y, and Z:

X	Y	Z
1	1	1
2	2	2
3	4	5
6	7	8

Does this provide a model in which equality and universality are possible which avoids fungibility? One could identify with the best interests had by each individual; and one could identify with the same number of different but compatible mere interests of the three individuals, so one could identify in total with three interests of each of X and Y and Z. Clearly, there is no fungibility. Notice, however, that this model does not allow a maximal love of any, and assumes that the best interests of each are the best interests of all.

A serious objection to the Equality model is that equality is not enough, as a failure to love in the deepest way would be a defect incompatible with perfection, since if God is to love in the deepest way, God must love some in a maximal way. It is clear that *maximally loving no one* would be a defect for a human. Just as lacking deep relationships would be intrinsically bad for a human, the same holds for God. If God is perfect, then God could not love every human to the same significant but submaximal way, as perfection could not require a property the possession of which would lead to a life defective in significant respects. If this argument succeeds, then the second model fails.

One might respond, however, that even if God loves no human maximally, God could still love maximally as the divine persons could love each other maximally. That is, given the Christian doctrine of the Trinity, God could love maximally without loving any human. Setting aside the doctrine of the incarnation, the idea that God's maximal love is only among the persons of the Trinity generates a problem. The problem is that this trinitarian-only view colors the divine love in a narcissistic shade. Anyone who loves himself only, or loves himself more than he loves others, is guilty of narcissism. Clearly enough, narcissism is a moral defect. Why? Narcissistic love is a self-centered love that is neither selfless nor disinterested; and so is not willing to sacrifice its own interests in order to advance the interests of another. Narcissistic love, rather, is willing to sacrifice the interests of others to advance its own. Keeping in mind that Christians are monotheists, the love shared within the Trinity is a self-love. Self-love, of course, is not identical with narcissistic love, and the maximal love shared among the persons of the Trinity could not be narcissistic.[16] A maximal love of another or others, then, is required if the divine love is not narcissistic. If we recall that the incarnation involved humankind, then there is reason to think that humankind is the proper focus of a maximal divine love. That is, there is reason to think that if God is to love another maximally, then God would maximally love some human or other, which means a

---

[16] Recall that the "second greatest commandment" requires that you love your neighbor as you love yourself. This command does not prohibit self-love; it prohibits narcissistic self-love.

divine love willing to sacrifice its own interests for those of others. As we saw, however, it is not possible that God maximally love every person, so God maximally loves some, which counters the Equality model. As with the Maximality model, the Equality model wilts under scrutiny.

4 A perfect love is a partial love

So far, the argument has been that God cannot maximally love all, as significant differences between persons make it in-principle impossible to love every person to the deepest degree. In addition, a second model in which the divine love is equally and impartially (but not maximally) extended to all also fails if that means that God loves no human maximally. So how should we understand a perfect love? Is there a third model available that survives scrutiny?

If perfection requires that a being loves maximally and if the early church was correct that God loved every human, then there will be variability in the divine love, with humans loved by God to a significant but varying degree. That is, God loves some maximally and others submaximally. This is our third model of divine love: God loves every human but loves some more than others. An important consequence of this model is that if God loves some more than others, then we have reason for thinking that God would not seek the same for each person as lovers do not act impartially between their dearests and others. So, any argument that implies that God, say as a loving parent, would ensure that every person would be treated the same by God (if God existed and loved perfectly) will be unsound given what we have argued so far. This model we will dub the "Variability" model. According to it, God loves all humans; and yet the divine love is variable, as God loves some more than others. The Variability model does not tell us whom God loves more or less, just that God's love must be variable. If God loves some more than others, then that love will not impartially manifest or express itself. With variability, we should expect partiality, as no one treats her beloveds the same as she treats those she loves less.[17] It is important to keep in mind that variability implies partiality as we move to examine the argument from divine hiddenness and the evidential argument from evil.

5 Applying the lesson[18]

An important argument for atheism is the argument from divine hiddenness. We can get a sense of this argument via a story about the Nobel Laureate Bertrand Russell (1872–1970), who, when asked what he would say to God if he should die and find himself in the divine presence, replied he would say, "Not enough evidence God, not enough

---

[17] Is there any scriptural support for the third model? There is. For example, see the annunciation passages in Luke, chap. 1; and Paul's Epistle to the Romans, chap. 9.

[18] For more detail on the divine hiddenness argument, see my exchange with John Schellenberg, a proponent of that argument, in the *European Journal for the Philosophy of Religion* 9/1 (2017): 187–207.

evidence."[19] On the other hand, the French philosopher and mathematician Blaise Pascal (1623–62) thought there was enough evidence. At least enough to condemn those who do not believe, but not so much as to overwhelm one's free will and reason:

> The prophecies, and even the miracles and proofs of our religion, are of such a nature that they cannot be described as absolutely convincing. But they are also of such a kind that one cannot say that it is unreasonable to believe them. Thus there is both evidence and obscurity to enlighten some and bewilder others. The evidence, however, is such that it surpasses, or at least equals, the evidence to the contrary. Therefore, since it is not reason that can persuade men not to follow it, only concupiscence and malice of heart can do so. Thus there is sufficient evidence to condemn, but insufficient to convince. Hence it appears that, as regards those who follow it, grace and not reason causes them to do so, and that, as regards those who shun it, concupiscence and not reason causes them to do so.[20]

Pascal held that too much evidence would overwhelm one's will and freedom. Pascal argued that there was enough evidence for a responsible belief, even if that evidence was not convincing in its quantity or quality. The point, however, of the argument from divine hiddenness is that there should be no controversy or debate whether there is enough evidence available for believing that God exists, if God were to exist. Consider:

(1) If God exists, then it is in the best interest of every human to be in a personal relationship with God. And,
(2) if God loved every human, then God would always seek a personal relationship with every human, as that would be in the best interest of every human. But,
(3) there are humans open to a relationship with God, who now lack enough evidence for a justified belief that God exists. But,
(4) if God exists, no one would ever lack the evidence necessary for a justified belief that God exists. Therefore,
(5) God does not exist.

This argument employs the agreeable proposition that God loves every human (if God exists). Even so, the argument rests upon a shaky assumption—that God's love must be invariable. God's invariable love, the argument assumes in premise (2), means that God would always treat every human the same by ensuring that God always seeks a personal relationship with every person. The argument cannot tolerate variability in the divine love because the argument requires that no human would ever lack the evidence necessary for belief. Notice, however, if there is variation in the degree of divine love—if God loves some more than others—then our reasons for supposing that God would always seek the same for each person evaporate, as lovers do not act impartially between their dearests and others. If there is variability in the divine love, then, for all we know,

---

[19] John Searle recounts being present when Russell uttered his evidential complaint. See Searle's book, *Mind, Language, and Society: Philosophy in the Real World* (New York: Basic Books, 1998): 36–37.
[20] Pascal, *Blaise Pascal Pensées*, trans. J. Warrington (London: J.M. Dent & Sons, 1960), 200.

relationships with those not so deeply loved could require that God not now be open to personal relationships with those deeply loved. Alternatively, if there is variation in the divine love, then, for all we know, relationships with those deeply loved could require that God not now be open to personal relationships with those not so deeply loved. The takeaway here is that, contra premise (2), we have no reason for thinking that a variable divine love requires that God would always be open to a personal relationship with every person. Since, for one thing, there may be, for all we know, great goods the accomplishment of which requires that God does not now seek a personal relationship with every human.[21] This variability, in other words, casts serious doubt on the soundness of the divine hiddenness argument. Any version of the argument from divine hiddenness implying that divine love requires invariability requires the Maximality model or the Equality model, but founders with the Variability model. With the ascendency of the Variability model, the argument from divine hiddenness sinks.

6 A second application

The evidential argument from evil is the strongest argument for atheism, and William Rowe (1938–2015) has been its most influential modern proponent since that argument's debut in David Hume's 1779 *Dialogues Concerning Natural Religion*. Rowe's work on the evidential argument began with his much-discussed 1979 article, "The Problem of Evil and Some Varieties of Atheism," and continued with more than a dozen articles on various versions and defenses of the evidential argument.[22] Evidential arguments from evil do not contend that evil is logically incompatible with the existence of God, but that certain facts about evil—in particular that some cases of suffering seem pointlessness—provide strong evidence that God does not exist.

Framed in a systematic way, Rowe's evidential argument from evil runs this way:

(6) There exist instances of intense suffering which an omnipotent, omniscient, perfectly good being could have prevented without thereby preventing the occurrence of any greater good. And,

(7) an omnipotent, omniscient, perfectly good being would prevent the occurrence of any intense suffering it could, unless it could not do so without thereby preventing the occurrence of some greater good. Therefore,

(8) there does not exist an omnipotent, omniscient, perfectly good being.[23]

[21] What possible goods could preclude God from now being open to a personal relationship with any who have not shut themselves off from such a relationship? While we are far from being able to itemize such goods, we can imagine some. One conceivable good, assuming that God exists, would be it is a great good for one to influence another to commit to the belief that God exists. Being instrumental in bringing others to saving belief would be a great service to others, and deepen one's own commitment. This conceivable good would be possible only if God has not now been open to personal relationships with all until some, with whom God has a personal relationship, have had the opportunity to seek to bring others to saving belief.

[22] Rowe's various writings on the evidential argument are collected in *William Rowe on Philosophy of Religion: Selected Writings*, ed. N. Trakakais (Burlington, VT: Ashgate Publishing Co., 2007).

[23] William Rowe, "The Problem of Evil and Some Varieties of Atheism," *American Philosophical Quarterly* 16 (1979): 335–41; reprinted in *William L. Rowe on Philosophy of Religion*, 61–67.

Although (6)–(8) is a deductive argument, the evidential aspect of it comes with the support offered by Rowe for premise (6): we know of innocent beings suffering for no known justifying reason. Consider, for example, a fawn, trapped in a forest fire, and horribly burned, lingering in anguish for days until dying. We know of no good that would justify God in permitting the fawn to suffer. This fact supports (6) as long as we have reason to think that we would be aware of a justifying good if there were one. The key idea of Rowe's evidential argument is not that horrendous evils occur, but rather that we lack knowledge why such evils occur. This key idea is expressible as an inference of proposition (Q) from (P):

P: No good we know of would justify an omnipotent, omniscient, perfectly good being in permitting the suffering of the fawn. So,

Q: there probably is no good at all that justifies an omnipotent, omniscient, perfectly good being in permitting the suffering of the fawn.

Since this inference is invalid, Rowe employed in his early articles an inductive generalization as a way of bridging the gap between (P) and (Q): since we do not know of any good that would justify God in permitting the suffering of the fawn, there probably is no good (known or unknown) that would justify God in permitting that suffering.[24] This simple inductive generalization attracted much criticism as some argued that Rowe provided no reason for thinking that our knowledge of goods is representative of all the goods there are, while others objected to the idea that we could grasp goods that would justify an infinite being in permitting evils.[25]

In reaction to this criticism Rowe offered a "loving parent" analogy in support of the inference of (Q) from (P), accepted, he says, by theists and atheists alike:

God, if he exists, is . . . to us as loving parents are to their children . . . Moreover, he is our loving father. What do loving parents do when their children are suffering for reasons they cannot comprehend? Loving parents do their best to relive the suffering of their children. . . . The point is this: love entails doing the best one can to be consciously present to those one loves when they are suffering. . . . And given the absence of any loving, heavenly father, the evil and suffering in our world only increases the likelihood that God does not exist.[26]

The "loving parent" analogy generates certain expectations, which our observations and experiences find unfulfilled. Among those expectations is proposition (R):

R: God, as a loving parent, would ensure that suffering persons are aware of his comforting presence.

---

[24] See for instance, William Rowe, "Evil and Theodicy," *Philosophical Topics* 16/2 (1988): 123–24; reprinted in *William L. Rowe on Philosophy of Religion*, 91–104.

[25] For example, see Stephen Wykstra, "The Humean Obstacle to Evidential Arguments from Suffering: Avoiding the Evils of 'Appearance,'" *International Journal for Philosophy of Religion* 16 (1984): 73–93.

[26] William Rowe, "Friendly Atheism, Skeptical Theism, and the Problem of Evil," *International Journal for the Philosophy of Religion* 59 (2006): 89; reprinted in *William L. Rowe on Philosophy of Religion*, 207–20.

Many human sufferers however report no awareness of the comforting presence of God. If the "loving parent" analogy via (R) adequately supports the inference of (Q) from (P), then Rowe's evidential argument is a formidable obstacle to theistic belief.

According to proposition (R), every sufferer should be aware of God's comforting presence. Proposition (R) implies a commonality among human sufferers—each should be aware of God's presence as long as God exists, and none of the sufferers has blinded themselves to that presence. Is the idea that God, as a loving parent, should present himself to each suffering person plausible? It is hard to see that it is, since however much plausibility proposition (R) enjoys via the Loving Parent analogy, would be shared also by proposition (R'):

> R': God, as a loving parent, would ensure that all persons are aware of his loving presence.

Proposition (R'), however, is plausible only if it is plausible that God would always seek a personal relationship with every human. We have reason, however, to doubt that God would always seek a personal relationship with every human. The idea of a divine love impartially and equally extended to all, as we have seen, breaks down. If God loves some persons more than others, however, then our reason for supposing that God would seek the same for each person evaporates, as lovers do not act impartially between their dearests and others. Moreover, if there were great goods the accomplishment of which requires that God not make his presence known to every person, then arguably those same goods would also require that God not make his presence known to every suffering person. In short, the same considerations that undercut proposition (R'), also undercut (R).

One might seek to dismiss the threat of variability by asserting that, for all we know, the variability would hold in but a very small number of cases. This objection misses the mark, as can be seen by recalling the logic of the situation: there are cases in which those suffering claim to be aware of God's comforting presence; and there are cases in which those suffering claim not to be aware of God's comforting presence. It is doubtful that any of us know the relevant aggregate numbers or the ratio here. In any case, those values are irrelevant. The point of proposition (R) is that we should expect that all who suffer would be aware of God's comforting presence. If, however, for all we know, it is not possible that all who suffer could be aware of God's comforting presence then (R) is in trouble—regardless of the numbers or ratios involved. Proposition (R) is viable only with the Maximal model or the Equality model, but not if the Variability model is our best approximation of the divine love. Simply put, given the Variability model, proposition (R) is false, and without (R), Rowe's loving parent analogy loses its relevance.

7 A conclusion

No love, whether perfect or not, can be universally maximal, as significant differences between persons make it impossible to love every person to the deepest degree. Moreover, any life, divine or not, lacking a maximal love is defective, so if the divine love is equally and impartially (but not maximally) extended to all would imply that a perfect being is defective. A result less than sanguine. Although the Maximality model and the Equality model enjoy a wide popularity among theists as well as atheists, both suffer from deep flaws. The Variability model alone is immune from those flaws and presents us with our best approximation of the divine love, conforming to the proclamation of the early church and, arguably, the witness of scripture. Even so, suspicion of the Variability model may remain.

Is a God who loves some more than others too small? Without maximal love, is God worthy of worship? It is important to remember that our argument has not been that God does not perfectly love, but rather that it is impossible for any being to love every other being in the deepest way possible. Our argument has been about the logical limits of God's love. Love, like power and knowledge, conforms to logic. If the "failure" of God to control the actions of those who enjoy significant freedom implies no diminishment of worship-worthiness, or, the "failure" of God to know a prime even number, greater than two, implies no loss of worship-worthiness, then likewise the "failure" of God to love all maximally, and his "failure" to love all equally is just as benign. These "failures" are not genuine defects as they are compatible with perfection. Could a perfect being love some more than others? Well, since no being can love all finite beings in the deepest way, then, if God is to love in the deepest way, God must love some more than others, as the failure to love in the deepest way would be a genuine defect incompatible with perfection and worship-worthiness. Finally, as we have seen, that God must love some more than others if God is perfect, undermines influential versions of the argument from divine hiddenness and the evidential argument from evil. This latter result, if nothing else, should count heavily in the Variability model's favor—at least in the eyes of those favorably inclined toward the Christian proclamation.[27]

Is it troubling that God might love some more than others? It is not if we keep in mind that we have no claim on God's love and, consequently, no claim that God love us all equally. Clearly, we are in no position to know whom God loves more or less. It is enough in any case that we are loved at all.[28]

---

[27] Do the Christian scriptures teach that God is the heavenly father of all humans? See the concise but informative discussion of this issue in Carson's *The Difficult Doctrine of the Love of God*. At the dawn of the twentieth century, the German church historian, Adolf von Harnack (1851–1930) held that the universal fatherhood of God was a major part of the essence of the Christianity. See his *What Is Christianity?* trans. T.B. Saunders (New York: G. P. Putnam's Sons, 1902), 68–74. In reaction, the American theologian, J. Gresham Machen (1881–1937), held that the proposition that God was the heavenly father of all was in fact constitutive of a religion other than Christianity. See his *Christianity and Liberalism* (Grand Rapids, MI: Eerdmans, 1946), 18, 58–62, 157–58.

[28] I thank Doug Stalker, Ross Parker, and Jordan Wessling for their comments on early versions of this chapter.

6

In Defense of the Loving Parent Analogy

Thomas Talbott

1 Introduction

A long-standing dispute within Christian theology, one that extends at least as far back as St. Augustine, concerns the nature and scope of God's love for the human race as a whole. Virtually all committed Christians view God's relationship to *themselves* as analogous to that of a loving parent; as William Rowe once remarked, "It is not for nothing that the common prayer begins with the words: 'Our *father* which art in heaven.'"[1] But not all Christians have believed that God's love extends to every human being. Augustine seems to have been the first Christian writer to have restricted God's love to a limited number of persons (a so-called limited elect),[2] and many of the most famous names in the Western theological tradition have followed him in this regard.

Jonathan Edwards was especially emphatic on the point. "The saints in glory," he wrote, "will know concerning the damned in hell, that God *never loved them*, but that he hates them, and [that they] will be for ever hated of God."[3] Edwards even held that the torments of those writhing in hell forever will increase the joy of those in heaven:

> When the saints in glory ... shall see how miserable others of their fellow-creatures are, who were naturally in the same circumstances with themselves; when they shall see the smoke of their torment, and the raging of the flames of their burning, and hear their dolorous shrieks and cries, and consider that they [the saints] in the

---

[1] Rowe, "Friendly Atheism, Skeptical Theism, and the Problem of Evil," 89; emphasis in original.
[2] See, for example, *Enchiridion*, sec. 103, in *Augustine: Confessions and Enchiridion*, ed. and trans. A.C. Outler (Philadelphia, PA: The Westminster Press, 1955), 401–02. Here Augustine seems clearly to have endorsed the following principle: for any human being *h*, God wills the salvation of *h* if, and only if, God successfully achieves the salvation of *h*. If God does not will the salvation of *h*, moreover, then he wills the eternal damnation of *h*; he wills, in other words, that *h* should come to a bad end and, at the very least, be miserable everlastingly. And that is surely inconsistent with any intelligible love for *h*. Augustine thus found it necessary to explain away 1 Tim. 2:4 and to deny its apparent teaching that God at least wills or sincerely desires the salvation of all humans; it teaches instead, he insisted, that God wills the salvation of only some humans from all nations, groups, and classes.
[3] Jonathan Edwards, "The End of the Wicked Contemplated by the Righteous: Or, the Torments of the Wicked in Hell, No Occasion of Grief to the Saints in Heaven," in *The Works of Jonathan Edwards in Two Volumes*, Vol. 2, ed. E. Hickman (London: William Ball, 1834), sec. III, 210. Emphasis added.

mean time are in the most blissful state and shall surely be in it to all eternity; how will they rejoice![4]

And finally, he made the following appeal an important part of his preaching:

> How will you bear to see your parents, who in this life had so dear an affection for you, now without any love to you. . . . How will you bear to see and hear them praising the Judge, for his justice exercised in pronouncing this sentence, and hearing it with holy joy in their countenances, and shouting forth the praises and hallelujahs of God and Christ on that account?[5]

Now in several articles written over the past decade,[6] Jeff Jordan has sought to occupy a middle ground, so it appears to me, between the harsh view of a Jonathan Edwards, which so many find appalling, and the early Christian understanding (prior to Augustine) of God's maximal love for every human being. For, on the one hand, Jordan writes, "According to Christian teaching . . . God's love flowed beyond the boundaries of ethnicity, tribe and place, to the Gentile as well as the Jew. In short, God loves every human."[7] On the other hand, however, he also argues vigorously against the claim that "God's love must be equally extended and maximally intense."[8] He also notes that "a venerable Christian theological tradition populated with names like Paul, Augustine, Thomas, Luther, and Calvin, asserts that divine love and grace are divine gifts, which are not uniformly distributed."[9] The fact that he includes St. Paul in this tradition suggests a basic agreement with it,[10] and he also seems to endorse the same tradition elsewhere when he writes, "If the divine love cannot be maximally extended and equally intense, it may not be surprising, or perhaps as surprising, that God saves a particular sinner but not another who is no less a sinner."[11]

In any case, Jordan makes two crucial claims—among others—that I wish to examine and challenge here: first, that "no one [not even God] can in-principle maximally love all persons,"[12] because "it is not possible to love or befriend every person equally given that persons have incompatible interests";[13] and second, that divine love, like human love, is a matter of degree in that "the more interests one identifies with and the greater

---

[4] Ibid., sec. II, 209.
[5] Ibid., sec. IV, 211.
[6] See Jordan, "The Topography of Divine Love," *Faith and Philosophy* 29, no. 1 (2012): 53–69; "The Topography of Divine Love: Reply to Thomas Talbott," 182–87; "The 'Loving Parent' Analogy," *International Journal for Philosophy of Religion* 82 (2017): 15–28; and "The Limits of Divine Love" in this volume. For a couple of replies to Jordan, see Talbott, "The Topography of Divine Love: A Response to Jeff Jordan," 53–69; and Parker, "Deep and Wide: A Response to Jeff Jordan on Divine Love," 444–61.
[7] Jordan, "The Limits of Divine Love," 97
[8] Jordan, "The 'Loving Parent' Analogy," 19.
[9] Ibid., 23.
[10] No Christian would likely place Paul in a tradition with which he or she disagrees. No Arminian, for example, would place Paul in the Augustinian/Calvinist tradition, and no Calvinist would place him in the Arminian tradition. For the correct interpretation of Pauline theology is precisely what is at stake in these very different traditions.
[11] Jordan, "The Topography of Divine Love," 68.
[12] Jordan, "The 'Loving Parent' Analogy," 17.
[13] Ibid., 20.

the concern for one's beloved, the more deeply one loves that beloved."[14] In addition to these two claims, I shall also examine Jordan's objection to an argument of mine concerning the inclusive nature of love, an argument that he misconstrues by replacing my own words with words that conceal the precise kind of love I had in mind.

2 Maximal love and incompatible interests

Jordan's most controversial claim, namely, that "no one [not even God] can in-principle maximally love all persons," rests upon two crucial concepts: that of a person's *interest* and that of one person's *identifying with the interest of another*. He understands a person's interest "as something the person cares about, or something the person should care about"; and in at least one place, he understands identifying with the interest of another "as, roughly, caring about what one's beloved cares about because one's beloved cares about it, or caring about what one's beloved should care about because one's beloved should care about it."[15]

Now Jordan's understanding of an interest, as just described, carries a noteworthy implication. For just as the actual world includes billions upon billions of people with incompatible wants and desires, so it also includes, given Jordan's understanding of an interest, billions upon billions of incompatible interests, where any two interests are incompatible if, and only if, it is logically impossible that both of them should be satisfied. When two children squabble over a toy, for example, their conflicting desires in this specific matter cannot both be satisfied; and similarly, when Jacob and Esau both sought to acquire the birthright and their father's blessing, their respective desires in this matter could not both be satisfied.[16]

But why should such incompatible interests (or desires) pose any difficulty at all for the view that God has a maximal love for every human person? That not even God can *satisfy* two incompatible interests in no way entails that he cannot identify with them in the sense of caring deeply about both of them. Having empathy for incompatible interests is one thing; having the power to satisfy both of them is something else altogether. And as Jordan himself has acknowledged, "The relevant sense of love . . . might be seen as a deep desire that the interests of one's beloved are advanced . . . [and] also as seeking to advance those interests *when feasible*."[17] In the case of two incompatible interests, however, advancing both of them is not even feasible. So given the loving parent analogy, a God with a maximal love for everyone would presumably handle such incompatible interests in much the way that a loving mother might handle a situation in which her two beloved children are squabbling over a toy. Because she identifies with both of their incompatible desires in the sense of caring about them,

---

[14] Jordan, "Reply to Thomas Talbott," 186.
[15] Jordan, "The 'Loving Parent' Analogy," 19.
[16] Given the conventions governing ancient Semitic society, only one of the twins could receive the birthright and the blessing; and given a different set of conventions, the birthright and the blessing would have had a very different meaning and would have been very different from the thing that both of them had desired.
[17] Jordan, "The 'Loving Parent' Analogy," 18. Emphasis added.

she will no doubt try to resolve this squabble as equitably as possible. If she previously resolved a similar dispute in favor of one child, she might resolve this one in favor of the other child; or she might try to compensate in some way the one who loses out, thereby proving that she cares about this child's frustrated desire; or she might even, perhaps, take away the toy from both of them in order to teach a valuable lesson. In the case of beloved children whom we love deeply and equally, we often appeal to some notion of fairness or non-retributive justice when we find ourselves unable to satisfy all of their incompatible desires. We also weigh their short-term interests over against what might seem best for them over the long run, employing as well as we can our highly fallible judgments concerning such matters. And similarly for God's love, with this important difference: unlike our loving mother, God would not be hampered by the same fallibility that hampers her as he works around both the incompatible and the short-term interests of those whom he loves maximally.

So far as I can tell, then, the impossibility of satisfying two incompatible interests in no way excludes the possibility of identifying with them in the sense of caring deeply about both of them. But Jordan also offers another account—a very profound one, I might add—of what it means to identify with the interests of another. He specifies two "conceptually necessary features" of the relevant love, the second of which is "taking the beloved's interest as one's own, or identifying with the interests of the one loved."[18] Here he equates two ideas: that of identifying with the interests of another and that of taking the interests of another as one's own. What makes this a different account is that our loving mother, above, can care deeply about each of her squabbling children's incompatible interests without taking either one of them as her own. She might instead seek to alter over time (perhaps in exceedingly careful, subtle, and tactful ways) the immature attitudes of her squabbling children and to cultivate more mature attitudes in them for the future. Indeed, her willingness to oppose, or perhaps to rechannel, both of their incompatible interests may be a better measure of her parental love than siding with one child over the other would be. And as Jordan himself points out, "Love does not require identifying with harmful interests or destructive interests or immoral ones."[19] In exercising her parental responsibility to correct *both* of her squabbling children, our loving mother thus adopts a more important underlying interest of which her children are probably both unaware: their long-term interest in acquiring more mature (and more loving) attitudes of a kind so essential to enduring happiness.

So why not say the same thing about God's purifying love for us? Has not the Christian religion always affirmed that God "disciplines those whom he loves and chastises every child whom he accepts" (Heb. 12:6)? The whole point here is that God is like a loving parent in just this respect: his maximal love for each of us often plays a corrective role in our lives. In no way, then, does the depth of God's love for us depend upon our present condition, that is, our present attitudes, desires, and character; neither does it depend upon our *present* fitness for intimate fellowship with him. To the contrary, God's love for us is just what leads him to seek our ultimate perfection, which is why he creates a host of opportunities over time for the kind of changes in us

[18] Ibid.
[19] Ibid.

that would make a more intimate fellowship with him (as well as with other people) genuinely feasible in the future. It is also why Paul distinguished sharply between the old person, which God sometimes opposes with sternness and severity, and the new creation in Christ, which is destined for perfect fellowship with him.

Essential to the Loving Parent Analogy, therefore, is the idea that God's maximal love plays a corrective role in our lives. It is, in that sense, a love that purifies, and the measure of such love lies in the interests he opposes as well as in the ones he takes as his own. For, according to the traditional Christian understanding of original sin, all of our natural attitudes, desires, and motives are tainted with selfishness and sin, and these undermine over time the most enduring forms of human happiness. Jesus thus came into this earthly realm, so Mt. 1:21 declares, to save us from these sins. He came, in other words, to replace our sinful interests with better ones. He also sought to accomplish this, so 1 Jn 2:2 declares, by actually dying "for our sins, and not for ours only but also for the sins of the whole world." If true, would that not be a clear indication of a maximal love for all people? As Jesus himself put it, "No one has greater love than this, to lay down one's life for one's friends" (Jn 15:13). So if Jesus laid down his life for each human sinner, there can be no greater love than that for anyone.

The Loving Parent Analogy also accords well with a classic soul-making theodicy of a kind that John Hick famously set forth.[20] It suggests that God would not have brought us into an environment in which people have incompatible interests, at least over the short run, unless that were itself an expression of his parent-like love for all of us. Loving parents typically understand the importance of their children learning how to get along with other children on a playground where incompatible wants and desires often arise; and for all we know, an environment in which people have incompatible earthly desires and therefore incompatible interests is one of the most important means by which God seeks to teach all of us the lessons of love. For what purpose would it serve outside the context of a good many incompatible interests (wants and desires) for Jesus to issue such commands as, "Thou shalt love thy neighbor as thyself" (Mt. 22:39, KJV), and especially, "Love your enemies and pray for those who persecute you, so that you may be children of your Father in heaven" (Mt. 5:44-45). As paradoxical as it may sound in our present condition, it is in each of our long-term interests, according to Jesus, that we sometimes be willing to sacrifice our own wants and earthly desires, particularly when these interests are incompatible with those of someone else, so that we might eventually become "perfect" even as our "heavenly Father is perfect" (Mt. 5:48).

Jordan thus adopts two premises that any proponent of the Loving Parent Analogy can happily accept:

(1) Many people in this earthly realm have a multitude of incompatible interests.
(2) It is logically impossible that, for any two incompatible interests, God should identify with them both in the sense of taking them both as his own.

---

[20] See Hick, *Evil and the God of Love*. I am not here assessing the anti-theistic argument from evil and am not, therefore, defending the Loving Parent Analogy as a successful response, all by itself, to that argument. I merely point out that, insofar as Christians believe that God's love plays a corrective role in our lives, such a belief accords well with a soul-making theodicy.

But it is also obvious that the conjunction of (1) and (2) above does not entail (C) below, which is Jordan's main conclusion:

(C) With respect to all of the people who in fact exist in this earthly realm, it is logically impossible on account of at least some of their incompatible interests that God has a maximal love for all of them.

A valid deduction of (C) thus requires, at the very least, some premise (or premises) connecting the impossibility of God identifying with incompatible interests, or certain specific kinds of them, with the impossibility of his having a maximal love for all people. And just one possibility he never excludes is this: for every case where two persons have incompatible interests, God takes as his own some deeper and more important interest that both parties share, whether either of them is aware of it or not. Just as our loving mother above might take as her own a more important interest that both of her squabbling children share—that is, their interest in acquiring more mature attitudes in the future—so God might use our incompatible interests as an opportunity to cultivate in us more spiritually mature attitudes, such as a willingness to live according to the law of love and in accordance with the principles set forth in the Sermon on the Mount.

3 Best interests and mere interests

Now Jordan takes a step in the right direction, I believe, when he draws a distinction between best interests and mere interests, as he calls them. He writes, "Let's understand the best interests of a person to be those interests that the person should care about, whether or not she knows those are her best interests, and whether she even in fact cares about those interests. Best interests are those one would acknowledge if one were fully rational and fully informed."[21] By contrast, a mere interest, as Jordan understands it, is any interest that does not qualify as a best interest, that is, does not qualify as something one would care about if one were fully rational and fully informed.

With this distinction, Jordan acknowledges that not all of our interests, as he understands them, are equal in the sight of God. To this, I would add two further comments. First, a perfectly loving God would care most about what is best for a loved one *over the long run*, and second, we humans often make mistakes about our own long-term best interest as well as that of others. We are not always fully rational, after all, and are rarely fully informed about someone's long-term best interest with respect to some specific matter. Certainly union with the divine nature is in everyone's best interest, according to the Christian faith, whereas neither everlasting torment in hell nor everlasting separation from the divine nature would be in anyone's best interest. Beyond that, however, we rarely know which temporal events are, or are not, in a given person's long-term best interest; we almost never know, in particular, what might in fact prompt someone to repent and submit to God in the end.

---

[21] Jordan, "The 'Loving Parent' Analogy," 20.

Immediately after drawing his distinction between best interests and mere interests, Jordan employs two assumptions in an effort to shore up his argument for (C) above. The first he makes explicit when he writes, "The point of this distinction is to pare the stock of relevant interests persons have down to a compatible few."[22] But how on earth does that follow from his own account of best interests? Why suppose that the number of interests we would acknowledge if we were fully rational and fully informed would be relatively small rather than indefinitely large? And if our best interests include things we should care about but do not, as Jordan says they do, how could this possibly "pare the stock of relevant interests persons have" down to a few? Consider again those selfish or sinful interests that we all still have. Presumably God never identifies with these, at least not in the sense of taking them as his own. But for every sinful interest we have, we also have, surely, an additional best interest, namely, something we should care about but may not. Hitler's hatred of the Jews and his evil intention to exterminate them from the earth illustrates the point nicely. For of course a maximally loving God could never have taken such an evil interest as his own, not even if he had permitted it to be satisfied for some reason or another. Still, the fact that Hitler ought to have cared about the welfare of those whom he hated and slaughtered is itself one of his best interests, given Jordan's account. So by what argument, I wonder, would Jordan justify his assumption that our best interests are few in number?

With respect to each individual person, to be sure, we might identify a single long-term best interest, namely an ultimate union with the divine nature, as the most important interest of all. But even that single long-term interest will no doubt include a host of more specific interests, some of which may lie entirely beyond our ken. We have no way of knowing in advance, for example, whether good physical health or poor physical health, if either, will do more to advance a given person's moral and spiritual growth in the end, or do more to prepare that person for union with the divine nature. I thus see no way to reduce the total number of a person's best interests to a relative few.

As for Jordan's second assumption, which is not quite as explicit as the first, I infer it from the following passage:

> If God loves individuals as regards their particularity and singularity, and not just as bearers of universal features, then advancing or identifying with a thinned set of best interests found among all hardly seems a sufficient fit, as neither our beloveds nor their cares are fungible. If divine love relevantly resembles the love characteristic of the best of human parenting, then simply meeting only those interests of a beloved child interchangeable with those of any other child falls short of the mark.[23]

Here Jordan appears to assume that our best interests are "universal features" common to all, that they are all somehow interchangeable, and that they are therefore independent of an individual's "particularity and singularity."

But that makes no sense to me at all. Why suppose that the best interests of a special needs child would always be interchangeable with those of a healthy athletic child? And

---

[22] Ibid.
[23] Ibid.

why suppose that interests cannot be compatible unless they are also interchangeable? Not all differences in interests—not even all radical differences—represent incompatibilities, after all. We can all agree, I presume, that, "God loves individuals as regards their particularity and singularity." For just as loving parents love each of their children in that way, so also would a perfectly loving God, who knows each of us from the inside out far better than we know ourselves, love each of us in that way. Would not the unique personality, character, and spiritual needs of each unique individual—not even to mention the issue of free choice—help to shape many of that individual's best interests over the long run? If so, then God could hardly take as his own someone's long-term best interest without, at the same time, taking as his own a host of that person's more specific interests that arise from his or her "particularity and singularity."

Accordingly, both assumptions that Jordan makes about our best interests seem to me manifestly false, and neither of them, so it again seems to me, provides any support at all for (C) above. Because our best interests are not few in number and are not independent of our "particularity and singularity," but are instead contextually dependent upon our unique personality and spiritual needs, and because we often make mistakes about what is best for us over the long run, or even over the short run, I prefer to distinguish between our *perceived* interests, as we humans might view them, and our best interests or *real* interests, as God himself might accurately view them. We can then acknowledge that some of our perceived interests are not real interests at all, because some of the things we care about are in fact bad for us. Neither do all incompatibilities between perceived interests constitute incompatibilities between real interests. And whatever incompatibilities may exist among various perceived interests, such as someone's narrowly conceived economic interests, these are relatively trivial, I would argue, when compared to the steps God has already taken, according to a widely held theory of the Atonement, to advance the long-term best interest of all people.

4 Are there degrees of divine love?

Consider next Jordan's statement that "the more interests one identifies with and the greater the concern for one's beloved, the more deeply one loves that beloved." How should we understand such a remark?

Suppose someone should say, "The greater the concern for one's beloved, the more deeply one loves that beloved." This shortened version of the above quotation, absent the expression "the more interests one identifies with," seems necessarily true, perhaps even true by definition. Applying it to God, we get: necessarily, God has a maximal love for all humans if, and only if, he has a maximal concern for each of them. But this hardly entails that God has less than a maximal love for some people. As a consequence, Jordan in effect combines a necessary truth about God's love with the hopelessly vague idea that we humans have a countable number of specific interests with which God identifies. What makes the latter idea so hopelessly vague is that we have no principled way of distinguishing between and enumerating a given person's overlapping interests. Consider again Hitler's best interests with respect to the six million Jews whom he effectively murdered in the gas chambers. Does not each one of these Jews represent someone whom Hitler should have cared about even though he clearly did not? Are we therefore to suppose, given Jordan's account of a best interest, that we have in this example six million countable best interests of Hitler? As it stands, the latter question has no clear meaning. For where does one specific interest end and another overlapping interest begin? And what are we to say about a host of more specific interests that are included in a more general interest, such as the true interest Hitler had in becoming more loving in his relation to the Jewish people? Until such questions as these are answered, we have no coherent way to claim that God takes as his own more of one person's interests than he does those of another. Why not suppose, instead, that each of us has an indefinitely large number of perceived interests that God opposes as well as an indefinitely large number of real interests that he seeks to advance?

What room does any consistent Christian theology leave, moreover, for degrees of divine love? If union with the divine nature and the *everlasting* fellowship it entails is the greatest possible human good; if the only alternative to such a union is separation from the divine nature; and if such separation is, in the words of C. S. Lewis, an objective horror, then there appears to be no middle ground in the end between eternal bliss and an objective horror. It is not as if Christian theology permits a variety of different destinies between these two final conditions. So neither is there any room left, it seems, for degrees of divine love.[24] With respect to any given person, either God has a maximal love for that person, willing that he or she finally achieve eternal bliss, or God has no love at all for this person. That is also the context in which we must understand the Calvinist doctrines of limited election and limited atonement. These doctrines clearly imply—as consistent Calvinists like Jonathan Edwards, Arthur W. Pink, Herman Hoeksema, David J. Engelsma, and many others have always insisted—that God never had any love at all for the non-elect.[25]

---

[24] Many Christians do, it is true, speculate that, as a matter of divine justice (not divine love), gradations of punishment will exist in hell; some sinners, they suggest, may experience greater *physical* pain than others, and some places in hell may be hotter than others. But if all of the sinners in hell are dead in the theological sense, if all have lost *forever* everything that might make life worth living, then all have received essentially the same punishment: everlasting separation from God and a permanent loss of happiness. One might also speculate that the redeemed can participate in the life of God to varying degrees. But again, unless one imagines this participation to be an eternally static affair instead of an unending process of greater and greater participation in the divine life, it is hard to see why this should imply degrees of divine love.

[25] Arthur Pink thus wrote: "When we say that God is sovereign in the exercise of His love, we mean that He loves whom he chooses. God does not love everybody" (Arthur Pink, *The Sovereignty of God*, 3rd ed. [Pensacola, FL: Chapel Library, 1999], 17). Similarly, Herman Hoeksema explicitly argued against the view that God generally has a favorable attitude toward all of humankind. In *Het Evangelie*, according to G. C. Berkower, Hoeksema thus spoke of the "sovereign hatred of God's good pleasure" and argued that the non-elect are an object of God's "eternal hatred" (see G. C. Berkower, *Divine Election* [Grand Rapids, MI: Eerdmans, 1960], 224). And finally, David Engelsma has argued that "reprobation is the exact, explicit denial that God loves all men, desires to save all men, and conditionally offers them salvation. Reprobation asserts that God eternally hates some men; has immutably decreed their damnation; and has determined to withhold from them Christ, grace, faith, and salvation" (David Engelsma, *Hyper-Calvinism and the Well-Meant Offer of the Gospel* [Grandville, MI: Calvary Press, 1994], 58). Engelsma also claims that this is not hyper-Calvinism, but instead *consistent* Calvinism. A Google search under "reprobation and eternal hatred" will likewise turn up many more examples of Calvinists who hold similar views.

According to many theological traditions, in any case, a community of love is a condition of the highest form of human happiness; indeed, love may be the only thing that makes any life worth living forever. So God must first purge us of all the selfishness and arrogance and lust for power that separates us from others before we can experience what Richard Swinburne has called "supremely worthwhile happiness."[26] And if "salvation" is the theological name for such a spiritual transformation, then God wills or sincerely desires the salvation of all humans, as 1 Tim. 2:4 explicitly declares he does, only if he has a maximal love for each one of them as well.

5 The inclusive nature of love

I said, above, that a valid argument for (C)—Jordan's main conclusion—requires a premise (or premises) connecting the impossibility of God identifying with incompatible interests, or certain specific kinds of them, with the impossibility of his having a maximal love for all. So perhaps we are now in a position to return to that issue. As we noted in the previous section, union with the divine nature is, according to Christian theology, the only possible means to one's eternal welfare and supreme happiness. Call that everyone's supremely worthwhile interest. Here, then, is a valid argument for (C):

(1*) There exist in this earthly realm at least two persons, A and B, such that A's supremely worthwhile interest and B's supremely worthwhile interest are incompatible.
(2) It is logically impossible that, for any two incompatible interests, God should identify with them both in the sense of taking them both as his own.
(3) Therefore, it is logically impossible that God should identify with both A's supremely worthwhile interest and B's supremely worthwhile interest.
(4) But necessarily, for any Person P, if God does not identify with P's supremely worthwhile interest, then neither does God have a maximal love for P.

Therefore,

(C) With respect to all of the people [including both A and B] who in fact exist in this earthly realm, it is logically impossible on account of at least some of their incompatible interests that God has a maximal love for all of them.

Now I am certainly not attributing this argument to Jordan, because he nowhere endorses (1*)—which, for reasons I will explain below, strikes me as necessarily false. But unless something like (1*) should be true, it is hard to see how various incompatibilities among lesser *earthly* interests could undermine God's maximally intense love for all humans. Accordingly, the real impossibility in this particular

---

[26] See Richard Swinburne, "A Theodicy of Heaven and Hell," in *The Existence of God*, ed. Alfred J. Freddoso (Notre Dame, IN: University of Notre Dame Press, 1983), 39–40.

neighborhood, I shall now argue, is that of God willing the best for one person even as he wills less than the best for some of that same person's own loved ones. For there is no escaping the inclusive nature of love (understood as willing the best for another) and the way it ties the interests of people together.

Jordan himself points in the right direction when he specifies his two "conceptually necessary features" of the relevant love. According to the first, "the lover desires good for her beloved," and this Jordan understands "as the lover having a disinterested or selfless concern for her beloved—that her beloved flourish or do well."[27] According to the second feature, which we examined above, one who loves another takes "the beloved's interest as one's own." Do not these two features already illustrate how love ties the interests of people together and thereby creates a common set of *real* interests? The more one is filled with love for others, the more the unhappiness of others is likely to jeopardize one's own happiness—as Paul illustrated when he commented concerning his fellow worker, Epaphroditus, "He was indeed so ill that he nearly died. But God had mercy upon him, and not only on him but on me also, so that I would not have one sorrow after another" (Phil. 2:27). Similarly, if a mother should love her child even as she loves herself, then any great evil that befalls her child is likewise a great evil that befalls the mother, and any great good that befalls her child is likewise a great good that befalls the mother. Or, as Jesus himself put it, "As you did it to one of the least of these my brethren, you did it to me" (Mt. 25:40, RSV).

It therefore looks as if Jordan's two "conceptually necessary features" of the relevant love support the idea that love ties the interests of people together in a way that creates a common set of real interests. But whereas Jordan identifies *desiring good for another* as a necessary condition of the relevant love, I have identified *willing the best for another* as a *sufficient* condition of a maximal love for another. For not even God can have a greater love for someone than to will the very best for that person. In a previous reply to Jordan, I therefore formulated the following Principle of Inclusive Love, as we might call it:

(IL) For any two persons S and S*, if S wills the best for S*, then no one (including God) can will less than the best for S* without also willing less than the best for S.[28]

In that reply, I also illustrated this principle with the supposition that a woman's possessive attitudes with respect to her only son should induce her to hatch a murderous plot against his fiancée whom she fears has stolen his heart. Is it not obvious that such a woman's murderous jealousy would be just as incompatible with any genuine love for her son as it would be with any genuine love for his fiancée. If her son genuinely cares for his fiancée and thus wills the very best for her, then anyone, including the man's own mother, who wills less than the best for his fiancée likewise wills less than the

---

[27] Ibid., 18.
[28] See my "Response to Jeff Jordan," 315. This section of the present chapter includes additional material from that same article.

best for the man himself. We might even imagine that the mother has deluded herself into believing that she genuinely loves her son, but that again merely illustrates how different loving someone in the sense of willing the best for that person is from that grasping possessiveness so often confused with love.

Neither, I might add, does such love require a context of perfect fellowship or full reconciliation. Full reconciliation between good parents and their wayward children, like full reconciliation between God and his wayward children, may sometimes require a context of repentance and forgiveness. But as the parable of the prodigal son illustrates so forcefully, bad (or even monstrous) behavior on the part of a son or daughter in no way diminishes a good parent's love for that rebellious son or daughter. I have seen no more poignant illustration of this truth than a television interview, just prior to Ted Bundy's execution in 1989, with his long-suffering mother. When the interviewer asked this dear woman—a committed Christian, by the way—whether she could continue to support a son who had become a monster (as a serial murderer of young women), her response was most telling. She began to shake uncontrollably, her eyes filled with tears, and she could barely be heard to whisper these words: "Of course I support him; he is my son; I love him; I have to support him." She did not, of course, support his monstrous crimes or even object to the severity of his punishment. But she still loved him as a mother loves a son, still yearned for his redemption, and was still prepared to do everything within her power to promote his best interest.

Even as love in the sense of willing the best for others ties the interests of people together, it also has a remarkable ability to replace incompatible interests with an ever-expanding arc of compatible interests. This is precisely why there can be no partiality and no exclusiveness in love over the long run. For as our own loved ones—our children, for example—acquire additional loved ones of their own, and as these in turn acquire still more loved ones, a common set of real interests continues to expand. And furthermore, given that every human is loved by someone or another (by God, if by no one else), we have every reason to believe that this common set of real interests will exclude no one in the end.

6 The Jordan critique

Now Jordan reconstructs my argument above in the following way:

P1: if S loves S*, then, for any person P, if P loves S then P must also love S*.
P2: for any person S, S will love someone and will be loved by someone.

Therefore,

C1: every person will be loved equally and fully as any other.[29]

---

[29] See Jordan, "A Reply to Thomas Talbott," 187.

But that, I think it is fair to say, misconstrues my argument entirely. The issue between us, as Jordan frames it himself, is whether the following proposition is true:

(L) If God exists and is perfect, then God's love must be maximally extended and equally intense.[30]

I accept (L), and he rejects it. He also prefaces his reconstruction with these words, "Talbott also supports (L) by a kind of transitivity of love argument."[31] If that is true, shouldn't the conclusion of his reconstruction look more like (L) than it does (C1), which fails even to mention the name of God? Beyond that, both premises above strike me as clearly false. (P2) is false, or at least not obviously true, because we have no reason to believe that every young child and every sociopath loves at least one person in the sense of willing the best for that person. And (P1) is false because some person P no doubt exists who loves some other person S in a context where (a) S loves some third person S* and (b) P is altogether unaware of S*'s existence. Even more bewildering to me is how different (P1) is from the principle I actually set forth, which is (IL) above. One important difference is that my (IL), unlike Jordan's (P1), restricts one's attention to cases where P knows of S*'s existence and nonetheless wills less than the best for S*. Another difference is that the word "love," which is highly ambiguous in so many ordinary linguistic contexts, never even appears in the principle I actually set forth. Instead, I tried to make it clear that I had in mind love in the sense of willing the very best for another.

So why, one might wonder at this point, did Jordan attribute to me (P1) rather than the principle I actually formulated? Here is the explanation he offers in a footnote: "I have substituted 'loves' for 'wills the best' in my reconstruction of Talbott's argument, since our discussion is about love, and we have been given no reason to hold that love and willing the best are interchangeable."[32] But that, surely, gets the matter exactly backward. If the terms "loves" and "wills the best for" were indeed interchangeable (or equivalent in meaning) in the relevant context, then replacing one of these terms with the other would be defensible. But if these terms are not interchangeable (or equivalent in meaning) in the relevant context, then Jordan has succeeded only in replacing my principle with one that I never intended. Jordan's stated objection to (P1), moreover, makes it abundantly clear that (P1), as he understands it, is in no way equivalent to my (IL). He thus insists that (P1) "looks manifestly false" and goes on to explain:

Suppose Jones loves Juliet and is a rival with Greene for her hand. In fact, Juliet loves Greene. Does it follow from loving Juliet, that Jones must also love Greene, his rival for her hand? This seems doubtful. Or suppose Juliet's love for Greene is pathological or harmful or imprudent. It surely cannot be that Jones too must love Greene, or will that Juliet love Greene.[33]

[30] Ibid., 182.
[31] Ibid.
[32] Ibid., note 11.
[33] Ibid.

Do we not have here a clear illustration of the extent to which Jordan confuses different senses of the term "love," or, more specifically, identifies *love* with something, such as an intense romantic interest in someone, that may have little or nothing to do with *willing the best* for that person? Suppose we replace my original expression, "S wills the best for S*," with the expression, "S has a romantic interest in S*." More than a few identify such a romantic interest with being in love with someone, and this seems to be what Jordan has in mind when he asks us to imagine that "Jones loves Juliet and is a rival with Greene for her hand." Following Jordan's strategy, then, we might formulate an obviously absurd Principle of Romantic Love:

(RL) If S has a romantic interest in S*, then for any person P, if P has a romantic interest in S then P must also have a romantic interest in S*.

No one, I presume, would need Jordan's example of a romantic triangle in order to appreciate the absurdity of (RL). That example also illustrates the unique challenge that romantic love presents to anyone seeking to obey the two great commandments that Jesus delivered to us. As I recall from my own high school and college days, the experience of "falling in love" was probably closer to a kind of paranoia, rooted in self-centered desires of the flesh, than it was to any kind of self-giving love. I have no doubt that romantic love, despite the jealousies it so often engenders, can also include (or at least mature into) a genuine caring for the welfare of another. So if Jones truly wills the best for Juliet and senses that her romantic interest in "Greene is pathological or harmful or imprudent," as Jordan implies it could be, then Jones might believe, quite apart from any selfish motives, that Juliet would be better off ending any romantic involvement she might have with Greene. But the issue is whether Juliet genuinely wills the best for Greene, and even if she does not (in part because her romantic interest in him is selfish or pathological), Jones would still be obligated on other grounds to will the best for his rival. For that obligation follows directly from Jesus's command that we are to love our neighbor, including any possible rival in a romantic triangle, even as we love ourselves. Even in a case where rivals in a romantic triangle become bitter enemies, as sometimes happens, there is no escaping the command that we are to love our enemies as well as our friends and even pray for those who persecute us (as romantic rivals sometimes do to each other).

Jordan also insists, by the way, that his reconstructed version of my argument is invalid because "(P2) can be satisfied even if Greene and Juliet love only each other, and are loved by no one else."[34] But even if it were *possible* that God should create someone he does not love—an assumption I categorically reject[35]—Jordan's example of two *actual* persons, Greene and Juliet, loving "only each other" and being "loved by no one else" (not even by God) flatly contradicts his own statement, quoted above, that "God loves every [actual] human." Neither can he establish the *possibility* of two people

---

[34] Ibid.
[35] I reject this assumption on the ground that love (in the sense of willing the best for created persons) is an essential property of God. If that is true, then there is no possible world, so I would argue, in which God fails to love some created person, whether that *person* (as opposed to an evil force of some kind) be human, angelic, or demonic.

not being loved by God merely by asserting it. He has so far failed to demonstrate, therefore, even the invalidity of his own faulty reconstruction of my argument. But since I do not endorse his reconstruction, the issue of its validity need not concern us any further here.

Still, it is at least possible, under certain specified conditions, that two people might "love only each other" and no one else. For suppose that, at some given time in the past, only two humans existed on earth—call them Adam and Eve—and that during some stretch of time they both willed the best for each other and no one else (i.e., no other human). As we have seen, the relevant point for my argument here is this: assuming that Adam and Eve willed the best for each other, God could not have willed less than the best for either one of them without also willing less than the best for the other. Similarly, if Isaac, the father of Esau and Jacob, willed the best for his beloved son Esau, then God could not will less than the best for Esau without willing less than the best for Isaac as well. Worse yet, neither could God will less than the best for Esau without also willing less than the best for Jacob, because the feuding twins finally came to love each other as brothers. In fact, the account of their reconciliation is one of the most moving stories in the entire Old Testament: "But Esau ran to meet him [Jacob], and embraced him, and fell on his neck and kissed him, and they wept" (Gen. 33:4). So complete was their reconciliation and so sincere was Esau's forgiveness that Jacob declared, "for truly to see your face is like seeing the face of God—since you have received me with such favor" (33:10). Yet, this man—in whom Jacob was able to see the very face of God—is one whom, as some would have it, God had already rejected and had destined for eternal perdition even before he was born.[36]

7 Conclusion

Where maximal love is identified as willing the very best for another, it is simply not possible, I have argued, that God should have a maximal love for one person—whether it be Isaac, Jacob, Ted Bundy's mother, or anyone else—even as he wills less than the best for that person's own loved ones. So, for that reason alone, the doctrine of limited election, particularly as someone like Jonathan Edwards understood it, is not only morally repugnant but logically impossible as well. And if, according to Christian eschatology, the only alternative to eternal bliss is an objective horror in the end, then neither is it possible that God's love for someone should be a matter of degree. Contrary to what Jeff Jordan has argued, therefore, the mere fact that God had a good reason to start us out in a context in which people have incompatible earthly interests carries no implication that God loves some people more than he does others.

---

[36] For why, in my opinion, God's love of Jacob and his so-called hatred of Esau are both instances of his willing the best for someone, see the section entitled "I Have Loved Jacob, But I Have Hated Esau," in *The Inescapable Love of God*, 2nd ed. (Eugene, OR: Cascade Books, 2014), 111–15. See especially page 114. In addition to the points made there, I would argue that the statement about Esau is a clear case of hyperbole, where hyperbole is by intention literally false.

Not even God, it is true, can *satisfy* incompatible interests. But in the absence of a principled way of differentiating between and enumerating interests, and then weighing them on some scale of importance, we have no reason to deny that everyone has an indefinitely large number of interests that God opposes and also an indefinitely large number of them with which he identifies. Neither do we have any reason to deny that, for every case where two persons have incompatible earthly interests, God takes as his own some deeper and more important interest that both parties share. Beyond that, the whole point of the Loving Parent Analogy is that God's love plays a corrective role in our lives, as it seeks to cultivate more spiritually mature attitudes in us. Accordingly, the depth of his love for us in no way depends upon our *present* fitness for intimate fellowship with him; it depends instead upon what he is prepared to do to secure a glorious future for each of us.[37]

---

[37] My thanks to Jordan Wessling for several excellent (and helpful) comments on a prepublication version of this chapter.

What Wideness, Whose Strictness? The Scope and Limits of Divine Love for Humankind

Marilyn McCord Adams

1 Truth in hymnody

I have to confess, my own understanding of divine love is aptly captured by the following verses of F. W. Faber's 1854 hymn:

> There's a wideness in God's mercy,
> Like the wideness of the sea;
> There's a kindness in His justice
> Which is more than liberty.
>
> There is no place where earth's sorrows
> Are more felt than up in Heaven;
> There is no place where earth's failings
> Have such kindly judgment given.
>
> For the love of God is broader
> Than the measure of our mind;
> And the heart of the Eternal
> Is most wonderfully kind.
>
> But we make His love too narrow
> By false limits of our own;
> And we magnify His strictness
> With a zeal He will not own.
>
> It is God: His love looks mighty,
> But is mightier than it seems;
> 'Tis our Father: and His fondness
> Goes far out beyond our dreams.

There is plentiful redemption
In the blood that has been shed;
There is joy for all the members
In the sorrows of the Head.

If our love were but more simple,
We should take Him at His Word;
And our lives would be all sunshine
In the sweetness of our Lord.[1]

If I were a musician, I could simply sing it and sit down. For better or worse, however, vocal music is not my gift, and a hymn is not a lecture. So it is incumbent on me to say more, and to say it in a different way.

2 What wideness, whose strictness?

2.1 Manifold strictness?

"There's a wideness in God's mercy," but how wide is it? Does divine love extend to everyone? Does it extend to everyone equally? Many Christian witnesses urge: both times, the answer is "no." Since we are philosophers, we might as well begin with Aquinas's argument for *metaphysical* strictness: to love is to bestow goods on the beloved. Creatable natural kinds form an excellence hierarchy, so that in creating a thing of a higher kind (e.g., an angel), God bestows more natural goodness than God gives to things of lower kinds (e.g., cows and earthworms). Aquinas concludes that God loves angels more than cows and earthworms, not to mention the elect more than the damned.[2]

Scotus argued for metaphysical *license*. Because creatures are only finite goods, they provide only defeasible reason to love them. What creatures are does not give God decisive reason to create them or decisive reason (at least in individual cases) to see to their well-being. God is not obliged to love creatures. Should God create, divine liberality is an option, but not one to which divine Goodness is bound.[3]

Scripture and tradition testify to de facto strictness. God's penchant for ordering creation by separation and division (Genesis 1) gets reflected in divine separation of Israel from the other nations by electing them to be God's own people. The division reaches back to their primal progenitors: "Jacob I loved; Esau I hated" (Rom. 9:13). Apocalyptic texts warn of the Judgment-Day Great Assize with double verdicts and dual destinies, when Christ will separate the sheep from the goats (Mt. 25:31-46), when the wicked will be consigned to a pit of fire prepared for the devil and all his angels, but the righteous will enter into eternal bliss of life together with God (Mt. 13:42, 49, 25:46).

---

[1] www.cyberhymnal.org/htm/t/h/e/therwide/htm First (accessed October 27, 2016).
[2] Aquinas, *Summa Theologica* I, 1.20, aa.3-4.
[3] Scotus, *Op.Ox.* III, d.18, q.u, nn.6-7; Wadding VII.1.415–18.

Traditional theologies of predestination struggle to balance providential sovereignty over against the charge of arbitrariness. Some (e.g., Ockham[4]) posit that divine policy to include creatures in the trinitarian friendship circle is naturally prior to, but that the actual division of saved and damned is naturally consequent upon the (fore-/eternally) known track record of earthly careers. Others (e.g., Scotus;[5] sometimes Aquinas[6]) hold to an asymmetry between predestination and reprobation: predestination to glory is prior but damnation is posterior to (however) known cradle-to-grave choices. God takes the initiative in benefiting, but God is not a punisher before humans are debtors! Sterner theologies insist on the symmetry of the dual destinies, so that divine division comes first, and graces are distributed to make sure that the earthly careers match the eternal destinies (for an infralapsarian version, see Aquinas;[7] for a supralapsarian version, see some Dutch Calvinists).

Experience of the human condition in this present earthly life supports the conclusion that—on Aquinas's metaphysical principle (that love is proportionate to good bestowed)—God loves human beings unequally. Even if—as I maintain—all but hermits are complicit, indeed share ownership in collectively produced horrors, not everyone is an individual horror-participant—not everyone individually participates in evils that are prima facie life-ruinous—horrendous evils, participation in which gives everyone prima facie reason to believe that the participant's life cannot be a great good to him/her on the whole.[8] If to love is to bestow goodness, does not God—in causing or permitting preventable horrors—give evidence (perhaps defeasible evidence, but evidence all the same) that God loves individual horror-participants less than those who manage to escape individual horror-participation? If—as Ockham suggests—the damned could reasonably hate God if they believed that God had condemned them to hell forever, cannot individual horror-participants reasonably wonder whether God hates them? Shifting to cultic categories, can they not reasonably ask whether God has cursed them by setting them up for ruin that cuts them off from God—for traumas and torment that destroy for them the psychological possibility of believing in, trusting, or loving God; that set up seemingly insurmountable obstacles to their becoming the kind of persons God says God wants us to be?

Scripture and tradition, reason and experience can all be aligned to suggest that God's mercy is not as wide as it could be. There *is* a strictness to it, and *God* owns it!

2.2 Maximum width?

Minority-report universalism begs to differ. On the contrary, universalists maintain, the doctrines of limited election and dual-destiny predestination simply "map up" "us

---

[4] Ockham, *Tractatus de Praedestinatione et de Praescientia Dei respectu Futurorum Contingentium*, qq.1, 4, 5; OPh II.507–19, 536–39.
[5] Scotus, *Ordinatio* I, d.41, q.u, nn.40-51; Vat VI.332–36.
[6] Aquinas, *Summa Theologica* , q.22, a.2 ad 2; q.23, a.3c.
[7] Aquinas, *Summa Theologica* I, q.23, a.5 ad 3.
[8] I expand upon the notion of horrors in my books *Horrendous Evils and the Goodness of God* (Ithaca, NY & London: Cornell University Press, 1999), chaps. 2–3, and *Christ and Horrors: The Coherence of Christology* (Cambridge: Cambridge University Press, 2006), chaps. 2–3.

versus them" tribalism. They are paradigms of making "God's love too narrow with false limits of our own"! Universalist John Hick's landmark book *Evil and the God of Love*[9] was notable, among other things, for framing the problem of evil, not in terms of divine rights and obligations, but in terms of divine love. Hick developed his soul-making theodicy around the question: In what sort of world(s) would a God who loved human beings place us, the better to achieve the divine goal of fitting every soul for union with God?

Nowadays, some perfect-being theologians contend that a perfect being would exhibit each pure perfection to the maximum degree.[10] They reason that if love (where love involves concern for the well-being of the beloved) is a pure perfection, perfect love would—in one sense—not "exceed the measure of our mind," because it would have an abstractly conceivable maximum. The perfect being would love its personal creatures maximally and so exhibit maximal concern for their well-being.

In a similar vein, John Bishop and Ken Persyk[11] insist that perfect loving relationality is a trait that would belong to a personal omni-God essentially. Showing an appreciation for how bad horrors (prima facie life-ruinous evils) are, they reason that—whether or not, even if (à la Hick) perfect loving relationality might teach the beloved a few painful lessons—perfect loving relationality would not allow the beloved to *go* through, much less *put* the beloved through horrors that it could prevent. Not preventing and/or not refraining from causing such horrors would constitute an indelible stain on the relationship, in the sense that there would be nothing God could do to make up for it. Bishop and Persyk conclude, not that individual horror-participants would be reasonable in thinking God hated them, but that we all would in consequence be reasonable in thinking that a personal omni-God does not exist. Put otherwise, the hypothesis that a personal omni-God is essentially such as to exhibit perfect loving relationality to its personal creatures combines with the horrors of our experience to constitute a new norm-relative atheological argument.

In the scholastic manner, pro and contra arguments frame the question: Is divine love for created persons maximally or even immeasurably broad? Or is it somehow narrow and restricted?

3 Love embracing horrors

3.1 Cruciform strictness

To continue with hymnody: Christians certainly believe in "Love Divine, all loves excelling, joy of heaven to earth come down." But is it really part of Christian belief

---

[9] John Hick, *Evil and the God of Love* (New York: Harper & Row, 1966).
[10] For an extensive discussion of this issue, see Mark Murphy, *God's Own Ethics: Norms of Divine Agency and the Argument from Evil* (Oxford: Oxford University Press, 2017), chap. 1.
[11] John Bishop, "How a Modest Fideism may Constrain Theistic Commitments: Exploring an Alternative to Classical Theism," *Philosophia* 35 (2007): 387–402; "Towards a Religiously Adequate Alternative to OmniGod Theism," *Sophia* 48 (2009): 419–33; John Bishop and Ken Perszyk, "The Normatively Relativised Logical Argument from Evil," *International Journal for Philosophy of Religion* 70 (2011): 109–26; and "Concepts of God and Problems of Evil," in *Alternative Concepts of God*, ed. Yugin Nagasawa and Andrei Buckareff (Oxford: Oxford University Press), 106–27.

that God loves human beings with Bishop-Persyk perfect loving relationality? Grant for the sake of argument Bishop and Persyk's notion that there is such a thing as perfect loving relationality (*pace* Mark Murphy[12]) and that it is essentially characteristic of Godhead (as Bernard of Clairvaux and Richard of St. Victor[13] thought). Still, one might expect—following ancient treatises on friendship—perfect loving relationality to be found only among peers, indeed, for Christians, among those paradigm peers, the persons of the Trinity.

What I want to focus on here, however, is whether the Bible or Christian theology generally advertises God as exhibiting Bishop-Persyk perfect loving relationality toward human beings? To face the issue more starkly, temporarily bracket disagreements about universal salvation and begin with biblical and traditional pictures of God's love for the elect. The question is, do Scripture and tradition really represent the Christian God as so prioritizing their well-being as to protect the elect from any and every horror? The answer is obviously "no." John's Jesus is confident that he loves the Father and the Father loves him. Yet, John's Jesus embraces his own crucifixion (a horror par excellence) as the climax of the Father's plan. John's Jesus warns Peter that he, too, will die a horrendous death (Jn 21:18-22). The Synoptic Jesus puts would-be disciples on notice: if any would follow him, they must take up their crosses daily (Lk. 9:23-25). Individual horror-participation and/or the risk thereof is a cost of discipleship.

According to the Gospels and the New Testament generally, divine love for the elect expresses itself by calling them to cruciform careers, in the confidence that God has/is the currency with which to more than compensate them for their troubles. Who and what God is, is infinitely more than we can ask or imagine (in the words of the hymn, Who and what God is, "exceeds the measure of our minds"). Intimate and beatific forever-after life together with God is incommensurably good *for* human beings, and so not only balances off but swamps the negative value of horrors. Moreover, insofar as the elect will risk suffering horrendous persecution and death for what they do right (i.e., because of their loyalty to God), their suffering will be caught up in their life together with God, which will overall and in the end be beatific, and so will have a dimension of positive meaning. Consequently, their horror-participation is not merely balanced-off but defeated.

3.2 Varieties of cases

Of course, horror-defeat varies with individuals and contexts. Scripture and tradition illustrate the dynamics of divine love toward the elect with a range of cases. (1) John's Jesus, saints, and martyrs whose relationship with God is intimate enough and/or who have experienced the Goodness of God often enough *do not hold horror-participation against God*, because they give horror-participation a dimension of positive meaning by undergoing it for God's sake, and because they *experience* how intimate life together

---

[12] Murphy argues that love is not a pure perfection because it has no intrinsic maximum. See *God's Own Ethics*, chap. 2.

[13] Richard of St. Victor, *De Trinitate*, Books III & IV, in *La Trinité*, intro. and trans. into French by Gaston Salet S.J (Paris: Les éditions du Cerf, 1959).

with who and what God is will defeat it. Think of the seven brothers butchered and fried by Antiochus Epiphanes for refusing to eat pork (II Maccabees 7), or St. Ignatius who rushed toward martyrdom eager to be ground by the teeth of the lions, or of Perpetua and Felicity in ecstasy as they were tossed by the wild beasts, or of Polycarp's matter-of-fact refusal to betray his lifelong friend and Lord. Their torture and death were horrendous because they were degrading and prima facie life-ruinous, but they knew all the while that what they were going through was not *ultima facie* ruinous because they were already experiencing how God defeats it.

(2) The Gospel passion narratives tell how in the Triduum Jesus's first disciples fell apart and betrayed their deepest loyalty. While Jesus suffers the horror of crucifixion, they suffer the horror of disintegration, which makes it clear that there is not enough to them to be faithful friends. Yet, in the Gospels, Jesus *does not hold it against them*. Their failures make no difference to his call on their lives. Jesus knew their immaturity and fully expected what happened (Mt. 26:32-35, 40-46; Mk 14:27-31, 37-42; Lk. 22:31-34, 45-46). Instead of shaming or blaming them, Jesus *heals them and empowers them* with the gift of Holy Spirit. They are "born again" "from above." Their personalities are restructured. Earlier, their personalities were managed by their autonomous ego's acting alone. That was the center that would not hold, the personal organization that went to smash in the crisis. But indwelling Godhead *resurrects them into perichoretic partnership*—I-not-I-but-indwelling Godhead in me, I-not-I-but-Christ—and *recommissions* them for Gospel proclamation (Jn 21:15-19; Mt. 28:18-20). The disciples' failure was prima facie life-ruinous. But their *experience* of the love of Jesus embracing them in their disintegration, acting to renew relationships and to recreate them for shared ministry, meant that their Triduum horror-participation was not *ultima facie* ruinous.

(3) The Hebrew Bible represents God as aiming for life together with human beings in an ideal society of which Israel is elected to be the prototype. God furnishes detailed legislation for how to organize and regulate communal life. But Israel fails to cooperate and develops social practices that spawn systemic evils. God sends prophets to warn and correct. But when the society becomes too invested in the *status quo* to make midcourse corrections, God brings it about that big powers invade and destroy Israelite society, shatter its infrastructures, deport its leadership, and so deny Israelite culture institutional embodiment. After a time, a time, and half a time—time-out for repentance, time-out for the body politic (partly through generational turnover) to let go of entrenched unjust practices—God allows a remnant to return to the land for a fresh start. God loves Israel with an everlasting love (Jer. 31:3), but there is a strictness to it. God not only permits but also perpetrates horrors on the beloved. In dealing with the body politic, the Bible's God uses horrors instrumentally, not to obliterate God's people altogether, but as a refiner's fire (Mal. 3:2). The meltdown is a condition of the possibility of their being in a position to reorganize. Divine faithfulness and determination mean that meltdowns will be repeated until Israel becomes a light to the nations by embodying God's social dreams.[14]

---

[14] In the past I have resisted the idea that horror-perpetration could ever be a legitimate means to an end. I still believe that this is true where human agents are concerned, inasmuch as we lack the

Thus, God's call portends horror-participation. What defeats horrors is perceived life together with God, sooner or later resolving into harmony of purpose and beatific intimacy. Divine love for the elect expresses itself by being with them always, wherever they go (Gen. 28:15, 20; Mt. 2:23, 18:20, 28:20), and by exercising divine powers for recreation, resurrection, and reversal.

4 The love of God, how mighty?

4.1 Uncalled for horrors?

In the world as we know it, however, individual horror-participation is not restricted to proto-saints and heroes who have tasted and seen the goodness of the Lord, or even to the immature and floundering whose horror-participation comes about in the training course for an explicit vocation. Consider Auschwitz. Transportation was no respecter of persons. Prisoners were rounded up without regard for their individual moral or spiritual preparation. Some inmates were lifelong atheists. Others believed but had not taken God with full seriousness. Still others had been devout but their experience of soul-killing trauma annihilated their faith in God's existence or good will (cf. Elie Wiesel's *Night*). Think of the fictional but true-to-life scene in Frank Cottrell Boyce's television drama *God on Trial*. The rabbi, who many had thought to be the messiah, reviews God's Hebrew Bible track record and concludes: "God was never good. He used to be on our side. Now he has switched sides." That is only to speak of the horror-*victims*. But Auschwitz society was dominated by horror-perpetrators. German commanders were often true-believer Nazi's, who disciplined themselves to be callous enough to carry out extermination as a necessary means to their ideological ends. Others were German patriots who were just following orders the way soldiers do in wartime. Kapos were co-opted into bettering their own lot by taking an active role in terrorizing and degrading fellow prisoners. Hapless others were confronted with the ghastly choice of shoveling bodies into crematoria or being incinerated alive. Most prisoners descended to the Darwinian episodically when they rejoiced at the death of relatives, because they could take their crumbs of bread.

Is the love of God mighty enough to defeat horrors within the contexts of such lives? Would there be any way for God to prove loving to them? Or does their psychological inability to believe and trust and/or their hard-heartedness and vice put them beyond the power of divine love to save? My own answer is that the love of God *is* able, because—on reflection—the second set of cases is not so different from the first, and because the Bible advertises God as making or as able to make the moves needed to defeat the ruinous quality of horror-participation within the context of any individual horror-participant's life.

> capital and resourcefulness to defeat the horrors we cause. But reflection on the texts of Scripture and the role of prophets has led me to the conclusion that God does sometimes destroy the meaning-making systems in which people have made sense of their lives, when those systems are too entrenched and perverse.

4.2 Implicit vocation, universal, and cosmic

Not all humans are believers. Not all humans experience themselves—like Saul of Tarsus on Damascus Road (Acts 9:1-22, 26:9-18) or Peter, Andrew, James, and John (Mk 1:16-20; Mt. 4:18-22; Lk. 5:1-11)—as called by God to a distinctive task. Nevertheless, Anselm[15] recognized a distinction between explicit and implicit vocation. All actual creatures, by the very fact that God creates them, whether or not they are or are even the kind of thing that could be aware of it, share a vocation to play a part in God's cosmic plan—as Anselm puts it, to be and to do that for which they were made (*ad quod facta sunt*). My cosmic hypothesis is that God loves material creation (in one way, this is trivial, because the material world would not exist unless God willed it into existence) and wants it to be as Godlike as possible while still being itself. Because God is active, God makes material stuff dynamic. Because God is life, God nudges material stuff into structures that can host life. Because God is personal, God nudges it some more into configurations that support personal life. Because God is holy, God aims at the perichoretic restructuring of material personalities, so that material persons become temples of the Holy Spirit (1 Cor. 6:19-20). God purposes life together, God with God's creatures, in the material world that God has made.

God's choice to create us in this world is not exotic, because this world is our natural home, the one in which our species evolved. But making us personal animals in a world such as this makes us radically vulnerable to horrors. The risk of individual and the certainty of collective participation in horrors are thus vocational hazards for humankind in this material world. Yet, our calling as human beings is to get through a human life in this material world the best way we can.

4.3 Presence and solidarity

Where the elect are concerned, perceived divine presence and divine favor are key to defeat. Perceived presence breaks into two components: the fact of divine presence and the individual horror-participant's perception of it and appreciation of its significance. God is omnipresent by nature: nothing could be anywhere, nor could there be anywhere to be, if God were not there. Medieval Christian theologians agree: God is cognitively present to each and every creature, knows the creature through and through. Charles Hartshorne understood omniscience kinesthetically, on analogy, not with vision but with feeling. Hartshorne declares that God is omni-sensitive in the sense of feeling all of our feelings and sharing all of our pain. Of course, God's feeling our pain will not have the same effect on divine subjectivity as our feeling our pain does on ours, because divine consciousness is full of so many other good things. Linda Zagzebski does Hartshorne one better when she argues that divine omniscience includes immediate knowledge of *our* subjectivity, not only of what it is like to be us but also of what it is like for us to be us.

The Christian God goes further still. On my cosmic hypothesis, divine love for material creation presses toward incarnation, in which God becomes as much like

---

[15] Anselm, *Monologion*, cc.68–69; Schmitt I.78–79; *De Veritate*, cc.5, 7, 12; Schmitt I.182, 185, 191–92.

material creation as God can while still being Godself! God becomes part of material creation by making an individual human nature God's own, and by acting and suffering through its powers. So far as God's human nature is concerned, God hands Godself over to the chances and changes of this material world and to life in a corrupt society of flawed human beings. God does so in a particular context, in which He has taken up a prophetic role, in consequence of which God is crucified.[16]

Saints and heroes with explicit vocations see their own horror-participation as a way to imitate Christ's sufferings on the cross, and rejoice to be counted worthy to suffer for the Name (Acts 5:41). Where horror-participants with merely implicit vocations are concerned, the relevance is reversed. God's own horror-participation in Christ is a divine initiative of solidarity with all human horror-participants, a way of showing that our God is no aloof Pentagon general but an officer in the trenches, a way of God's saying: "I am not asking more of you than I ask of myself." The world as we know it is God's project, in which each and every human being is implicitly called to take part. God's project carries horrendous costs for human beings. Outside the context of an explicit preestablished friendship, horror-participants would have no reason to believe that God could be trusted to be *for* them. Indeed, they would have reason to believe that God was not *for* them but at best *indifferent* to them and at worst *against* them. A crucified God lays the foundation for trust by sharing the costs. Ironically, within the biblical frame, the manner of Jesus's death puts Christ in solidarity with all of the cursed, with people who—by what they suffered, were, or did—were cut off from God and the people of God. This is a central ingredient in horror-defeat, because if God takes God's stand with the cursed, the cursed are not cut off from God after all.

4.4 Perceptual dysfunction

God is omnipresent by nature. God is Incarnate and crucified by choice. Likewise, being *for* any or all created persons is a divine policy option. Divine omnipresence and favor manifested in for better or for worse solidarity constitute a foundation of defeat, because they turn horror-participation into a shared experience and so catch it up into the horror-participant's relationship with God, which—if God so wills—can resolve into something beatific.

For defeat to take hold, however, the horror-participant must perceive divine presence and solidarity and appreciate its meaning-conferring significance. The Bible seems to acknowledge: divine hiddenness is what makes horrors so bad. Bible stories also remind how bringing human beings to have ears that hear and eyes that see is a nontrivial problem even for God, at that twice-over.

4.4.1 Entrenched latency

First, while human beings do have an innate capacity to perceive God, quite apart from individual horror-participation, the *sensus divinitatis* is more difficult to evoke and bring up to always-or-for-the-most-part functional engagement than our other faculties are.

---

[16] For a more extensive elaboration, see my *Christ and Horrors*, chap. 3.

Even with the senses, infants require time to achieve focus. Tradition and developmental psychology declare that children do not reach the age of reason until six or eight, after which long and deliberate education (courses in philosophy and critical reasoning) are required to perfect it. But even where there are episodic "wow" experiences, lifelong training and spiritual practices are needed to awaken our sensitivity so that we can perceive the world as God-infested, recognize good things as personal gestures of divine favor, experience the bigness of divine Goodness as ready, willing, and able to make good on the worst that we can suffer, be, or do. Jesus's first disciples illustrate the challenge, even with eager pupils. By word and deed, Jesus gives them intensive tutorials. But mid-ministry, they still see human beings as walking trees (Mt. 8:22-25).

4.4.2 Damaged capacities

Worse still, where horrors occur outside the context of deep and preestablished friendship with God, horror-participation easily stunts or aborts the awakening of the individual's *sensus divinitatis*, at the very least blurs and distorts vision. Many individual horror-participants find it psychologically impossible to believe *that* God exists. Others may credit cosmological reasoning in theory, but find that trust in God's love for them is definitely not a live option. For many, the only honest move is Ivan Karamazov's moral indignation that returns the ticket. Others are consumed by rage, become convinced that God hates them, and with all of their might hate God back. Their individual horror-participation furnishes reason not to trust, indeed provides grounds for mistrust, and—other things being equal—makes it reasonable to believe that God is at best indifferent and at worst sadistic. Is divine love mighty enough to restore our powers and correct their vision?

4.4.3 Biblical adverts

Gospel healing miracles are sacraments of the scope of divine power. Thus, *the Synoptic Jesus heals the blind and the deaf as an outward and visible sign of divine power to reverse human spiritual perceptual dysfunction.* In John's Book of Signs, Jesus begins by healing a man born physically blind. But the story goes on to tell how the newly sighted man has his *sensus divinitatis* awakened, how he moves from latency to explicit confession and worship of the Son of Man ("I followed his directions and now I can see" [Jn 9:9-11]; "he is a prophet" [Jn 9:17]; he is "from God" [Jn 9:31-33]; "Lord, I believe" [Jn 9:35-38]). The dramatic story of the conversion of Saul of Tarsus makes the same shift. Saul, the persecutor of the church, by his own account the worst of sinners (I Tim. 1:15), has been spiritually blinded by his own misplaced zeal (Gal. 1:13-21; 1 Tim. 1:12-17). On the Damascus Road, he is physically blinded by the light, as an outward sign of his inward condition. His old worldview shattered, Saul spends three days in tomb-like darkness, prayer, and fasting. When Ananias arrives, something like scales falls from Saul's bodily eyes. He receives the Holy Spirit along with his spiritual sight, is baptized, and starts proclaiming that Jesus is the Son of God (Acts 9:9-20). The Bible includes no real-time accounts of divine success with bodies-politic, but we are told that on the day of Pentecost some of Jesus's religious establishment enemies heard Peter's Pentecost sermon and were "cut to the heart" (Acts 2:37-42).

Jesus healed the Gerasene demoniac and restored disintegrated personalities to their right mind (Mk 5:1-20). With the gift of Holy Spirit, the risen Jesus resurrected and recentered the first disciples and St. Paul. Neurotic upbringings, dysfunctional workplaces, the rough and tumble of human life bottoming out in horror-participation—all of these distort our perceptions and disable us from making good sense of the world and our lives. God's general strategy for reforming human beings into people who can trust God to be *for* them involves finding many and various ways to experience divine Goodness. *Jesus healed the mute* (Mt. 9:32-33), signaling divine power to make horror-participants articulate, able to assess and reconfigure meanings by using their experience of divine Goodness and their growing sense of God as Emmanuel to re-sort what was really happening and how they and God were related in the worst and best of times.

4.5 Divine power to defeat horrors among the callous and the cruel?

Meaning-making is an essential human function that organizes life around goals and values. Because human subjectivity is developmental, our ways of making sense of who we and others are and what we are meant to do, naturally falls apart in the developmental cycle (think of the transition from childhood to adolescence, from adolescence to young adulthood, of midlife crisis and later of retirement with the diminishments of old age). But if we are naturally built to outgrow old ways of being in the world, we are also equipped with resources to reintegrate the pieces into something richer or at least more age appropriate, albeit with help from our social surroundings and through a very messy process.

The callous and hard-hearted may have their lives tightly organized around goals and objectives. They may be highly efficient in selecting means through which to skillfully pursue their ends. Many mafia bosses would boast that their lives are filled with meaning; they have successfully built an empire, enriched family and associates, and creatively extended their reach into new fields. Nazis had reason to think their lives meaningful, that they were spending energy and ingenuity for a cause in which they believed, and that—for a time—was winning. The trouble was not their prudential effectiveness, but that their lives were organized around the wrong values. Their meaning-making system required them to accept the destruction and degradation of other human beings as an acceptable price of reaching their goals.

Can—how can—divine love defeat horrors within the lives of Corleone, Hitler, and Pol Pot? By repeatedly orchestrating the destruction of their entrenched but perverse meaning-making systems. For divine love to restore positive meaning to the lives of cruel and callous horror-perpetrators, the individuals will have to face up to what their actions and acquiescence meant for other people. They will have to become people who take the dignity God confers on every human being with full seriousness. This means that their old meaning-making systems will have to go to smash and that they will have to flounder with God's help for new ones. As with human development, the callous and the cruel will have to choose their way out of vice toward virtue by successive approximations. There will be many rounds of confronting the truth about their choices and values, many rounds of letting go of the old frame, many rounds of repentance and new beginnings. For many, this will require drastic changes of environment and a postmortem career-extension!

5 Trust, paradoxical, and expansive

5.1 Trust among the elect

God aims for beatific intimacy; God with the people of God. But beatific intimacy is built on trust. With saints and heroes, trust issues do not arise. Their experience of horrors does not call God's trustworthiness into question, because it is accompanied by an experience of divine Goodness and favor. As for the first disciples right after the Triduum, they need to be assured that Jesus still believes in them and wants to be their friend. Confronted with how untrustworthy their autonomous-ego-centered personalities are, they have to enter into and learn to trust their newly perichoretically reconfigured selves. Israel always had trouble trusting God enough not to worship other gods as insurance against bad weather, infertility, and foreign invasions. Israelite powers-that-were rarely trusted God enough to put divine social-justice legislation into practice. After prophetic warnings and denunciations culminating in destruction and deportation, even with God's dramatic exit from the temple and the city, the relationship had to be renegotiated. The Sinai covenant is explicitly conditional (Deut. 11:26-29, 28:1-68), and Israelite national apostasy called down covenant curses. Exile was a time for the relationship to be revived and rebuilt, until it was strong enough to try life together in the land again.

5.2 A paradox of trust

What about the second group of horror-participants? I have argued that horrors are too ruinous to be defeated by any package of merely created goods, that the only credible defeater is divine solidarity integrating individual horror-participation into the person's on the whole and in the end beatific and intimate relationship with God. My claim that this is plausible rides on the intuition that beatific intimacy with God is incommensurately good *for* created persons.

Nevertheless, paradox threatens the implementation of this proposal. For beatific intimacy presupposes trust. But it is not reasonable for individual horror-participants to trust God to be *for* them unless and until they see how their individual horror-participation is being defeated. They need to see defeat in progress, or at least the makings of horror-defeat. Indeed, absent such evidence, it is reasonable for them not to trust God to be *for* them. So there is a circle: trust presupposes horror-defeat which presupposes beatific intimacy which presupposes trust! Horrors will be finally defeated only if we trust without reservation, but it is not reasonable for us to trust; it is reasonable for us not to trust without reservation so long as horrors have not been decisively defeated.

One answer to this paradox is that the circle is not vicious because relationship development in general and reconciliation in particular involve a process. Given who and what God is, harmonious relationship with God will make everything alright. Divine love can achieve this (as above) by finding many and various ways for the horror-participant, wittingly or unwittingly, consciously or unconsciously to experience divine Goodness. Divine assistance will be required to midwife a dialectic that puts experienced goodness up against experienced horror, and struggles to articulate what this can all mean within the context of a single life. Divine solidarity, appreciation of the horror-participant's costs, the reversal of damages, and eventually (in the eschaton) removing us from recurrent danger, can be put into play to spiral this process toward completion. With the callous and cruel, a winning pedagogy would cycle and recycle between shattering confrontations with the truth and dawning reassurance that the worst that they had been or done had no power to separate them from God and were no match for divine resourcefulness to compensate their victims.

5.3 Human-to-human solidarity

The love of God is mighty, but whether or not God uses divine power to defeat individual horror-participation in every case is a function of free and contingent divine policy. There is a wideness in God's mercy, but how wide is it actually? Does divine love act to the limit of its power? The Bible offers a clue in divine commands to the people of God to widen the scope of our loves.

Torah and Gospel declare God's command to love our neighbors as ourselves (Lev. 19:18; Mt. 22:38). Torah explains that "neighbor" is not restricted to our ethnic in-group but extends to sojourners—that is, to resident aliens or immigrants, who live and work here, who share our common life (Lev. 19:33-34). Sermon-on-the-Mount Jesus commands disciples to go further to love enemies (Mt. 5:43-48). These add up to a command to universal human sympathy, to love each and all other human beings as ourselves. Christian ethics is full of arguments about the meaning of such commandments. But surely, even on a minimalist interpretation, they imply that God wants us to want individual horror-participation to be defeated in the lives of each and all human beings as much as we want it for ourselves.

It is not reasonable for me to trust God without reservation; indeed, it is reasonable for me not to trust God without reservation absent evidence that God is *for* me— evidence that God is defeating my individual horror-participation within the context of my life. But if I am altruistic, I will care as much about horror-defeat for others as I do for myself. It will, therefore, not be reasonable for me to trust God without reservation unless I have good evidence that God is *for* everyone else as well—evidence that God is busy defeating their horror-participation within the context of their individual lives, too. In short, I cannot trust God to be *for* me if I cannot trust God to be *for* by being good *to* everyone. Otherwise, divine favor might be temporary and teasing. God might let me down in the crunch by switching sides!

Obeying divine commands to be altruistic binds horror-defeat for each to horror-defeat for all. For an altruistic person cannot trust God without reservation unless he or she has reason to think that God is benefiting everybody, and he or she cannot enter into the horror-defeating beatific intimacy without unreserved trust in God. But God wants the elect to trust God without reservation. And God is the one who has commanded the elect to love other human beings as themselves. Thus, *divine commands to the elect to be altruistic set God up for a situation in which God cannot get what God wants without being for everybody, without defeating individual horror-participation within the context of the individual horror-participants' lives.*

I do not claim that my argument is demonstrative. Some would point to Bible stories where God (like olden-days kings) issues commands that God does not intend to be obeyed. Did God really intend Abraham to kill Isaac, or was it only a test (Genesis 22)? Did Jesus really mean for the people he healed to keep quiet about it? Abelard insisted not.[17] Even if we grant such interpretations, however, it seems unlikely that the second great commandment or the Golden Rule number among the commands God does not want us to obey. Others might claim that divine commands to universal human sympathy and "do unto others" are pedagogical. Trying to obey them helps the elect become the sort of people they need to be to enter into bliss, but God will tell them at the last minute that God's love is narrower and that they should (as Michelangelo's painting shows) imitate God in despising the damned. Still, we should hesitate. Does not Scripture warn that "with the crooked"—that is, with the still twisted agency of all human beings except possibly for a few saints and heroes—"God is wily" (Ps. 18:27)? Jesus commands us to love our enemies, the better to "be perfect" as our "heavenly Father is perfect" (Mt. 5:48). Faber's hymn also stands as a caution: the more energetically we scramble for explanations why God would command us to love everybody when God does not, the more we might wonder whether we are magnifying God's strictness with a zeal God will not own!

---

[17] Abelard, *Peter Abelard's Ethics*, ed. with intro. and English trans. D. E. Luscombe (Oxford: Clarendon Press, 1971), 29–33.

8

Impassibility, Omnisubjectivity, and the Problem of Unity in Love

R. T. Mullins

Before the turn of the twentieth century, a debate arose over the doctrine of divine impassibility. Though impassibility had been held as orthodox Christian teaching for many centuries, the doctrine found itself under a newfound scrutiny.[1] In 1900, Marshall Randles commented that this modern rejection of divine impassibility is merely a passing mood that "will probably turn out to be one of those temporary reactions which come and go."[2] Randles's prediction turned out to be deeply mistaken. Far from a passing mood, the doctrine of divine passibility eventually came to be declared as the new orthodoxy within twentieth-century theology.[3] Despite the apparent orthodoxy of divine passibility today, the doctrine of divine impassibility continues to have support from theologians and philosophers.[4]

In the contemporary debate over impassibility and passibility, a great deal of reflection has focused on the definition of divine love. Anastasia Philippa Scrutton notes that passibilists in the twentieth century have tended to argue that the nature of love entails the denial of impassibility.[5] A typical line of argument is that perfect love entails suffering with the beloved in certain circumstances.[6] For example, Thomas Jay Oord argues that the biblical definition of love is "to act intentionally, in sympathetic/

---

[1] Cf. J. K. Mozley, *The Impassibility of God: A Survey of Christian Thought* (Cambridge: Cambridge University Press, 1926).
[2] Marshall Randles, *The Blessed God: Impassibility* (London: Charles H. Kelly, 1900), 5.
[3] Richard Bauckham, *Jesus and the God of Israel: God Crucified and Other Studies on the New Testament's Christology of Divine Identity* (Grand Rapids, MI: Wm. B. Eerdmans Publishing Co., 2008); Jürgen Moltmann, *The Crucified God: The Cross of Christ as the Foundation and Criticism of Christian Theology* (London: SCM, 2001); Alan Torrance, "Does God Suffer? Incarnation and Impassibility," in *Christ in Our Place: The Humanity of God in Christ for the Reconciliation of the World*, ed. Trevor A. Hart (Eugene, OR: Wipf and Stock Publishers, 1989); and Fretheim, *The Suffering of God* (Philadelphia, PA: Fortress Press, 1984).
[4] Richard E. Creel, *Divine Impassibility: An Essay in Philosophical Theology* (Cambridge: Cambridge University Press, 1986); Weinandy, *Does God Suffer?* (Notre Dame, IN: University of Notre Dame Press, 2000); and Eric Silverman, "Impassibility and Divine Love," in *Models of God and Alternative Ultimate Realities*, ed. Jeanine Diller and Asa Kasher (New York: Springer, 2013).
[5] Anastasia Scrutton, "Divine Passibility: God and Emotion," *Philosophy Compass* 8 (2013): 870.
[6] Paul Fiddes, *The Creative Suffering of God* (Oxford: Oxford University Press, 1988), 16–25.

empathetic response to God and others, to promote overall well-being."[7] The passibilist argues that the current state of the sin-stained world contains many such circumstances where a perfectly loving God's response toward His beloved creatures must involve empathetic suffering.[8]

While I think there is something to be seriously considered in this line of reasoning, it is worth noting that this definition of love rules out impassibility from the start. This is because proponents of divine impassibility explicitly deny that God's love is responsive, and that God is empathetic.[9] As such, impassibilists do not typically find this line of reasoning convincing because they wish to affirm a different conception of divine love that better supports their position. This would seem to put the debate between impassibility and passibility at a standstill.

Scrutton explains that, "Arguing for either position from divine love has, so far, only resulted in a stalemate, since both arguments rest on opposing ideals of love." According to Scrutton, the passibilist will appeal to the lover who suffers with the beloved out of solidarity, while the impassibilist will favor the wise Stoic who is blissful and charitable in his actions.[10]

Is there a way out of this stalemate? I believe that there is. In this chapter, I propose to offer a modified strategy for moving the passibilist versus impassibilist debate forward. Instead of considering opposing views on love, I believe that the passibilist can grant the impassibilist her favored fundamental definition of love, and then argue that this definition of love pushes one toward a passible God. In order to build this argument, I must do several things in this chapter. In Section 1, I shall briefly articulate the doctrine of divine impassibility and its connection to the attribute of divine blessedness. In Section 2, I shall discuss the doctrine of divine passibility and the attribute of omnisubjectivity. In Section 3, I shall briefly explain the need for finding a common ground on the nature of love in order to advance the debate. In Section 4, I shall examine the impassibilist's definition of divine love as developed by Eleonore Stump. In Section 5, I shall argue that Stump's account of love is incomplete without omnisubjectivity. Thus, if God is going to be loving, He must be omnisubjective. If God is omnisubjective, He must be passible.[11]

1 Impassibility

IMPASSIBILITY is a pre-eminent mode of the Essence of God, according to which it is devoid of all suffering or feeling; not only because nothing can act against this

---

[7] Oord, *The Nature of Love: A Theology*, 17.
[8] Bertrand R. Brasnett, *The Suffering of the Impassible God* (London: The MacMillan Co., 1928), 118.
[9] Arthur W. Pink, *The Attributes of God* (Grand Rapids, MI: Baker Books, 1975), 77–78. Cf. *The Whole Works of the Rev. W. Bates*, Volume 1, ed. W. Farmer (Harrisonburg: Sprinkle Publications, 1990), 289; and Girolamo Zanchius, *Life Everlasting: Or, The True Knowledge of One Jehovah, Three Elohim, and Jesus Immanuel* (Cambridge: John Legat, 1601), 357–58.
[10] Scrutton, "Divine Passibility: God and Emotion," 872.
[11] Along the way, readers will also need to count the musical references in the chapter. Hint: there are six references.

Essence, for it is of infinite Being and devoid of external cause; but likewise because it cannot receive the act of any thing, for it is of simple Entity.—Therefore, Christ has not suffered according to the Essence of his Deity.

—James Arminius[12]

The doctrine of divine impassibility is best understood within the classical conception of God which includes attributes like timelessness, immutability, and simplicity. To be sure, classical theism also affirms attributes like aseity, self-sufficiency, omnipotence, omniscience, and so on, but such attributes are also affirmed by modified or neoclassical theists, open theists, and some relational theists.[13] What makes classical theism unique is its commitment to divine timelessness, immutability, simplicity, and impassibility since these attributes are held to be systematically connected. It must also be understood that classical theism affirms certain principles, assumptions, and divine attributes that other Christian theists will deny. Since I have articulated and explored these issues elsewhere, I shall here seek to offer a brief discussion of the doctrine of divine impassibility and its entailments for the emotional life of God.[14]

There are two common claims made by classical theists about the doctrine of divine impassibility. First, there is a widespread agreement among classical theists that the impassible God cannot suffer. The "cannot" here is quite strong. It implies that it is broadly logically, or metaphysically, impossible for God to suffer.[15] Second, underlying this notion is the assumption that God cannot be moved, nor acted upon, by anything *ad extra* to the divine nature. Again, the "cannot" is quite strong. It implies that it is broadly logically, or metaphysically, impossible for God to be moved, or acted upon, by anything outside of God.[16] Adherence to these two impassibilist commitments will help one understand certain claims about the emotional life of the impassible God.

The emotional life of the impassible God has often been caricatured in contemporary debates. Sometimes passibilists accuse the impassible God of being apathetic in the sense of lacking all emotions. To be sure, this is not an accurate portrayal of the impassible God. While it is true that the impassible God lacks passions, it is false to say that the impassible God lacks emotions.[17] For example, the nineteenth-century theologian William Shedd affirms the impassibility of God. Shedd denies that God has any passions, but he holds that God has two emotions: love and wrath. Shedd says that these two emotions are in fact one and the same moral attribute of God—holiness.[18] Shedd is not alone in affirming that God lacks passions, and yet is full of

---

[12] Arminius, *Disputation* IV.XVII. James Nichols, trans. *The Works of James Arminius: The London Edition, Volume 2* (Grand Rapids, MI: Baker Book House, 1986).
[13] See my "The Difficulty of Demarcating Panentheism," *Sophia* 55 (2016): 325–46.
[14] R.T. Mullins, "Why Can't the Impassible God Suffer?" *TheoLogica* 2 (2018): 3–22.
[15] Paul Helm, "The Impossibility of Divine Passibility," in *The Power and Weakness of God*, ed. Nigel M. de S. Cameron (Edinburgh: Rutherford House Books, 1990), 120–21.
[16] Richard E. Creel, "Immutability and Impassibility," in *A Companion to Philosophy of Religion*, ed. Philip L. Quinn and Charles Taliaferro (Malden, MA: Blackwell Publishing, 1997), 314.
[17] Anastasia Philippa Scrutton, *Thinking through Feeling: God, Emotion and Possibility* (New York: Continuum International Publishing Group, 2011), chap. 1.
[18] W. G. T. Shedd, *Dogmatic Theology*, Vol. 1. (New York: Charles Scribner's Sons, 1888), 174.

love and wrath. This is a fairly common claim throughout church history, though not all agree that God literally has wrath because it appears to conflict with the blessedness or happiness of God.[19] More on divine blessedness below.

How are we to make sense of this claim that the impassible God lacks passions, but has emotions? Shedd claims that the happiness of God is a pleasurable emotion that arises from the harmony of the emotion and its proper object.[20] Shedd seems to be assuming something that contemporary philosophers call the *perceptual theory of emotions*. According to the perceptual theory of emotions, some emotions are cognitive, or intellectual, in that emotions are judgments about the world.[21] Not all emotional experiences are cognitive, but some are. The cognitive emotions can be rational or irrational depending on how well they track reality, and how well in line they are with one's pattern of commitments and considered judgments.[22] The claim is that cognitive emotions allow one to perceive the value of objects in the world. An emotional response to an object is partly constituted by the way the individual perceives the value of the object.[23] An object has value to an agent if she perceives it to be worthy of her attention, and worthy of her to act on behalf of the object.[24] If an emotional response fails to properly track the value of the object, the emotional response is not rational. If an emotional response properly tracks the value of the object, the emotional response is rational.[25] What impassibilists like Shedd are claiming is that God has whatever cognitive emotions are rational for a perfect being to possess.

The divine passibilist and impassibilist agree that God has whatever cognitive emotions are rational for a perfect being to possess. Where the passibilist and impassibilist disagree is over which emotions can be literally predicated of the divine life. Elsewhere I have identified three criteria that impassibilists use to discern which emotions can be literally predicated of the divine life.[26] Here I shall summarize that discussion. The impassibilist claims that God cannot have any emotions that are inconsistent with His perfect rationality, moral goodness, and blessedness.[27] In other words, it is metaphysically impossible for the impassible God to have an emotion that is irrational, immoral, or that disrupts His perfect happiness.

I shall assume that the claim that God is perfectly rational and morally good will be familiar to most contemporary readers, so I shall say no more about this. My guess is that contemporary readers will be less familiar with the doctrine of divine blessedness as understood by classical theists. Understanding blessedness will help one understand the emotional life of the impassible God.

---

[19] Cf. Paul L. Gavrilyuk, *The Suffering of the Impassible God: The Dialectics of Patristic Thought* (Oxford: Oxford University Press, 2004), 51–60.
[20] Shedd, *Dogmatic Theology*, Vol. 1, 176–77.
[21] Scrutton, *Thinking through Feeling*, chap. 3.
[22] Bennett W. Helm, "Emotions and Practical Reason: Rethinking Evaluation and Motivation," *Nous* 35 (2001): 190–213.
[23] Cain Todd, "Emotion and Value," *Philosophy Compass* 9 (2014), 706.
[24] Helm, "Emotions and Practical Reason," 195.
[25] Todd, "Emotion and Value," 704.
[26] Mullins, "Why Can't the Impassible God Suffer?"
[27] Shedd, *Dogmatic Theology*, Vol. 1, 174. Cf. Gavrilyuk, *The Suffering of the Impassible God*, 51–62; Lister, *God Is Impassible and Impassioned*, chap. 3; and Scrutton, *Thinking through Feeling*, chaps. 1 and 2.

What exactly is this attribute of divine blessedness? The classical theist James Ussher explains blessedness as follows: "It is the property of God, whereby he hath all fullnesse [*sic*] of delight and contentment in himself." According to Ussher, all felicity, happiness, endless bliss, and glory arises from God's perfect nature. Thus God has no need for anything else because He is perfectly happy in Himself.[28]

How does blessedness connect with impassibility? To start, a perfectly happy God is incapable of suffering, but Ussher has more to say than this. Ussher explains that, because God is perfectly happy, nothing outside of God can move His will. With creatures like you and I, we are moved to act by external factors. For example, if I see someone who is in a state of pure misery, I will hopefully be moved by this toward an action that will help alleviate this person's misery. Yet, according to Ussher, God is not like this. Since God is perfectly happy, He cannot be moved to act by anything outside of Himself. Instead, God can only will to act toward His own glory.[29]

2 Passibility and omnisubjectivity

Proponents of divine passibility tend to reject the attributes of timelessness, immutability, and simplicity.[30] Passibilists who are neoclassical theists or open theists typically agree with classical theists that God is a necessarily existent being whose existence and essential nature are not dependent upon anything external to the divine nature.[31] However, passibilists claim that the everlasting God undergoes various kinds of changes over time as He expresses His essential nature in new ways in response to His creatures.[32]

Although I find these sorts of differences between impassibility and passibility interesting, there are more salient differences for the argument of this chapter—that is, differences over the emotional life of God. The passibilist and impassibilist both agree that God cannot have any emotions that are irrational or immoral.[33] Where they disagree is over the nature of divine blessedness and creaturely influence on the divine life. The passibilist maintains that God can be moved or influenced by things external to the divine nature. This is because God has willingly created a universe in which He is capable of responding to, and cooperating with, His creatures in order to satisfy His purposes for His creation. Given this, the passibilist maintains that God is capable of suffering. The passibilist affirms that God is as happy as one can be in any given

---

[28] James Ussher, *A Body of Divinitie, or the Summe and Substance of Christian Religion* (London: M.F., 1645), 34. Cf. Thomas Aquinas, *Summa Contra Gentiles*, I.90; and Silverman, "Impassibility and Divine Love," 168.
[29] Ussher, *A Body of Divinitie*, 34.
[30] For a critique of these classical attributes, see R.T. Mullins, *The End of the Timeless God* (Oxford: Oxford University Press, 2016).
[31] For example, Brasnett, *The Suffering of the Impassible God*; and Francis J. McConnell, *Is God Limited?* (London: Williams and Norgate, 1925).
[32] Cf. John S. Feinberg, *No One like Him: The Doctrine of God* (Wheaton, IL: Crossway Books, 2001). Bruce A. Ware, *God's Greater Glory: The Exalted God of Scripture and the Christian Faith* (Wheaton, IL: Crossway Books, 2004).
[33] Charles Taliaferro, "The Passibility of God," *Religious Studies* 25 (1989): 217–24.

circumstance.[34] Yet, she claims that God's happiness is disturbed by what transpires in the universe.[35]

The passibilist has more to say about the differences between her position and the impassibilist over the nature of God's knowledge. Recall that the impassibilist claims that God cannot be moved, nor acted upon, by anything external to the divine nature. This has a particular entailment for understanding God's knowledge. As I have discussed elsewhere, on classical theism, God's knowledge is in no way dependent upon, nor derived from, creation. Instead, God has a perfect comprehension of His own nature, and thus God possesses all propositional knowledge.[36] Passibilists have tended to find this account of omniscience less than satisfactory.[37] Allow me to explain.

In recent years, Linda Zagzebski has been exploring a possible divine attribute that she calls *omnisubjectivity*. According to Zagzebski, "Omnisubjectivity is, roughly, the property of consciously grasping with perfect accuracy and completeness the first-person perspective of every conscious being."[38] Zagzebski claims that omnisubjectivity is entailed by God's omniscience or maximal cognitive perfection. An omniscient God is typically said to know the truth-value of all propositions, but several philosophers and theologians have complained that this does not do justice to God's cognitive perfection.[39] There is more to know in the world than *de dicto* propositions. There is also knowledge by acquaintance or experiential knowledge.

What is experiential knowledge? There is a common story that philosophers tell about a scientist named Mary in order to explain this kind of knowledge. The story can go something like this. Mary has had a very unusual upbringing. She has been locked in a room her entire life, and this room is decorated in only black and white. Mary has never seen any other colors besides black and white. Mary has at her disposal reading material about the entire world outside of her room. She has spent her life studying this material closely, and she knows a great deal about many different subjects. Yet Mary has a particular interest in roses. She reads everything that she can about roses. She comes to know all of the propositional facts about roses, yet she has never seen a rose in person. She knows that roses are red, but this concept of *red* puzzles her. She therefore reads everything she can about color theory in order to get a better grasp on "redness." She eventually comes to know all of the propositional facts about the color red. Yet her curiosity still pulls at her. One day Mary discovers a way out of her black and white room. A fellow scientist has heard of her bizarre living situation, and offers to break her out. She accepts the fellow scientist's offer, but on one condition—she wants to see a rose in person as soon as she is out. The fellow scientist smuggles Mary out of the room in a trunk under the cover of darkness. Once the fellow scientist feels

---

[34] Brasnett, *The Suffering of the Impassible God*, 73.
[35] Nicholas Wolterstorff, *Inquiring about God* (Cambridge: Cambridge University Press, 2010), chap. 10.
[36] Mullins, *The End of the Timeless God*, chap. 4.
[37] McConnell, *Is God Limited?*, 290.
[38] Linda Zagzebski, "Omnisubjectivity," in *Oxford Studies in Philosophy of Religion, Volume 1*, ed. Jonathan L. Kvanvig (New York: Oxford University Press, 2008), 231.
[39] Yujin Nagasawa, "Divine Omniscience and Knowledge *de se*," *International Journal for Philosophy of Religion* 53 (2003): 73–82.

that they are far enough away from Mary's captors, he opens the trunk and hands her a rose. For the first time in Mary's life she sees a rose in person. She sees the color red.

Does Mary's knowledge grow when she sees the rose? There are a fair number of philosophers who wish to answer in the affirmative. She has not grown in propositional knowledge, but she has grown in experiential knowledge. There is something that it is like to see the color red that Mary could not know by merely reading about color theory. There is something that it is like to see a rose, to smell its fragrance, to feel the weight of the rose in one's hand. This kind of experiential knowledge is not something that Mary had in her black and white room. The propositional facts do not capture all there is to know about the world. Thus Mary has truly grown in knowledge.

If there is this kind of experiential knowledge to be had in the world, Zagzebski argues that God must have it. An omniscient God must know all there is to know, and that includes knowing things other than mere propositions. God must have experiential knowledge as well. When Mary comes to experience a rose for the first time, there is a change in her mental states that reflects this new experience. Zagzebski holds that this change in Mary's mental states is not fully captured by propositions. So if God is going to be omniscient, God must be able to know this change in Mary's mental states, which entails God knowing more than mere propositions about Mary.[40] God must be able to consciously grasp her first-person perspective of what it is like for Mary to experience seeing a red rose.

In developing her account of omnisubjectivity, Zagzebski focuses on the nature of empathy as a kind of knowledge that God must have. A somewhat rough and ready account of empathy is that it is the transference of emotion from one person to another. As Scrutton explains, empathy is "the mechanism by which we imaginatively construct the feelings of others, and therefore are able to put ourselves in their shoes."[41] Yet this needs to be nuanced a bit. To this end, Zagzebski outlines five different features of empathy. I shall discuss each in turn.

The first feature of empathy is that empathy is a way of acquiring an emotion like that of another person. It is not identical to the emotion of the other person, but it is similar enough to help the empath understand what the other person is experiencing.[42]

The second feature of empathy is that there is something about seeing that the other person has this emotion that gives the empath a reason to acquire a similar emotion token. Otherwise, the transference of emotion is an emotional contagion, and not empathy. Empathy is not an unconscious, accidental transfer of emotions.[43] Empathy is intentional. The empath may have several reasons for wanting to acquire a similar emotional state to another person. Perhaps she wants to come to a better understanding of the other person. As Zagzebski explains, "Empathy is a way of making the emotional states of others intelligible to us. Understanding their emotions is often important if we want to understand their actions, and we can have many reasons for wanting to do that."[44] More on this below when I discuss the fourth feature of empathy. The main

---

[40] Zagzebski, "Omnisubjectivity," 233.
[41] Scrutton, *Thinking through Feeling*, 77.
[42] Zagzebski, "Omnisubjectivity," 238.
[43] Ibid., 237–39.
[44] Ibid., 238–39.

point, at the moment, is that the empath has reasons for intentionally empathizing with others and that these reasons are grounded in the perceived desirability of understanding the other person's emotional state.

The third feature of empathy is that the empath takes on the perspective of the other person as best as she can. She imaginatively reconstructs the other person's perspective on the world to the best of her abilities.[45] Yet she does not make her perspective identical to the other person's perspective. There are several reasons for this being the case. The most obvious reason being the nature of personal identity over time, but I shall set that aside as it will take us off topic. A more relevant reason has to do with the fact that empathy involves the empath receiving subjective states from another person. As Scrutton explains, "Even if we can, through empathy, imaginatively reconstruct the experiences of the other accurately (and most of the time this will only ever be partial or approximate), the experiences of the other remain, first and foremost, the experiences of the other, and are only experienced by the self in a secondary and derived way."[46]

The fourth feature of empathy has been touched on above, but it is worth making explicit. When the empath empathizes with another person, she is motivated to empathize for her own reasons to assume the other individual's perspective.[47] The motivation to try on someone else's perspective comes from within her own perspective, thus preventing it from being identical to the other person's emotional state.

The fifth feature of empathy is that the empath is consciously aware that she is trying on a copy of the other individual's perspective. The empath is aware that the emotion she is acquiring is through the process of perceiving that another person has this emotion. The empath does not lose her own awareness of herself in the process of empathizing. As such, she will have her own perspective on, and judgments about, the conscious states that she is empathizing with. Zagzebski goes so far as to say that one must have empathy in order to make a fair and accurate moral judgment of another person.[48]

When it comes to God, Zagzebski says that God must possess something she calls *perfect total empathy*. This "is the state of representing all of another person's conscious states, including their beliefs, sensations, moods, desires, and choices, as well as their emotions."[49] Indeed, God will have perfect total empathy for all of His creatures. In other words, God is omnisubjective. The attribute of omnisubjectivity requires having perfect total empathy. Why must God possess this attribute? Zagzebski gives various reasons for God being omnisubjective, but one will suffice for my purposes here. It is epistemically superior to have an exact representation of all conscious states than to not have an exact representation.[50] An omnisubjective being knows more than a being who lacks this attribute.

---

[45] Ibid., 239.
[46] Scrutton, *Thinking through Feeling*, 78.
[47] Zagzebski, "Omnisubjectivity," 239.
[48] Linda Zagzebski, "Omnisubjectivity: Why It Is a Divine Attribute," *Nova et Vetera* 14 (2016): 448.
[49] Zagzebski, "Omnisubjectivity," 241.
[50] Ibid.

Where does this leave us with regard to the impassibility debate? Zagzebski notes that omnisubjectivity is incompatible with impassibility.[51] An impassible God is a being who is not moved by anything external, and an omnisubjective God is moved to some extent by creation. What this account of omnisubjectivity seems to have built into it is an unstated truth condition for God's empathic knowledge. It is worth making these truth conditions clear. In order for God to have empathic knowledge of some other person S, God's knowledge must be grounded in and derived from S. In other words, God's empathic knowledge involves God having an empathic perceptual experience of S. The passibilist is not merely saying that God understands what it is like to be S in some abstract sense that does not involve any emotional engagement with S, if such a sense there be. Instead, the passibilist is claiming that God has a deep emotional engagement with S and that there are certain things that God simply cannot know about S without actually empathically experiencing her. This is because empathic knowledge, like experiential knowledge in general, is a form of knowledge by acquaintance.[52] One cannot have such knowledge without being acquainted with the world in some way. Hence, God is moved by the world that He has created.

The passibilist has more to say about the way that God is moved by His creation. According to Zagzebski, "A person cannot empathize with an emotion or a sensation without feeling the emotion or sensation because a copy of an emotion is an emotion, and a copy of a sensation is a sensation."[53] Any copy of a creature's emotional suffering will be emotional suffering. As Zagzebski puts it, "A perfect copy of pain is surely ruled out by impassibility, as is a copy of every other sensation or emotion, whether positive or negative. A perfectly empathic being is affected by what is outside of him."[54] A perfect copy of a creature's emotional suffering would quite obviously disturb God's perfect bliss. It does not seem coherent to say that God is experiencing perfect, undisrupted happiness while also experiencing a perfect representation of emotional suffering, turmoil, and pain. Thus, it would seem that an omnisubjective God cannot be an impassible God.

3 What is love? The search for common ground

As I mentioned at the beginning of this chapter, Scrutton explains that the twentieth-century debate over impassibility has focused on arguments over competing ideals and definitions of love. Divine passibilists emphasize notions of love where the lover is responsive and empathetic toward the beloved. This is something that an impassible God cannot do because it would entail that God suffers with His beloved. Further, this would entail that God is influenced by, and responsive to, His beloved. So impassibilists

---

[51] Linda Zagzebski, *Omnisubjectivity: A Defense of a Divine Attribute* (Milwaukee, WI: Marquette University Press, 2013), 45.
[52] Zagzebski, "Omnisubjectivity: Why It Is a Divine Attribute," 442.
[53] Zagzebski, "Omnisubjectivity," 242–43.
[54] Zagzebski, *Omnisubjectivity*, 44–45.

tend to emphasize notions of love where God acts beneficently and non-responsively toward His beloved.

This being the case, I wish to develop a different sort of argument. I believe that one can grant the impassibilist her own understanding of love, and then argue that the impassibilist account of love entails a kind of compassion that impassibility cannot allow for. This avoids the stalemate noted by Scrutton between competing accounts of love offered by passibilists and impassibilists. This strategy avoids the stalemate because it starts with the impassibilist's own understanding of love and then draws out logical entailments that lead one toward a rejection of impassibility.

What is this impassibilist account of love? Eric Silverman, and others, explain that love involves two desires: first, a desire to will the good for the beloved, and second, a desire to will union with the beloved.[55] For the sake of argument, I will grant the impassibilist that love involves these two desires. With this common ground on the nature of love, I believe that the debate between passibility and impassibility can move forward.

However, there is a cautionary note worth considering. Silverman complains that passibilists tend to focus their critiques on the impassibilist understanding of the first desire of love. He claims that passibilists typically ignore the desire for union and focus solely on benevolence.[56] Silverman believes that many of the passibilist's criticisms will fall flat once the impassibilist brings in the desire for union.

In an effort to avoid Silverman's complaint, I shall argue that in order to satisfy the desire for union with the beloved, God must be maximally empathetic. Call this the Unity Problem for divine impassibility. I shall articulate the Unity Problem in Section 5.

4 There is XXXX within my heart: The desires of love

Before delving into the Unity Problem, we need to get clear on this understanding of love that Silverman points toward. In her recent work, *Wandering in Darkness*, Eleonore Stump develops a nuanced account of the desires of love (which, in ways that we cannot currently discuss, is based upon Aquinas's understanding of love).[57] In this section, I shall explore Stump's account because it is the most detailed discussion that I am aware of.

The first desire of love is a desire for the good of the beloved. Goodness is being used here broadly to cover different kinds of goods related to morality, beauty, and metaphysics.[58] The good of the beloved is objective in that there is something objectively good for a person based on her nature. The "good of the beloved has to be understood

---

[55] Silverman, "Impassibility and Divine Love," 171. Cf. Aquinas, *ST* II, II.27.2. See also Randles, *The Blessed God*, 53.
[56] Silverman, "Impassibility and Divine Love," 172.
[57] Eleonore Stump, *Wandering in Darkness: Narrative and the Problem of Suffering* (Oxford: Oxford University Press, 2010), 91.
[58] Ibid., 93.

as that which truly is in the interest of the beloved and which truly does conduce to the beloved's flourishing."[59]

With regard to human persons, a human person can flourish in a variety of ways. She can flourish by growing in wisdom, moral knowledge, and virtue. A human person can also flourish by growing in physical strength and health, or by learning a new skill. So when it comes to promoting the good of a human person, one has a variety of potential actions to perform that would be conducive to the flourishing of the beloved. For example, a set of parents might wish to see their daughter grow in wisdom, so they hire her a personal tutor to help her with her homework. Or perhaps the parents have a child with a stunted emotional development, so they take their child to see a specialist who can help their child grow in emotional knowledge and sensitivity.

There is more nuance to Stump's account than I am offering here related to the epistemic limitations of human persons, and distinctions between intrinsic and derivative goods. Also, on Stump's account of love, anything that contributes to the objective good of the beloved draws the beloved closer to God.[60] Though interesting, a full discussion of such things would take us off track for the purposes of this chapter. So I shall move on to consider the second desire of love—union with the beloved.

Union of love requires two things: personal presence and mutual closeness.[61] Personal presence is a necessary condition for mutual closeness, so I shall discuss it first. Personal presence comes in degrees. In order to be minimally present a person must be aware of another individual, and see him as a person. This other individual must be conscious and functioning relatively well.[62] This is not a particularly interesting kind of presence for Stump's purposes. Sally could be aware of a small child in the room with her, but not have any particular concern or affection for the child. Further, the child is completely unaware of Sally. In this situation, Sally is minimally present to the child.

In order to develop this account of union, Stump says that we need *significant* personal presence. For significant personal presence, Stump says we must add something called *joint* or *shared attention*. Let us return to Sally. Say that Sally is aware of the small child in the room and does have some degree of concern toward the child. Further, say that the child is aware of Sally, and gestures emphatically toward a toy that he wants Sally to pick up. As Sally turns her attention toward the toy, her and the child are both aware of each other, and yet focused on the toy. They are aware that each other are both focused on the toy. This kind of awareness is shared attention. As Stump points out, shared attention comes in degrees.[63] What ultimately matters for our purposes here is that shared attention involves a mutual awareness between two or more persons, that each person is aware of the other as a person, and that each exhibits some degree of concern toward the other.

Recall that union requires personal presence and mutual closeness. With a discussion of personal presence on the table, we can turn our attention toward mutual closeness. As already noted, shared attention comes in degrees. The richer the

---

[59] Ibid.
[60] Ibid.
[61] Ibid., 109.
[62] Ibid., 112.
[63] Ibid., 113–18.

shared attention is between two persons, the greater their mutual closeness will be.[64] Yet Stump says that more is needed. One necessary feature of mutual closeness is an openness of mind. This is where one person is open and willing to share her important thoughts and feelings with another person. Not any old thought will do. Most people who know me are aware of my love for delectable cheeseburgers. I have even discussed my love for delectable cheeseburgers in several of my writings. One does not have to be particularly close to me to know this fact about my life. Knowing this fact about me does not really shed much light on who I am as a person. But there are other facts about me that I am not willing to share with just anyone. These are facts that I only share with a select few. If I were to share these facts with you, I would be actively revealing my innermost thoughts, desires, and passions with you. This sort of active self-revelation is one of the necessary components of mutual closeness that Stump has in mind.[65]

Again, more is needed for *mutual* closeness. Say that I am on a date, and I believe that it is going quite well. I decide to share some of my innermost thoughts: thoughts that are really important to me. If my date shows no interest in this self-revelation, there will not be another date. Why? Because the potential for mutual closeness seems dim. In order for the closeness to be mutual, my date will need to show an interest in my self-revelation. She has to exhibit an ability to comprehend and a willingness to receive what I am sharing with her.[66] These claims about comprehension and willingness need to be unpacked a bit further.

Consider first comprehension. If my date is unable to comprehend what I am revealing to her about myself, the potential for closeness in our relationship will be quite minimal. Comprehension comes in degrees, and comprehension involves more than mere propositional knowledge. My date could have a great deal of propositional knowledge about me, but that does not mean that she really knows me. Perhaps she stalked me online before agreeing to go on a date with me. During her internet search she could acquire a fair bit of propositional knowledge about me, but she will not know me in the deepest sense. She will not know what it is like to experience my presence, witness my quirks and mannerisms, or hear my laugh. She will also not have a deep understanding of my mental states, and the emotional weight that I place on certain things in my life. In order to know me in the deepest way she needs to be able to get into my shoes, so to speak, and see things from my perspective. In other words, she needs to have some degree of empathy and emotional intelligence in order to understand my perspective on the world. She does not have to agree with my perspective on various things, but she must have some comprehension of what it is like to be me in order to be close to me. I, in turn, must have the same comprehension of her in order for the closeness to be mutual.

This capacity to understand another person in this deep way is one thing, but there also needs to be a willingness to open up oneself to this kind of closeness. Say that my date has a highly refined capacity for empathy and a staggering emotional intelligence. She is able to comprehend my self-revelation to her. Yet, say that she is unwilling to

---

[64] Ibid., 119.
[65] Ibid., 120.
[66] Ibid.

accept my self-revelation. Perhaps I misjudged the situation, and she is really not that into me. In revealing myself to her, she might have no interest in being that close to me. Without her willingness to accept what I am revealing about myself, there can be no mutual closeness between us.

This willingness component of mutual closeness can be quite scary. There is a kind of vulnerability that comes with this openness of mind. As Stump explains, a person makes herself vulnerable to her beloved in the very act of opening up. In revealing my innermost thoughts to someone, I am demonstrating my desire for union with this person. The satisfaction of that desire is now in her hands.[67] I might make myself an open book to my date, and she might show a willingness to understand who I am as a person, but then reject what she sees in me. This rejection can come in several different forms, and each comes with varying degrees of associated pain. For instance, a person might be put off by my love of heavy metal. Once this person willingly comes to know who I am, she might decide that she is no longer willing to be close to me. Thus, the satisfaction of my desire to be close to her is now cut off.

This discussion of mutual closeness brings up issues related to experiential knowledge of other persons as discussed in Section 2. In the next section, I shall try to bring these threads together and develop the Unity Problem for divine impassibility.

5 Love rhymes with hideous car wreck: The unity problem

I shall argue that the union of love is incomplete without omnisubjectivity. Since omnisubjectivity is incompatible with impassibility, this will be a problem for impassibility.

Stump makes it clear that unity and mutual closeness can be hindered by the makeup of one or more parties in the loving relationship.[68] For instance, there might be something wrong with Sally that prevents her from drawing closer to God. Perhaps some horrible sin she refuses to repent of, or perhaps some lack of trust in God grounded in previous experiences of betrayal by loved ones. But what about the other way around? What if there is something wrong with God that prevents Him from being united to us?

I imagine that an impassibilist will wish to say that there is nothing wrong with the impassible God, but I beg to differ. According to Stump, the intrinsic characteristics of the lovers will determine the character and extent of union that is possible.[69] It seems to me that the impassible God is going to be severely limited in the possible extent of His union with creatures compared to the possible extent of union between a passible, omnisubjective God and His creatures.

Recall that a lover cannot be fully, or perfectly, unified with her beloved if she does not have the deepest possible epistemic understanding of her beloved. As Zagzebski

---

[67] Ibid., 122.
[68] Cf. Eleonore Stump, *Atonement*, Oxford Studies in Analytic Theology (Oxford: Oxford University Press, 2019).
[69] Stump, *Wandering in Darkness*, 99.

makes clear, "Love is premised on understanding the other, and the fuller the understanding, the greater the possibility for love."[70] As noted earlier, unity comes in degrees. Also, epistemic comprehension or understanding likewise comes in degrees.[71] Surely an omniscient God has complete epistemic understanding. Surely in the eschaton God will be fully unified with His beloved creatures. Then God will have a complete epistemic understanding of His creatures.

In order to have a complete epistemic understanding, God will have to understand creaturely mental states. Recall that one of the conditions for unity with the beloved is the ability to comprehend the beloved's mental states, and the emotional weight that the beloved places on certain things. If God is going to have the kind of comprehension needed for unity, God will need to have empathy. One cannot have this kind of comprehension without empathy. As should be clear by now, an omnisubjective God can have this kind of comprehension. According to Zagzebski, the "omnisubjective God is the most intimately loving because he is the most intimately knowing."[72]

An impassible God, on the other hand, cannot have empathy in any meaningful sense of the term. Classical theists, like Anselm, explicitly deny empathy and compassion of the impassible God.[73] As the impassibilist Girolamo Zanchius makes clear, empathy can bring suffering, and this is something an impassible God cannot do. This is because an impassible God is perfectly happy, and nothing can disturb God's perfect happiness.[74] Thus it would seem that impassibility prevents God from being able to comprehend His creatures, and thus prevents God from being united with His creatures in love.

Consider the following example to see how an impassible God is prevented from being fully united with His creatures in love. An impassible God can know all of the propositions about His creatures. For instance, an impassible God will know that Sally has mental states x, y, and z. He will also know that Sally places a certain amount of emotional weight on these mental states. Say that Sally has certain mental states associated with her son Ben. Perhaps mental states such as "I love my son Ben," and "I would do anything for Ben." Ben is currently suffering from cancer, and is on death's door. Naturally, Sally is in emotional anguish. She is deeply disturbed by what is happening to her son because she has placed a great amount of emotional weight on her son's well-being.

An impassible God can know all of the propositional facts about Sally and her current mental and emotional state. However, an impassible God cannot be united in love with Sally, since an impassible God cannot satisfy the conditions of comprehension needed for mutual closeness. As I shall argue, an impassible God fails to satisfy the conditions of comprehension in at least two ways.

---

[70] Zagzebski, "Omnisubjectivity: Why It Is a Divine Attribute," 449.
[71] Robert C. Roberts, *Intellectual Virtues: An Essay in Regulative Epistemology* (New York: Oxford University Press, 2007), 43.
[72] Zagzebski, "Omnisubjectivity: Why It Is a Divine Attribute," 450.
[73] Anselm, *Proslogion* VIII.
[74] Zanchius, *Life Everlasting*, 357–58.

5.1 The impossible God cannot comprehend suffering

The first reason that the impossible God cannot satisfy the conditions for mutual closeness is because the impossible God cannot comprehend what it is like to suffer. An impossible God cannot suffer because an impossible God is necessarily in a state of undisturbed bliss. For such a God, it is metaphysically impossible for Him to comprehend what it is like to be Sally in her situation of agony. Sally is in a state of deep mental anguish, and that is a mental state that an impossible God cannot possibly understand.

Recall that the classical theist maintains that God has a perfect cognitive grasp of His own nature. In grasping His own nature, God experiences perfect, undisturbed bliss. Thus, the impossible God knows that it is metaphysically impossible for Him to suffer.[75] As Randles explains, "Perfect blessedness excludes everything contrary to happiness." Any "happiness mingled with unhappiness is imperfect blessedness."[76] For Randles, the impossible God cannot have any hint of uneasiness, conflict, weakness, limitation, or sorrow in His emotional life since such a thing is incompatible with perfect blessedness.[77] Any experiential knowledge of "suffering would be a loss of inherent excellence, and is therefore impossible to Him who is absolutely perfect."[78]

Thus, the impossible God is a God who cannot comprehend what it is like to be Sally in her suffering. Comprehension of Sally's emotional states is necessary for mutual closeness. Thus the emotional life of the impossible God prevents Him from possessing mutual closeness with Sally.

5.2 The impossible God cannot be moved

There is a second reason that the impossible God cannot comprehend what it is like to be Sally, and thus is prevented from enjoying mutual closeness with her. It is metaphysically impossible for an impossible God to be moved or acted upon by anything outside of God. His emotional state of perfect happiness is based entirely upon Himself. Since an impossible God's emotional state is based purely and entirely on Himself, it is metaphysically impossible for an impossible God to comprehend what it is like to have one's emotional states wrapped up in another person. As Randles explains, "The happiness of God is from the perfection of His nature independently of all other beings . . . it is not in the power of the creature to spoil or diminish His infinite blessedness."[79] To further drive home the impossible God's emotional independence from creatures, Stephen Charnock reminds us that it is impossible for creatures to add to, or subtract from, the infinite blessedness of God as well.[80]

---

[75] Silverman, "Impassibility and Divine Love," 168.
[76] Randles, *The Blessed God*, 43–44.
[77] Ibid., 48.
[78] Ibid., 50.
[79] Ibid., 44.
[80] See Stephen Charnock's essay in *God without Passions: A Reader*, ed. Samuel Renihan (Palmdale, CA: Reformed Baptist Academic Press, 2015), 144–54. Cf. Ussher, *A Body of Divinitie*, 35.

An impossible God cannot possibly comprehend what it is like for Sally to place the emotional weight that she does on her son Ben because it is metaphysically impossible for God to have His emotional states depend upon something external to the divine nature. It is metaphysically impossible for an impassible God to be emotionally invested in another person because such an investment would render God's emotional life dependent upon something *ad extra* to the divine nature. Such a dependence would be in clear violation of divine impassibility. So an impassible God cannot possibly understand what it is like to be Sally in her emotional vulnerability toward her son. Consequently, an impassible God cannot be united to Sally fully, as would be expected from the God of perfect love.

5.3 Responding to possible rejoinders

The Unity Problem arises from an internal conflict between impassibility and the desire for union with the beloved. An impassibilist might try to respond to the Unity Problem by saying that an impassible God can understand what it is like to be Sally without God ever having to experience suffering.[81] I find this suggestion to be implausible. The impassible God is necessarily in a state of undisrupted, and undisturbable, joy. The suggestion that such a being could possibly understand what it is like to experience suffering seems like it deserves nothing more than an incredulous stare. This is so because such a being has never once suffered, nor can such a being ever suffer. How could such a being possibly understand what it is like to be Sally in her suffering?

However, the impassibilist might try to argue that some person P could have an understanding of what it is like to suffer without ever having suffered. Perhaps something like the following scenario will get your intuitions pumping in the impassibilist's favor.

> Imagine that the universe popped into existence only five minutes ago. The universe came into existence with all of the appearance of age, including a whole host of memories and psychological states, etc., that led the inhabitants of the universe to believe that it is in fact 13.5 billion years old. Imagine that Bill finds himself in this universe with the distinct memory of having his foot caught in a bear trap 15 years ago. The memory of this experience does not cause Bill any pain or discomfort at present. Nevertheless, Bill does understand what it is like to experience having his foot caught in a bear trap.[82]

The impassibilist might insist that Bill understands what it is like to suffer even though his understanding of suffering is not based on any actual experience of suffering. The goal of this thought experiment is to demonstrate the possibility of the impassible God comprehending Sally's suffering without God actually experiencing Sally or her conscious states, thus helping the impassible God satisfy the desire for union with the

---

[81] This has been suggested to me by audiences at Fuller Theological Seminary and the University of St Andrews.
[82] Thanks to Peter van Inwagen for this colorful thought experiment.

beloved. The passibilist finds this suggestion perplexing, to say the least. This is because there is a deep disanalogy in the thought experiment between Bill and God.

In the thought experiment, above, Bill is not in an analogous epistemic situation to that of an impassible God. Even though Bill does not actually experience suffering, Bill is at least capable of suffering. The ability of Bill to suffer is one way a philosopher might try to justify the claim that Bill understands what it is like to suffer.[83] This is where the disanalogy rests: Bill has the ability to suffer whereas the impassible God lacks the ability to suffer. Further, an omniscient and impassible God knows that it is metaphysically impossible for Him to suffer. The impassible God can never be in the same epistemic state as Bill because He knows His nature well enough to know that such a thing is impossible. Thus, the Unity Problem remains.

5.4 Love rhymes with sympathy

Given the failures of impassibility to satisfy the conditions for mutual closeness, the possible unity between God and Sally seems quite limited, if not impossible. Things are quite different for a passible God who enjoys omnisubjectivity. A passible God can enjoy a range of emotions that are consistent with God's rational and moral nature. A passible God with omnisubjectivity can understand what it is like to be Sally, and so can enjoy a deep epistemic comprehension of her, thus making the passible God able to enjoy a significantly deeper degree of unity with Sally than an impassible God. Zagzebski goes so far as to say "that omnisubjectivity is a condition for the perfect love God has for us."[84]

Francis McConnell agrees that the sympathy of God is needed in order to have a fully loving God. He claims that a God who cannot suffer with and for His creatures is morally lower than the thousands of men and women who have willingly suffered for the well-being of others. He writes, "There is no way for God to escape sorrow if he is a God of love. We must repeat that we are not trying to glorify suffering on its own account, but we are trying to preserve the moral fullness of the Divine Life."[85]

According to McConnell, the passibilist is not claiming that there is some intrinsic virtue in God suffering simply for the sake of suffering. Instead, the Christ-like God sympathetically suffers in order to reconcile creatures to Himself. As McConnell explains, "If we are to reconcile men to the God of pain, we must show that God does not ask men to undergo experiences which he is not, as far as possible, willing to undergo himself."[86] This is because humans "want to feel that their suffering means something at the center of the universe. It means that they crave at least to be understood through the understanding which comes out of sympathetic sharing of distress."[87] God and humanity bear the cross with one another. "It is cross-bearing together which provides

---

[83] Cf. Yujin Nagasawa, *God and Phenomenal Consciousness: A Novel Approach to Knowledge Arguments* (Cambridge: Cambridge University Press, 2008), 64–71.
[84] Zagzebski, "Omnisubjectivity: Why It Is a Divine Attribute," 449.
[85] McConnell, *Is God Limited?*, 287–88.
[86] Ibid., 289.
[87] Ibid., 290.

the closest unions between man and God." This union may start in pain, but it ends in an abiding joy in the eschaton.[88]

6 Conclusion

In this chapter, I have accepted the impassibilist's own understanding of divine love. I have argued that the impassible God cannot satisfy the desire for union with the beloved because the emotional life of the impassible God has no room for empathy. It seems that the tainted love of the impassible God actually pushes us to run into the loving arms of an empathetic God. The desire for unity with the beloved cannot be satisfied without empathy. A maximally empathetic God can far better satisfy the desire for unity than an impassible God. The impossible God can only offer a love that is completely uninfluenced by us, and this, so say I, is a sick way to love.[89]

---

[88] Ibid., 293.
[89] I do hope that some readers are able to catch all six music references. I would also like to thank audiences at Fuller Theological Seminary and the University of St Andrews for helpful comments on earlier drafts of this chapter.

9

A Love that Speaks in Harsh Tones: On the Superiority of Divine Communicative Punishment*

Jordan Wessling

According to the book of Acts, King Herod refused to give glory to God, and, as a result, "the angel of the Lord struck him down, and he was eaten by worms and died" (12:23). Though uncomfortable to think about, this event should not entirely surprise those who are familiar with the Bible. "Vengeance is mine, I will repay, says the Lord" (Rom. 12:19; cf. Deut. 32:35-36); and Jesus is presented as saying that he will return in glory to judge the nations (Mt. 25:32-33), the result of which will lead to a penalty of "outer darkness" (e.g., Mt. 22:13), the "weeping and gnashing of teeth" (e.g., Lk. 13:28), and even a "furnace of fire" (e.g., Mt. 13:41-50).[1] In such biblical passages we are confronted with a punitive God, even a violent God, that makes many of us extraordinarily uneasy. Besides running roughshod over our modern sensibilities about what is good and praiseworthy, it is difficult to discern how the God of love revealed in Christ might match these vengeful depictions. After all, it was God in Christ who taught us to forgive at a magnitude of seventy times seven (Mt. 18:22), who cried "Father, forgive them" while being unjustly crucified as a criminal (Lk. 23:34), and who reveals a God that deigns to share his life with those who were once his enemies (e.g., Jn 17:1-28; 1 Jn 4:7-20). How can *this* God of love also be a punitive, vengeful God?

---

* Research for this chapter was supported by the John Templeton Foundation by way of the Analytic Theology for Theological Formation project, which was led by Oliver Crisp at Fuller Theological Seminary. Many thanks to Oliver, Fuller Theological Seminary, and the John Templeton Foundation for making this chapter possible. Thanks also goes to James Arcadi, J. T. Turner, and Oliver for comments on an earlier version of this chapter. Finally, I also owe a debt of gratitude to David Cannon and Timothy Scheuers not only for providing comments on an earlier version of this chapter but also for helping me with its preparation.

[1] Which of Jesus's sayings actually apply to hell is disputed. For overviews of contemporary literature on Jesus's view of hell, see David Powys, *"Hell": A Hard Look at a Hard Question* (Milton Keynes and Waynesboro, GA: Paternoster, 1997), 17–41; and Anthony C. Thiselton, *Life after Death: A New Approach to the Last Things* (Grand Rapids, MI: Eerdmans, 2012), 151–59.

Speaking very generally, reflection upon this question, and others like it, has produced two competing paradigms concerning God's love and punitive wrath.[2] According to the first paradigm, the aims or motives corresponding to God's love and wrath sometimes diverge from one another. In particular, it is thought that God (sometimes) punishes creatures in a manner that is not motivated by love for those punished, but is instead motivated by that which is contradictory to such love—typically, a desire for an entirely non-remedial form of retribution. This first paradigm might be called the *divergent account* of God's love and punitive wrath, and it is to be contrasted with the *unitary account*. The proponent of the latter account maintains that any observed conflict between the noted divine attributes is merely apparent and that divine punishment is always ultimately motivated by love for the one that is penalized.[3] The present chapter focuses on how theologians should make sense of the unitary account.

A particularly influential version of the unitary account can be named the *natural consequences view*. According to it, God is too loving to impose external penalties on wrongdoers through special divine action; so, instead, God allows sinful humans to undergo the terrible yet eventually inevitable consequences of their own behavior. It is said that this more "removed" approach to dealing with human sin is befitting of God's love, as the approach manifests a way in which God respects the autonomy and choices of even his wayward creatures. Advocates of the natural consequences view often admit that the position has difficulty explaining certain kinds of biblical data, but many believe that this view is the best available way of preserving our image of the perfect God of love revealed in Christ.[4]

The natural consequences view is not the only way to envision the unitary account, however. An alternative version of this account relies upon a communicative theory of divine punishment (call it, *divine communicative punishment*).[5] According to this theory, God's punishment aims to communicate to offenders the censure they deserve, with the purpose of trying to persuade these individuals to start down the path of spiritual transformation. So understood, God's wrath is at root an expression of God's love, intent on revealing to sinful creatures the error of their ways, so that they might repent, be reformed, and be reconciled to the God who never stopped loving them.

The goal of this chapter is to demonstrate that divine communicative punishment is worthy of serious consideration by those who are committed to the unitary account. I will take it that I have accomplished this goal to the degree that I show that divine communicative punishment is a more plausible rendition of the unitary account than the natural consequences view. For the purposes of this chapter, then, I will suppose that the unitary account is true, and I shall endeavor to show, not that divine

---

[2] For a contemporary overview of several ways in which God's love and wrath are conceptually related, see Tony Lane, "The Wrath of God as an Aspect of the Love of God," in *Nothing Greater, Nothing Better: Theological Essays on the Love of God*, ed. Kevin J. Vanhoozer (Grand Rapids, MI: Eerdmans, 2001), 138–67.

[3] To label "wrath" an "attribute of God" is not to suggest that wrath is an essential divine attribute or that God experiences literal anger. Rather, the label is merely a placeholder for something like *that feature of the divine character that motivates God to punish humans on account of their sin*.

[4] To cite just two examples, see Gregory Boyd, *The Crucifixion of the Warrior God: Interpreting the Violent Old Testament Portraits in Light of the Cross* (Minneapolis, MN: Fortress Press, 2017), 155–58.

[5] See my "How Does a Loving God Punish?: On the Unification of Divine Love & Wrath," *International Journal of Systematic Theology* 19 (2017): 421–43.

communicative punishment is the most accurate way of conceiving of God's punitive wrath, but that divine communicative punishment provides, in crucial respects, a more satisfying understanding of how the God of perfect love deals with sin than does the rival understanding of the unitary account.

Before we proceed to that argument, however, an initial clarification is required concerning the nature of divine wrath under consideration. There are at least two ways in which God can be said to dispense wrath, each of which has biblical precedent and each of which likely has implications for how we think of the unitary account. There is, on the one hand, a kind of corporate expression of God's wrath, wherein God visits calamity on entire people groups (e.g., the killing of the firstborn children of Egypt or the Israelite conquest of Canaan). Corporate expressions of divine wrath are extremely difficult to reconcile with God's love (not to mention justice) because they often involve bringing suffering and even death to those who did no wrong of the relevant sort. On the other hand, Scripture describes God as one who punishes individuals for their personal transgressions with, for example, death or consignment to hell (as we have already seen). These two kinds of biblical phenomena are rather different, and it may turn out that the two phenomena merit radically different kinds of analyses vis-à-vis the love of God. Whatever the case, this chapter focuses exclusively on God's punishment of individuals for their misdeeds, and how this punishment relates to God's love. Consequently, all subsequent references to "wrath," "retribution," and like notions refer to God's punishment of individuals, not the ostensible biblical record concerning God's indiscriminate penalization of entire people groups. By extension, the examined versions of the unitary account should be understood in this light.

1 The natural consequences view

In his widely read essay published in 1955, "Is There a Doctrine of Retribution in the Old Testament?," Klaus Koch argues that the God of the Old Testament rarely, if ever, steps into human history for the purpose of doling out punishment.[6] On the contrary, God is depicted as one who does little more (but a bit more) than create and sustain a milieu in which misdeeds have "built-in consequences" that are often unpleasant.[7] Koch compares these built-in consequences to "laws of nature which operate so that an action inevitably is followed by a reaction," which "inevitably results in disastrous consequences" for those who refuse to live in harmony with the moral structure of the universe.[8] As an example of my own making as to how this might work, God's wrath can be expressed toward an egoist not by imposing external punishment upon him, but by allowing him to persist in his self-centered ways until his selfishness repels all companions, leaving him miserably alone. More generally, the natural penalty of a vicious life is becoming a vicious person, and the vicious person ultimately cannot flourish. Going a bit beyond what Koch

---

[6] Throughout this chapter, I refer to the version of Koch's article that has been translated by Thomas H. Trapp and appears in *Theodicy in the Old Testament*, ed. James L. Crenshaw (Philadelphia, PA: Fortress Press, 1983), 57–87.
[7] Koch, "Is There a Doctrine of Retribution in the Old Testament?," *passim* (e.g., 66, 69, 75).
[8] Ibid., 58.

explicitly says, the basic idea is that God does not impose external punishments through special divine action; rather, God allows sinful humans to undergo the terrible, even if natural, consequences of their own misbehavior.[9]

Koch is not the only biblical scholar to affirm that significant segments of Scripture indicate that God's punitive wrath is expressed via natural consequences. Approximately two decades before Koch, the renowned New Testament professor C. H. Dodd found this teaching in St. Paul. Noticing that Paul, in Rom. 1:18-32 in particular, describes God's wrath in terms of giving the sinful over to their own devices, Dodd claimed that Paul uses the concept of the wrath of God "not to describe the attitude of God to man, but to describe an inevitable process of cause and effect in a moral universe."[10] In Dodd's mind this indicates that Paul stands in basic theological continuity with Jesus, in whose teachings "anger as an attitude of God to men disappears, and His love and mercy become all-embracing."[11]

Though Dodd perhaps has been the most influential advocate of the natural consequences view in the English language, his treatment of it spans just a few pages. So far as I am aware, the most thorough biblical defense of the natural consequences view appears in A. T. Hanson's monograph, *The Wrath of the Lamb*. Moving from the preexilic period to the close of the New Testament canon, Hanson contends that on the whole Scripture does not depict God's wrath as a personal attitude directed toward sin, but instead that which "is simply the impersonal process of the consequences of men's sins working itself out in history."[12] "The wrath of God," Hanson says, "is the punishment of God, and the punishment of God is what he permits us to inflict on ourselves. God loves the most obdurate infidel as much as he loves the most devoted saint. He permits wrath, but he is love."[13] Hanson adds that there is no place within the New Testament "in which a tension appears between the love and the wrath of God."[14]

It is possible to understand the natural consequences view in terms of the divergent account. It could be, for instance, that God passively allows creatures to taste the bitter, and often irredeemable, consequences of their behavior as a way of giving up on the rebellious. We can envision God saying, "I love you no more, and that is why I leave you to yourselves." But this is not how most advocates of the natural consequences view understand their position—it is certainly not the view of Hanson and Dodd, as we have seen. Instead, these advocates often present their position as a moral improvement upon the perceived vindictiveness of certain classical retributivist views of divine wrath, whereby God steps into the regular causes of human history and places an external penalty on wrongdoers as an expression of

---

[9] Koch's concern is with describing what the various biblical authors thought about God's wrath, not with providing a systematic account of it (see, in particular, "Is There a Doctrine of Retribution in the Old Testament?," 83). Thus, Koch may not affirm these last two sentences, which go beyond Koch's exact characterization of the biblical depiction of divine wrath.

[10] C. H. Dodd, *Epistle of Paul to the Romans* (London: Hodder & Stoughton, 1932), 23. Also see Hanson, *The Wrath of the Lamb*, and G. H. C. MacGregor, "The Concept of the Wrath of God in the New Testament," *New Testament Studies* 7 (1960–1961): 101–09.

[11] Dodd, *Epistle of Paul to the Romans*, 23.

[12] Hanson, *The Wrath of the Lamb*, 194.

[13] Ibid., 198.

[14] Ibid., 179.

his justice.¹⁵ The natural consequences view, we are told, is preferable because it fully takes into account the God of love revealed in Christ, who shows us a God that could not possibly punish in opposition to his love.¹⁶ Conceived in this way, the natural consequences view is a version of the unitary account; and in keeping with my stated purposes, this is how I will understand the view within this chapter.

The question remains as to how giving someone over to his or her own sinful devices can be understood as an act of love. The most plausible way of making sense of this of which I am aware concerns God's respect for human free will. Let us agree, if only for the sake of argument, that God has created humans with the tremendously valuable ability to rise above the causal influences of their environment and internal impulses and choose what they shall do and, ultimately, whom they shall become. It is often said that granting creatures this kind of freedom enables them to be morally responsible and to enter a richer kind of love relationship with God and each other than would otherwise be possible, even though it makes disobedience and rejection of God an all but inevitable reality. Now, if freedom is a great good that God bestows upon creatures as an act of love, then it is not too difficult to imagine why one might maintain that God's permission for humans to become vicious persons is, paradoxically, also an act of love. God has given humans the remarkable ability to choose what kinds of persons they shall become. Were God to give humans the gift of freedom only to take it back once it was misused, we might doubt the gift had ever been genuinely given. Moreover, if this is a gift of love, then so too is God's patience with those who exercise this gift in ways in which God does not approve—or so it is often argued.¹⁷

Someone might object that the natural consequences view is not really a view of divine punishment. For punishment, says the putative objector, requires performing one or more discrete actions for the purpose of placing hard treatment on those who have done wrong. Yet the natural consequences view does not meet this requirement. On the contrary, it looks as if God's giving creatures over to their sinful inclinations requires little-to-nothing more from God than his allowing humans to perform morally virtuous actions. God just stands back, and lets the creature choose as she may.¹⁸

I am not terribly impressed with this kind of objection. God, after all, can work through secondary causes. He can set up a system that is purposely structured in such a way that good behavior is rewarded and bad behavior leads to unhappiness. Similar to the way in which God can be said to be the creator of all biological species within an evolutionary system, God can be said to be the author of dire consequences

---

[15] For example, see Ibid., 181–201; Dodd, *Epistle of Paul to the Romans*, 23; MacGregor, "The Concept of the Wrath of God in the New Testament," 107–09; and, with some modification, Steven H. Travis, *Christ and the Judgment of God: The Limits of Divine Retribution in New Testament Thought*, 2nd ed. (Peabody, MA: Hendrickson Publishers, 2008).

[16] See Boyd, *Crucifixion of the Warrior God*, especially p. 796; Hanson, *The Wrath of the Lamb*, 195–201; and Dodd, *Epistle of Paul to the Romans*, 23. Compare these volumes with Eric A. Seibert, *Disturbing Divine Behavior: Troubling Old Testament Images of God* (Minneapolis, MN: Fortress, 2009), chap. 10.

[17] For just two discussions of the idea that God gives humans freedom as an act of love, see Gregory Boyd, *Satan and the Problem of Evil: Constructing a Trinitarian Warfare Theodicy* (Downers Gove, IL: InterVarsity Press, 2001), 343–57 (cf. Boyd, *Crucifixion of the Warrior God*, passim), and Jonathan Kvanvig, *The Problem of Hell* (New York: Oxford University Press, 1993), chap. 4.

[18] I here leave to one side concerns about Pelagianism.

for those who do evil. (And, crucially, maybe God has good independent and non-vindictive reason for setting up such a system.) Moreover, withholding certain goods from someone on account of his or her wrongdoing can be described as a kind of punishment, and it seems compatible with the natural consequences view to say that God does not grant wrongdoers certain goods that he otherwise would if they had not sinned. For such reasons, the natural consequences view is plausibly thought to be an account of divine punishment.

However, it is best not to quibble over the meaning of the word "punishment." For if it should turn out that the advocate of the natural consequences view does not articulate a view of divine punishment, strictly speaking, the proponent of this viewpoint nevertheless does describe certain biblical phenomena in a manner that takes the place of what has been classically understood as punishment. Hence, at minimum, the natural consequences view provides an alternative analysis to certain kinds of theological accounts of divine punishment and is thus worth engaging as a competing understanding of the way in which God directs his wrath against sinful individuals. Since nothing of substance relevant to the purposes of this chapter turns on the precise categorization of the natural consequences view, I will continue to speak of the view as a theory of divine punishment for the remainder of this chapter. Those who prefer to categorize the view differently can make the terminological amendments that they see fit.

2 An evaluation of the natural consequences view

The natural consequences view is attractive in part because it appears to explain a remarkable amount of biblical material and theological data.[19] At present we cannot begin to do justice to the kind of cumulative case that one might provide for the natural consequences view; nevertheless, we can arrive at a basic sense of its apparent plausibility.

First, return to Rom. 1:18-32, the passage that so was influential on C. H. Dodd. The passage begins with the striking claim that "the wrath of God is revealed from heaven against all ungodliness and wickedness of those who by their wickedness suppress the truth" (v. 18). Yet the description of wrath that follows is not one of famine and flood but God's act of *giving the sinful over* to their "degrading passions" (1:26; cf. vv. 24, 28). Here we have what is among the most detailed expositions of God's wrath in the New Testament, and what we find is not the presence of externally imposed retribution but God allowing creatures to go their own way. Some have claimed that this passage provides a window into God's normal way of dealing with the rebellious.[20]

The ministry of Christ is also used to support the natural consequences view. Christ taught an ethic of nonviolence, and in Christ we see a God who refuses to crush his enemies; on the contrary, he is willing to die for them. The supposed implication is that the God revealed in Christ is not the kind of God that is interested in settling scores by

---

[19] One need only read Hanson's *The Wrath of the Lamb* to be convinced of this.
[20] For example, Hanson, *The Wrath of the Lamb*, 68-69, 83-86, and 193-95.

breaking sinners through externally imposed penalties. Importantly, this implication is said to provide a kind of theological backdrop that should raise one's credence in the truth of the natural consequences view.[21]

Finally, there is the aforementioned idea that the natural consequences view meshes neatly with the widely held theological tenet that God respects the autonomy of his rational creatures. On this conception of things, God, out of love, grants freedom to humans so that they can choose what kinds of persons they will become, or whether or not they want to be united with God. And, some say, since God deeply values the freedom that he gives to humans, God would rather allow humans to wreck themselves through their own poor choices than take back his generous gift of autonomy by crushing the human will through retribution.[22]

So, the natural consequences view is believed to be supported by three strands of reasoning. There is a kind of strictly biblical or exegetical case for the natural consequences view (here represented by Rom. 1:18-32), a certain kind of appeal to the ministry of Christ as that which provides evidential grounds for this view, and, finally, the conviction that God values human freedom is believed to provide some manner of indirect confirmation for the natural consequences view of divine wrath. However, each of these strands suffers from a point of significant weakness. Let us consider them in turn.

The problem with the strictly biblical or exegetical case for the natural consequences view (as opposed to the appeal to the ministry of Christ or the value of human freedom) is that it does not explain *all* of the relevant biblical data, even if we are prepared to agree that it explains large swaths of it. This has been argued forcefully by a number of biblical scholars,[23] and even A. T. Hanson grants the point.[24] Once again, we cannot get into the details now, but to see where the natural consequences view looks to be at odds with Scripture, recall the first biblical passage cited within the present chapter: God's killing of King Herod (Acts 12:20-25). The text stresses that "immediately" after Herod put himself in the place of God, he was struck down. At an earlier stage within the same book, something similar is said to happen to Ananias and Sapphira. "Immediately" after receiving the apostolic judgment that they lied not merely to the church but to God about a certain sum of money, they fall to the floor and die (Acts 5:1-11). Luke does not explicitly say that they were killed by God, but the narrative leaves the implication unambiguous. Accordingly, Hanson admits that "the death of Ananias and Sapphira appears to be an instance of direct divine punishment."[25] Though it may be possible to interpret passages such as these in a manner that is compatible with the natural

---

[21] See Boyd, *Crucifixion of the Warrior God*, especially chaps. 4, 15-17; Dodd, *Epistle of Paul to the Romans*, 23; Hanson, *The Wrath of the Lamb*, x; and J. Denny Weaver, *The Nonviolent God* (Grand Rapids, MI: Eerdmans, 2013), 47-50.
[22] See note 17 for modes of reasoning that run along such lines.
[23] See, for example, D. A. Carson, "The Wrath of God," in *Engaging the Doctrine of God: Contemporary Protestant Perspectives*, ed. Bruce L. McCormack (Grand Rapids, MI: Baker Academic, 2008), 37-63 (see especially pp. 42-47); and H. G. L. Peels, *The Vengeance of God: The Meaning of the Root Nqm and the Function of the Nqm-Texts in the Context of Divine Revelation in the Old Testament* (Leiden: Brill, 1995), especially pp. 302-05.
[24] Hanson, *The Wrath of the Lamb*, 131, 155-58.
[25] Ibid., 131.

consequences view, that view certainly does not sit well with these texts and others like it (e.g., 1 Cor. 27-31; 2 Pet. 2:1-16; Rev. 16). This mismatch has led some theologians to contend that whenever a biblical passage strongly implies that God performs abrupt retributive actions of the kind that do not mesh with the natural consequences view, we should suppose that the human authors of Scripture are wrongly interpreting the events of history.[26] However, I submit that, all other things being equal, it is better to have a theory of divine wrath that does not require us to cut out the bits of Scripture we simply do not care for. One need not be an advocate of biblical infallibility to suppose as much.

What about the Christological case for the natural consequences view? The defender of the natural consequences view is right to suppose that God's revelation in Christ should color how we see God's wrath. Indeed, I maintain that it should lead us to hold that the unitary account is true.[27] Nevertheless, the proponent of the natural consequences view goes too far in thinking that her preferred view can be read off the ministry of Christ.

Suppose we take a completely pacifistic reading of the ministry of Christ, according to which Christ taught and exemplified an ethic of love that requires complete nonviolence. Even still, one has the difficulty of moving from this ethic to the claim that God only punishes via natural consequences.[28] After all, God became human for us, to show us how to live, and thus what Jesus does *qua* human may not always represent what he does *qua* God. This is not to say that God calls humans to love others more deeply than he does. Instead, it is to say that, given the differences between God and humans, God's love may move him to behave in ways that would be inappropriate for humans, analogous to the manner in which a mother's love may require her to act in ways toward her children that she prohibits for them.[29] In keeping with this, Paul indicates that God's punitive methods are not always to be imitated by humans (e.g., Rom. 12:19), and Jesus uses fairly frightening imagery to describe his return in glory to judge the living and dead (e.g., Mt. 25:31-46). Hence, even when one adopts a pacifistic reading of Christ's ministry (which is controversial in its own right), this is a far cry from showing that God always punishes by way of nonviolent natural consequences.

---

[26] For two examples, see Hanson, *The Wrath of the Lamb*, 157-58; and Weaver, *The Nonviolent God*, 127, 149. Cf. Seibert, *Disturbing Divine Behavior*, chap. 10.

[27] See my "How Does a Loving God Punish?"

[28] The most thorough and thoughtful defense of the inference from Christ's nonviolent ministry to the essentially nonviolent character of God comes from Boyd's *Crucifixion of the Warrior God* (see especially pp. 223-27). Central to Boyd's defense of this inference is the idea that Jesus's self-giving love found at the cross puts "the Father's character, and therefore the Father's way of responding to evil, on full display. If we assume anything different, we undermine the cross as the decisive revelation of the kind of love that characterizes [God's] eternal nature" (p. 225). (Cf. Paul Alexander, "Violence and Nonviolence in Conceptualizations of Godly Love," in *The Science and Theology of Godly Love*, ed. Matthew T. Lee and Amos Yong [Dekalb, IL: NIU Press, 2012], 77-93.) It is one thing, however, to affirm that the cross demonstrates God's preferred means of dealing with wayward creatures (all of whom he loves). It is quite another to suppose that the cross shows that God is *always* nonviolent. In my view, Boyd is too quick to think that the latter option is to be preferred over the former.

[29] See my "How Does a Loving God Punish?"

It seems to me that God in Christ reveals not that God is nonviolent but that he is unsurpassably loving. Unfortunately, some theologians conflate the two and suppose that a loving God is ipso facto not violent toward those he loves. But this need not be the case as fans of the superb television program, *The Walking Dead*, can attest.[30] Consider episode 1 of season 3, where the beloved Christian character Hershel is bit on the ankle by a zombie. If nothing is done, the bite will lead to Hershel's zombification in a matter of minutes. Aware of this unfortunate reality, Hershel's friends waste no time. Not knowing if he can be saved, they restrain a protesting and writhing Hershel and began to hack off his leg with a blunt axe. The job takes more than one swing, and Hershel does not receive so much as an aspirin. If any act is violent, this is a violent act. Yet it is also an act of deep love, done with the relentless desire to save Hershel. I dare say that cases such as this one reveal that sometimes it takes more love to act violently than it does not to.

It should be clear how the compatibility of love and violence applies to the present issue. The proponent of the unitary account need not maintain that God's punishment is nonviolent; instead she needs to maintain that God's punishment is loving, whether violent or not. Thus, insofar as the natural consequences view relies upon a conflation of love and nonviolence, it remains unconvincing. After all, it could be (for all we know) that God must sometimes act violently toward us, for our good, and it could be that he is willing to act in violent ways precisely because his love is unsurpassable.

On a parenthetical note, it is worth mentioning that the idea that God's love can lead him to violence is not something that was lost on the early church. For example, Gregory of Nyssa was willing to compare God's punishment to "knives, cauteries, and bitter medicines,"[31] and yet he insisted that this punishment, even that which takes place in hell, is a "healing remedy provided by God"[32] that must not be divorced "from the noble end of the love of man."[33] Similarly, Origen of Alexandria before him spoke of God's "punishment of fire," not as a means of destroying humans, but as a means of painfully healing the souls of sinful men and women.[34] These metaphors point toward the idea that God is sometimes violent precisely because he is perfectly loving.

The upshot is that it is not apparent that a loving God is not violent in the manner suggested by certain proponents of the natural consequences view. Crucially, nor it is apparent that dealing with sinful creatures in the way specified by the natural consequences view is the most loving way in which God can deal with sinners. That view says that God lets the perpetually rebellious experience the bitter consequences of their own evil behavior. Sometimes this may be a reasonable course of action, but,

---

[30] The claim that *The Walking Dead* is superb requires qualification. The earliest seasons of the program are quite good, but, in my opinion, the quality soon deteriorates dramatically.

[31] Gregory of Nyssa, *An Address on Religious Instruction*, in *Christology of the Later Fathers*, ed. Edward Hardy, trans. Cyril C. Richardson (Louisville, KY: Westminster John Knox Press, 1954), 26 (p. 284).

[32] Ibid., 26 (p. 284).

[33] Ibid., 26 (p. 303). Compare with 8 and 40 (pp. 282–85 and 324–25) of the same work, as well as Gregory's *Making of Man* (specifically, 21–22) and *Soul and Resurrection* (specifically, 46).

[34] See, e.g., *First Principles* 2.9.2. For commentary on Origen's view of punishment, see Mark Scott, *Journey Back to God: Origen on the Problem of Evil* (New York: Oxford University Press, 2012), chap. 4.

in our experience, letting the vicious go their own way rarely helps them reform. No, humans often require externally imposed discipline if they are to grapple with the depths of their wrongdoing and begin the process of change. We recognize this most especially with undisciplined children, but we also realize that it is a morally unfortunate circumstance when an adult's resources allow him to rise above the law and social pressures and enable him to have a fair measure of unbridled freedom. Both kinds of circumstances engender individuals who wreak havoc not only on the lives of others but on themselves. The natural consequences view is inadequate insofar as it suggests that God has not set up a world where punitive actions call evildoers back to himself.[35]

What about the idea that God respects human freedom? Does not that notion require something like the natural consequences view? I doubt it. There is a difference between curtailing and influencing someone's freedom and allowing wholesale autonomy. It is best, I submit, to have an understanding of divine punishment whereby God does not override human freedom entirely (in the sense of taking away one's ability to choose between good and evil), but instead guides, or even pressures, those who are punished toward reform. At least this is preferable up to a certain point. There might be circumstances where it is advisable to allow sinners simply to go their chosen way. Nevertheless, to allow sinners only to experience the outcomes of their own choices seems to be a much too passive form of disciplinary love.

Of course, the proponent of the natural consequences view has resources. Using the parable of the Prodigal Son as her guiding metaphor, she can suggest that God has structured the cosmos such that those who choose the path of evil will eventually find their worlds crashing down on them, which will provide numerous opportunities to change. In fact, it is compatible with the natural consequences view to suppose that one day, in this life or the next, *everyone* will realize that life apart from God is hopeless and will enter the saving embrace of God.

Perhaps God could have set up the world like this. However, as already suggested, the biblical data does not paint this picture. While I am prepared to grant that God sometimes uses natural consequences to teach lessons and bring people to himself, Scripture also suggests that God imposes external penalties on wrongdoers in a manner that does not seem to fit within the framework of the natural consequences view. The defender of the unitary account should not feel the need to resist this, given that it is a common feature of human experience that imposed penalties can actually be good for the one punished. Certainly, there remains the question as to whether any kind of unitary account can make sense of God striking people dead, and other such acts of apparent retribution. But in light of the biblical shortcomings of the natural consequences view, the proponent of the unitary account at minimum should be open to an alternative rendition of this account. With this in mind, we now turn to such a rendition.

---

[35] As I subsequently explain, I do not mean to suggest that the natural consequences view excludes the idea that God created the world in such a way that unpleasant natural consequences impinge upon sinners their need to turn to God. My claim is more modest: the natural consequences view is inadequate *insofar as* it suggests that God has not set up a world where punitive actions call evildoers back to himself, and, furthermore, mere natural consequences seem to have limited utility in this respect.

3 Divine communicative punishment

What I am calling divine communicative punishment can be found in embryonic form in the work of some of the early church fathers,[36] but the understanding of punishment that undergirds the theory finds maturity in the writings of the contemporary philosopher and legal theorist R. A. Duff.[37] Though Duff's concern is with the state's punishment of humans, not with the theology of divine punishment, the basic theory he propounds can be transformed into a theory of divine punishment with very little alteration. My proposal is that Duff's theory is worth considering as a model of how God punishes, whatever one makes of the theory as a model of how the state should punish.

According to Duff, punishment "should communicate to offenders the censure they deserve for their crimes and should aim through the communicative process to persuade them to repent [of] those crimes, to try to reform themselves, and thus to reconcile themselves with those whom they wronged."[38] Duff maintains that this means that punishment should direct wrongdoers' attentions to the values they have flouted, while condemning the perversion of these values. Done correctly, punishment forms a context in which wrongdoers can discern, and palpably experience, the error of their ways. In the typical case, such a context is painful, as it involves the aim of getting transgressors to understand in heart and mind why their actions are morally unacceptable. Yet the communicative punishment points beyond itself as well. It is meant to persuade transgressors to change by creating an environment in which the wrongdoer can focus on "the nature and implications of his crime, face up to it more adequately than he might otherwise (being human) do, and so arrive at a more authentic repentance."[39] Authentic repentance will in turn lead to reform and, when possible, reconciliation.[40]

As a noncriminal example of how communicative punishment might work, consider a case where a child arbitrarily forbids one of his peers from playing with him and his friends. In such a scenario, the child's mother might put her son on an excluded "time-out" in the attempt to communicate to him the detrimental nature of his behavior, and she might, after the time-out period is complete, demand that her son apologize to the one he has alienated and offer an invitation to rejoin the group of children at play. In accordance with communicative punishment, the mother's hope might be that by causing her son to suffer the pain of exclusion from his peers, he will experience the badness of this exclusion and will come to see that he should not be the cause of similar sorts of suffering in others. Alongside this goal, the mother's demand that her son apologize and invite the excluded child into the group might be for the

---

[36] See, for example, my "How Does a Loving God Punish?" for an examination of Gregory of Nyssa's thought on this issue.
[37] For a brief explanation of Duff's view, see his "Punishment," in *The Oxford Handbook of Practical Ethics*, ed. Hugh LaFollette (New York: Oxford University Press, 2003), 337–40.
[38] Antony Duff, *Punishment, Communication, and Community* (New York: Oxford University Press, 2001), xvii.
[39] Ibid., 108.
[40] Ibid., 107–08.

purpose of showing her son how to repent, how to begin to change his ways, and how to take steps toward reconciliation with the one he alienated.

To appreciate the internal structure of Duff's communicative theory, it will prove helpful to draw the well-known distinction between forward- and backward-looking justifications for punishment. Those who maintain that the justification of punishment rests on forward-looking principles point to some future good that punishment is likely to produce—such as deterrence from wrongdoing, reformation of the transgressor, and the like. Here punishment is not typically understood to be morally good in itself, but for the consequences it can potentially yield. By contrast, those that believe that the justification of punishment is backward-looking hold that punishment is morally justified because of the guilt accrued by the past misconduct of an individual. The view that punishment is sufficiently justified in terms of backward-looking considerations is often labeled "retributivism," and those who hold to retributivism maintain that there is something intrinsically good about punishing those who deserve it with the fitting level of severity.[41]

Both exclusively backward- and forward-looking justifications of punishment have their respective challenges.[42] If, on the one hand, punishment is done simply because it is deserved, without taking into consideration how the punishment might harm or benefit the person punished, then the punishment looks to be uncaring toward that individual. While punishing in an uncaring way may or may not be problematic when carried out by the state, the defender of the unitary account will need to resist any view of divine punishment that has this implication. To embrace this implication, after all, would be to deny the unitary account. On the other hand, if it is contended that the justification of punishment is based entirely upon the production of some future good, then, as many legal theorists have stressed, punishment becomes disconnected from desert in a way that leads to injustices.[43] For example, if deterrence from future wrongdoing is the goal of punishment, and the severity of this punishment is not guided by what the offender deserves, then one would be justified in imposing incredibly burdensome sanctions for the smallest peccadilloes, if that is what will deter best. But such punishment is manifestly unjust.

Duff's model of punishment is neither entirely backward- nor forward-looking, but a combination of the two. His model contains a backward-looking, even retributivist, component in that stern communicative treatment is understood as an intrinsically good and justified response to an individual's past failings. However, unlike standard

---

[41] See, for example, Michael S. Moore, "The Moral Worth of Retribution," in *Responsibility, Character, and the Emotions: New Essays in Moral Psychology*, ed. Ferdinand Schoeman (Cambridge: Cambridge University Press, 1987), 179–219.

[42] See Duff, "Punishment," 337–40.

[43] For a clear overview of many of the relevant issues, see C. S. Lewis, "The Humanitarian Theory of Punishment," in *God in the Dock: Essays on Theology and Ethics* (Grand Rapids, MI: Eerdmans Publishing Company, 1973), 287–94. For more rigorous contemporary treatments of such issues, see David Boonin, *The Problem of Punishment* (New York: Cambridge University Press, 2008), chap. 2; H. L. A. Hart, *Punishment and Responsibility* (Oxford: Oxford University Press, 1968), chaps. 1–2; H. J. McCloskey, "An Examination of Restricted Utilitarianism," *The Philosophical Review* 66 (1957): 466–85 (especially pp. 468–89); and Igor Primoratz, *Justifying Legal Punishment*, 2nd ed. (Atlantic Highlands, NJ: Humanities Press, 1999), chaps. 2–3.

retributive theories, Duff maintains that punishment should aim to persuade the wrongdoer to repent and reform, which will hopefully engender reconciliation between the wrongdoer and his victim, and, ideally, everyone else affected by the wrongdoer's actions.[44] But, importantly, Duff's use of a forward-looking constituent differs from the characteristic way in which this component is conceived.[45] Those who stress a forward-looking justification of punishment often claim that it is the contingently related outputs of punishment (deterrence, remediation, etc.) that justify the means. Against this, Duff maintains that it is the holistic communication of punishment that is intrinsically appropriate. Punishment puts the transgressor's heart and mind in contact with the values he has flouted, while also directing his gaze toward the way of change and restoration. The communicative content by itself, and not so much the outcomes, is a worthwhile endeavor that warrants punishment. Certainly, one should not be surprised if communicative punishment routinely achieves the goals of repentance, reform, and reconciliation. However, for Duff, these outcomes are not what make punishment essentially fitting, or even successful. Rather, an instance of punishment is successful if it is implemented in the correct communicative manner: for those who are receptive, the punishment brings a deep understanding of the appropriate values and it illumines the path to change. As free moral agents, wrongdoers may refuse to accept the message of punishment. Still, communicative punishment remains justified since it treats transgressors as rational and moral individuals who are worth engaging through communicative treatment, even if stern and unpleasant.

The way in which Duff integrates both backward- and forward-looking components into his theory of punishment avoids the mentioned problems that hinder those understandings of punishment that have us looking only in one direction. Because Duff's model of punishment is based upon a backward-looking, retributivist component, there is no fear that the one who punishes as Duff prescribes would punish someone beyond what she deserves. At the same time, because the punishment has the forward-looking aims of persuading moral transgressors to repent and seek reform and reconciliation, the proposed view of punishment cannot be labeled as uncaring either (assuming that these outcomes are good for the one punished).

To help us get a better handle on Duff's communicative view of punishment, I turn to speech act theory. According to this theory, the primary function of language is to *do* things with one's words and other communicative actions. My wife, for example, might say "it's time to go," or she might covertly tap her watch, and either of these actions—these speech acts—might be done for the purpose of persuading me to wrap up my conversation so that we might leave the party. Speech acts are typically thought to include, but are by no means limited to, (i) *statements*, which indicate what is the case, (ii) *exclamations*, which express feelings or attitudes, and (iii) *commands*, which attempt to persuade or command people to do or believe certain things.[46]

---

[44] Duff, *Punishment, Communication, and Community*, 107–08.
[45] See Duff, "Punishment," 347.
[46] For just two examples from prominent speech act theorists, see William Alston, *Illocutionary Acts and Sentence Meaning* (Ithaca, NY: Cornell University Press, 2000), chaps. 4–5, and John Searle, *Mind, Language, and Society: Philosophy in the Real World* (New York: Basic Books, 1998), 146–52.

On J. L. Austin's version of speech act theory, a specific speech act (or "illocutionary act") is to be distinguished from the *illocutionary force* of that speech act. To label something a speech act, we have seen, is to refer to what is being said or communicated (a statement, command, exclamation, or what have you). By contrast, a specific speech act's illocutionary force refers to the effect the speaker (or more generally, communicator) aims to accomplish by carrying out the relevant speech act.

Suppose that you are disgusted by a crude and insensitive joke that your colleague Bill makes. You respond by saying, "You filthy, small man!" In saying this, we may suppose that you mean to perform a three-part speech act: (i) express/exclaim your distaste for Bill's joke, (ii) make the statement that Bill should not have made the joke, and (iii) command/direct Bill not to make such jokes in the future. In addition, we may suppose that the intended illocutionary force of your insult is threefold: (i) cause Bill to feel emotions of guilt and shame about his joke, (ii) make Bill believe that he should not have made that joke, and (iii) persuade Bill to form the intention not to make such jokes in the future. If Bill ends up feeling, believing, and intending as you hope in response to your insult, the illocutionary force has hit the mark.[47]

On the communicative view of punishment, the act of punishing can be seen as a multifaceted speech act. This punitive speech act can be implemented through official decree (e.g., the judge says, "I hereby sentence you to five years in prison for your crime") and/or through the particulars of the punishment itself (e.g., being forced to perform community service for defacing public property makes a statement about the value of the property that was defaced). On Duff's communicative view, moreover, punishment can be understood to include two basic kinds of speech acts intended for the wrongdoer. There are those that pertain to the censure of the wrongdoer and there are those that pertain to directing the wrongdoer. Regarding the censure, the implementation of punishment makes one or more statements about the badness of the wrongdoer's actions, and it expresses certain attitudes of disapproval of them. The intended illocutionary force is to make the wrongdoer understand or believe that his behavior is wrong/bad, and to elicit feelings of guilt (i.e., the sense that one has committed a bad action), shame (i.e., that sense that one has a defective moral character), and the corresponding remorse for one's actions and state of character. Regarding the directive, the punishment commands the wrongdoer to repent and form the intention to reform and seek reconciliation (as appropriate). The intended illocutionary force here is to persuade the wrongdoer that genuine repentance is a good action that should be done, as are the noted intentions to seek reform and reconciliation.

Consider a case where someone is punished for defacing a mom and pop shop downtown. When the communicative theory of punishment is paired with speech act theory in the manner described, the aim of punishment would then be twofold: (i) to state and exclaim the censure the person deserves for her bad behavior and (ii) to command her to repent and seek reform and reconciliation. Furthermore, both of these communicative acts would have the intended illocutionary force that was

---

[47] See J. L. Austin, *How to Do Things with Words*, 2nd ed., ed. J. O. Urmson and M. Sbisá (Cambridge, MA: Harvard University Press, 1962), chaps. 8–9.

previously mentioned, namely, the objective of producing a deep understanding of the error of one's ways—complete with feelings of guilt, shame, and remorse—and the goal of engendering the sense that it would be good to repent and seek reform and reconciliation (again, as appropriate). There are perhaps many ways that all of these punitive ambitions can be achieved, but one way might be to force the vandal to compensate the shop owners financially and to spend long hours restoring that store front and others. Being forced to compensate the shop owners might communicate to the vandal that she is guilty of ruining something that does not belong to her, and being forced to repair storefronts might communicate to her the financial and emotional resources that are involved in shop ownership. This experience may furthermore lead her to repent and present her time and money to the shop owners as a means of indicating to them that she is sorry, wants to change, and wants to be reconciled.

Although the communicative view of punishment is perhaps initially attractive, there remains the question as to whether this view of punishment can account for the kinds of hard treatment and corresponding suffering that we normally recognize as appropriate in punishment. For example, most of us think that it is (at minimum) right to incarcerate someone for a brutal and premeditated physical assault. Yet one might think that a judge could communicate the relevant censure and issue the relevant directive without any imprisonment. The judge, for instance, could simply tell the assaulter that what he did was bad and command him to repent and seek reconciliation and reform. Such a sentence might be uncomfortable, maybe a bit embarrassing, but it does not seem to be much of a punishment. Hence it may look as if the hard treatment and suffering that typically and rightly characterize punishment are needless addendums, on the communicative view.[48] But if this is so, it is reasonable to conclude that it is the idea of communicative punishment that must be jettisoned, rather than our common notions about hard treatment and suffering.

My preferred response to such a concern is to suggest that the communication involved in punishment should be much more holistic than the individual who raises this kind of objection perhaps thinks. On communicative punishment, the goal is not merely to teach or reinforce the truth of some proposition. Instead, and as we have seen, the goal is to help the wrongdoer deeply understand, in a holistic way that involves heart and head, the depth of his sin, and to provide the opportunity for the wrongdoer to break his connection with evil and alienation by repentance, reform, and reconciliation. In many cases, it seems, there would be something communicatively incomplete about punishment that does not make the wrongdoer feel, often "from the inside," the horror of his ways. Typically, this will be painful. Additionally, genuine repentance, reform, and reconciliation often cannot take place unless the evildoer makes certain efforts toward reparation and even penance (where penance refers to doing something above and beyond mere repayment to show that one is deeply sorry for one's wrongdoing).[49] But reparation and penance involve some kind of loss to the person offering them, and thus regularly will be painful.

---

[48] Relevant here is Nils Christie, *Limits to Pain* (London: Martin Robertson, 1981), 98–105.
[49] See Richard Swinburne, *Responsibility and Atonement* (Oxford: Oxford University Press, 1989), 81–89.

To illustrate the point about the suffering involved in holistic communicative punishment, consider a chilling example involving a society where eye transplants are a reality. (Think of the film *The Minority Report*.) Suppose a man named Phil, with much forethought and enjoyment, intentionally gouges out the eyes of an innocent man named Samson. Phil is a hardened "eye-gouger" who is always on the prowl for his next victim. How would a society that cares about Phil get through to him, hardened as he is? Not implausibly, one might suppose that the best way to get through to Phil regarding the horror he has caused Samson is by turning Phil's actions back on himself, such that Phil not only comes to form new beliefs about what he has done to Samson but also comes to feel some of what Samson felt when Phil stole his eyes. In step with this, the advocate of communicative punishment who lives within this society might suggest forcing Phil to have his eyes removed surgically and ceremoniously present them to Samson for a transplant. This advocate of communicative punishment might say that the goal of forcibly removing Phil's eyes and having Phil give his eyes to Samson is not merely to compensate Samson or to cause Phil to suffer, but also to provide a context in which Phil can own up to his wrongdoing, change his ways, and gesture toward reconciliation. For the sake of penance, this advocate might also suggest that Phil should pay for the eye removal and implantation surgeries and present an additional gift beyond that.

Though uncomfortable to think about, the communicative power of this form of punishment is difficult to miss. By turning Phil's actions back on himself, he experiences, from within, the evil of his behavior. Because he has blinded, he must now live a life of blindness. Because he has taken something dear from another, he must give something dear to himself to the one from whom he has stolen. As a free agent, Phil may refuse to internalize the message of punishment and refuse to apologize and offer his own eyes and financial resources as an expression of his longing for change and reconciliation. Yet, it is reasonable to maintain that this severe form of punishment is among the most effective forms of holistic communication to Phil—a form of communication that, one may hope, will lead to moral transformation.

The upshot, then, is that it is far from obvious that the consistent application of communicative punishment would lead to forms of punishment devoid of much hard treatment and suffering. On the contrary, taking communicative punishment seriously may push us to consider forms of punishment that seem much too harsh for our liking.

Before applying the discussed view of punishment to God, it is worth making a final remark, albeit all too brief. Thus far we have been focusing on how punishment of the wrongdoer might in some way be good or an act of care for the one punished. Nothing has been said about how punishment might be good or caring for the victim of the one punished. But surely the relevant punishing authority should factor into her penal sentence the claims of the victim.[50] With communicative punishment, it is easy to see

---

[50] Consider the case of a child who is killed in cold blood, but in which the murderer's lawyer is able to hoodwink the judge and jury into thinking he is innocent of the crime. The man responsible for the child's death shows no remorse; he even mocks the parents of the child he has killed. The cry of the parents becomes the cry of the Psalmist, "Vindicate me, O LORD, my God, according to your righteousness, and do not let [my adversaries] rejoice over me" (Ps 35:24), "put [them] to shame" (v. 4), "may ruin overtake them by surprise" (v. 8). Understandably, the parents want the smirking

how this might be done. If nothing else, punishment can be used to say to the victim that his victimization will not be overlooked. Because the victimizer has not treated the victim with the respect he deserves, the victimizer will be required to pay for her evil deeds. Communication to the victim might be formulated in terms of stating to the victim that he should not have been treated as he was, expressing certain feelings of sympathy for the victim, and promising that one will do what one reasonably can to decrease the likelihood that the individual will be victimized by the wrongdoer again in that way.

With the basic contours of this Duff-inspired communicative theory of punishment before us, we can now see how the theory can be transformed into a general account of divine punishment. Accordingly, divine punishment is that which aims to communicate to offenders the censure they deserve for their sins, and it commands them to repent of their evil, to reform themselves (with God's help), and thus (when possible) to reconcile themselves with those whom they have wronged. However, punitive success is not essentially dependent upon the change of sinners, but on the punishment's intrinsic communicative effectiveness—that is, it is the kind of punishment that provides a context in which transgressors can, if they allow it, palpably discern the depth of their sins and understand how they should respond to the fact that they have committed these evils. As a secondary aim, God's punishment intends to communicate to those who have been wronged, letting them know that he will not stand by when their value is disrespected. God can administer communicative punishment through secondary agents (think Rom. 13:1-5)[51] or in a more immediate fashion (think of the final judgment), and being omniscient and omnipotent, God likely has means of communicating through punishment that outrun our imaginative capacities (e.g., maybe God communicates diachronically by weaving together premortem and postmortem events).

It should be clear that with the communicative theory of divine punishment the preservation of the unity account is straightforward. Divine punishment aims to communicate to offenders the censure they deserve for their sins, but this punishment is an expression of God's severe mercy, internally directed toward bringing repentance,

---

murderer to be "put in his place," and to understand the bitter evil he has committed against them and their child. In other words, the parents have "a truly ethical demand that . . . the right should be asserted, the flag planted in this horribly rebellious soul," as C. S. Lewis once characterized the phenomenon. (See Lewis's *The Problem of Pain* [New York: Harper Collins Publishers, 1973], 94.)

Some Christians object to the idea that the desire for vengeance is ever appropriate. But whatever one thinks about this issue, notice that the communicative view of punishment enables (at least in principle) one to cry for vengeance and yet do so out of love. The parents of the murdered child can want the murderer to pay for what he did to their child, while hoping that paying for this crime will also lead to him becoming a changed man. Hoping for vengeance *might* be dangerous territory that we best not encourage. Still, I consider it a benefit of the communicative view that punishing in this way can speak to the victim as well as those who are victimized.

[51] Rom. 13:1-5 reads, "Let every person be subject to the governing authorities; for there is no authority except from God, and those authorities that exist have been instituted by God. Therefore whoever resists authority resists what God has appointed, and those who resist will incur judgment. For rulers are not a terror to good conduct, but to bad. Do you wish to have no fear of the authority? Then do what is good, and you will receive its approval; for it is God's servant for your good. But if you do what is wrong, you should be afraid, for the authority does not bear the sword in vain! It is the servant of God to execute wrath on the wrongdoer" (NRSV).

reform, and reconciliation to those who are willing to respond appropriately to the message of punishment. In addition, this punishment communicates to the victims that their victimization will not be tolerated. So, given divine communicative punishment, God's punishment does not diverge from his love, rather his punishment is borne out of it.

4 The explanatory advantages of divine communicative punishment

In my view, divine communicative punishment offers an attractive model of God's punishment that integrates backward- and forward-looking components and explains why the God who is unsurpassable in love might perform special punitive acts that are fairly severe. As stated at the outset, however, the goal of this chapter is not to argue that divine communicative punishment is true. Instead, my goal is to show that this model of punishment has certain explanatory advantages over the natural consequences view, which is a leading alternative understanding of the unitary account. What, then, are these advantages?

First, recall that the natural consequences view has difficulty accounting for the biblical data which depicts God as performing direct or discrete acts of punishment that appear retributive. Punishment by immediate death has been the primary example. Divine communicative punishment does not face comparable problems regarding apparent retribution or immediate implementations of capital punishment by God. With respect to apparent retribution, it has been shown that divine communicative punishment is a modified form of retributivism. Thus, divine punishments that appear retributive within Scripture can be regarded as such by proponents of divine communicative punishment. Crucially, however, the defender of divine communicative punishment proposes a way in which retribution is not opposed to love.

Moreover, the proponent of divine communicative punishment can claim that immediate executions by God are powerfully communicative, notwithstanding the initial appearances to the contrary. The reason we normally do not see instantaneous capital punishment as communicatively redemptive is because we tend to think that death ends all ability to reflect on the nature of such punishment in a manner that allows for change. But this ought to be regarded as a failure of imagination.[52] An omnipotent and omniscient God can surely construct the cosmos in a way that allows for postmortem reflection on life and death, and, so far as I can tell, there is nothing that would keep God from offering postmortem opportunities for salvation, should he desire to do so.[53]

My purpose here is not to defend the idea that God offers postmortem opportunities for salvation. Rather, my point is simply that abrupt capital punishment by God does

---

[52] That said, one does not necessarily evince a lack of imagination if one limits all opportunities for salvation to this terrestrial life on the basis of Scripture and/or sacred tradition. See, for example, the *Catechism of the Catholic Church*, 2nd ed. (Washington, DC: Libreria Editrice Vaticana, 2000), 393 and 1,021.

[53] For additional discussion and resources, see my "How Does a Loving God Punish?"

not count against divine communicative punishment if we are open to the idea that God is willing to communicate through punishment beyond this terrestrial life. However it is that God chooses to distribute opportunities for salvation, though, it seems that the defender of the unitary account should be open to postmortem chances for salvation, given that this account places a premium on God's love.

But, if one believes that the authority of Scripture and/or tradition should lead theologians to limit God's redemptive communication to this terrestrial life, perhaps the defender of divine communicative punishment can propose that God sometimes acts in miraculous ways to communicative redemptively in the process of death by punishment. For example, God might meet people mystically in the process of dying and give them a final opportunity to turn to him. It is often said that one's entire life runs through one's consciousness in but a flash in the process of death, and maybe God is behind this phenomenon, often weaving together events in such a way that they confront the dying and call them, one last time, to repentance from their sins. Additionally, and in consonance with the unitary account, maybe God is careful to punish individuals in this way only when the subjects of punishment are so morally hardened that there is no superior option. On this way of thinking, abrupt capital punishment by God constitutes a final drastic measure to turn his sinful children back to himself. The details, to be sure, remain to be worked out, but if something like this "last chance" option is viable, then the mere fact that Scripture records God striking persons dead should not lead one to abandon hope in divine communicative punishment.

Whichever option one prefers, the important implication is that there are two ways in which divine communicative punishment has an apparent advantage over the natural consequences view regarding abrupt executions by God. The proponent of the natural consequences view must deny that God abruptly imposes external punishments of death, even though Scripture appears to indicate otherwise. By contrast, the defender of divine communicative punishment can affirm the apparent biblical teaching that God sometimes retributively kills, but submit that God provides postmortem opportunities for salvation and/or that God redemptively communicates to sinners via miraculous and mystical means in their final moments.

Another advantage of divine communicative punishment concerns divine discipline. Recall that the proponent of the natural consequences view seems to overlook the value of intervening disciplinary punishment. Loving parents sometimes let their children experience the painful consequences of their behavior, but certainly this is not always the case. Instead, parents are often quick to correct their children through disciplinary means. Divine communicative punishment has no difficulty accounting for disciplinary action. In fact, a corrective element is built into the theory.

In addition to these two explanatory advantages, the proponent of divine communicative punishment can assimilate what the natural consequences view gets right. If it true that the latter view explains much of the relevant biblical data, this is no threat to the defender of divine communicative punishment. As parents know, sometimes allowing children to reap what they sow is an effective way of teaching them valuable lessons. Similarly, certain kinds of natural consequences can be seen as a way in which God communicates to his creatures and calls them back to himself. But, on divine communicative punishment, there is no reason to maintain that the only way in which God expresses his wrath is through natural consequences.[54]

What about respect for human free will? Does divine communicative punishment allow for this? I believe it does. While it might be said that punishment restricts the range of free actions the creature can perform (something we do with one another on a daily basis), there is nothing about divine communicative punishment that suggests that human freedom should be overridden. Recall that for Duff punishment is about rightly communicating. What justifies punishment are *not* the outcomes of repentance, reform, and reconciliation, but rather the punishment's intrinsic communicative effectiveness. (It must be the kind of punishment that provides a context in which a transgressor can, if he allows it, holistically discern his sins and understand how he should respond to the fact that he has sinned.) Because punishment is not justified by the outcomes, there is no reason to think that God would crush the freedom of the creature in order to achieve the ends of repentance, reform, and reconciliation. Instead, how humans respond to God's punishment is something that he can choose to leave to them.

Of course, questions remain. Does divine communicative punishment provide the best explanation of all the pertinent biblical data? Is this form of punishment philosophically tenable? And to what extent can the defender of divine communicative punishment affirm a classical doctrine of hell?[55] Such questions will need to be addressed on another occasion. For now, I hope I have shown that divine communicative punishment is preferable to the natural consequences view in important respects, and thus merits serious consideration by those who adhere to the unitary account.

---

[54] There are at least two ways in which the defender of divine communicative punishment might incorporate the insights of the natural consequences view. She might maintain that God teaching his children lessons via natural consequences is but one form of communicative punishment. Alternatively, she might hold that allowing one to be harmed via natural consequences is not punishment strictly speaking, but another way, alongside communicative punishment, in which God teaches lessons to his children.

[55] On this last question, see my "How Does a Loving God Punish?"

10

The Indwelling of the Holy Spirit as Love

Adonis Vidu

1 Introduction

Christians have universally affirmed that salvation entails an intimate relationship of union with the trinitarian God. The language of evangelical piety includes phrases that refer to this union, such as "accepting Jesus into your heart," "the Holy Spirit lives within you," "being born again," and so on. Such language, however, is puzzling for many reflective persons. What might it mean for the transcendent God to enter one's heart, or for the Holy Spirit to take residence within the human soul? The problem of the presence of God to finite reality is also encountered in the perplexities of the Eucharistic doctrine, where the question has to do, partly, with the capacity of the finite for the infinite. There are differences, though, between the two discussions. In the case of the Eucharist, the bread and wine are in some sense the body and blood of Jesus Christ, thus human parts of the incarnate Son of God. There is, furthermore, a material mediation of these parts by the Eucharistic elements. In the case of the indwelling of the Holy Spirit, however, there is no such mediation. This fact complicates matters somewhat, since here the aim is union with a transcendent, rather than an incarnate (and thus already embodied) reality.[1]

A first difficulty, then, is constituted by the distinction between created reality and the uncreated, transcendent God. The difficulty does not primarily consist in the possibility of the union, something the Christian tradition readily grants, but in how to conceptualize the union metaphysically such that the distinction between God and creatures is preserved. At this point I will note that there is a historical suspicion in Protestantism of certain ontological accounts of such a union, a suspicion that is largely not shared in either Catholic or Orthodox theology.

But there is a second difficulty related to the inhabitation of the Holy Spirit. Christians confess that all trinitarian persons inhabit the believer in their hypostatic character. In other words, the persons of the Son and Holy Spirit are being given to

---

[1] This chapter was presented as part of the Analytic Theology Seminar at Fuller Theological Seminary. I am grateful for the participants' comments on the chapter. Additionally, Jordan Wesling, James Arcadi, and Kimberley Kroll provided invaluable feedback on a draft. Finally, gratitude goes to my research assistant, Mark Hertenstein, who offered valuable comments and assisted with the editorial process.

us, and the Father is giving himself to us. The persons are present with us, moreover, in their hypostatic particularity, as distinguished from one another in their particular identities. For the classic Western tradition of trinitarian theology, however, this presents a problem. In this tradition—but not exclusive to it—the external operations of the Trinity are axiomatically inseparable. In virtue of the unity of the divine substance, which is the foundation for its operations, all external works of the Trinity must be common to the three persons.[2] Now, an invisible mission of the Spirit (which is how this tradition often refers to the indwelling) is an *opus ad extra* and thus must be taken as common to all trinitarian persons. The perplexity becomes clear at this point: How can the Spirit, and the Father and the Son, be given to us in his hypostatic uniqueness, given that his operations are supposed to be common to all the persons?

Although the Western tradition holds that all the economic works of the Trinity are inseparable, it also employs the so-called principle of appropriation.[3] Simply defined, the principle holds that although such works are common to all trinitarian persons, certain works are appropriated to certain persons. Such appropriation does not indicate any unique causality of that particular person, but rather that this or that particular work—or particular effect, to be more precise—manifests a specific trinitarian person. Thus, for example, we speak about sanctification as being a work common to the whole Trinity, yet appropriated to the Holy Spirit.

In the case of the indwelling, however, we do not have to do simply with an external effect—such as "sanctification"—but with a self-giving of the person. The Western strictures seem to foreclose precisely what is religiously significant about the concept, namely that the persons are being given to us distinctly, not simply in an appropriated manner.

The question naturally arises whether the Western rule of inseparable operations inherently contradicts the faith that we are united distinctly to the Father, Son, and Holy Spirit as the end of our salvation. The thesis of this chapter is that this conflict is resolvable. It is possible to give an account that both preserves the important strictures about inseparability of action and affirms the indwelling of the trinitarian persons in their hypostatic character. I propose to reach this goal through the following steps: (1) I start with the biblical testimony to the notion of indwelling and its traditional Thomistic interpretation in terms of love. (2) I then present a number of important objections and Karl Rahner's alternative interpretation of the indwelling in terms of a "quasi-formal"

---

[2] For patristic defenses of inseparable operations, see Gregory of Nyssa, *Ad Ablabius*: "On 'Not Three Gods,'" in Gregory of Nyssa, *Dogmatic Treatises*, Nicene and Post-Nicene Fathers, Vol. 5, ed. Philip Schaff and Henry Wace (New York: Cosimo Classics, 2007); Augustine, *The Trinity*, trans. Edmund Hill, O.P., ed. John E. Rotelle, O.S.A. (Hyde Park, NY: New City Press, 2011); and Augustine, *Sermon 52*, in *Sermons III (51–94)*, trans. Edmund P. Hill, O.P., ed. John E. Rotelle, O.S.A. (Brooklyn, NY: New City Press, 1991). For modern interpretations of the patristic sources, see Lewis Ayres, "Remember That You Are Catholic (Serm 52:2): Augustine on the Unity of Triune God," *Journal of Early Christian Studies* 8, no. 1 (2000): 39–82; Michel René Barnes, *The Power of God: Δύναμις in Gregory of Nyssa's Trinitarian Theology* (Washington, DC: The Catholic University of America Press, 2001).

[3] For additional work on appropriation, see Augustine, *The Trinity*, books VI–VII; Gilles Emery, O.P., *The Trinitarian Theology of Thomas Aquinas* (Oxford: Oxford University Press, 2007), 312–38; and Adonis Vidu, "Trinitarian Inseparable Operations and the Incarnation," *Journal of Analytic Theology* 4 (2016): 106–27.

presence of the persons. (3) The next section argues that Rahner's interpretation fails to preserve important theological assumptions. (4) Following this, I return to the Thomistic interpretation and argue that it is able to address the objections formulated by Rahner and others through its notion of exemplary causality. (5) Finally, I respond to a number of objections, some of which have been inspired by Protestant dogmatic sensibilities.

2 The Western interpretation of the indwelling: The appropriation tradition

The Scriptural witness to the operation of the Trinity upon the justified seems to imply that there is a presence of the divine persons to the just that transcends the effects of God's actions. In Catholic theology, this presence extends beyond created sanctifying grace to the supernatural elevation of the soul into communion with the whole Trinity. For Protestants, this refers to a union with Christ in sanctification. For the Orthodox, this refers to the deification of the believer. The universal affirmation of the Christian faith is that salvation amounts to much more than either the communication of a moral property, or forgiveness, or justification. More than simply a restoration to an original state, or even the resumption of a process of development, salvation's ultimate aim is ontological communion with God. All Christians affirm that such communion is not simply eschatological, but it is already inaugurated in some way. While there are differences in how this communion is related to other elements of salvation, in how realized it might be, or in how it is connected to the ultimate *visio Dei*, there is universal agreement on the fact that the Christian is indwelt by the whole Trinity.

The scriptural language for this indwelling is sometimes cultic: "Do you not know," the Apostle Paul asks the Corinthians, "that your body is a temple of the Holy Spirit within you, whom you have from God?" (1 Cor. 6:19; cf. 1 Cor. 3:16).

The Apostle John states that God lives in us and we know this by his Spirit: "Whoever keeps his commandments abides in God, and God in him. And by this we know that he abides in us, by the Spirit whom he has given us" (1 Jn 3:24). At the same time, the other persons of the Trinity are not merely represented by the residing Spirit, but are also indwelling, as Jn 14:23 implies: "Jesus answered him, 'If anyone loves me, he will keep my word, and my Father will love him, and we will come to him and make our home with him.'" As seen here, John especially likes to relate the divine indwelling to love, while also connecting love to the keeping of Christ's commandments. In John 17, Jesus prays for the apostles (and their followers) that they "may be one," that "they may be in us." In v. 23 he says: "I in them and you in me, that they may become perfectly one, so that the world may know that you sent me and loved them even as you loved me." And then, in v. 26: "I made known to them your name, and I will continue to make it known, that the love with which you have loved me may be in them, and I in them." John further argues (1 Jn 4:12-13), "If we love one another, God abides in us, and His love is perfected in us. By this we know that we abide in Him and He in us, because He has given us of His Spirit." Here love is some form of condition of God's abiding in us, and thus of the indwelling Spirit.

Paul seems to be echoing a similar theme in Rom. 5:5: "God's love has been poured into our hearts through the Holy Spirit who has been given to us." Moreover, the presence of the Spirit is what vivifies our bodies (Rom. 8:9-11). Importantly, it is the reason for our confidence in our ultimate vindication. Paul uses the language of seal, of down payment, of earnest to make this point, as in Eph. 1:13-14. It is precisely through the Spirit that we become sons. This theme is replete in Paul (Rom. 8:9-10, 15-16; Gal. 4:6).

To summarize this much too brief glimpse at Scripture, the Holy Spirit lives in believers as in temples, unites them to the Father and the Son, and seals them in Christ. His indwelling seems especially connected to the love that has been poured into our hearts, just like Christ's indwelling seems especially connected to faith (Eph. 3:17). Not only is the Spirit given but the other trinitarian persons are also given as they come to make their home with us. This presence of the Trinity, of the Holy Spirit in particular, is taken as an earnest, as an anticipation of what is yet to come. The language of Scripture on this matter seems intensely ontological: we do not merely have gifts from the Spirit, but the Spirit himself. We do not merely have the benefits of Christ, but Christ the Son himself.

The question is, can the Western tradition handle these texts? How can the Spirit inhabit us, be possessed, received, and so on, if he does not have his own exclusive operation? The answer given by the Western tradition, especially in its Augustinian-Thomistic version, is that the manner in which the Holy Spirit inhabits us is through love. Now is the time to briefly expound this interpretation.

For ease of reference, I will refer to this tradition as the "appropriation tradition," even though I will argue that, in this case, the tradition takes us significantly beyond mere appropriation. This tradition understands a divine mission (such as the sending of the Spirit into our hearts) as being primarily a manifestation of a divine person. Two important features[4] of the divine missions need to be stressed at this point. A divine person sent on a mission does not leave the place from which he is sent. Being sent does not imply a change in the immutable divine person, who remains invested in his immanent relations. For that reason, a mission has been called an external procession, or the extension of a procession. A second feature is that the sent person does not "arrive" at a location that he did not previously occupy. Divine missions assume divine omnipresence, in its various forms.[5] As a consequence of these assumptions, a mission entails no change for the divine person. But it does involve a change for the creature.

These assumptions are not to be underestimated. They are crucial to this outlook and produce a very peculiar understanding of divine action in the world. Rather than conceiving divine action in terms of divine persons coming down or going up an "ontological ladder," which amounts to a mythological view of such action, it correlates divine action with divine omnipresence and predicates change not to the divine persons, but to the created natures upon which it acts. As such, the very concept of a divine action will be parsed in such a way that the production of created effects

---

[4] See, for example, Aquinas, *ST* I q. 43 art. 4, 6; cf. Gilles Emery, O.P., *The Trinity*, trans. Matthew Levering (Washington, DC: The Catholic University of America Press, 2011), 178ff.
[5] Aquinas, *ST* I. q. 43 art. 3.

is brought about without it implying change on the divine side. A certain kind of commensurability or proportionality between effect and cause is thus resisted.[6]

A mission is thus defined as a procession (a relation of origin, for example, the procession of the Son, or the spiration of the Holy Spirit) that is extended to include a created effect. More precisely, a created effect is drawn into a procession, without change to the procession. Or, a created effect is brought to participate in one of the divine immanent relationships. It will be stressed that, though the creature is brought into relation with the trinitarian persons, the relation is real for the creature only, and conceptual for God.[7] In other words, due to the creator-creature distinction and divine immutability, the new relation is not constitutive for God's identity, although it is constitutive for the creature's identity. In Aquinas's parlance, God does not depend on his relation to his creatures, while the latter are dependent on this relation.

Now, all such created effects, since they are created, involve efficient divine causality. But efficient divine causality is the causality common to all the trinitarian persons.[8] Thus, as far as the production of the effect is concerned, the trinitarian persons are its common authors. Nonetheless, some of these created effects can make certain divine persons "manifest," due to an affinity to their personal property. We enter now the territory of the doctrine of appropriation.

Augustine understands that the inseparability principle makes it difficult to understand revelation, in which we have distinct persons apparently being revealed to us through their unique (not common) operations. Take the baptism of Jesus.[9] While to some it might be a great proof for the Trinity, from the perspective of inseparable operations it might pose quite a difficulty. The reason is that we seem to be presented with different divine persons actually doing different things: the Son is getting baptized, the Father speaks from heaven, and the Spirit comes down in the form of a dove. Augustine is at pains to explain how this revelatory event is consistent with the common operation of the three divine persons. He applies precisely the conceptuality of "created effects" in the process. The created effects (the human nature of the Son, the voice from heaven, the dove) are efficiently caused by the common operation of the Trinity, yet they are referred to and reveal distinct persons of the Triune God.

Augustine also provides another analogy that explains the same procedure of appropriation: the three faculties of memory, understanding, and will are commonly producing the effect of the words "memory," "understanding," and "will."[10] Yet even though each of these individual words are produced by all the faculties together (I cannot say "memory," without willing to say it, without understanding that I have said it, or without remembering that I have said it), the words themselves relate to and identify just one of the faculties. We have here a way of talking about missions that transcends the efficient causality. The distinctions between missions are not given in

---

[6] See Aquinas *ST* I.43.5.
[7] Aquinas, *De Veritate* 4.5; *ST* I.13.7; *De Potentia Dei* 3.3.
[8] For different types of causality, see Michael E. Dodds, *Unlocking Divine Action: Contemporary Science and Thomas Aquinas* (Washington, DC: Catholic University of America, 2012).
[9] See Augustine's discussion in *Sermon 52*.
[10] See Augustine, Sermon 52.20 (p. 60).

terms of the persons performing different actions, but in terms of being given distinctly through the common operation of the Trinity.

Aquinas's distinction between visible and invisible missions preserves the same basic definition of mission. A visible mission is the manifestation of a trinitarian person through a created effect that is brought about by the common trinitarian agency, yet related to and revelatory of just one of the persons. An invisible mission, likewise, is a new relation between the soul and the Trinity, whereby something is produced in the soul by the common agency of the trinitarian persons, yet that something relates the soul distinctly to one of the divine persons.

This provides us with the basic framework for understanding the idea of the inhabitation of the Holy Spirit by love. While the divine love in our soul is the common production of the three persons, it disposes us specifically to receive one of them, the Holy Spirit. As I will explain below, this is a so-called intentional or exemplary solution to the problem. The Holy Spirit is given to us in his hypostatic uniqueness as the end term of a relation to which we are elevated and disposed by the created effect of love. Love, as the common production of the Trinity is, in scholastic language, the "formal reason" of the inhabitation of the Holy Spirit. In other words, love is the form in our soul through which we are disposed to enjoy God and the third person specifically. Our participation in the divine nature takes place precisely through the formality of the divine gifts of love, wisdom, and so on, as the Apostle Peter puts it: "so that through them [these promised gifts] you may become partakers of the divine nature, having escaped from the corruption that is in the world because of sinful desire" (2 Pet. 1:4). In this way, Aquinas hopes to have provided an account by which we are related distinctly to the third person, all the while preserving the traditional principle of inseparable operations. I will return to this account once I have discussed some major objections to it.

3 Objections to the appropriation approach

James P. Mackey objects to Augustine's notion of appropriation:

> Once again a flat and undifferentiated formula, if rigidly applied in accordance with its own logic, will yield only the sense that the one God "creates" voices, clouds, fire, or human flesh, to make visible one of the "persons" and to reveal them thus in their relationships to one another, but no visible means of manifestation has, or could have, any intrinsic relationship to any particular "person." *Opera ad extra sunt indivisa* is now so much in possession that it makes all detectable means of distinguishing the "persons" suspect.[11]

The problem identified by Mackey is one of individuation of the persons. If every action *ad extra* belongs to their common causality, there is no way of discriminating between

---

[11] James P. Mackey, *The Christian Experience of God as Trinity* (London: SCM-Canterbury Pres. Ltd., 1983), 157–58.

the persons. We thus seem to have been robbed of any possible basis for ascribing real distinctions to the persons within the Godhead.

Most Latin trinitarians would hesitate to call for efficient causalities that are exclusive to particular divine persons. However, many theologians in this tradition would affirm the reality of distinct relations to distinct divine persons. But is it possible to conceive of such distinct relations on a basis other than efficient causality? Or, to put it more simply, can one relate distinctly to Father, Son, and Holy Spirit even if they always act inseparably? If we cannot assign different actions *ad extra* to them, can we nevertheless assign different relationships between them and creatures like us?

But what other kinds of relations of presence may be conceived other than in terms of efficient causality? A number of modern Catholic theologians have suggested a return to formal causality as a means of showing a presence of the trinitarian persons in terms of their hypostatic character, that is, in their uniqueness and not just in terms of their common operation. The appeal to formal, or rather quasi-formal, causality is made in a number of variations. Here is a brief summary:

Dionysius Petavius argues for a quasi-formal presence of the Holy Spirit, who unites himself to the human person (or the person's will) in a manner analogous to the Son's uniting himself to human nature. According to Petavius, it is the Holy Spirit alone who unites himself to the just in this way: "The three persons dwell in the just man, but only the Holy Spirit is, as it were, the form that sanctifies and renders a man an adoptive son by its self-communication."[12] The presence of the other trinitarian persons in the soul of the just is mediated through the formal presence of the Holy Spirit. Such a view has been called the "exclusive proprium view."[13] For Petavius, there is a kind of equivalency between the way in which the Son possesses his divine nature and how the Spirit possesses our natures.

Matthias Joseph Scheeben has proposed a so-called nonexclusive proprium view. Scheeben argues largely within an appropriation approach, yet crucially expands it to allow for non-appropriated, quasi-formal relations between the just and the trinitarian persons. His account is nonexclusive in that he argues that each trinitarian person may possess the soul in a manner analogous to how he possesses the divine nature.

> Although the divine substance and activity is common to all the persons, the possession of the substance is peculiar to each person. As each distinct person possesses the divine nature in a special way, He can possess a created nature in His own personal way, and to this extent exclusively. We know that this is the case with the Son in the Incarnation. If the Son alone takes physical possession of a created nature, why should not the Holy Spirit be able to take possession of a created being in a way that is proper to His own person, by means of a less perfect and purely moral possession?[14]

---

[12] Quoted in David Coffey, *Did You Receive the Holy Spirit When You Believed?* (Milwaukee: Marquette University Press, 2005), 16.

[13] As by Malachi J. Donnelly, for example, "The Inhabitation of the Holy Spirit: A Solution According to De La Taille," *Theological Studies* 3 (September 1947): 450ff.

[14] Matthias Joseph Scheeben, *The Mysteries of Christianity* (New York: The Crossroad Publishing Company, 2008), 166.

Scheeben further argues that this new possession is of a formal kind: "We shall perceive that by dwelling in our soul as a guest the Holy Spirit is in a most exalted and marvelous manner not only the efficient and exemplary cause, but in a certain sense also the formal cause of our supernatural sanctity, of our dignity as sons of God, and of our union with the divine persons."[15]

While there are other important voices in this conversation, the focus in this chapter will be on Rahner.[16] Scripture and the Greek Fathers, Rahner argues, challenge the received scholastic solution to the problem (which appeals to appropriation and makes the created grace the form of the indwelling). Though the Scriptural statements about the divine self-communication include a created effect, Rahner feels that the order should be reversed. Created grace, he argues, should be understood as the consequence, not as the form, of uncreated grace.[17] In other words, the love we have for God (and for each other) is the consequence, not the basis, of the inhabiting Spirit.

Rahner perceives a clear advantage of this solution. The whole Trinity is given to us really, the persons in their hypostatic character, even now before the eschaton, as it were. Grace is intrinsically supernatural because it consists precisely of the indwelling of the persons in their *propria*. As Rahner puts it,

> The life of grace, that is to say, and the life of future glory do not stand in a purely moral and juridical relation to each other, such that the latter is the reward of the former as merit; the life of glory is the definitive flowering (the "manifestation," "the disclosure") of the life of divine sonship already possessed and merely "hidden" for the moment.[18]

Let me explain. On the appropriation model, Rahner and others suggest that we only have the Spirit, and the Son, and the Father in a way that is mediated by created realities. Their indwelling really consists in this new "entitative" (pertaining to an essential element of the soul) transformation. The beatific vision and our life of glory, on the other hand, consist in an unmediated participation in the triune being which, consequently, is qualitatively different than our fellowship with the Trinity in this life, and which can therefore only be understood as reward. At any rate, our relationship to the persons of the Trinity is, as Mackey also has noted, extrinsic, not intrinsic.

Rahner believes that such a new relationship between God and the creature exceeds the order of efficient causality. It is, first, anticipated in our beatific vision, where we shall contemplate God not through created species, but through God's own essence.

---

[15] Ibid., 167.
[16] Rahner discusses the inhabitation in terms of God's threefold self-communication in several places: first, in "Some Implications of the Scholastic Concept of Uncreated Grace," in *Theological Investigations*, Vol. 1, trans. Cornelius Ernst, O.P., (Baltimore, MD: Helicon Press, 1961); then in *The Trinity* (New York: The Crossroad Publishing Company, 1997), 24–45; and finally in *Foundations of the Christian Faith*, trans. William V. Dych, S.J. (New York: The Crossroad Publishing Company, 1982), 117–26.
[17] Rahner, "Scholastic Concept," 321–22.
[18] Ibid., 326.

Moreover, such a relationship is already understood in the case of the hypostatic union. They

> have this in common, that in them there is expressed a relationship of God to a creature which is not one of efficient causality (a production *out* of the cause [...]), and which must consequently fall under the head of formal causality (a taking up *into* the ground [*forma*] [...]): the ontological principle of the subsistence of a finite nature in this case, the ontological principle of a finite knowledge in the other.[19]

Rahner is aware that there is a problem with God entering into formal composition with creation. As Aquinas argues, God does not enter into such relations, since it would make God a composite being and dependent on matter. Any relationships into which God enters must be construed in such a way as to preserve divine immutability and aseity. Consequently, Rahner prefixes his notion of causality with "quasi." He feels that, despite all the risks, "it cannot be impossible in principle to allow an active formal causality of God upon a creature without thereby implying that this reactively impresses a new determination upon God's being in itself, one which would do away with his absolute transcendence and immutability."[20]

This has consequences for the logical relation between created and uncreated grace: "God communicates himself to the man to whom grace has been shown in the mode of formal causality, so that this communication is not then merely the consequence of an efficient causation of created grace."[21] On the contrary, "the communication of uncreated grace can be conceived of under a certain respect as logically and really prior to created grace: in the mode namely in which a formal cause is prior to the ultimate material disposition."[22]

The category of formal causality suggests a presence of the Holy Spirit in a different sense than his presence by his own efficiency. But what kind of presence, and what kind of causality, is this? If efficient causation concerns the production of an effect *out of* a cause, formal causality concerns the particular actualization of a potentiality that resides in the object. We have seen Rahner calling it a "taking up into the ground." Thus, for example, the form of fire causes the wood to burn. The form of *statue* causes this marble to become a statue, and so on. Let us take this second example. In terms of efficient causality, what causes the statue to exist is the sculptor. In terms of material causality, what causes the statue to exist is the particular matter from which it is sculpted (marble, indeed, is already a formed matter, and thus a substance, but a substance may become the matter to be informed by higher form). Formal causality, in turn, refers to that by which this particular marble is a statue. Aristotle argues that we can speak of causality here because the form of statue accounts for this marble being a statue.

---

[19] Ibid., 329.
[20] Ibid., 330.
[21] Ibid., 334.
[22] Ibid.

Rahner and others want to be able to individuate a self-communication of one of the persons that is proper to that person alone, in this case, a self-donation of the Holy Spirit to the human being. This self-donation must be more than mere appropriation, but it must not be conceived along the lines of an exclusive efficiency.

The Holy Spirit comes to live in the human person, as in a temple, and comes to make us partakers of the divine nature. Rahner et al. interpret that participation in the divine nature as the self-communication of each of the divine persons to the just, along the lines of formal causation.

It must be admitted that there is at least a prima facie plausibility and attractiveness to this model, beyond enabling us to preserve the principle of inseparable operations in the case of efficient causality. It has been argued that the language of formal causality seems better suited to explain our supernatural elevation. If we become partakers of the divine nature, and are sanctified and deified, this is best explained through the reception of some supernatural form. A mere created effect—such as supernatural grace—cannot really account for the supernatural in the natural. Malachi J. Donnelly expresses this well: "How can a created physical accident make us truly sharers of the divine nature, and how can uncreated grace, which surely does not inform the soul, truly sanctify?"[23] It thus becomes attractive to think of our supernaturality in terms of the formal reception of the triune persons inside of us. Moreover, explaining our supernaturality in terms of the formal self-communication of the persons (either just the Holy Spirit as in Petavious, or all three persons as in K. Rahner and M. Scheeben, M. J. Donnelly and others) has the advantage of making uncreated grace the basis of created grace (sanctifying grace).

To be sure, as Catholic theologians, all of the above will insist on the consequent necessity of created grace. On occasion the language of seal is used to express the point.[24] Created grace is the concave consequent condition upon our created reality of the uncreated, convex formal self-communication of the persons.[25] In this case, love is the concave created effect of the convex formal self-donation of the Holy Spirit. Moreover, they will insist, with the rest of the tradition, and against the Lutheran and Reformed theologians,[26] that this love is a habitual love and not simply an actual love. However, at least in the case of Rahner, his prioritizing of uncreated grace has made some of his Catholic peers suspicious of coming too close to a Lutheran position (see the Finish School of Luther interpretation).

4 Problems with the alternative view

Rahner is aware of at least one issue with the language of formal causality, and he devotes most of his energy responding to it. I am not aware (yet) of whether he addresses some of the other substantial difficulties that I will flag below.

---

[23] Donnelly, S. J., "The Inhabitation of the Holy Spirit," 452.
[24] Cf. Scheeben, *The Mysteries of Christianity*, 168–72.
[25] M. J. Donelly uses this pair of concepts in "The Inhabitation of the Holy Spirit," 463.
[26] See the discussion in the final section of the chapter.

The tradition has consistently rejected a formal interpretation of the inhabitation of Trinity in the just (preferring the appropriation approach) for one fundamental reason. In any formal causation there is a certain act-dependence and act-limitation of the form itself. In other words, the form depends on and is limited by its actualization in its own identity. Thus, the form of fire is dependent on the matter of wood or other combustible materials for its essence.

Thomas rejected the idea that God (as form) might enter into composition with matter,[27] since that would yield another substance, with God as a component of it, thus making it superior to God. Even if God were to drive such a process of composition, he would still be dependent on the matter itself and his relationship to matter would be real, rather than merely conceptual. Thomas is quite clear that what is at stake here is precisely divine transcendence and aseity.

Now, Rahner et al. are aware of this issue. But they will not stop this rational consideration from allowing them to do justice to what they take to be a data of revelation. First, such a formal communication has already taken place in the person of Jesus Christ (the hypostatic union); second, the beatific vision also entails it, since then we will behold God through his own essence, and thus a certain actuation of our knowledge by the divine essence will take place.

Rahner appeals to something like Maurice de la Taille's notion of "actuation," which the latter develops in his work on the hypostatic union.[28] Although in the natural order any actuation is an in-forming,[29] which implies act-dependence and act-limitation, this need not be the case, de la Taille argues, in the case of a supernatural actuation. In such a case, the form does not depend on the matter, or its potentialities, but simply creates these. In the hypostatic union, for example, the union does not depend on the prior existence of the human nature of Jesus Christ. In fact, the union actuates precisely the human nature of Jesus Christ as existing in the Logos. Or, rather, the Logos himself actuates the human nature of Jesus Christ as his own. Again, it should be noted that this actuation is not in the order of efficient, but formal causality. The eternal Logos, in other words, actuates the human nature of Jesus Christ.

At least in the case of the incarnation, then, we have a precedent for a formal actuation that does not entail in-formation, and thus the Thomistic hesitations about formal causality do not apply in this case. We can thus treat the hypostatic union as a paradigm case of the inhabitation of the divine persons. The created realities that are being actuated by the supernatural form of the divine persons (knowledge and faith in the case of the inhabitation of the Son, love in the case of the inhabitation of the Holy Spirit) are the form of the self-communication of the divine persons. The Son comes to exist in our knowledge as its very form and the Holy Spirit comes to exist in our love as its very form. The divine persons do not in-form these capacities; if they did, the

---

[27] *ST* I.3.2.
[28] See Maurice de la Taille, *The Hypostatic Union and Created Actuation by Uncreated Act: Light of Glory, Sanctifying Grace, Hypostatic Union* (West Baden Spring, IN: West Baden College, 1952), *passim*. For a discussion of the problems of "information," see p. 29.
[29] Rahner also stresses that "such a formal causality of God (a Trinitarian hypostasis, his Being) is not known to us in the realm of nature" ("Scholastic Concept," 330).

persons themselves would depend upon them for their own (new) identity. Instead, such capacity is a "created actuation" by "uncreated act."

Nevertheless, serious difficulties remain. We may grant, for the time being, that what takes place in the incarnation is in fact a case of quasi-formal causation, a created actuation by uncreated act. But should the analogy of the incarnation reassure us, or should it worry us? A number of theologians are certainly worried about it.[30] The problem has to do precisely with the dis-analogy that is entailed here. Though in the case of Christ the prior nonexistence of his created capacities is essential in avoiding Nestorianism, in our case it must remain the case that our created capacities (knowledge and love) already exist. And thus to speak about the persons themselves becoming the form of these capacities sounds very much like in-forming, since the relationship seems to depend upon a prior reality. The Thomistic tradition for this very reason prefers to speak about an "adaptation," or elevation, or disposing of our already existing realities to enjoy the supernatural persons. But the very reception of the form of the persons into these created capacities either leads back to in-formation, or it confuses the ontological orders, of created and uncreated. Let me explain: if the form is received into a matter, the matter is informed. To avoid this, the matter must not exist prior to the actuation—but this does away with the fact that our existence is already hypostatic. On the other hand, if our already hypostasized beings are to be raised to the level of the divine communion, such adaptation must be created, or connatural, adapted to its own nature.[31] But what is suggested is that the adaptation is itself supernatural, and that our (already existing) capacities are actualized by a transcendent form, in fact by a triune person. What appears to transpire here is confusion between the created and the uncreated orders. How may the Holy Spirit be communicated to an already hypostasized love, except by the adaptation of that love?

Thus the first problem associated with the quasi-formal approach seems to be that it blurs important distinctions between the natural and the supernatural, between created and uncreated.[32] In the case of the hypostatic union, the human knowledge and love of Christ were brought into existence exclusively as they were hypostasized in the Logos. Such logic may not apply in the case of the human persons, who are

---

[30] See, for example, Yves Congar, *I Believe in the Holy Spirit*, Vol. 2, trans. David Smith (New York: The Crossroad Publishing Company, 2013), 88, who is otherwise sympathetic to ascribing a logical and causal priority to uncreated grace.

[31] Aquinas writes (*In Sent.* I, dist. 17, Paris version): "Whatever is received into a thing is received according to the recipient's mode. But uncreated love, which is the Holy Spirit, is participated in by the creature; therefore he must be participated in according to the creature's mode. But the creatures mode is finite; thus what is received into the creature must be some finite love. But every finite thing is created. Therefore, in the soul having the Holy Spirit, there is a created charity." Thomas Aquinas, *On Love and Charity*, trans. Peter A. Kwasniewski, Thomas Bolin O.S.B., and Joseph Bolin (Washington, DC: The Catholic University of America Press, 2008), 10.

[32] The work of Bernard Lonergan on this issue might be mentioned. As Doran explains, he was having hesitations about the perceived priority of created grace at roughly the same time as Karl Rahner, but resolved the issue in the opposite direction from him. See the excellent discussion in Robert Doran, *The Trinity in History: A Theology of Divine Missions*, Vol. 1 (Toronto: University of Toronto Press, 2012), 25–26. Lonergan discusses the issue in several places, most centrally in *Early Latin Theology: Collected Works of Bernard Lonergan*, Vol. 19, ed. Daniel Monsour, Michael G. Shields, and Robert M. Doran (Toronto: University of Toronto Press, 2011); see especially "Part 7: Supplementary Notes on Sanctifying Grace."

already hypostasized natures. For us, a formal actuation is out of the question, since it would necessarily imply in-formation and thus act-dependence and act-limitation. The only option left for us would be that our own hypostases, remaining what they are, would receive something commensurate with our created existence. Clearly, what they receive cannot be the divine essence, since that would entail our becoming divine.

There is an additional problem with the quasi-formal suggestion. Simply put, persons are concrete particulars and thus do not become the form of a matter, though they may certainly be informed by an additional substance. Thus, for example, when the marble is sculpted, it takes the form of a statue; it becomes a statue. The form it takes is not this or that statue, but the universal form, statue. The resulting composite is certainly *this* statue, rather than statue in general, since the form is actualized in the production of the statue.

William Hill explains this concept well: "A person cannot be a form in any proper sense. Form belongs rather to the realm of essence and is a determinative principle of composite being which can be 'had' only as constituting an intrinsic aspect of the receiving subject's own being."[33] In other words, a form configures determinate being. To say that a person can come to exist in another matter, or to inform another matter is a categorical confusion, since the person is already a configured thing, a nature that is "closed off," or actualized.

At this point an objection might be formulated on the basis of a particular metaphysics of the soul. Eleonore Stump is arguing for a particular Thomistic metaphysics of the human soul:

> For Aquinas, the metaphysical world is ordered in such a way that at the top of the metaphysical hierarchy there are forms—God and the angels—which are configured but which aren't configurational constituents of anything else. These forms are configured but non-configuring. Near the bottom of the hierarchy are forms that configure matter but don't exist as configured things in their own right. The form of an amethyst is like this. Such forms are configuring but non-configured. And in the middle are human souls, the amphibians of this metaphysical world, occupying a niche in both the material and the spiritual realm. Like the angels, the human soul is itself configured; but like the forms of other material things, the human soul has the ability to configure matter.[34]

Why is this significant? Because this ontology might present us with the possibility of a form, the human soul, which exists as configuring matter, but which can also itself be configured. The implication is that the soul can exist independently of the body. The soul is, thus, both a particular (configured) and something that can inform matter (configuring). Putting it differently, the soul is both person and form. It thus seems possible that persons do inform.

---

[33] William Hill, O.P., *The Three-Personed God* (Washington, DC: The Catholic University of America Press, 1983), 293. For a lengthier treatment, see Hill, O.P., "Uncreated Grace – A Critique of Karl Rahner," *The Thomist* 27 (1963): 333–56.
[34] Eleanore Stump, *Aquinas* (London: Routledge, 2003), 514.

Closer attention to this discussion will quickly reveal that it is not an authentic counterexample. Stump defines the soul as something that "emerges" from the body. Even as the soul informs the matter of the body, making it *this* body, the soul can survive the expiration of the body, thus creating the appearance that it does not depend on the body. However, it can be argued that the soul that survives the body is this particular soul because of its having informed this particular matter (which became this body, now dead). The very particularity of this soul is its having informed this matter/body. The soul's surviving the body is conceptually distinct from its being independent, as a particular, from the body.

The soul emerges from the matter, which becomes this body through the emergence of the soul. Thus, the soul does not preexist the body, as something configured, but becomes something configured (a particular something) precisely through its configuring the matter of the body. It is not at all clear, then, that a person, as a concrete particular actualization of some matter, can be also a form of something. In the case of the human soul, the soul only informs the matter/body as something emerging from it.

It is not true that a person can be both a concrete particular as well as a form for a matter. The soul, which is at one point a concrete particular, having emerged from the matter, only informs the matter by having emerged from it. It remains the case that this particular soul is dependent on the matter that it configures, since it emerges from it and is not imposed upon it, as in problematic views of the preexistence of souls.

When this putative counterexample is applied to our problematic, the difficulties are insuperable. To say that the person of the Spirit is both a concrete particular mode of existence of the divine substance, as well as the (quasi-)form of a concrete human created reality is only consistent with identifying the divine substance with the human created reality, or with claiming that the eternal Holy Spirit is an emergent property of the human soul. To say that one of the triune persons becomes the form of a concrete created substance in an actuation takes us far beyond the accepted use of the categories of person and nature.

I have identified two fundamental problems with using the framework of quasi-formal causality to explain the inhabitation of the divine persons in the souls of the just. The first problem consists in the blurring of the ontological distinctions between created and uncreated. Francis Cunningham puts it well: "All things outside of the Trinity Itself are being by participation, dependent for their very existence on the productive and sustaining power of the subsistent Being."[35] Consequently, we can only participate in God in the order of operation, not in the order of nature.[36] But God's operation is common to the three persons. Avoiding the pitfalls of quasi-formal causality has led these theologians to affirm that the trinitarian persons

---

[35] Francis L. B. Cunningham, O.P., *The Indwelling of the Trinity: A Historico-Doctrinal Study of the Theory of St. Thomas Aquinas* (Dubuque, IA: The Priory Press, 1955), 194.

[36] Some proponents of the quasi-formal approach hesitate to describe the invisible missions as *ad extra*, thus confirming the impression that the distinctions between created and uncreated are blurred. Thus, M. J. Donnelly writes, "The uniting of the creature with the divine Person (or Persons) is not strictly an *opus ad extra*, but rather *ad intra*[!]" ("The Inhabitation of the Holy Spirit," 459). For a similar critique, see Ralph Del Colle, *Christ and the Spirit* (Oxford: Oxford University Press, 1994), 74.

form our created capacities (faith and love) in a supernatural way. But this begs the question of whether these capacities remain recognizably created and human, or at least proper to us.

The second problem consists in a categorical confusion between person and nature. A divine person cannot become the form of something else simply because a person is already a nature existing in a certain manner. Cunningham explains it well:

> The rational creature in the line of essence is a complete being, with his own subsistence, not merely a principle of being. Once can, accordingly, find no explanation for his union with the Trinity in the line of nature: God cannot be present to him as a hypostatic term because his nature is closed by his own personality, whereas the human nature of Christ was open to the divine personality. Only in the line of operation, then, can God exist as a term for the rational creature.[37]

Given that a quasi-formal approach to the problem of the inhabitation seems to be plagued with considerable difficulties, it is time to revisit the "appropriation" approach.

5 Salvaging the appropriation approach

For Aquinas and the tradition, there are strong trinitarian reasons why the indwelling may not take place in the order of nature, along the lines of a formal causality, for instance. An inhabitation in the order of nature renders the creature passive, which is acceptable in the case of the hypostatic union. Our natures are "closed off" (Cunningham) by our personalities and therefore cannot be actuated in the order of nature, where they are already actuated. It follows that the inhabitation can only take place in the order of operation.

The problem, of course, is that in the order of operation no distinct notional (or hypostatic) causality can be detected. It becomes difficult, if not impossible, in this scenario to distinguish between the persons in the life of grace, or to speak about the presence of the persons in their hypostatic uniqueness. But is this really the case? To answer this question we need to look more closely at the answer Thomas gives to the problem of the inhabitation.

Aquinas provides two explicit accounts of the inhabitation. The first one appears in various places throughout his *Commentary on the Sentences*, book I. The second account appears in his treatment of the divine missions in the *Summa Theologiae* I, Q. 43. The two treatments approach the topic from two different directions. The analysis in the *Sentences* is from the standpoint of the processions, while the analysis in the *Summa* is from the standpoint of the created effect. It would help to reacquaint ourselves with the definition of the divine missions that Thomas retains from Augustine: a mission is

---

[37] Cunningham, *Indwelling of the Trinity*, 189–90.

a prolongation of a procession in a new relationship to a created effect. Approaching the mission from these opposite directions is thus natural and helpful.

There has been some discussion in the scholarship about whether Thomas's analysis in the *Sentences* may leave some room for a quasi-formal approach. I am not equipped to enter into that conversation, so I will simply appeal to Emery's verdict. The analysis in the *Sentences* commentary is ontological, he argues. It discusses the divine missions in light of the trinitarian processions as causes. In the *Summa*, an operational or intentional analysis is given from the standpoint of the believer's operations. In this second account, God is taken to be present in grace in the manner in which a thing known and loved is present in the subject.

Even in the *Sentences*, however, the principle is clearly enunciated that the effects, which are the formality of the divine indwelling, are the product of the whole Trinity. Much of the discussion in I *Sent* d. 17 (Paris version) is given to a correction Thomas makes to Peter Lombard's understanding of charity. Lombard understands the charity by which the Holy Spirit resides in us to be an act, not a habit.[38] Aquinas's response makes three important points.

The first point is that the reception of uncreated love must itself be created:

> Whatever is received into a thing is received according to the recipient's mode. But uncreated love, which is the Holy Spirit, is participated in by the creature; therefore he must be participated in according to the creature's mode. But the creatures mode is finite; thus what is received into the creature must be some finite love. But every finite thing is created. Therefore, in the soul having the Holy Spirit, there is a created charity.[39]

The second point is: "Every assimilation [of one thing to another] comes about through some form. But it is through charity that we are made conformed to God himself, and when charity is lost, the soul is said to be deformed. Therefore, it seems that charity is a certain created form remaining in the soul."[40]

Finally, God is present in the saints differently than how he is present in other creatures. But "that diversity cannot be placed on the side of God himself, who stands uniformly to all things." In other words, the effect that is brought about does not involve a change in God himself, but in the operations of the creature. Further, this effect, must be a habit in the soul "which habit is indeed from the whole Trinity as efficient cause, but flows from love, which is the Holy Spirit, as exemplar cause: and therefore it is frequently found that the Holy Spirit is the love by which we love God and neighbor."[41]

This is where the confusion of certain modern theologians lies. For they would argue that we have here an instance where the Great Doctor himself understands the Holy Spirit to be the form of our love, implying something like a quasi-formal

---

[38] Peter Lombard discusses this in *The Sentences*, book 1, dist. XVII, chap. 6.8–9, 97 in the edition translated by Giulio Silano (Toronto: Pontifical Institute of Medieval Studies, 2007).
[39] Aquinas, *In Sent.* I, dist. 17, in *On Love and Charity*, 10.
[40] Ibid.
[41] Ibid., 11.

communication. By now it should be clear why this will not do. Love is a created capacity that is already hypostasized. To have the Holy Spirit to be the (quasi-)form of our love implies in-formation, with all its attendant dangers. If there is a perfection of our love, it cannot be from its being informed by uncreated love, which is the case in the incarnation (by nature).

Aquinas explains the difference:

> For the union of human nature in Christ has its term in the one being of the divine Person, and therefore an act numerically the same belongs at once to a divine person and to the human nature assumed. In contrast, the will of a saint is not assumed into unity of suppositum with the Holy Spirit. [. . .] Hence one cannot understand that there is a perfect operation of the will through which it is united to the Holy Spirit unless one also understands that there is also a habit perfecting the operative power itself.[42]

Thus, in the *Sentences*, a certain causality is ascribed to the Holy Spirit as the notional love (uncreated love). But this is not a formal causality.

As I have mentioned, the perspective on the divine missions is different in the *Summa*. Aquinas unpacks the notion of a divine mission in the sense of a manifestation of a triune person, for the purpose of bringing the creature back to God. In q. 43, art. 2, he responds to the question "Whether the invisible mission of the Divine Person is only according to the Gift of Sanctifying Grace?" Thomas rehearses his conception of mission as a temporal procession. He invokes the authority of Augustine that the Holy Spirit proceeds for the creature's sanctification. But since the creature's sanctification is by sanctifying grace, the mission is by sanctifying grace. The same principle enunciated in the *Sentences* can be observed here: the assimilation of uncreated love takes place through a certain created form. No other effect can bring about such an attaining to God, but sanctifying grace, Thomas argues. Though all creatures participate in God in the very act of existing—God already being in all things by his essence, beyond this mode of presence—God is present in the rational creature in the same way that the known is present in the knower.

Thomas argues that the rational creature attains to God by knowledge and love. Moreover, in response to the objection that the divine person is not given, but only his gifts, God not only exists in but also dwells therein as in His temple, Aquinas argues. "Yet the Holy Ghost is possessed by man, and dwells within Him, in the very gift itself of sanctifying grace."

The very gift, then, appears to become the formality of the indwelling of the person. Aquinas articulates this idea in terms of an adaptation of the creature, such that it might *enjoy* the divine person that is sent. The just person has not merely the gift, without the person, since to have the person is to be able to enjoy the person, which is what the gift precisely does.

But how can one "enjoy" the Holy Spirit if one is unable to individuate the Spirit in its causality *ad extra*? Francis Cunningham helps us understand this. The gift of

---
[42] Ibid., 12.

sanctifying grace, he argues, produces a certain adaptation of the creature such that it enjoys an "experimental knowledge" of God.[43] God is thus substantially present and attained, inasmuch as he is known and loved. However, this knowledge is not a discursive knowledge; it is not knowledge by inference. Such knowledge may be present in unbelievers as well. It thus cannot be the form of the inhabitation of the Word, as wisdom and faith.

Cunningham cites Aquinas:

> The experiencing of a thing is gained through the senses; but in one way, of a thing present, in another, of an absent thing. Of an absent thing, by reason of sight, smell and hearing; but of a thing present, by touch and taste—of a thing extrinsically present, by touch; by taste, however, of a thing intrinsically present. God, however, is not far from us nor outside of us but in us . . . and therefore the experiencing of the divine goodness is called a tasting.[44]

Thus, Cunningham comments, this formality of the divine presence "must be an effect within man, an effect to which God is immediately perceptible, an effect supremely expressive of God."[45]

The intrinsic connection desired by Mackey is thus established in the fact that the gift represents an imprint of a divine person. But the imprint is not in the order of formal, or efficient causality, but in the order of exemplary causality. As Emery puts it, the "proper relation belonging to the divine person is represented in the soul through a sort of received likeness, whose exemplar and origin is the property of this same eternal relation."[46]

Aquinas's notion of exemplary cause presents some ambiguity. On the one hand, he treats it as a type of formal cause; on the other hand, it is not an intrinsic cause, much like final causes. It seems to straddle the usual distinction between extrinsic and intrinsic causes. Arguably, Aquinas is compelled to introduce the exemplary variation into the neat distinction between the four causes because he regards creation as being intentional. The ideas in the divine mind are the exemplary causes and the blueprint of creation. The forms, on the other hand, inhere in the creatures.

An example from Aquinas's *De Veritate* will help clarify the distinction between formal and exemplary causes. Reflecting on the goodness of creatures, Aquinas argues that "all things are good by a created goodness formally, as by an inherent form, but by uncreated goodness, as by an exemplary form."[47] God, as uncreated goodness, is the *terminus ad quem* of creatures, while the inherent form of goodness, as created, is *that by which* creatures are good. The distinction between formal and exemplary serves to identify God as the end of creation, while preserving the ontological distinction between creator and creature.

---

[43] Cunningham, *Indwelling of the Trinity*, 197.
[44] Ibid., 198.
[45] Ibid., 200.
[46] Emery, *The Trinitarian Theology of Thomas Aquinas*, 376.
[47] *De Veritate*, Q. 21, art. 4 [accessed at http://dhspriory.org/thomas/english/QDdeVer21.htm#4]

As to the Holy Spirit, created love is the form through which we come to become more like the Holy Spirit in our union with the Father and Son by love. Through created love we come to enjoy the personal property of the Holy Spirit, which is love.[48]

We are distinctly related to trinitarian persons since "the divine person is sent to transmit a participation in his eternal property."[49] But the eternal property of the Holy Spirit is precisely love. And so love, as a created effect and *opus ad extra*, is the formality in which we come to enjoy uncreated love. We participate in the distinct triune persons not because our created capacities are informed by the respective triune person (our knowledge by the Logos, our love by the Holy Spirit). In other words, we participate distinctly in the persons not because the persons are the form of our souls, or various components of our souls. We participate in them because we participate in their notional relations and imitate them.[50] We are sharers in the Holy Spirit not because the Holy Spirit becomes our love, but because our love comes to resemble the Holy Spirit. In this sense, and in this sense alone, can one speak about an "imprint" of the divine person. The divine person bears fruit *ad extra* in our enjoyment of the Trinity. The gifts assimilate us to their exemplars.

In a very real sense, while remaining firmly in the appropriation tradition, when the invisible mission of the Spirit is regarded from the standpoint of its *terminus*, it reveals a relationship that is proper to the Spirit, and not simply appropriated to him. The relationship, however, is in the order of human operations, augmented by the created habits that make it possible for us to enjoy the distinct persons. This is also consistent with the reorientation of our understanding of divine action in terms of creatures being drawn to their ends, as opposed to ontological change in God. Distinct possession of a trinitarian person refers not to a separation among trinitarian actions, but to their common production of a return to God whereby the creature comes to resemble their distinct relations. To be distinctly related to a trinitarian person is, in this key, understood as participating in his distinct personal property, which in turn is the personal fruition *ad extra* of the immanent processions.

The Scriptures also indicate that our ultimate transformation according to the likeness of the Son takes place in the operational order: "What we will be has not yet appeared; but we know that when he appears we shall be like him, because we shall see him as he is" (1 Jn 3:2). Our becoming like Christ takes place through our operation of seeing him. This transformation is not an exclusively eschatological reality, in that we are already being remade in his likeness (2 Cor. 3:18). Although the form of our ultimate destiny is not yet known or accessible to us ("what we will be has not yet appeared"), the exemplar of our present transformation is the same as that of our ultimate destiny. For the wayfarer, Christ truly is given, yet in a mirror darkly, since our seeing him is by faith, not sight.

Just as the form by which we relate distinctly to the Son and are assimilated to him is our sonship, so also our distinct enjoyment of the Holy Spirit has the form of

---

[48] See, for example, Augustine's appeal to 1 John 4 as the basis for calling the Holy Spirit "charity," in *The Trinity*, book xv.31, 424.
[49] Emery, *The Trinitarian Theology of Thomas Aquinas*, 376–77.
[50] Admittedly, this approach dovetails more nicely with a definition of an eternal person as a subsistent relation.

our sanctification. God has poured his love into our hearts through the Holy Spirit (Rom. 5:5) so that, through this love, God and the human person mutually abide in one another (1 Jn 4) or become mutually assimilated to one another through love. Moreover, not only do we come to enjoy the Holy Spirit but our love for God is necessarily also a love of others (1 Jn 4:19-21). Furthermore, we become purveyors of the Spirit after a manner analogous to Christ's sending the Spirit. Jesus says, "Whoever believes in me, as the Scripture has said, 'Out of his heart will flow rivers of living water.'" As John explains (7:38-39), Jesus is referring to the Spirit who at that time had not yet been poured out.

6 Does love "buffer" the Spirit?

I have argued that the formality by which the Holy Spirit indwells believers is love. I have further suggested that metaphysical and trinitarian strictures are compelling us to give such an account. Careful reflection on the metaphysics of the indwelling raises some caution about the danger of blurring the distinctions between created and uncreated realities. The solution proposed by Rahner and others, suggesting that the Spirit is quasi-formally present in the believer, risks ignoring those cautions.

It may be retorted, however, that the proposed alternative is guilty of the opposite danger, namely of buffering the real presence of the Holy Spirit. Sometimes it is charged that the Thomistic account overreaches in its attempt to give a metaphysical description of an incomprehensible mystery. Protestant dogmatic sensibilities sometimes account for the suspicion that an intermediary is interposed between God and the human person, which is supposed to enable the former to be received by the latter. In response, such a reaction vigorously insists that God is in no need of such intermediaries; no prior disposition needs to be created to enable God to act upon the human soul.

The issues and assumptions involved in this dispute are multiple, ranging from broader metaphysical frameworks (Aristotelianism vs. Platonism) to divergent conceptions of the relationship between justification and sanctification. I will have to restrict my remarks to the issues I have addressed in the chapter.

Protestant theologians would typically side with Rahner on the issue of the priority of uncreated over created grace. John Owen, for instance, argues that "all gracious habits are effects of the operation of the Spirit, but not the well itself."[51] Similarly, Herman Bavinck insists that the infused habits "are distinguished [. . .] from the Holy Spirit, who effects them but does not coincide with them."[52]

Owen and Bavinck's willingness to even speak of infused habits, however, represents a possible correction to Luther and Calvin's[53] proclivity to avoid the language of habits

---

[51] John Owen, Appendix in *Pneumatologia*, abridged by G. Burder from the 3rd London Edition (London: Towar & Hogan, 1827), 327.
[52] Herman Bavinck, *Reformed Dogmatics*, Vol. 4 (Grand Rapids, MI: Baker Academic, 2008), 94; see p. 114 for a discussion of how faith is related to love. See also Bavinck, *Reformed Dogmatics*, Vol. 3, 574ff.
[53] See Calvin's discussion of habits in *Bondage and Liberation of the Will*, ed. A. N. S. Lane, trans. G. I. Davies (Grand Rapids, MI: Baker Books, 1996), book. 6, 378; cf. Charles Partee, *The Theology of John Calvin* (Louisville, KY: Westminster John Knox Press, 2010), 91.

altogether. Both magisterial reformers were in fact explicitly siding with Lombard against the broader Western approach.[54] As it has been pointed out, Lombard argues that the Holy Spirit is the very form of the love we have for God, as opposed to the later tradition which insisted that the habit of love is the form of the Holy Spirit's presence.

Part of the reason for the Protestant suspicion of "created grace" is precisely the fear of an intermediary that is "entitative" (or pertaining to an essential quality of the human soul) and thus appearing to lead to semi-Pelagianism. With Augustine and Lombard, Luther and Calvin insist that human love of God is directly caused by God. Consequently, Protestantism tends to regard grace as a divine action, rather than a substance, or a reality that is distinct from God's action.

This is a legitimate and significant worry. But it fundamentally misunderstands the proposal. To say that created love is the way in which the Holy Spirit is received is not to say that this love is present in the soul prior to and independently of the presence of the Holy Spirit itself. This would indeed require the Spirit to prepare the creature in advance of his coming. But the creature does need to be prepared in a very carefully circumscribed sense. This is a widespread assumption made by Catholic theologians, rejected by Luther and Calvin, but subsequently accepted by, for example, Peter Martyr Vermigli and Jerome Zanchi.[55] While this may be part of their Aristotelianism (or Thomism),[56] it intends to safeguard the ontological difference between creator and creature by the principle that any activity of God upon the creature must take place according to the creature's nature.

However, this adaptation to the creature is not an additional *ens completum*, but merely the consequent effect of the divine presence itself. The assimilation of the Holy Spirit to some creature must take place through a form, as we have seen. But this form does not preexist the presence of the Spirit. It is precisely the manner of its assimilation.

Grace, therefore, is not something reified, a "something" turned into a substance. Moeller and Philips explain this well:

> The love of God works effectively—a man is changed if the Spirit dwells in him; the *habitus* is the result of this; there is no question, therefore, of a *habitus* being required in advance, or produced by any other causality than that of God himself at the very moment He gives Himself. One must speak in this case of a *reciprocal causality*, an idea that expresses the unbreakable union between God sanctifying and the soul really changed by God's entering it. In other words, the idea of created grace simply expresses the reality of regeneration; it is in no way an intermediate reality, a thing, complete in itself, which man possesses as his own.[57]

---

[54] For more on this, see J. Todd Billings, *Calvin, Participation, and the Gift* (Oxford: Oxford University Press, 2008), 49; and William B. Evans, *Imputation and Impartation: Union with Christ in American Reformed Theology* (Eugene, OR: Wipf and Stock, 2008), 43–52.

[55] See the discussion in Evans, *Imputation and Impartation*; Norman Shepherd, "Zanchius on Saving Faith," *Westminster Theological Journal* 36 (1973–74): 31–47; Marvin W. Anderson, "Peter Martyr on Romans," *Scottish Journal of Theology* 26 (1973): 408; and J. P. Donnelly, "Calvinist Thomism," *Viator* 7 (1976): 441–55.

[56] See Donnelly, "Calvinist Thomism."

[57] Charles Moeller, *The Theology of Grace and the Ecumenical Movement* (New York: St. Anthony Guild Press, 1961), 19.

Some examples of assimilation may provide some clarity here: in the process of digestion food becomes assimilated into the human body in the form of tissues and fluids; in photosynthesis, carbon dioxide and water are assimilated through the form of organic molecules; blue paint is assimilated into yellow paint in the form of green paint; in visual perception light is assimilated into the knower through a sequence of forms, both physical (sense impressions) and cognitive (concepts). The presence of an element in another is realized in a way that accords with the nature of the receiver. As these examples show, the resulting form is not what makes possible the assimilation, but is its very form. It may be said that the form is not a constitutive condition, but a consequent condition. Strictly speaking, the form does not *enable* or cause the assimilation, anymore than the tissues and fluids cause the food to be present in the body. Neither is it, however, a remote consequence or effect of the assimilation. This is what Moeller and Philips's idea of "reciprocal causality" intends to convey.[58]

We can, in conclusion, affirm a priority of uncreated grace over the infused habits, including love, but still wish to insist that these habits are precisely the form of the Spirit's presence. As created, they are efficiently caused by the inseparable operation of the Trinity, even as they dispose the person to enjoy the trinitarian persons as distinct from one another.

---

[58] Cardinal Charles Journet prefers to call created and uncreated grace "correlative," in *The Theology of the Church*, trans. Victor Szczurek, O. Praem. (San Francisco, CA: Ignatius Press, 1987), 79.

11

Love and Resentment

Leigh Vicens

Do loving relationships necessarily involve a susceptibility to resentment on the part of the lovers? Many philosophers since the publication of Peter Strawson's seminal essay "Freedom and Resentment" have thought so. Strawson argued that resentment is part of a larger network of "reactive attitudes"[1] that are "'inextricably bound up' with our involvement in personal relationships and 'thickly woven into the fabric' of our lives."[2] While the connection between loving relationships and the reactive attitudes is not, on Strawson's view, a conceptual one, he maintained that the reactive attitudes have deep roots in "our human nature and our membership of human communities,"[3] so that the repudiation of resentment would be "practically inconceivable," "something of which human beings would [not] be capable."[4] While Christian philosophers have paid little attention to Strawson's claim that love and resentment go hand in hand, this claim should concern them, since the model of love central to Christian thought and practice would seem to involve the repudiation of resentment (cf. 1 Cor. 13:5).

In this chapter, I examine the connection between love and resentment. I begin by considering one objection to Strawson's claim about this connection raised by Derk Pereboom. On Pereboom's view, humans are not *ultimately* morally responsible for what they do, or *deserving* of praise or blame in a way that would make them appropriate targets of the reactive attitudes. Pereboom bases his denial of "basic-desert" moral responsibility on a complex series of philosophical and empirical arguments for free will skepticism,[5] but he also suggests that his view has theological

---

[1] Strawson uses the phrase "participant reactive attitudes" for our natural human reactions "to the quality of others' wills towards us, as manifested in their behavior," and distinguishes such attitudes from what he calls "vicarious reactive attitudes," which are "reactions to the qualities of others' wills, not towards ourselves, but towards others." He calls "resentment" the participant reactive attitude to a display of ill will or indifference, and "indignation" the vicarious analogue of resentment. I follow his usage in this chapter, and focus only on the participant reactive attitude of resentment. See Peter Strawson, "Freedom and Resentment," in *Free Will*, 2nd ed., ed. Gary Watson (Oxford: Oxford University Press, 1963), 83.
[2] Seth Shabo, "Where Love and Resentment Meet: Strawson's Intrapersonal Defense of Compatibilism," *Philosophical Review* 121, no. 1 (2012): 116.
[3] Strawson, "Freedom and Resentment," 85.
[4] Ibid., 81.
[5] Derk Pereboom, *Living without Free Will* (Cambridge: Cambridge University Press, 2001); and Derk Pereboom, *Free Will, Agency, and Meaning in Life* (Oxford: Oxford University Press, 2014).

motivation.⁶ Recognizing the importance of the reactive attitudes in the present-day system of social relationships, Pereboom nevertheless proposes that they be replaced by "nonreactive" attitudes, such as sadness, which do not assume basic-desert moral responsibility. However, both Seth Shabo and Justin Coates have defended Strawson's claim, maintaining that Pereboom's proposal fails to recognize an essential element of loving relationships that connects them to the reactive attitudes: "normative expectations" (on Coates's view) or "personal caring" about another's attitudes (on Shabo's view). I investigate these lines of reasoning and argue that, in fact, a person can suspend her reactive attitudes toward another on the grounds that the other is not ultimately responsible for what he does without sacrificing these elements of loving relationships. In defending this point, I appeal to a Christian ideal of love. Of course, it may be that the Christian *ideal* of love is just that—a model that is admirable but not humanly possible. However, although the Christian ideal admittedly assumes that perfect love between human beings is "supernatural," in the sense that it cannot be achieved without divine grace, I maintain that it is a realistic and attainable model for human beings. In support of this claim, I discuss Christian teaching on the practices by which one can learn to relinquish resentment.

To begin with, then, let us consider Pereboom's views on moral responsibility and the reactive attitudes, to which Coates and Shabo object. On the grounds that there is no evidence that humans are indeterministic agent-causes of their actions,⁷ Pereboom concludes that we are unjustified in believing that humans have the sort of free will required for "basic-desert" moral responsibility. He defines basic desert as follows:

> For an agent to be morally responsible for an action in this sense is for it to be hers in such a way that she would deserve to be blamed if she understood that it was morally wrong, and she would deserve to be praised if she understood that it was morally exemplary. The desert here is basic in the sense that the agent would deserve to be blamed or praised just because she has performed the action, given an understanding of its moral status, and not, for example, merely by virtue of consequentialist or contractualist considerations.⁸

Though Pereboom is skeptical that we are ever morally responsible in the "basic-desert" sense, he does not deny that we may be morally responsible in *some* sense. In fact, he endorses "an answerability notion of moral responsibility that invokes three non-desert involving and forward-looking moral desiderata: protection of potential victims, reconciliation in personal relationships and with the moral community, and reform and formation of moral character."⁹ Pereboom maintains that the fact that

---

⁶ Derk Pereboom, "Theological Determinism and Divine Providence," in *Molinism: The Contemporary Debate*, ed. Ken Perszyk (Oxford: Oxford University Press, 2011), 262–80; and Derk Pereboom, "Libertarianism and Theological Determinism," in *Free Will and Theism: Connections, Contingencies, and Concerns*, ed. Kevin Timpe and Daniel Speak (Oxford: Oxford University Press, 2016).
⁷ Pereboom, *Free Will*, chaps. 2–4.
⁸ Ibid., 2.
⁹ Pereboom, "Libertarianism and Theological Determinism," 117.

we are likely not indeterministic agent-causes of our actions does not undermine our ability to recognize and respond to reasons, and on the answerability account of moral responsibility, it is the agent's responsiveness to reasons, together with the moral desiderata just mentioned, that make it appropriate to praise and blame her.[10]

However, as Pereboom notes, the non-basic-desert view of moral responsibility is not compatible with "the practice of holding responsible in the sense that involves making agents targets of moral resentment," since resentment involves not just a *feeling* of anger, but also the *belief* that the targeted agent deserves—in the basic-desert sense—to be blamed for her action.[11] Pereboom maintains that resentment and other such reactive attitudes that assume basic desert should not be retained for consequentialist reasons, since, if we accept free will skepticism, such retention would amount to "our thinking and acting as if agents are morally responsible in a sense in which they are not," which would be both "doxastically irrational" and unfair to the targeted agents.[12] Thus, he recommends that we strive to eliminate reactive attitudes like resentment. Acknowledging that "expressions of resentment . . . play an important communicative role" in our personal relationships, Pereboom does not recommend simply abandoning these attitudes, but rather replacing them with alternative attitudes "whose expressions are not threatened by the skeptical view and can also communicate the relevant information," such as shock, disappointment, concern, and "moral sadness."[13] He insists that, "far from threatening good interpersonal relationships, [basic-desert moral responsibility skepticism] holds out the promise of better relationships through the release of anger that underlies so much human misery."[14]

In response to Pereboom's claim that we can do without reactive attitudes like resentment, Coates and Shabo have both defended versions of Strawson's thesis that this is not practically possible or desirable, given the important role that such attitudes play in loving relationships. On the version of the thesis that Coates defends, which he calls "love internalism," it is not that we *couldn't* engage in meaningful loving relationships while denying each other's moral responsibility; it's that such relationships—or certain forms of them, anyway—would be *inappropriate* if moral responsibility skepticism were true.[15] In particular, Coates contends that moral responsibility skepticism would undermine the appropriateness of mature "reciprocal" loving relationships—those, that is, between close adult friends or romantic partners that involve "normative expectations." Coates's basic line of reasoning for this conclusion (which he takes to be Strawson's own) may be summarized as follows:

(1) Relationships constituted by reciprocal love involve mutual normative expectations for respect and good will.
(2) A person's normative expectations for respect and good will from another are constituted by her susceptibility to reactive attitudes toward that other.

---

[10] Ibid.
[11] Pereboom, *Free Will*, 128.
[12] Ibid., 128–30.
[13] Ibid., 146.
[14] Pereboom, *Living without Free Will*, 188.
[15] Justin Coates, "In Defense of Love Internalism," *Journal of Ethics* 17 (2013): 250.

(3) To be an apt target of the reactive attitudes is to be a morally responsible agent.
(4) Thus, it is appropriate for two people to engage in a relationship constituted by reciprocal love only if they are morally responsible agents.[16]

Coates takes premise (1) to be fairly uncontroversial, so he says little in its defense; and premise (3)—the central plank of Strawson's theory of moral responsibility—is accepted by moral responsibility skeptics such as Pereboom as well. (Indeed, this is why Pereboom thinks it is irrational for a moral responsibility skeptic to nurture resentment.) Thus, Coates spends the bulk of his paper defending premise (2). In response to Pereboom's contention that one person might hold another to normative expectations through nonreactive attitudes such as sadness and disappointment, Coates notes:

> Sadness and disappointment can be fitting responses to hurtful events even if those events are not caused by agents. It seems to follow, then, that if we were to *exclusively* respond to another's ill will or disrespect with sadness or disappointment—the very same emotions with which we might fittingly respond to the destruction caused by a tornado or a hurricane—we would be failing to take seriously their agency. After all, in such a case we are emotionally exercised in a way that makes insufficiently fine-grained distinctions between the causal role an agent's will plays in the production of a hurtful event and the causal role that swirling winds and rain play in the production of a hurtful event.[17]

Failing to take a loved one's agency seriously, by responding to her behavior as one might to a tornado—this is a serious charge to lay against the moral responsibility skeptic. But is it true that the moral responsibility skeptic cannot take agency seriously? To answer this question, we need to ask whether, on Pereboom's view, the disappointment one might feel in response to another person's behavior is of the same sort that one might feel in response to some impersonal event. Let us compare, for example, a case in which I get upset because my computer crashes and I lose the paper I have been working on to a case in which I get upset because my partner recycles the handwritten notes I have prepared for a paper.

When students encounter free will or moral responsibility skepticism for the first time, they tend immediately to conclude that if it is true, we are all just like computers (or robots). But while it seems true that computers lack free will, they also lack other capacities that would seem essential to human agency, such as consciousness, rationality, and emotionality. Given the lack of such capacities, when a computer malfunctions and thwarts my purposes, I may feel disappointed and frustrated, but I do not take the computer's behavior to reveal anything about its thoughts, feelings, or intentions toward me. In contrast, when my partner recycles the notes I need for a paper, I may take this to reveal something about his will or character: perhaps a sort of negligence (he does not care enough about my work

---

[16] Ibid., 243.
[17] Ibid., 247.

to be attentive and careful when handling my papers), or a willful disrespect of my property (if he got fed up with my messy piles of paperwork crowding the kitchen table and chucked them).

So while Coates is obviously right, that the disappointment I experience in response to my computer crashing "provide[s] an insufficient basis for normative expectations," the disappointment I experience in response to my partner's behavior *can* constitute the normative expectation in question, since it may involve—or at least be accompanied by—a richer set of cognitive states.[18] Perhaps this is why Pereboom speaks of "moral" sadness, in contrast to the nonmoral sort, in his discussion of the nonreactive attitudes. The sadness I feel may be *moral*, since it may involve a judgment that the harmful thing my partner has done is *wrong* or reveals something vicious about his character. It should be noted that I might make this judgment *without* taking him to be ultimately morally responsible for his behavior or character. For, recall that basic-desert moral responsibility skepticism of the sort Pereboom defends does not rule out other non-basic-desert forms of moral responsibility. In sum, then, I may indeed take seriously a person's *agency*—the fact that he has reasons for acting, and a will that moves him to act according to those reasons—without taking this to secure his basic-desert moral responsibility.

These points, I think, constitute a sufficient response to Coates's claim that a susceptibility to nonreactive attitudes cannot ground a person's normative expectations toward another, since they are no different from the attitudes we experience in response to impersonal events. Because Coates thus seems to lack justification for premise (2) in the argument reconstructed above, I conclude that his Strawsonian thesis, that reciprocal loving relationships are only appropriate between lovers who are morally responsible in the basic-desert sense, and thus apt targets of reactive attitudes like resentment, also lacks justification.

Shabo, however, offers a slightly different argument for the connection between love and resentment. Shabo's version of Strawson's thesis differs from Coates's in that, whereas Coates is concerned with the *appropriateness* of reciprocal loving relationships in the absence of reactive attitudes, Shabo questions their practical *possibility*. According to Shabo's "Inseparability Thesis," "Our continued involvement in personal relationships precludes us from losing or relinquishing our ordinary susceptibility to reactive attitudes."[19] His argument for this thesis may be summarized as follows:

(1) Caring about how one's romantic partner or close friend treats or regards one "is partly constitutive of mature, reciprocal love."[20]
(2) "The sort of caring at issue is essentially *personal*" in the sense that one cares about one's friend's or partner's attitudes "in their own right, quite apart from what they portend" for one's own interests.[21]

---

[18] Ibid., 248.
[19] Shabo, "Where Love and Resentment Meet," 99.
[20] Ibid., 111.
[21] Ibid., 112.

(3) "Someone who cares in this essentially personal way . . . will be prone to hurt feelings in response to certain kinds of treatment,"[22] feelings that one "cannot reliably bring [oneself] to forgo or disavow."[23]
(4) Someone who experiences such hurt feelings will be susceptible to resentment, which one likewise cannot reliably bring oneself to forgo or disavow.[24]
(5) Therefore, one's involvement in a mature, reciprocal loving relationship precludes one from forgoing or disavowing a susceptibility to resentment.

Shabo takes premises (1) and (2) to be conceptual truths, and (3) and (4) to be psychological. He explains the connection between personal caring, proneness to hurt feelings, and susceptibility to resentment in premises (3) and (4) in terms of the emotional vulnerability that such caring involves:

> Given this emotional vulnerability, individuals will normally have limited control over whether their susceptibility to take hurtful behavior from the other personally is manifested in hurt feelings. This is especially evident when the hurt behavior is damaging to one's self-esteem. And, the thought continues, hurt feelings often beget resentment; for, like resentment, they are a reaction to the sense that one has been treated rudely, inconsiderately, disrespectfully, callously, and so on. Finally, . . . in practice, we often can't forgo or disavow resentment without forgoing the feelings that prompt it.[25]

Shabo admits that there might be exceptions to these psychological claims. He writes, "Perhaps some individuals *are* exceptionally self-sufficient [or] emotionally secure . . . and thus rarely if ever take it personally when a close friend or romantic partner insults or wrongs them . . . And some individuals who have an ordinary susceptibility to hurt feelings may lack an ordinary susceptibility to resentment." Not wanting to base his argument on "a denial of these possibilities," Shabo says his argument concerns "a community whose members overwhelmingly *do* possess ordinary susceptibilities to resentment and hurt feelings."[26] He thus ends up qualifying his Inseparability Thesis as follows: "Among individuals who have an ordinary susceptibility to resentment, few (if any) of us could strive to shed this susceptibility without undertaking a broader emotional divestment than is compatible with involvement in personal relationships."[27]

One way to read this "qualification" is as a watering down of the original thesis so that any supposed counterexample—any individual who has succeeded in overcoming a susceptibility to resentment—might be considered to have had a *non-ordinary* susceptibility to begin with. The problem with such a thesis, of course, is that it would be unfalsifiable. Thus, a more charitable interpretation of Shabo's qualification would read it as excluding, not individuals who have *overcome* their natural susceptibility to

---

[22] Ibid., 113.
[23] Ibid., 114.
[24] Ibid.
[25] Ibid.
[26] Ibid., 116.
[27] Ibid., 117.

resentment, but those who were not *born* with an "ordinary" susceptibility, or who did not manifest such a susceptibility in childhood. I will assume this latter interpretation, which implies that the Qualified Inseparability Thesis may be falsified by (some or many) examples of adults who seem to have developed an ordinary susceptibility to resentment, but then, through some means or other, succeed in overcoming it. Of course, there are other versions of the thesis we might consider, and important questions about such versions. For instance, if it is true that most people are born with a tendency to develop a certain susceptibility to resentment, might it be possible to socialize them out of it in childhood? Shabo considers whether "an intergenerational effort ... to curb the reactive attitudes" might have some success, but notes that such a proposal would still need to address how we could help children overcome their natural tendencies—such as "for hurt feelings to reinforce resentment."[28] While it might be easier to see how children could overcome an ordinary susceptibility to resentment—and so, how an intergenerational effort to rid society of this reactive attitude might have more success than one focused on changing the ingrained cognitive and emotional responses of adults—I will focus solely on the question of adults in this chapter.

In response to Shabo's claim that the emotional vulnerability essential to loving relationships may make inevitable a resentful response to certain behavior, Pereboom points to a kind of loving relationship in which such reactive attitudes tend to be replaced with nonreactive ones, namely, that between parents and teenagers. He writes:

> Adolescents often go through a phase in which they have attitudes of disregard and disrespect for parents, expression of which often occasions hurt feelings. Yet sometimes such expressions of disregard and disrespect do not occasion the parents' resentment, but rather disappointment and sadness. Although these emotions do not qualify as reactive attitudes, they are nevertheless manifestations of vulnerability on the part of the parent. They are also personal, since the teenager's attitudes toward his parents matter to them in their own right, apart from the consequences of these attitudes for their interests.[29]

An objection one might raise to this response is, as Pereboom himself puts it, "that this absence of resentment is an artifact of the specific nature of the parental relationship, and that it will not carry over on a significant scale to close relationships among adults on an equal footing."[30] Indeed, one might think that several features of the parental relationship disqualify it from consideration. First, and most importantly, the relationship is *nonreciprocal*; the parents love their teenager in spite of the teenager's evident lack of love for his parents. Second, and relatedly, the parents continue to love their teenager in part because the teenager is *not a mature adult*, but rather someone whose disregard or disrespect may be taken as a sign that he has not fully developed,

---

[28] Ibid., 122.
[29] Derk Pereboom, "Love and Freedom," in *The Oxford Handbook of Philosophy of Love*, ed. Christopher Grau and Aaron Smuts (Oxford: Oxford University Press), DOI: 10.1093/oxfordhb/9780199395729.013.34 (accessed June 8, 2018).
[30] Ibid.

intellectually and emotionally, to a stage at which he might appreciate what his parents do for him and what he owes them in return.

In response to this objection, Pereboom notes, first, that some relationships of reciprocal love between mature adults also feature disappointment in the place of resentment. He writes:

> A change to this sort of emotional profile may be an option for those of us who currently have the resentful reactions. The past several centuries have witnessed very significant changes in attitudes toward criminals, those who suffer from mental illnesses, and children, and thus it cannot plausibly be argued that significant emotional change over time is not possible for us. Second, the feature that stands to rule out the legitimacy of the reactive attitudes in parental relationships is the parents' role in the moral formation of not fully morally mature children. However, adults also stand in need of moral formation.[31]

Thus Pereboom suggests that, while teenagers may present something of a special case in the respects I have outlined, "mature" adults share with them a need for further moral formation; and this need, when we take note of it, might serve to soften our responses to each other's bad behavior, just as it does in parents of a teenager. In what follows, I develop this idea within the framework of a Christian conception of "mature" adult human beings and relationships. The focus of my discussion will be on Shabo's premise (4), which makes the claim that resentment cannot be untethered from the hurt feelings caused by "personal caring" in the sense he has in mind. Given the similarities between their arguments, my discussion of Shabo's reasoning will also further call into question premise (2) of Coates's argument, discussed above.

Many passages in the New Testament counsel the overcoming of anger and related negative reactive attitudes of the sort at issue between Pereboom, Coates, and Shabo. Jesus warns the crowds in Matthew's Gospel, "if you are angry with a brother or sister, you will be liable to judgment" (5:22); the author of Ephesians urges his readers, "Put away from you all bitterness and wrath and anger . . . and be kind to one another, tender-hearted, forgiving one another, as God in Christ has forgiven you" (4:31); and in one of the most oft-quoted passages from Scripture, the Apostle Paul writes to the church at Corinth, "Love is patient; love is kind; love is not envious or boastful or arrogant or rude. It does not insist on its own way; it is not irritable or resentful. . . . It bears all things . . . endures all things" (1 Cor. 13:4-7).

Although such passages suggest that loving relationships are both possible and desirable without anger or resentment, many questions might be asked about the applicability of these passages to the present discussion. First, are they really meant to characterize the intimate love between romantic partners and close friends, rather than the more disinterested love one might possess for all people—or even the benevolent love God has for humankind? Second, if applicable to reciprocal human relationships of the sort of interest here, is the New Testament picture of love supposed to be an attainable ideal for human beings in this life, or only a vision of perfected relationships in the age to

---

[31] Ibid.

come? Third, are we to interpret these passages as advocating that we strive to *eliminate* anger, resentment, and so on, or rather that we simply manage them in certain ways (e.g., Eph. 4:26: "Be angry but do not sin")? Finally, do these passages assume that we should refrain from anger—if indeed we should—because those with whom we are in relationship are not apt targets of the reactive attitudes, or for some other reason?

I think there is room for much (reasonable) disagreement in answer to such questions, but on one interpretation that I find especially plausible, these passages are quite applicable to the discussion at hand. On this interpretation, though some passages, such as 1 Corinthians 13, may primarily characterize divine love for human beings, such love is set as a model for reciprocal relationships between human beings. (I take this to be why 1 Corinthians 13 is read in marriage ceremonies—because it offers a model for love that applies to married people.) I also think that, although the passages just cited may be taken to offer a vision of perfected love not fully realizable by humans this side of the grave, Jesus and the biblical authors would not have done so much advising and exhorting of people to let go of their anger if this were not an ideal we were at least meant to *strive for* here and now.

In answering the other questions—whether we are to strive to *eliminate* negative reactive attitudes like resentment, or just manage them, and how, and why—it will be instructive to consider a "model" of Christian forgiveness described by Marilyn McCord Adams, since on her model, the process of forgiveness includes the choosing to let go of, and the praying to overcome, negative reactive attitudes. This model, I will argue, gives a realistic picture of how one might strive to eliminate resentment through a kind of prayerful meditation on God's perspective. I will also contend that this model is compatible with the assumption that the one forgiven is not (at least known to be) ultimately morally responsible for the wrongs he has done—but that this assumption need not motivate the forgiver to adopt what Strawson called an "objective attitude" toward the wrongdoer.

Adams describes "forgiveness from the heart" (as opposed to "performative forgiveness") as "a *process* of letting go of one's own point of view ... and entering into God's point of view."[32] The process has several steps, the first of which involves the victim of an "offense"—which signifies some falsehood about her worth—sharing with God how things look from her perspective: "All of the pain and humiliation, all of the retributive and vindictive feelings and attitudes, will be put on the table between the victim and God in prayer."[33] Then, the victim will pray to see how things look to God. Adams writes,[34]

> Usually, the victim's attempt to enter God's point of view will involve shifting from a one-dimensional picture of the offender qua offender to a more complex characterization, which recognizes him (i) as a person with problems, (ii) in response to which he has deployed inefficient adaptational strategies, (iii) resulting in behavior harmful to himself and others. The victim will also acquire deeper insight into how

---

[32] Marilyn McCord Adams, "Forgiveness: A Christian Model," *Faith and Philosophy* 8, no. 3 (1991): 294; emphasis in original.
[33] Ibid., 295.
[34] For ease or reading, I have taken the liberty of changing Adam's gender-neutral pronouns ("him/her," "s/he," etc.), so that the victim is female and the offender is male.

> God sees herself, sometimes (but not always) as a person with similar problems and comparable faults. Moreover, the victim's prayerful exchange with God will bring her to a deeper realization of *God's love* for her and the overwhelming worth conferred on her thereby.... Such appropriations of Divine power and love to herself free the victim to appreciate and enter into God's love for the offender and the overwhelming worth thus conferred on him, and God's power to heal, redeem, and educate him.[35]

Since, Adams insists, "God is not interested in retribution, but in reform," the process of taking on God's perspective will also lead the victim to choose to let go of, and pray to overcome, "various retributive feelings and attitudes."[36]

The process outlined by Adams is, no doubt, a difficult one, given that we are often unaware of the assumptions about another person's behavior under which we are operating, or the depth of feelings we have about what we assume—and given that we have natural instincts to blame and punish offenders, as well as self-serving biases that blind us to our own faults. The kind of self-disclosure and change of perspective that Adams proposes may require the help of others, including spiritual directors and counselors, as well as a good bit of grace. But I believe the process is a feasible one, as evidenced by the fact that many Christians are able to moderate their negative reactive attitudes through such practices of prayer and meditation, as well as "performative" acts of forgiveness and reconciliation. Pereboom makes a similar observation, noting that, "for many centuries now human beings have developed communities in which training and teaching methods are employed to diminish resentment and indignation. . . . Christian monastic societies, and Radical Reformation groups such as the Amish come to mind."[37] While Adams's model of forgiveness presupposes that one will initially experience reactive attitudes that one must then work to diminish, such Christian communities as Pereboom cites are a testament to the fact that, if this process becomes a regular habit, it can even serve to dampen the resentment one initially experiences. Though not cases involving "reciprocal relationships," the immediate forgiveness which the Amish of Lancaster County showed after the 2006 school shooting that left ten of their children dead—or which survivors of the 2015 Charleston AME church shooting bestowed upon the gunman who killed nine of their own—suggests that members of these communities, under the influence of their religious teachings and practices, were able to change their cognitive and emotional responses to wrongdoing in the ways outlined by Adams.

So far I have contended that it is psychologically possible for human beings with an "ordinary" susceptibility to resentment to overcome this reactive attitude by developing a habit of "forgiveness from the heart," as described by Adams. I would also now note that, though she does not go as far as Pereboom to deny that anyone is ever morally responsible in the "basic-desert" sense for what they do, Adams's model of forgiveness is amenable to this view. While she identifies what a person undertakes to forgive as an "offense," Adams expressively denies that one can forgive

---

[35] Ibid., 296.
[36] Ibid., 297.
[37] Pereboom, *Free Will*, 149.

only "responsible wrongdoing," in the sense of a fully intentional harm or insult. She writes, "My Christian model recognizes that some of the deepest wounds are inflicted on their victims by agents who in important senses 'know not what they do.'"[38] A significant component of the process of forgiveness involves what Adams calls "role release"—relinquishing the role of judge, jury, and executioner to God. This release is grounded in the recognition that "no human being is *competent* to evaluate another human person" since "only God can see deeply enough into the human heart."[39] This suggests a kind of "local skepticism" about moral responsibility, in the sense that we cannot know, for any *particular* action that a person takes, whether or to what extent she is responsible for the action—though it does not go as far as the "global" skepticism defended by Pereboom. In any case, as already noted, Adams maintains that "God is not interested in retribution, but in reform," suggesting that even if people sometimes are fully responsible in the "basic-desert" sense for their wrongdoing, God is working with the "answerability" notion of moral responsibility endorsed by Pereboom, which aims at reformation and reconciliation.

This brings us to a question of concern to Strawson in "Freedom and Resentment": if one renounces one's resentment toward another on the grounds that the other is not ultimately morally responsible, does it follow that one must take an "objective attitude" toward the other? Strawson characterizes the objective attitude as follows:

> To adopt the objective attitude to another human being [is] to see him, perhaps, as an object of social policy; as a subject for what, in a wide range of cases, might be called treatment; as something certainly to be taken account, perhaps precautionary account, of; to be managed or handled or cured or trained.... The objective attitude may be emotionally toned in many ways, but not in all ways: it may include repulsion or fear, it may include pity or even love, though not all kinds of love. But it cannot include the range of reactive feelings and attitudes which belong to involvement or participation with others in inter-personal relationships; it cannot include resentment, gratitude, forgiveness, anger, or the sorts of love which two adults can sometimes be said to feel, reciprocally, for each other. If your attitude towards someone is wholly objective, then though you may fight with him, you cannot quarrel with him, and though you may talk to him, even negotiate with him, you cannot reason with him.[40]

Given Strawson's stark characterization of the objective attitude, it seems obvious to me that one need not take this attitude toward another person simply because one thinks the other is not ultimately morally responsible for what she does. Strawson has presented us with a false dilemma: either view an individual as ultimately morally responsible, or view her as not a *person* at all, but rather an *object*. He seems to have been led to think in these dilemmic terms by the kinds of individuals he considers who we would deem not responsible for their behavior: a young child, a "hopeless

---

[38] Adams, "Forgiveness," 293.
[39] Ibid., 295; emphasis in original.
[40] Strawson, "Freedom and Resentment," 79.

schizophrenic," someone whose behavior is "purely compulsive," or someone whose mind has been "systematically perverted."[41] It is revealing that he says, at the end of his discussion of the objective attitude, that we cannot reason with an individual who is the target of such an attitude. One consideration that may lead us to deem both a young child and a schizophrenic adult as not responsible for their behavior is that they lack some basic ability to recognize and respond to reasons. But, as mentioned already in discussing the difference(s) between human beings and computers, the ability to recognize and respond to reasons is not one that basic-desert moral responsibility skeptics need deny of "normal" adult human beings. Instead, they might base their skepticism, as Pereboom does, on the belief that human character and behavior is universally shaped by forces—genetic, psychological, social, or whatever—over which we have little awareness or control. And the theological conviction that "all . . . are under the power of sin" (Rom. 3:9) may likewise push those who find the inevitability of wrongdoing incompatible with basic-desert moral responsibility toward such skepticism. But neither of *these* possibilities—the universal determinism of human behavior, or the general "fallenness" of humankind—precludes the kind of cognitive and emotional capacities that make us eligible for treatment as persons and not objects, and capable of the kind of reasoning (and quarrelling!) which form an important part of (flawed) interpersonal relationships.

In this chapter I have called into question premises of Coates's and Shabo's arguments for the conclusion that two people cannot (appropriately) have a reciprocal loving relationship without being morally responsible (in the basic-desert sense) and thus, without being susceptible to resentment in response to perceived offense. The premises against which I argued were that one cannot have "normative expectations" for respect and goodwill from another, or "personally care" about another's attitudes toward oneself, without being susceptible to resentment. Following Pereboom's suggestion, I proposed that we think of "mature" adults in such reciprocal relationships as similar to older children or adolescents in that they are still in need of moral formation. I drew a connection between this suggestion and a Christian view of human beings offered by Adams—as "people with problems" who have developed "inefficient adaptational strategies" that may lead to wrongful action. I further argued that Adams's "model of Christian forgiveness," which counsels us to see those who wrong us—and to see ourselves—from God's perspective, and to relinquish the roles of "jury, judge, and executioner" to God, can empower us to forgo resentment while remaining in reciprocal relationships with those who might wrong us.

---

[41] Ibid., 78.

12

Is There a Christian Duty to Love?

Kent Dunnington

1 Introduction

In this chapter, I contend that there is no Christian duty to love one's neighbor as oneself. At first glance, the thesis appears obviously false. In each of the Synoptic Gospels, Jesus enjoins his disciples to observe the two greatest commandments: love God with all your heart, soul, mind, and strength; and love your neighbor as yourself (Mk 12:30-31). But I will argue that whatever Jesus was doing in so enjoining his disciples, he was *not* obligating them to love their neighbor as themselves; he was *not* saying that if they failed to love their neighbor as themselves they would be violating their moral duty.[1]

It is not just standard interpretations of the love commands that seem to contradict my thesis, however. Much of the tradition of Christian ethics appears to disagree with my claim as well. Elizabeth Anscombe[2] famously identified the concept of duty as among Christianity's *contributions* to the history of ethics, and many proponents of Christian love ethics treat "agapism" as a duty-based moral theory differing from other duty-based theories only in its rule of application.[3] Exceptions to the trend include a trio of Lutheran theologians: Dietrich Bonhoeffer,[4] Anders Nygren,[5] and Robert Jenson.[6] For each, although in different ways, the law-gospel antithesis prompts the rejection of duty as a central category for Christian ethics. I am sympathetic with their claim, but I want to see about another way of grounding it. I want to examine whether duty is displaced by the New Testament revelation of divine love as the regulative ideal for human love.

---

[1] I will treat "duty" and "obligation" synonymously, and unless otherwise indicated I always mean *moral* duty/obligation.
[2] Elizabeth Anscombe, "Modern Moral Philosophy," *Philosophy* 33, no. 124 (1958): 1–19.
[3] See Søren Kierkegaard, *Works of Love*, ed. Howard V. Hong and Edna H. Hong, repr. (Princeton, NJ: Princeton University Press, 1995); Paul Ramsey, *Basic Christian Ethics* (New York: Charles Scribner's Sons, 1950); Gene Outka, *Agape: An Ethical Analysis* (New Haven, CT: Yale University Press, 1972); and Nicholas Wolterstorff, *Justice in Love* (Grand Rapids, MI: Eerdmans, 2015).
[4] Dietrich Bonhoeffer, *Ethics*, repr. (Minneapolis, MN: Fortress Press, 2005), 299–338.
[5] Anders Nygren, *Agape and Eros: A Study of the Christian Idea of Love*, Part 2, Vol. 1, trans. Philip S. Watson (London: SPCK, 1938), 31–37.
[6] Robert Jenson, *Story and Promise: A Brief Theology of the Gospel About Jesus* (Philadelphia, PA: Fortress Press, 1973), 81–102.

In Sections 2 to 3 of the chapter, I defend and develop the claim that the New Testament reveals divine love as the regulative ideal for Christian "ethics." Then, in Sections 4 to 7, I argue for four implications of the claim, moving from the weakest to the strongest implication. In Section 4, I argue, against Søren Kierkegaard, that duty is not the only legitimate motive of Christian love; in Section 5, against Nicholas Wolterstorff, that duty is not an equally legitimate motive of Christian love; and in Section 6, that duty is at best a possible motive of Christian love. These conclusions seem to follow from the revelation of divine love as a regulative ideal. In Section 7, I argue that there is no Christian duty to love. This bolder claim is open to strong objections, so in Section 8 I consider several of those objections.

2 Divine love as the regulative ideal for human love

The second love command (which I will henceforth refer to simply as "the love command") enjoins disciples to love their neighbors, but how should we love? How do we know what motives and actions are appropriate to the love commanded? The command appears to contain a clue: love your neighbor *as yourself*. But the "as" is ambiguous. Which of the following is Jesus commanding?

(A) Love your neighbor *as much as* you love yourself.
(B) Love your neighbor *in the same way as* you love yourself.

Surely Jesus means (A). Most of us love ourselves *very much*, but we do not love ourselves *very well*. The alcoholic may love himself very much, but he certainly does not love himself very well. Far from condemning self-love, Jesus assumes it as the ideal *intensity* for the love we are to show for others. But he does not assume it as the ideal *way* in which we are to love others. So, again, how do we know what motives and actions are appropriate to the love commanded? What ideal should regulate how the disciples attempt to love as Jesus commands?

God's love, especially as displayed in the person of Jesus, is the ideal. Consider Jesus's call to love one's enemies. Here the disciples are given an example to imitate, namely, the "Father in heaven," who "makes his sun rise on the evil and on the good, and sends rain on the righteous and on the unrighteous" (Mt. 5:45). Notice the different use of "as" that sums up the call to enemy-love in Matthew and Luke.

Be perfect, therefore, *as* your heavenly Father is perfect (Mt. 5:48).
Be merciful, just *as* your Father is merciful (Lk. 6:36).

Clearly, each is an instance of "as" in the sense of (B) above. Be perfect *in the same way as* your heavenly Father is perfect. Be merciful *in the same way as* your Father is merciful. Similarly, Jesus sets up his own love for the disciples as the ideal *way* in which disciples are to love. "Just *as* I have loved you, you also should love one another" (Jn 13:34). Love one another *in the same way as* I have loved you, Jesus says. To sum up: if Jesus's followers want to know *how much* they should love others, they should look to the intensity of their own self-love. But if Jesus's followers want to know *how* they should love others, they should look to the love of God, especially as displayed by Jesus.

Taking the love of God as its ideal standard for the way in which Christians are to love, Christian love ethics must examine what is characteristic of God's loving actions *and* what is characteristic of God's motives to love. It seems to me that prominent agapists have done better at the former than at the latter. They mostly agree that the actions proper to Christian love are those that promote as an end in itself the good of anyone who is a neighbor. They disagree widely, however, about the motives proper to Christian love. Kierkegaard says duty is the only proper motive of Christian love. Wolterstorff says duty is one among several proper motives of Christian love, all equally legitimate. And Nygren says Christian love should be utterly spontaneous and unmotivated. My contention is that their disagreement is partly due to a failure to privilege divine motivation as the regulative ideal for the motives proper to Christian love.

Motives for love sometimes differ according to the object of love. For instance, the motives proper to parental love differ from the motives proper to romantic love. The desire to procreate might be a proper motive of romantic love, but clearly not of parental love. So if divine motivation is supposed to be the regulative ideal for the disciple's motives to love, a question arises about the objects of God's love. Two possibilities occur: first, God's love for creatures, especially human persons; second, God's love for God. Scripture is replete with references to the first object of divine love, the created order. The second can be inferred from Jn 17:20-23 and most obviously from 1 Jn 4:16: "God is love." This passage led Augustine and others in the West to posit love as "some kind of key to the inner reality of God," as Andrew Louth contends.[7] But Louth shows that this idea was not shared by the Greek Fathers. For the Greeks, God loves us but love is not characteristic of the divine life itself. I am drawn to the Augustinian claim (see *de Trin.* 8.8.12) but it does not matter for the argument of this chapter. For, whether focusing on God's love for us or the love between the members of the Trinity, duty is not among the motives of divine love.

3 Duty-free divine love

In *Love and Justice*, Wolterstorff lists among the possible motives of neighbor-love attachment, attraction, compassion, solidarity, and duty.[8] His thesis is that it does not matter which of these motivates us, as long as we love our neighbor. I will examine his thesis in Section 6, but first I want to observe that the final motive listed, duty, is not among the motives of divine love. The first four motives Wolterstorff lists plausibly characterize the love of Jesus at some point in Scripture. Jesus has a special love for the twelve over against the other disciples that follow him, and this we might think of as a love motivated by attachment. He has a special love for John among the disciples, and this we might think of as a love motivated by attraction. He has a special love for

---

[7] Andrew Louth, "Love and the Trinity," *Augustinian Studies* 33, no. 1 (2002): 14.
[8] Wolterstorff, *Justice in Love*, 110.

the many that he heals, and we are often told this love is motivated by compassion. He has a special love for the people of Israel, as depicted in his interaction with the Syrophoenician woman, and this we might think of as a love motivated by solidarity. Except in the case of compassion, I am speculating about Jesus's motives, but they make some sense. What does not make sense, I am inclined to think, is assigning the motive of duty to any of Jesus's displays of love in the gospel.

This may seem too quick. Assigning motives is notoriously tricky. Consider what is involved in being motivated by duty to perform an act. Kant, for whom duty was the only morally praiseworthy motive, distinguished between acting in accordance with duty and acting from duty. The shop owner who wants to maximize profit will treat his customers honestly and thereby fulfill his duties to them, but he may do it from selfish motives (profit). As such, he acts *according to* duty but not *from* duty. How would we know he acts *from* duty? The obvious case is one in which the shop owner thinks, "I would rather not do x, it will cost me, but I must; it's my duty." So the motive of duty is apparent when one acts against one's desire in conformity with duty; the duty-motive acts as a constraint or imposition on one's natural and recalcitrant inclinations.[9]

Does Jesus ever act against his own desires, under constraint of duty? The Garden of Gethsemane jumps to mind, where Jesus clearly acts against his desires (his first-order desires, at least), but here it appears that what motivates Jesus is his loving personal relationship with the Father: "Not my will but yours" (Mt. 26:39). Jesus acts in opposition to his first-order desires for survival because he seeks alignment between his will and that of someone he loves. The only way to interpret this action as motivated by duty is to presuppose that Jesus had a duty to align his will with the Father's, but this seems question-begging. What is clear is that Jesus suppressed some of his desires in deference to the desire to align his will with the Father, a motive that is characteristic of love. This shows that there are things other than duty that constrain us, like love. So love can appropriately name both an action (beneficent care for a beloved) and a motive (the desire to be in alignment with a beloved's will): one may love from love, and one may love from duty. In the Garden, Jesus makes clear his intention to obey God from love. We still have no evidence that Jesus acted from duty, let alone loved from duty.

Even if there is no evidence that Jesus acted from duty, this does not establish that Jesus never acted from duty, because people can act from more than one motive, and one motive can mask another. For instance, Gary may bring his girlfriend hot chicken noodle soup when she is ill because he is attracted to her and also because he feels compassion for her. And one of these motives may mask the other. Whether both motives are present is determined through counterfactual assessment: Would Gary bring her soup even if he were no longer attracted to her? Would Gary bring her soup even if he felt no compassion for her? Maybe Jesus was loving from duty all along, with

---

[9] To be more precise, I could distinguish between first- and second-order desires. On most accounts of human action, a desire is essential to act. So, you describe the shopkeeper as experiencing a contradiction between his first-order desire to cheat his customers and his second-order desire to comport with the moral law. If you think this is the right way to understand motivation, you can see how I could precisify my statements in what follows.

that motive being masked by others. All we can say at this point is that Jesus, who is our exemplar in love, never *appears* to act from duty.

It is worth asking why the gospel-writers attributed to Jesus the motives they did. More than any other motive, they attributed compassion to Jesus. Why? Was it because Jesus announced he was feeling compassion? Did they interview Jesus about his motives? Likely not. I suspect three reasons the gospel-writers depict Jesus's motives in the way they do. First, Jesus often displayed emotions demonstrating that his love was motivated by something other than duty. His tears at the death of Lazarus are an example of this. Second, when Jesus described what neighbor-love looked like, he described the motive at work. I am thinking here in particular of the parable of the Good Samaritan, in which we are told that the Samaritan came to the aid of the wounded man *because* "he felt compassion for him" (Lk. 10:33). Third, Jesus affirms the Hebrew call to love God with one's whole heart, which appears to require more than a dutiful determination of the will.[10] The gospel-writers never see duty as a motivation behind Jesus's love because they inferred from his emotional life and from his oral depiction of love of God and love of neighbor that other motives were key. Still, that is not enough to rule out the possibility that duty was lurking in the background. Can we rule that out?

Insofar as Jesus is God and the perfect human being, it is difficult to see how Jesus could have loved from duty. Consider why the motive of duty is important, why we need it as a fallback. The motive of duty is important because of the opposition between what is best for us to do and what we most want to do. When faced with such opposition, duty can motivate us to do what is best for us to do. But duty is not the only such motive that can overcome an opposition between what is best and what we want. I mentioned earlier that love is such a motive. The last thing Gary wants to do right now is bring his girlfriend some soup, but he adores her, so he brings her soup. Duty does not come into the picture. So duty is important especially when we lack any other motive that could close the gap between what is best and what we want.

Think, then, about times when duty is the only fallback. It is either because (a) we cannot see how the right thing for us to do is really in our best interest all things considered or (b) we know it is not. Can a Christian think (b) is *ever* the case? Can a Christian say, "It is not *ultimately* for my good that I do the right thing, but nevertheless I must"? Simone Weil seemed ready to countenance (b). She wrote, "I am always ready to obey any order [from God], whatever it may be. I should joyfully obey the order to go to the very center of hell and to remain there eternally."[11] This strikes me as perverse. Weil is out-Kanting Kant. Even Kant had to bring in a rewarding God to make the sacrifice demanded by duty tolerable. But then it is not really an ultimate sacrifice, is it? So I think (b) is off the table from a Christian perspective, which is why any Christian morality can be accommodated to a form of eudaimonism.

---

[10] See Robert C. Roberts, "Situationism and the New Testament Psychology of the Heart," in *The Bible and the Academy*, ed. David Lyle Jeffrey (London: Paternoster Press, 2008), for a careful treatment of the psychology of the biblical notion of the heart.

[11] Simone Weil, *Waiting for God*, trans. Emma Craufurd, repr. (New York: HarperCollins Publishers, 2009), 31.

And although (a) is on the table for all of us, it is certainly off the table for an omniscient God. If you think Jesus was omniscient, and you do not think doing the right thing can contravene our best interest all things considered, then Jesus could never require the motive of duty because there would never be a gap between what was right and what he wanted all things considered. But even if you do not think Jesus was omniscient, or if you think when he acted in his human nature he was not acting from omniscience, it is difficult to see how he would need duty as a fallback. After all, his is a perfectly loving relationship with the Father. Even if there were a gap between what Jesus thought obedience required and what he wanted all things considered, his perfect love of the Father would be sufficient to close the gap. All told, then, it is hard to imagine duty as a motive of divine love.

4 Is duty the only legitimate motive of Christian love?

In *Works of Love*, Kierkegaard argues that duty is the only legitimate motive of Christian love. He offers two arguments, which I will compress here.

First argument. Christian love is perfect love. Perfect love is free from fear. Love motivated by inclination is always susceptible to change. Love susceptible to change cannot be free from fear of love's loss. Therefore Christian love cannot be based on inclination. Only love motivated by duty escapes the impermanence of inclination.[12]

Second argument. Inclinational love, for example erotic love and friendship, is triggered by personal preference—one prefers some quality of the beloved. The only explanation for personal preference has to do with how the beloved somehow affects the self—either by satisfying or mirroring the self.[13] Thus all inclinational love is self-referential, and self-referential love is selfish. But Christian love is not selfish. Hence Christian love cannot be motivated by inclinations. It must be motivated by duty if it is to express Christian self-denial.[14]

Both arguments are problematic, but what strikes me is that Kierkegaard never raises the question of divine motivation. He starts at the other end, so to speak, attending to the imperfections that afflict our inclinational motives to love and thereby ruling them out as proper motives of perfect Christian love. But this gets things backward. Should we not begin with divine love? Divine love is perfect without being motivated by duty. Divine love is the regulative ideal of Christian love. There are other available motives of Christian love that are featured in displays of divine love as well as displays of human love, for instance compassion. Therefore duty cannot be the only legitimate motive of Christian love.

If we start with the motives of divine love, we can see what goes wrong in Kierkegaard's two main arguments. Kierkegaard is right that impermanence is a bad-making property of love. Ideally Christian love will be unwavering. But being motivated by duty is *also* a bad-making property of love. Suppose the husband loved

---

[12] Kierkegaard, *Works of Love*, 29–43.
[13] As the ancients noted, in *eros* and *philia* we have to do with the "other self," the "other I."
[14] Kierkegaard, *Works of Love*, 44–60.

the wife only from duty, the parent loved the child only from duty, God loved the world only from duty—this feature makes each love less valuable than it could be. If the lover tells his beloved he will love her forever, and she responds, "You can't guarantee that," is the situation made better if he responds, "then I will make it my duty"? Such a response misses the point of the beloved's anxiety, which is precisely the fear that her lover may cease to be inclined toward her. So, being duty-motivated is no solution to the imperfection of Christian love, although it may be a solution to its impermanence.

Consider the second argument from the perspective of divine love. It is difficult, as I have argued, to understand how divine love for the created order could be duty-motivated.[15] It is not difficult, however, to understand how God's love for the created order is in some way self-referential. Aquinas holds, for example, that all created being exists by participation in the being of God (*ST* 1.44.1), that God created many different creatures "because His goodness could not be adequately represented by one creature alone" (*ST* 1.47.1), and that "in all creatures there is found the trace of the Trinity" (*ST* 1.45.7).[16] It is hard to see, then, how God's love of the created order is not in some sense self-referential. But why should this make it *selfish*? God communicates his being and goodness to creatures and loves these things in them, but this is not selfish. So, starting from the perspective of divine love, Kierkegaard's attempt to link self-referential love with selfish love is confused. Christians may have a duty to love, but contra Kierkegaard, they do not have a duty to love from duty.

5 Is duty an equally legitimate motive of Christian love?

Wolterstorff rejects Kierkegaard's privileging of duty as the only legitimate motive of Christian love. In *Justice in Love*, he puts forth a more modest thesis:

> It makes no difference whether we care about the other because we are attached to her, because we are attracted to her, because we feel solidarity with her, because we are moved by compassion, or because we see it as our duty to care about her. Just see to it that you not care only about yourself but also about your neighbor.[17]

In other words, although not the only legitimate motive of Christian love, duty is an equally legitimate motive, alongside the other "inclinational" motives of attachment, attraction, solidarity, and compassion.

This is wrong, too, for reasons that have already been stated. Duty never appears to motivate Jesus, and duty is never recommended by Jesus as the proper motive of love. Other inclinational motives—especially compassion—are both ascribed to Jesus

---

[15] One way to rule out divine duty-motivation is to rule out the possibility of divine duty. But I am impressed by the arguments of Wolterstorff, *Justice: Rights and Wrongs*, 281–84, who thinks sense can be made of the notion of a divine duty. It is a further step, however, to argue that in addition to having duties God could act from duty.

[16] Thomas Aquinas, *Summa Theologica* (1274), trans. Fathers of the English Dominican Province (New York: Benziger Brothers, 1948).

[17] Wolterstorff, *Justice in Love*, 118.

and recommended by Jesus. And divine love, exemplified most clearly by Jesus's love, is the regulative ideal for Christian love. Therefore, duty, even if a possible motive of Christian love, is not on a par with other inclinational motives of Christian love such as compassion.

Other inclinational motives are better from the perspective of both the agent and the patient of Christian love. Supposing duty is a possible motive of love (a supposition we will consider shortly), it is better to be loved from duty than loved not at all; but it is better still to be loved from an inclinational motive (like compassion) than from duty. Why? Two reasons, I think. First, it is better to receive a good from someone who wants to give it than from someone who has to give it. Second, to be the object of an inclinational motive is to be *seen* and *experienced* as significant and worthwhile, not merely rationally acknowledged to be so. It is the difference between receiving the following two compliments: "My God, you're beautiful!" *versus* "You don't strike me as beautiful, but I accept on the basis of principle that you are."

And inclinational motives are better from the perspective of the agent of Christian love because our neighbors really are worthy of our love. If we saw them truly, as God sees them, we would be mightily inclined to care for their good. Thus to love from inclinational motives is to more fully embody our destiny as perfected lovers of God and one another.

6 Is duty a legitimate motive of Christian love at all?

All agapists agree that

(1) Jesus says his disciples should love their neighbors as themselves;
(2) ought implies can;[18] and
(3) natural inclinations to Christian love are weak and limited in scope.

But they disagree about whether or not

(4) duty is a psychologically coherent motive of love.

Those who accept premise 4 reason thusly: "If I am able to love my neighbor as myself, but I am not able to do so through insufficient (because weak and limited) natural inclinations, there must be another available motive. Duty is such a motive. Therefore, one may exercise Christian love from duty." Kierkegaard and Wolterstorff both fall in this camp. Those who reject premise 4, like Nygren, have to explain how Christian love is possible when inclinations to Christian love fail *and* when duty is not a psychologically coherent motive of genuine love. Nygren does so by positing an infusion of the love of God into every believer, which makes believers capable of

---

[18] Some agapists will qualify this claim to read: ought implies at least indirect ability; that is, although we may not always be able to do what we ought to do, we are always able to act so as to eventually position ourselves to do what we ought to do.

Christian love, neither from inclination nor from duty, but rather from the love of God shed abroad in their hearts. It is important to Nygren's view that the love that is enacted as a consequence of this infusion is utterly spontaneous, never responsive to the perceived good in another (or else it would be inclinational).

I do not deny that Christian love is assisted by the Holy Spirit, but I cannot see how it would be a good-making property of love if it were to be utterly spontaneous in the way envisioned by Nygren. Thankfully, though, we need not go Nygren's route, because there is no good reason to deny premise 4. I have argued that duty is neither the only legitimate nor the ideal motive of Christian love, but I see no reason one cannot perform (imperfect) acts of Christian love from duty. There is an apparent tension between love and duty because duty is so far from the ideal motive of love. Nevertheless, I do not think we should conclude that when duty-motivations are at work genuine love is ruled out. Suppose parents have a duty to love their children and, as sometimes happens, a mother feels no natural affection at all for her newborn baby. She may (and should) shower her baby with care, motivated by duty. I see no reason to deny that the care showered on her baby counts as love. Her love is imperfect, but it would be false, I think, to claim that the mother is failing to love her baby.

So there is no logical or psychological impediment to enacting Christian love from duty. Indeed, there is something noble about duty-motivated Christian love, as there always is when persons act from duty. It seems perfectly legitimate that a Christian would love from duty. But *must* Christians love from duty when all other motives fail? If we think of this as a question parallel to "*must* the mother love her newborn when all other motives fail?" the answer is an obvious and resounding "yes." The mother has a duty to love her newborn; therefore if she can find no other motive to love, duty must be the fallback. Similarly, Wolterstorff argues, it does not matter if you are not inclined to love your neighbor: just see to it that you do, even if you have to fall back on duty. But the parallel holds only if Christians have a duty to love, that is, only if premise 1 is to be read as Jesus laying a moral obligation upon his disciples.

7 Is there a Christian duty to love?

If loving one's neighbor as oneself is a moral obligation, we are morally obligated to give to those in need all our possessions beyond the minimum required to satisfy the basic standards of health and human dignity that comprise the biblical notion of *shalom* (Lk. 12:33, 14:33).[19] We could quibble about the specifics, but I suspect the moral obligation that would fall on us would be at least as severe as the one Peter Singer tried to impose in his famous "solution to world poverty."[20] After all, there are always persons in reach

---

[19] See Nicholas Wolterstorff (*Until Justice and Peace Embrace* [Grand Rapids, MI: William B. Eerdmans Publishing Company, 1983], 69ff) for a careful development of the biblical notion of shalom along these lines. *Shalom* is the state in which there is enough food, clothing, shelter, rest, safety, and relationships of care, for anyone concerned. To seek the *shalom* of another is to seek *their* inclusion in this state of affairs.

[20] Peter Singer, "The Singer Solution to World Poverty," *The New York Times Magazine*, September 5: 60–63.

of our care who are not experiencing the *shalom* that, according to the love command, we are to seek for our neighbors *to the same degree as we seek for ourselves*. Almost all of us are failing to pursue the *shalom* flourishing of those within reach of our care to the same degree that we pursue our own *shalom*. Assuming it is a moral obligation to pursue the *shalom* of anyone in reach of our care with the same intensity that we pursue our own *shalom*, it follows that, with respect to giving away most possessions, almost all of us

- are morally blameworthy;
- should experience consistent guilt;
- should expect to be morally upbraided; and
- should aim to call others to account for the same failure.

And this is only the tip of the iceberg. Jesus's call to enemy-love (Mt. 5:38-45), which is included within neighbor-love, enjoins us to even more demanding acts: welcoming potential enemies into our nations, neighborhoods, and homes; refraining from service in the military (since it uses lethal violence against enemies); refraining from taking someone to court or voting "guilty" on a jury or joining the police (since state punishment is predicated on violence); and on and on. And for each of these duties, it is appropriate that we should be morally blamed and upbraided for our failures, feel guilty about them, and so on.

"You're overstating things," many will say. "The love command does not require all that." Maybe not *all* that—perhaps I have made a mistake in my interpretation here or there—but does anyone really want to argue that the love command is not exceptionally, almost unimaginably, demanding? Yes, some do. For example, in his book *God and Moral Obligation*, C. Stephen Evans says, "The command to love the neighbor as oneself is, I believe, equivalent to the Kantian principle that all human persons have an intrinsic dignity that ought to be acknowledged."[21]

This cannot be, or at least it is so vague as to be misleading. Kant took himself to be offering an account of commonsense morality, which decidedly does not demand that each of us pursue the *shalom* of anyone in reach of our care to the same degree of intensity as we pursue our own *shalom*. The love command, on the other hand, does enjoin this upon us, at least on its most straightforward reading. The only way to align Kantian morality with the love command is by countering the straightforward reading of the command with a thousand qualifications and clarifications, walking the love ethic all the way back until it squares perfectly with conventional, middle-class, commonsense morality.

I understand the impulse. I suspect it stems from the assumption that the love command lays moral obligations on Christians. We are obligated to follow the love command, but the straightforward reading of the love command enjoins things that no person can be rationally obligated to do; therefore, the straightforward reading is wrong. But I think the straightforward reading is exactly right. The love command calls for a radical way of life that is sure to lead to immense self-sacrifice, the death of

---

[21] C. Stephen Evans, *God and Moral Obligation* (Oxford: Oxford University Press, 2013), 143–44.

conventional dreams for human happiness, and, in many cases, actual death. Rather than insisting that the love command lays moral obligations upon us and then trying to make the love command square with the limits of what persons could be rationally obligated to do, what if we considered the possibility that the love command is not laying obligations upon us at all?

Only Jesus issues the love commands. Only Jesus fulfills the love commands. Only Jesus loves with no shadow of fear. Only Jesus is resurrected. Resurrection, freedom from fear, the perfection of love, the fulfillment of the love commands—these are interwoven. Robert Jenson writes that, in the New Testament, "'Love' is not so much the name of a personality trait, as shorthand for a narrative: death and resurrection."[22] Though cryptic, the insight is essential. Narratively, the love commands are issued, then fulfilled perfectly by the fearless love of Jesus, then ratified in the resurrection. But logically and psychologically, the order is the other way around. Resurrection means freedom from death, freedom from death means freedom from fear, freedom from fear removes every obstacle to love. Resurrection is not the *reward* of Jesus's love; it is the *ground* of Jesus's love. It proves that love may be free from fear of death.

Consider the way that death, and our right to protect ourselves against it, functions as the limit of duty in commonsense morality. Of course, commonsense morality demands some sacrifice, but it does not demand that I sacrifice my life. It demands at times that I do that which I cannot immediately see to be to my benefit, but it never demands that I do what I can see is evidently to my own dissolution and death. I always have a right to self-defense, self-preservation, even self-realization. We valorize police officers, firemen, and soldiers because they go *above and beyond* the call of duty. I suspect that what finally grounds the line between duty and supererogation in commonsense morality is exactly the line between what can rightfully be asked of us without unduly risking death, and what cannot. To save a drowning man near the shore of a placid pond is a moral duty; to save him from a raging sea is supererogatory. To give occasionally and from my surplus to a person in need is a duty;[23] to give always and up to the limit of what I need here and now for my own *shalom* is supererogatory, for such generosity imperils my future self who may need surplus to survive a bad turn of fortune.

Precisely its antagonism to our reasonable hedges against the threat of future neediness and death makes the love command so extreme. "Do not be anxious about your life, what you shall eat or what you shall drink" (Mt. 6:25). And this is why it is foolish abstracted from resurrection. But if the love command requires resurrection for its intelligibility, in what sense is it properly understood as a moral obligation? Can we have moral duties to perform acts that require the fulfillment of a promise *by someone else* for their intelligibility? A father says to his young son at the edge of the pool, "I promise I will catch you; you *must* jump." No. He more likely says, "I promise I will catch you; you *may* jump." A promise issues an invitation to act in faith, in trust. A

---

[22] Jenson, *Story and Promise*, 55.
[23] This is why the duty to care for the needy, in commonsense morality, is called an "imperfect duty." You do not have a duty to give to the needy *always if able*. Rather, you have a general duty to assist the needy, but you have leeway to decide when and how it is satisfied.

promise does not issue categorical imperatives. Resurrection is a promise. The gospel promises that death does not have the final word; therefore we *may* love without fear.[24]

The love command is grounded in divine love. It invites us to love the neighbor *as God loves*. When we recognize that divine love is the ideal of the actions and motives of the love enjoined, the love command makes sense. For love that does not fear death can rationally fulfill the love command. On the other hand, when we recognize it presupposes a divine kind of love, we are thrown into crisis. Is there really such a love as the love promised? The gospel claims that there is such a love. Those who believe the promise may risk such love. But I cannot see how it is anyone's obligation, even those who hope in the promise, to risk such love.[25] The love command is an invitation to live in another, promised reality. It is not a categorical imperative.

8 Objections

My thesis is open to several objections, the most obvious of which goes as follows. Jesus issues love *commands*. Scripture is clear that they are commandments. Divine commandments generate moral obligations. Therefore, the love command lays upon us a moral obligation.

Commandments can fail to generate moral obligations for a number of reasons, sometimes because the one commanding lacks authority, other times because the context is not right. Go back to the father enjoining his child to jump from the edge of the pool. Does the father have authority? Yes. But is the context right for generating a moral obligation? I said he probably would not say, "You *must* jump." But he could say that. Suppose he did, and the child jumped. Now suppose he praised the child by asking, "Where did you find the courage to jump?" and the child responded, "You gave a command, and I have to obey you, therefore I had to jump." I think the father would be saddened by this response. He might say, "Son, I didn't mean it that way. You didn't *have* to jump. I was just emphasizing how utterly trustworthy I am, and also telling you that if you want to experience that trustworthiness, you would have to jump." In other words, in certain contexts, commands do not generate moral obligations but rather (a) implore trust and (b) generate hypothetical imperatives.

The love command is a hypothetical imperative: if you want x, then you must fulfill the love command. But what would the x be? What is conditional on fulfilling the love command in the gospel? Salvation? There are some who read Matthew 25 in this way, but this is at odds with the Christian doctrine of justification by grace alone. Perhaps *sanctification* is conditional on obeying the love command. If you want to be unified in holiness with God, then you must fulfill the love command. Or perhaps *experiencing the fullness of Kingdom life* is conditional on obeying it. Something

---

[24] I am indebted to Jenson, *Story and Promise*, for the ideas in this paragraph.

[25] What if we do more than *hope* in the promise? What if we *believe* the promise or, better yet, *know* the promise will be fulfilled. Suppose the child *believes* his father will catch him—does he thereby become obligated? I do not see how. Of course, if the child responds, "I promise I will jump, father," then the child obligates himself.

along these lines seems to me to be the best way of interpreting the love command. It lays a hypothetical imperative on Jesus followers. And this is supported by the biblical text. "Come to me, all you that are weary and are carrying heavy burdens, and I will give you rest," Jesus invites. Then he continues, "Take my yoke upon you" (Mt. 11:28-29). Jesus commands his followers to take his yoke upon themselves, and presumably this yoke refers to the love command. Yet the command is in the context of an invitation, and thereby becomes something other than a categorical imperative. Jesus says: if you want to live in the resurrection rest of the Kingdom, then you must love as I love.

Let us consider next a philosophical objection to my thesis. I said earlier that inclinational motives are better from the perspective of the agent of Christian love because our neighbors really are worthy of our love. If our neighbors are worthy of our love, to fail to love them would be to fail to treat them in a way appropriate to their worth. Perhaps it follows that if our neighbors are worthy of such love, then we have a duty so to love them (and they have a right to our love). Our duties to others, the objection claims, are grounded in their inherent worth. So if our neighbors are truly *worthy* of our love, we have a duty to love them. By issuing the love command, Jesus was simply making clear how radical our duties in fact are, how much the moral dignity of other human beings demands of us. The command does not *generate* the duty to love, but it *reveals* the duty to love, which is grounded in the worth of human persons.

In response, I want to draw a distinction between subjective and objective duties or, to use Wolterstorff's more precise distinction, between culpability duties and full-cognition duties.[26] Was the ancient physician who prescribed the harmful practice of bloodletting violating his duty? In one sense, no; in another, yes. He was not violating any culpability duties—he could not be blamed, for example, for prescribing bloodletting instead of antibiotics. But he *did* violate his full-cognition duty. Had he possessed ideal knowledge of human illness, he would have prescribed antibiotics; his full-cognition duty was to prescribe antibiotics. I think something along the same lines is true of the duty to neighbor-love. It is a full-cognition duty, but most of us, even Christians, see through a glass darkly. Because of our obscured vision, we cannot really *see* that what Jesus says is true; we do not possess ideal knowledge of the worth of our neighbors. We may take it on faith that they have immense worth, and strive to live as if they do, but we have nothing like a clear vision of their worth. Given these limitations, most of us are not culpable when we fail to love our neighbor as ourselves. Our most customary ways of talking about duties track culpability duties, and in that sense it is true that we have no duty to love our neighbor as ourselves.[27] This seems to me to be compatible with the claim I made above that the primary function of the

---

[26] Wolterstorff, *Justice*, 257.

[27] To put the point differently: our most typical ways of thinking about duties assume that if you have a duty you could reasonably be expected to know you have it, a principle related to the "ought implies can" thesis. But there is another way of thinking about duties according to which you can have duties you could not reasonably be expected to know you have. I am denying that neighbor-love is a duty in the first sense.

command is to implore trust in Jesus and to issue a hypothetical imperative in the context of a promise.[28]

Finally, let us consider a theological objection. The love command is "all the law and the prophets" (Mt. 22:40); it is the restatement of the second table of the Decalogue, as John Calvin thought. And since the Decalogue laid moral obligations on God's covenant people, the love command lays moral obligations on Jesus's followers.

The objection depends on a certain interpretation of the relationship between law and gospel, between the Old the New Covenants. This is theologically contentious territory. Some (like the Reformers) insist on an antithesis between the Old and New Covenants with respect to what each required for salvation. Some (like the Anabaptists) insist on an antithesis between the two with respect to normative content; so, for instance, the Old Covenant might have permitted just violence but the New does not. I am suggesting there is an antithesis of normative *form*: the Old Covenant set forth moral obligations, but the New sets forth hypothetical imperatives. And I am suggesting the difference here is to be traced to the way in which the resurrection of Jesus makes possible a radical kind of self-sacrificial love that violates the death-determined boundaries of natural moral reasoning but makes sense if (but only if) death has been swallowed up by resurrection. Jesus claimed to be fulfilling the law and the prophets, but the reception he received indicated that he was fulfilling it in a way that could only appear perverse to those, like the Pharisees, who loved the law because it made possible the pursuit of the good in a way that did not risk death. I am not quite sure how to relate my outlook to the various proposals made in the tradition about the relationship between the two covenants, but given the extreme variety in the tradition, I see no reason to think my view would go beyond the pale.

9 Conclusion

I have argued that the connection between duty and the love command is not what it is often thought to be. At the very least, I hope I have established my weaker thesis that duty is not the proper motive of Christian love; at best it is a possible motive. But I suspect that, in addition to the two objections raised above, there is a practical concern about my stronger thesis that there is no duty to Christian love. The practical concern is that if Christians really believed they had no such duty, they would be even less inclined than they already are to practice the works of mercy. There is no way to know; it is an empirical question. But I am struck by the way that the love command, interpreted as it generally has been as a duty, filtered down into the post-Christendom West in such a way that the dignity of human persons became an ethical axiom. Once it had become an axiom, human dignity was taken to be discernible abstracted from the promise the gospel makes (Kant). And once that happened, there was nothing to back up the assertion of human dignity except enlightened intuition. From my

---

[28] Even if the command does not generate a duty, it does generate a responsibility of some kind. On my view, if you do not live according to the command, you sin against God despite not violating a moral duty. Sin encompasses more than the failure to fulfill moral duties.

perspective, the rise of populism and nationalism represents an aggressive challenge to such enlightened intuition (by no means the first), and in the shrill and self-righteous anti-populism of the elite left, we encounter the folly of the valorization of neighbor-love abstracted from any ultimate hope that our love will not destroy us. Of course, this does not show there is no Christian duty to love. But it does suggest there is little to be gained by insisting on neighbor-love as a duty. Our task, as ever, is to remember that neighbor-love depends for its intelligibility and future on God's love for us.[29]

---

[29] Thanks to Tom Crisp and Ben Wayman for reading and helpfully commenting on this chapter. Thanks as well to the members of the Analytic Theology seminar at Fuller Theological Seminary for helpful responses to a talk based on an earlier draft of this chapter.

13

"Sex Is Really about God": Sarah Coakley and the Transformation of Desire

Erin Dufault-Hunter

I recently received an email from a brother in Christ who had found my name on the Internet. He addressed me as a Christian ethicist and, among other things, asked the following:

> If God is the creator of both morality and nature, why are there aspects of human physiology that push us away from being moral (such as the extra high libido in some men making faithfulness difficult) because while humans have the freedom to choose why give them a physical handicap?[1]

---

[1] Given I did not know this man, here is what I wrote in response to this part of his question: I don't see this so much as a handicap; men's "extra high libido" (met in many women by an "extra high" desire for relational connections of other sorts) is both an opportunity and a sign. First, it is an opportunity to have our desires trained into faithfulness. Longing (and sometimes even lust) is an appetite. How do we train and discipline that appetite so that we are nourished, so we don't just gobble up what is in front of us and then slowly become compulsive consumers of (say) porn or of others' lovers or the like? Rather, we ask for God's help and take action as we do in eating. We seek to be obedient to God, trusting in his grace to train us to "eat wisely and well" so our love of others (rather than our use of them to meet our needs) is nurtured and becomes—slowly, over time—our own nature. We become like God in this way, generous rather than consumptive and needy. *Eros* reminds us of our genuine need to be fed; we literally ache in our hunger for affection as for food. Christians turn to God, so that by grace he can train us to "eat wisely and well." How can we love others, rather than use them to meet our (real) needs? Coakley's consistent refrain about our desires is that finally only God fills them (even when he does so through the care of other people). In this way, we can become better lovers in and through God. But if we close ourselves off from God's generosity, then our appetites drive us to consume others rather than tend to them.

So that moves us to the sign part: Why such profound longing or even orgasmic release that feels so good and then (usually) fades or must be fed again? I would say that the erotic is a sign of how we are made to be in union with God and with others. We mistake the sign for the end; we think that sex is what we need, that God is not interested in our sexual life (or is angry at us for having the desire in the first place). But the erotic is a powerful recollection that we want a space in which we are "known and not ashamed," to be utterly so, to submit to another even in an embarrassingly needy way. Good lovers can do this, but often only partially. They, too, become signs of the ways that God will be "all in all," including in and for us—united with us. Gregory of Nyssa speaks about this among the church fathers; see Sarah Coakley's *The New Asceticism* for her ponderings on desires, prayer, and God.

I suspect that this inquiry highlights much of what is presumed about *eros* and the Christian life, particularly among those who identify as conservative, serious, or traditional ("evangelical") in their belief. What assumptions does he make? First, that our bodies mislead us *qua* its appetites, especially if those appetites are strong ones. The accompanying presumption is that faithfulness requires weakening these desires. Second, the body's sexual appetite—here noted in Freudian terms of the "libido" or sex drive—provides a particularly compelling example of how bodily desires handicap us in our pursuit of a life marked by fidelity to others and love of God. Finally, it is the *male* body that threatens to make a mockery of human freedom, at least in seasons binding men by leading them by the loin rather than by a pure heart.

In this chapter we interrogate this interplay of desire, freedom, and love guided by the sensibilities of Sarah Coakley. One of today's leading analytic theologians, Coakley asserts that sexual desire and desire for God are inevitably intertwined and calls for a "rethreading" in the Christian tradition of divine and human desire:

> *We need to turn Freud on his head.* Instead of thinking of "God" language as being really being about sex (Freud's reductive ploy), we need to understand sex as really about God, and about the deep desire that we feel for God—the precious clue that is woven into our existence about the final and ultimate union that we seek. And it matters in this regard—or so I submit—that the God we desire is, in Godself, a desiring trinitarian God: the Spirit who longs for our response, who searches the hearts, and takes us to the divine source (the "Father"), transforming us Christically as we are so taken.[2]

Coakley's first volume of her systematic theology (and much of her other writings) explores the interplay between contemplative prayer, the Trinity, sexuality, and gender. For her, a key link of these concepts is Rom. 8:26: "Likewise the Spirit helps us in our weakness; for we do not know how to pray as we ought, but that very Spirit intercedes with sighs too deep for words (NRSV)." This ceding of ourselves to the Spirit in prayer echoes the vulnerability of good sexuality; this is not mere rational assent but embodied submission before God that lays bare our souls. Thus Coakley's entre into the tangle of desire, sex, and God begins with experiences of bodily longing that is initiated in the wordless vulnerability of contemplative prayer. This chapter untangles sexuality from the other end, so to speak. That is, we will begin where our inquisitive emailer began, with the mundane and embarrassing experience of sexual desire and explore if it, too, can lead us into the Triune God in whose love we find the freedom that comes only through our surrender in defenseless dependence. In this sense, I hope to make Coakley's work more accessible to those of us who pray poorly, whose spiritual life (to the extent we have any) offers no easy path for the conjoining of this practice and sex, or who cannot imagine a link between our formidable erotic energy before our lover and our paltry passionless pleas before God.

---

[2] Sarah Coakley, *The New Asceticism: Sexuality, Gender and the Quest for God* (London: Bloomsbury, 2015), 96, emphasis in original.

Invigorated by Coakley's confidence that "sex is really about God," we discover that our erotic lives matter in two crucial ways: as an embodied sign of humanity's true end in communion with the Triune God and as a space in which we are shaped for fidelity to this God through the ordinary attentiveness that faithful sexuality demands.

1 Assumptions of our context: Conservative and liberal visions of sex misread the clues about God in our desiring bodies

On the whole, Christians in both "progressive" and "conservative" camps foreshorten the meaning of the erotic and thus often silence the testimony sexuality would bear. If we group most approaches to sexuality into these camps, we see that each follows a good impulse that never bears the fruit that wise attentiveness to the erotic produces. While seemingly distant from one another, both prove barren because at their root is the poison of fearfulness about pressing into sex's entanglements with the Spirit. That is, neither wants to admit that working the soil of sexuality requires arduous and potentially embarrassing labor, a dirtying of the hands in the muck of human vulnerability, loneliness, fragility, neediness, and greed. On one side, some Christians are reticent to admit that the erotic often feeds in frenzy on others' bodies (real, imagined, or virtual); they may not articulate enough that sexual appetites must be tamed in order to truly sate us. On another side, other Christians so fear the appetite itself that they sometimes rip at even its most tender sprout, suspicious of any sexual desire or at least of any desire springing up outside the box of opposite-sex marriage.

One set of responses to our emailer might come from a "sex-positive" Christian—perhaps in liberal theological guise but also potentially in an evangelical one—who would rush to soothe his sexual anxiety. In response to a supposedly repressive and gloomy past, Christians across the theological spectrum trip over themselves to affirm sexual desire, with few asking about its texture or its repercussions for their intimacy with God (and hence of their ability to love others well). Thus the usual litmus test—"Does it hurt anyone? Are you consenting adults?"—opens a wide cavity through which our brother's libido can happily and haplessly drive. His connection of high libido with difficulty in fidelity would likely be met with hasty confirmations of it as "natural," with scant questioning as to what his "nature" craves or asking him how he may need to tend this intense impulse of sexual desire.

The sensibility of affirmation that animates this response stems from a good gone awry. The clear good is an openness to sex, a confidence that the God who desires makes desiring animals—and sex is one key form of our desire. The problem then arises in the rather shocking positivity about sex's vigor; for many Christians eager to affirm consensual (committed?) adult sex, there seems little awareness that the erotic as it arises within us requires pruning if it is not to harvest heartache, violence, or isolation.

Conservatives too often preclude discussion and interrogation, utilizing rules or codes of behavior to foreclose on ponderings about sexuality's meaning. Liberal or progressives (including evangelicals who want to be "relevant") drown any doubt about the erotics' need for expression under mandates to liberation from oppressive systems of patriarchy or puritanism. But to aid our emailer requires a conviction that sexuality offers us clues for faithfulness and a context for learning love—not merely soothing, shunning, or forbidding it. We must press into explorations of what an "extra high libido" means for our brother concretely. Is this fantasy, masturbation (too extensive, too often?), porn use, betrayal of spouse or lover, or endless interruptions of tasks with visions of women (or men) and ideations of sexual intimacy of various sorts? Or is it a nagging, ceaseless longing, and distraction that sex can cause in us in seasons? We could also explore why he assumes that men's libido is "extra high," while women seemingly skate away unscathed by the pesky weight of erotic desire (and thus belie his presumed belief in "gender equality," a given even for a traditionalist who should affirm equality in our sinfulness).

A major attraction of Coakley's presumptions about sex is that they push against these settled impulses of conservative and liberal camps. Because we lack Coakley's confidence that sexuality bears a clue for our life with God, Christians back away from interrogations of the nitty-gritty of our libido's content and context. Throughout her writing, she resists the ruts into which much theological and ethical reflection easily runs. Coakley breaks open a new way of engaging our brother by refusing to baptize his libido or to clamp down on its eruption. Instead, it is just at this point that she surprises, affirming his sense that desires require discipline. But she also invites him to see that though raw desire naturally draws us toward easy, dangerous, or unhealthy "fixes," our freedom lies not in squelching desiring. Instead, we must embrace it in order to channel it into a less-worn and narrower path, a way opened by submission to the Triune God. When we intentionally focus even "extra high" desires in this way, they do not diminish. Rather, they become streams that nourish us, sating us by connecting us to God's love and making freedom to love others truly possible. How might we cross-examine desire theologically so we get to such a space, in which our brother can imagine that his sexual life becomes a resource for connection with God and a space of freedom, rather than an albatross of shame around his sinful neck?

2 A precious clue: *Eros* as desiring the desiring God

Too often, Christians approach sexual desire (and much bodily existence) as tangential to the spiritual life. We assume our appetites are *merely* animal and thus to be indulged without consideration as to God's involvement. In some conservative literature, they arise as dangerous diversions to our devotion or as an opportunity to prove that we can meet God's high standard through dogged denial of desire.[3] But Coakley reminds us that Christian faith is an all-in proposition, as the God who creates us from the dust also creates us in her image and likeness for eternal

---

[3] See, for example, the way male desire is described in the popular evangelical series that begins with Stephen Arterburn and Fred Stoeker, *Every Man's Battle: Every Man's Guide to Winning the War on Sexual Temptation One Victory at a Time* (Colorado Spring, CO: Waterbrook, 2004).

friendship. The above quote from Coakley regarding Freud and sex can be parsed out to show how central convictions of orthodox faith matter for sexual desire. One might lay out Coakley's assumptions thusly:

(1) The Triune God, as love, desires communion with her creation.
(2) This God creates humankind in her image and likeness, that is, as desiring animals whose ultimate desire is communion with her in the redeemed creation.
(3) Erotic desire names the drive in us toward communion and as such is a sign of our true end.
(4) This *eros* arises in us in raw force and requires tending if it is to become an aid rather than hindrance to loving union with others, God, and God's creation.
(5) Because Triune love requires that we offer ourselves for union rather than be forcibly taken into it, God invites us to nurture and train our sexual appetite so that we desire union with *this* God and with *this* God's redeemed creation.
(6) Finally, because we are created in the image of the desiring God whose desire constantly breaks forth in creative energy, redeemed humanity is marked by expansive desire rather than diminishment or mere "control."

This last claim about desire's effusiveness is not directly noted in Coakley's quote above, but we will see that this necessarily follows from her convictions about the nature of embodied life with the Triune God.

The first two claims offer nothing new for those of us who have attended to analytic theology's concerns.[4] What might be contested is how we understand the relationships of the Trinity, or whether the love of the persons necessarily expands outward and creates. What Coakley encourages us to recall in our doctrine of the Triune God emerges amid this third claim, that God *desires* union with her creation and hence, fourth, plants the erotic in us like a seed. Although an uneasy Augustinian might balk at this formulation, Coakley presumes that a *desiring* God creates *desiring* humans, and so all appetites—including the powerful realm of sexual yearning—can be received as arenas for training in love of the God who longs for our fidelity. As she notes on this point,

> If human loves are indeed made with the imprint of the divine upon them—*vestigia* [track, trail] of God's ways—then they too, at their best, will surely bear the trinitarian mark. Here we have to take off afresh where Augustine left us, at that crucial moment in his *De trinitate*, at the end of book VIII, when he rejects finally the analogy of "the lover, the loved one, and the love that binds," as inadequate to the Trinity because it is bound to bodies. "Let us tread the flesh under foot and mount up to the soul," as he puts it. But sexual loves are of course bodily as well as "psychic," and if they are also to be godly, then should they not themselves mirror

---

[4] For example, Thomas Aquinas asserted that love desires the good of the beloved and union with the beloved. For a short overview of this influential view, see Eleanor Stump, "Love, By All Accounts," *Proceedings and Addresses of the American Philosophical Association*, 80, no. 2 (November 2006): 25–43. See especially pp. 27–30 for a brief summary of Thomas's account of love.

forth the trinitarian image in some sense? And what would that involve? Surely, at the very least, a fundamental respect of each "person" for the other, an equality of understanding and exchange, and the mutual *ekstasis* of attending on the other's desire as distinct, as other. Such a vision is the opposite of abuse, the opposite of distanced sexual control.[5]

Here Coakley nods to fears running from Augustine into today about the erotic, and affirms the training all *eros* must undergo. In exploring claims 3–5 about the erotic in more detail, we must consider its nature not only in this lofty theological dress but also "from below," so to speak. As our emailer reminds us, it is far from obvious that the erotic can be such a good and redemptive space, let alone become a trail to something as exalted as the Trinity. While some theologians mock Augustine's reticence, others seem blithely incautious about the erotic's need for Christian discipline; for every Nygren who sets *eros* in opposition to *agape*, another comes along to claim it as a "positive power."[6] How might we enter into renewed consideration of sexual desire in a way that avoids blithe ignorance of its dangers and yet wrestles from its fraughtness unique clues for love of God?

3 "Kiss me—full on the mouth!": The Song of Songs and erotic desire as a clue to our end

I asserted that erotic desire names the drive in us toward communion and as such is a sign of our true end (claim 3). Anyone wanting to explore the erotic from within the Christian tradition has a resource in the Song of Songs. Coakley's theological guides spend considerable time in this poem, with Gregory of Nyssa a crucial companion.[7] While we cannot explore this rich Scripture in depth, we can let its opening lines wash over us as a refreshing recollection of what was once one of the most commented upon texts in Christendom:

Song 1:1 The Song of Songs, which is Solomon's (NRSV)
The Woman

2   Let him kiss me with the kisses of his mouth!
    For your love[making] is better than wine,

3   your anointing oils are fragrant,
    your name is perfume poured out;
    therefore the maidens love you.

---

[5] Coakley, *The New Asceticism*, Kindle locations 1613–1623.
[6] Some feminists too hastily affirm *eros* and speak of it as if it were itself a transformative force arising in us untrained. See Kathleen M. Sands, "Uses of the Thea(o)logian: Sex and Theodicy in Religious Feminism," *Journal of Feminist Studies in Religion*, 8 (1992): 7–33.
[7] Coakley frequently and appreciatively draws from church fathers—Pseudo-Dionysius, Origen, and Augustine among them—while she also points out ways their anxieties about sexual desire and gender misshape their understanding of the Trinity and human communion.

4   Draw me after you, let us make haste.
    The king has brought me into his chambers.
    We will exult and rejoice in you;
    we will extol your love more than wine;
    rightly do they love you.[8]

The open sensuality of the Song catches many of us off guard and the shameless sexuality of the *woman's* speeches throughout the poem surprise those who presume a univocal oppression of women in Scripture. Whatever we make of hermeneutical decisions (such as whether the text alludes to oral sex or that it must be read strictly as an allegory for Christ and the church), the poem's tenor beckons to us at our level of longing—a longing that is both an aching appreciation of the other and a yearning to be taken by another. As Ellen Davis and others point out about the Song, total satisfaction remains allusive and thus the poem echoes our own experience. Most importantly, we cannot deny that here we have testimony to the entanglement of desire with sexuality and of sexuality with the sacred. More importantly for our intuitions about the erotic as sign, the Song recalls for us the three interdependent arenas of erotic longing, three ways humans as *imago dei* crave communion: communion with God, communion with other humans, and communion with creation itself. In this way, the Song highlights various levels of erotic experience: the craving in our bodies for another body, for someone more satisfying than another (mere) human body, and for connection with the wonder of the created order itself. In interweaving these three arenas seamlessly, the Song invites us into the tangle of sexuality and deeper longings that Coakley affirms. More to the point for our brother, "extra high libido" scarcely interrupts whatever faithfulness the Song as Scripture intends to foster.

While Coakley has not written extensively on the Song, she alludes to the text throughout her writings, often utilizing the insights of church fathers. In her work, Davis recounts the Song's history of interpretation and helps us comprehend the Song's unique place in the canon. The Song has alternatively been understood to be *only* properly interpreted as an allegory of the love of God and of Israel (or of Christ and the church), then *only* as a celebration of human sexual love. Davis insists that the Song itself presses against both such limitations. Like Coakley and so many other faithful readers before us, Davis links the mystery of divine communion with fleshy human love.[9]

In making these connections, she notes that the Song alludes to many other Scriptures and as such pushes readers back into the biblical story of Israel's covenantal arrangement with YHWH, even as its obvious sensuality recalls human *eros*. Because

---

[8]   Ellen Davis notes that the Hebrew word in v. 3 usually translated "love" implies physicality, and she translates it as "lovemaking." She seems to use this word in terms of its older sense, not equating it with "sexual intercourse." See Davis, *Proverbs, Ecclesiastes, and the Song of Songs* (Louisville, KY: Westminster John Knox Press, 2000), 242.

[9]   For a short essay summarizing her views on the Song, see Davis, "The One Whom My Soul Loves: The Song of Songs," in *Getting Involved with God: Rediscovering the Old Testament* (Lanham, MD: Rowman & Littlefield, 2001), 65–88.

she refuses to delimit how such sacred poetry might work, Davis cannot sever these two interpretations but rather determines that they are interdependent—to comprehend the love of God and Israel one must attend to that of human lovers and vice versa. "Yet the Bible itself often allows the two realms of human love and religious experience to interpenetrate."[10] She goes on to note that the prophets record the wandering of Israel away from her first love, but here and here alone in the Song we have mutual admiration, requited love in sheer celebration, and delight in one another. This mutuality works humanly (man/woman) and religiously (God/Israel or Christ/church). In this sense, the Song extends hope to those of us too willing to cave to either the bentness of gender relations in our current world or to the tragedy of humanity's continued dysfunctional rejection of YHWH's covenantal love. However, Davis introduces a final suggestion about the Song's significance as regards the land and creation. For all its language of human love and supposed eroticism, the Song never describes the lovers (or their parts) in terms that map onto physical characteristics. (She observes that these lovers are curiously absent from Western art, despite the ways painters consistently searched for biblical themes and subjects.) Instead, we find allusions to creation itself—to animals, flowers, and trees that express the beloved's attractiveness or strength. These allusion abound, but as examples consider the following:

Your cheeks are like halves of a *pomegranate* . . . (4:3).

Your two breasts are like two *fawns*, twins of a *gazelle*, that feed among the *lilies*. . . . (4:5).

His head is the finest gold; his locks are wavy, *black as a raven*. His eyes are like *doves* beside *springs of water*, bathed in milk, fitly set. His cheeks are like *beds of spices*, yielding fragrance. His lips are *lilies* . . . His appearance is like Lebanon, choice as the *cedars* (5:11-13).[11]

In sum, the Song expands the way we comprehend the erotic and the longings that it signifies. Erotic desire names the magnetic, internal draw humans have toward union with God and toward union with one another—and indeed toward all that is good (including the redeemed creation). It recalls that we cannot shun our bodily longings for a supposedly disembodied ecstasy, nor can we abandon ourselves to bodily joy without regard to our craving for union with God. This dual interplay of human and divine love echoes a theological anthropology that insists that we are indeed "a little lower than the angels" as another biblical poet insists.[12] Finally, the Song's exultation in nature and what Davis dubs the "confusion" of the beloved person and the land recalls that, as humans made of humus we are mortals, material beings whose very breath is

---

[10] Davis, *Proverbs, Ecclesiastes, and the Song of Songs*, 234.
[11] These are the lines, of course, that make us chuckle and also tend to distance us from engaging in the Song. When comprehended as articulations of our mysterious longing to see in human love something beyond our reach or merely perceived in moments of stunned beauty in creation, these images can draw us back into the Song's openness to *eros* in the ordinary.
[12] Ps. 8:5.

borrowed and whose end includes participation amid creation as its servant.[13] While to my knowledge Davis does not overtly connect embodiment and our bodies' erotic longings to creation in this way, she observes that the land's exuberance becomes the means for expressing the lovers' desirability. For her this entails a recollection that we are to pray for peace and *shalom* in Israel as elsewhere, and that clearly the earth now "suffers precisely from our lack of love."[14] I suggest that what the Song recalls is an *eros* usually exalted in new age spirituality or the vague spirituality flourishing in many parts of the United States, such as the Pacific Northwest.[15] We could reject as utterly mistaken so-called tree huggers or granola-loving hipsters who top off a hike with another sort of high that accents "communing with nature." Yet the Song encourages us to sniff out in this experience a trail that leads not to an abstract mother nature but rather to the Triune God who beckons us to image her to her world, including in joyful, ecstatic attentiveness to its wonder as well as its own longings for restoration.[16] Just as Israel's welfare was inextricably joined to that of the land, so, too, Paul claims that our restoration to full humanity in Christ overflows, taking in the world that waits for our glory as partners with God.

4 *Eros* erupting in raw force: Orgasmic ecstasy and the need to tend our longings

Even if it is true that sexual desire expresses our ultimate longing to be joined to God and one another in a redeemed creation, our emailing brother may well balk at such an appeal. It is a sign, perhaps, but not a clear one, especially when sexual desire erupts unbeckoned as I presume he or others he knows experience. In this sense his caution is wiser than that of many others who rush from claim 3 to 5, as if there is a straight line from raw erotic desire to God.[17] Instead, we must acknowledge that every appetite

---

[13] Davis suggests that humans/humus provides a way of capturing the play in Hebrew of *adam/adamah*.

[14] See Davis, "The One Whom My Soul Loves," 85.

[15] I love the Pacific Northwest, and my family is from this region. However, many here repeat the sin Paul notes in Romans, mistakenly (and often rather limply) worshipping the created rather than the Creator. Sometimes "spiritual but not religious" translates to, "I like stroking my erotic longings but don't want anyone to tell me what to do with them."

[16] Thus, not coincidentally, we return to the text immediately preceding Coakley's key text, Rom. 8:19-22: "For the creation waits with eager longing for the revealing of the children of God; for the creation was subjected to futility, not of its own will but by the will of the one who subjected it, in hope that the creation itself will be set free from its bondage to decay and will obtain the freedom of the glory of the children of God. We know that the whole creation has been groaning in labor pains until now; and not only the creation, but we ourselves, who have the first fruits of the Spirit, groan inwardly while we wait for adoption, the redemption of our bodies."

[17] Claims 3–5: (3) Erotic desire names the drive in us toward communion and as such is a sign of our true end. (4) This *eros* arises in us in raw force and requires tending if it is to become an aid rather than hindrance to loving union with others, God, and God's creation. (5) Because Triune love requires that we offer ourselves for union rather than be forcibly taken into it, God invites us to nurture and train our sexual appetite so that we desire union with *this* God and with *this* God's redeemed creation.

emerges in humans not in some pure form but rather arises in our bodies shaped by our personal and cultural context.

In our era, many Christians affirm sexual desire as natural, and further profess their personal, particular flavor of it as "authentically" one's own. In doing so, they seek to offer freedom to those who have been ruthlessly hammered because of their desires (e.g., LGBTQI persons) or to extend relief to those crippled by embarrassment over any sort of expression of sexuality—including an absence of desire. The impulse to prevent this bludgeoning is exactly right, but the assumption that most of our appetites come to us unsullied and ready-made for indulgence turns out to be faulty. (Of course, we still balk at certain arguably "natural" appetites; in our culture pedophilia, pederasty, abuse, and sexual harassment remind us that desires *qua* desires cannot be read as trustworthy signs toward a fulfilling life for ourselves or others.) We leap from the awareness of sexual desires to advocating for indulgence as necessary, because we have wrongly swallowed the myth in the West of a good "self" that lies deep within us, an authentic "me" whose voice always accurately guides me toward my true end, if only I could attend to her.[18] We fail to recognize what social scientists as well as neurologists would tell us: before we are conscious of them, our context forms much of what we find appealing and deeply influences our visceral responses. For example, in my culture we find insects repulsive as food, while other cultures enjoy them as snacks; in other societies, my habit of walking around my home in the same shoes with which I just walked the street is disgusting and clearly unsanitary.

It may be easier to see the interplay between the goodness of desire and its need for tending if we consider another appetite, such as that of food. I did not grow up with vegetables, unless they came in a can or in a frozen bag (usually "succotash" that mysteriously all tasted like bad peas). Raised on iceberg lettuce and salt-and-peppered meats, I found most deeply green food items unappealing. Nothing. No draw to join my body to them in happy consumption; kale looked like a terribly bad idea. On the other hand, we also very seldom had desserts, and when my sisters baked my father chocolate chip cookies or made him pecan rolls, I ate as much as I was able to get my hands on. I did not particularly *want* to alter my diet, and I was not deeply unhappy in my iceberg-frozen-veggie existence. But I came to realize that the food I craved and found tempting was not actually nourishing me. So later in life, I had to learn to cook the vegetables that were in season and, further, to enjoy them by both relishing their flavor and drawing out their taste. To do this became a matter of faithfulness to God, as it became apparent that my appetite for food related to my love of God through self-control, attentiveness to God's earth, hospitality, and care for my family's well-being (to name but a few).

---

[18] I make this comment not to deny that there is a genuine and unique self or "me" who will one day be raised from the dead. Rather, I deny that our internal voices or consciousness is unproblematic as a moral guide, even while as an Anabaptist I resist certain conceptions of depravity. Whatever our Christian doctrine, I take it the "self" is growing, changing, and becoming more (or less) Christ-like throughout our life and thus more (or less) likely to perceive my desires honestly and channel them wisely.

The same is true in sexual appetite. If our emailer experiences in himself or sees in others a craving for pornography, for example, that idealizes sexual violence or panders to fantasies he finds abhorrent as a believer, he recognizes that personal habits conflate with social contexts to foster in him a taste for sexual desires he rationally rejects, especially as one who wants to obey God's commands. What he also hints at here is the penchant of our libido for that forbidden "it"; whatever "extra high" means to him, he finds certain sexual desires so strong that they threaten to choke off his sense of moral freedom. (One almost hears him pleading, "Forget freedom Lord! Give me slavery and chain me to the good.") We need to highlight two things about the likeness of appetites to one another: first, we must *learn* to taste God and find the taste of God good; this is a process and not a moment in time. Part of acknowledging our dependence upon God in that shorthand we dub "grace" means that moral determination is never enough. Willingness, openness to God always means willingness and openness to forgiveness, to admission of failure. We do this while fostering gratitude that happily grasps any lifeline the Spirit offers us and that celebrates slow reformations (such as when I finally savored a kale quinoa salad or received the gift of the man I married instead of measuring him against an imagined alternative). Among Christians, much angst about the sexual life occurs precisely because we fail to acknowledge *both* that appetites arise deeply influenced by our context *and* that this implies a retraining of our tastes over time. To draw out the metaphor a bit more: as I painstakingly needed to learn how to cook to draw out the flavors buried in vegetables in such a way that they nourished my body, I also need to learn how to enact my sexual life in way that pulls out its sweetness and sustains me over the long haul for faithfulness to God and to others.

The Song reminds us that our erotic energies find their source in God and thus find their flourishing there. But sexual desire also frequently holds up a mirror to our consumptiveness; because of its force and stubborn insistence on satiation (in fantasy as well as physically), we may well find the Song's celebration naive. (Notice, however, that there is no final consummation in the Song; arguably the Song ends open to future union, beckoning us as readers to imagine what it entails to be welcomed as Christ's bride.) Of course, what makes the Song such a relief and such a shock is that the rest of the Bible finds none of this mutuality and celebratory, noninstrumental *eros*. Instead, we see reflected in Scripture much of what we see in our own lives and in those around us: sexual consumptiveness (often by men) and sexual manipulation (sometimes by women).[19] Yet what our emailer and each of us need to recall about the

---

[19] As a feminist, I do not think this is because women are inherently less violent or greedy. I take this to reflect general patterns, as women have less opportunity for consumptiveness and have learned to weaponize limited access to assets, such as our sexuality. Contrary to many stereotypes is the righteous Joseph of Matthew's Gospel, who links his life to God in obedience and, in so doing, refuses to shame Mary. Instead of harming her, he allows his life to be disrupted by willingly aligning himself to his adopted son begotten by the Spirit. For Joseph, this includes waiting to have intercourse with his wife until after the child is born. This is apparently Joseph's own choice, not mandated by God, and an embodiment of his determination to honor Mary and YHWH (and perhaps of acknowledging their strange, wonderfully intimate collaboration in bearing Christ).

erotic is that it is precisely the force of the erotic-in-the-raw that also makes it such an important arena for formation in self-offering love of the other. Whether we are in a relationship and must regularly temper our desires to suit our lover, or if we are celibate and must resist making others into servants to our appetites, practicing resistance to unchanneled sexuality forms us profoundly because of the strength it requires to tend it well. Of course, for Christians both of these are merely forms (whether in intimate relationships or not in them) through which we submit to being molded for love of God. All loves require loss and denial; love of God also entails loss, a giving up—of others' expectations, and of our own illusions. In the end, Christians will almost always anger others, especially those who have some claim on our sexuality, because as humans they need (or think they need) our embodied fidelity. Others want to tell us how to love; our society provides expectations about how our sexual identity must be performed and our lovers tell us what caring for them necessitates. While important to consider, for those attached to Love Herself these commands are not unequivocally obeyed. What friends, lovers, and our neighbors actually need is a loyal love, always refracted through the Triune God and nourished by him. Like all intimacies, this movement into God builds slowly, painstakingly, yet eventually we become free: our hearts yearn in rhythm with God's own, and thus we do not ultimately *need* another to fulfill us nor our society to affirm our sexuality. Rather, we love freely, because we are not driven or directed by the other's demands on us. Instead, we receive others as gifts from God, but these gifts are endlessly complex in how to receive them well. Such gifts sometimes become enfleshed conduits of her gracious love and joyous communion. At other times, erotic relationships become spaces in which we recognize our finitude or duplicity. We may see in them reflections of our own and others' propensity to manipulation. But in all such relationships we must comprehend that our obligation is to love, not as others demand, but rather as God's loving kindness directs us, "through" God rather than strictly "as" God. In other words, in order to care for ourselves and others with generosity, we must depend upon and attach to the One who is the originator of "free love."[20]

5 Christ as fully human one: Can a celibate Messiah guide us to erotic freedom?

Our era often mistakenly conflates desire and freedom, as if indulging our wants defines liberty. In doing so, we forget that we are shaped by social forces in our "natural" appetites.[21] Such a vision also presumes that the touchstone for ordering

---

[20] For a discussion of how God loves us without needing us—yet also with affection and longing—see Miroslav Volf, *Free of Charge: Giving and Forgiving in a World Stripped of Grace* (Grand Rapids, MI: Zondervan, 2005). We cannot explore here the complexity that loving another as ourselves requires dying to ourselves. For some of us, living into such love necessitates resistance of temptations to self-hate on one hand or to denial of our limitations on the other.

[21] For how the sexual desires of young adults in the United States have been shaped by the larger cultural landscape, see Mark Regnerus and Jeremy Uecker, *Premarital Sex in America: How Young Americans Meet, Mate, and Think about Marrying* (New York: Oxford University Press, 2011). See the example of anal sex on pp. 32–33 as an increasingly common expectation in emerging adults' relational script.

our desires lies within, that the true self buried within each of us directs us to the good and does this in large part by giving us longings.[22] Against such confidence in our self-supervision and despite other feminists' resistance to the language, Coakley consistently links our freedom as creatures to our surrender to God.[23] Before exploring her reading of Gregory of Nyssa and the intensification of desire through submission, we should ponder the resource Christians have in the life of Christ for comprehending how we train ourselves to become lavish, free lovers. In Christ we see how raw desires (including, if not especially, good ones) must be submitted to a God who is trustworthy, whose love proves powerful over all other forces, and whose sometimes puzzling and difficult commands nonetheless train us for love of self, other, and of course God herself. As one way of examining the interconnectedness of desires, discipline, and freedom, consider the temptations of Christ. By setting these temptations within the larger context of his life, we see that our savior's celibacy cannot be severed from his celebration of communion with friends; we recall that Jesus, too, had to develop habits of setting aside his own appetites in order to love himself and others fully.

After being baptized and claimed as the beloved Son of God, the Spirit leads Jesus into the wilderness where he is tempted by the devil.[24] Remarkably, even Jesus cannot passively receive an affirmation of his identity as king-heir nor merely mentally assent to what such intimacy with God will mean. An enspirited body like all humans, Jesus must *practice* resistance to what might seem natural if bent way of responding to appetites by exercising the muscles of self-restraint in conditions of genuine stress. Rather than control as exclusively inwardly determined and resourced, "self-restraint" for Christ and his followers means learning to interrupt usual patterns of response through applied reliance on God's guidance and help.[25]

Consider how each of the temptations requires a retooling and aiming of basic human drives. Even when famished, he denies himself food, because fidelity to the Father requires costly trust in God's provision—and to that provision in God's own time. Hunger as a drive is not bad, but to be free means we resist feeding ourselves at the cost of our allegiances or for our own benefit. Even though it could secure others' acceptance of him, he rejects the showy display of exceptionalism that would mark him off as untouchable and thus render him a safe, desirable ally. To want to be known for who we are and to be desired as such is a natural enough longing, but Jesus must learn to seek friends by joining in our vulnerability rather than by manipulating our longing for security apart from the God of Israel's peculiar ways

---

[22] Charles Taylor has written extensively on this, including in *Sources of the Self: The Making of the Modern Identity* (Cambridge, MA: Harvard University Press, 1992).

[23] This is a major theme of Coakley's collection of essays, *Powers and Submissions: Spirituality, Philosophy, and Gender* (Oxford: Blackwell, 2002). See, in particular, chapter 1, "*Kenosis* and Subversion: On Repression of 'Vulnerability' in Christian Feminist Writing."

[24] Matthew states that the Spirit does this so that Jesus can be tempted by the devil (4:1); Luke's version simply states that this occurred (4:1-2). This account draws from Matthew's account in terms of the order of the temptations.

[25] Use of the term "enspirited" does not necessitate a verdict on the dualism/non-dualist views of the human person nor on Augustine's understanding of the resurrected body that can be translated in this way. Instead, I am recalling that orthodox Christians affirm that we are bodies (here including mind) and spirit together.

of salvation. When shown that certain forms of power could overthrow Roman oppression and institute justice by force, Jesus turns toward the One who brings *shalom* in his own way and time. An eternal reign of justice and peace flows only from the heart of the Righteous One, a heart joined only through adoration and utter dependence.

The reason these are genuine temptations and not playacting is that the devil taunts with the desire's usual path to seeming satisfaction: feed yourself so you can fulfill your calling to serve others; assert yourself by exuding confidence and displaying power so others will follow you into the good future you have planned; free others by controlling the field of play and seizing authority however we must.[26] Like all humans, Jesus must *enact* rejection of culturally mediated fulfillments and of self-referential ways to satisfy our deep longings to control our relationships, to live an effective and meaningful life, and to fulfill our intimacy with God and others. In order to be loved and love freely, Christ must submit to God's direction. Christ shows us how to be fully human and fully free as desiring humans, as those whose bodies necessitate that we willingly submit them to partnership and participation.[27]

What is crucial about Jesus's own journey is that he seeks to "remain in the Father's love," despite the sacrifices such love entails. In this submission he becomes released to enact his Messiahship as befits this identity as Son; he does not superimpose on his identity the Roman vision as the one who is the "son of god" and who secures *Pax Romana* by force.[28] But neither does Jesus play the victim nor does he remain hopelessly intimidated by such rule. The crowd responds, "He isn't like others! He teaches with authority!" (Mk 1:22) and this speaks to the way submission to the Father frees the Son to be the Son in a manner that mirrors divine power that is nonetheless noncoercive and vulnerable to human interaction.

Jesus is what love looks like: confidently resting in love Himself, he seeks the lost, comforts those in need, and speaks truthfully to those who risk alienation from their Creator in their refusal to embrace him. We, too, find that only in abandonment to the Father do we become Christoform. To do so means all our appetites are not theoretically or abstractly transformed. As in the temptations, they are exposed, and

---

[26] Like all rich texts, the temptations raise many important theological and ethical concerns. The interpretation here does not exclude those, particularly understandings of them in light of Israel's liberation from Egypt, her wandering, her failures, and finally with Matthew's portrayal of Jesus as God's faithful son.

[27] Such a connection between the training of desire and a deeply good human life must be true if Jesus is not merely putting on humanity but rather *is* human. Irenaeus's point is well taken: "Life in humankind is the glory of God; the life of humankind is the vision of God"; other translations read, "The glory of God is a living man [human]; the life of man [human] consists in beholding God." For translations and implications of Ireaneus's insight, see Veli-Matti Kärkkäinen, *Creation and Humanity: A Constructive Theology for a Pluralistic World* (Grand Rapids, MI: Eerdmans, 2015), 284. I want to highlight that Jesus is God's glory and reveals God's praiseworthiness. But as the fully *Human* One, Jesus's contemplation of God's goodness provides the lens through which he must view and respond to his desires so that his life enacts the interrelatedness of God and humanity that Irenaeus describes.

[28] Coins in Jesus's day bore the stamp, "Caesar Augustus, Divine Son of God." Among other places, one of his altars proclaims Augustus as the one who brought "peace and prosperity to the entire inhabited world."

we are given opportunities to practice how to fulfill them in the desert of our own earthly wandering.

In this understanding, Jesus's celibacy does not hobble us but rather recalls for us (contra much current assertion that abstinence is an unhealthy and meager human state) that great lovers focus their appetites through lifelong training. Lest one wonder if connecting sexuality and self-control with other appetites seems a stretch, social science research finds an interrelatedness of self-regulation and capacity to restrain oneself, including in our sexual behavior.[29] Because he practiced self-restraint through dependence on God, Jesus proved remarkably boundless in his relationships. He entered into close companionships with friends, ate at table with those whose own appetites were questionable, received sensual expressions of gratitude from women, and taught women like Martha and Mary. Cultural expectations and constraints on his sexual life—such as pressure as a faithful Jew and oldest son to marry and produce children—do not arise raw in him and thus become his guide. Instead, we see in the wilderness Jesus's continued openness to the Father's love through disciplined, intentional resistance (and, also, indulgence—whether it is angels that minister to him or women who offer him water). In Christ's transformed desires, we see that our own end (married or unmarried, virginal or not) is marked by a freedom to embrace others without self-consciousness, to choose indulgence or restraint not because others demand it of us but rather because sharing of divine *agape* requires it—and importantly, provides love's shape. So, love incarnate could be seen as a drunkard and a man of questionable company; in part, this is because his appetites run through the Father, refracted through God's care. This not only provides the form of Christ's love ("cruciform" in large part) but also allows his love to expand beyond what marriage might have rightly corralled. Whatever our doctrine of the incarnation, surely we see in Christ a controlled, intense burn of divine love and the promise that this, too, could be our own, by God's grace and our willingness.

6 Coakley and Gregory of Nyssa: Intensification of desire through focused attention to it

Through Christ as Lover par excellance, we return to Coakley's affirmation that rather than seeking to shrink or repress our erotic desire, as with any appetite we intentionally receive it as an opportunity for training in divine love for our good and the good of the world. Gregory of Nyssa provides a metaphor for this in *On Virginity*, a text that addresses married and unmarried people as equally challenged to lifelong ascesis for the sake of love. Gregory was probably married at the time he wrote the treatise, and he

---

[29] Some research suggests that self-control is a "unitary faculty," so that deficiencies in one area—say money management—result in insufficient discipline in another, such as sexual behavior. See, for example, Matthew T. Gailliot and Roy F. Baumeister, "Self-Regulation and Sexual Restraint: Dispositionally and Temporarily Poor Self-Regulatory Abilities Contribute to Failures at Restraining Sexual Behavior," *Personality and Social Psychology Bulletin* 33, no. 2 (February 2007): 173–86.

displays little of Augustine's anxiety about loss of male "control" in sex. Rather, Gregory offers the following image:

> Imagine a stream flowing from a spring and dividing itself off into a number of accidental channels. As long as it proceeds so, it will be useless for any purpose of agriculture, the dissipation of its waters making each particular current small and feeble, and therefore slow. But if one were to mass these wandering and widely dispersed rivulets again into one single channel, he would have a full and collected stream for the supplies which life demands. Just so the human mind . . . as long as its current spreads itself in all directions over the pleasures of the senses, has no power that is worth the naming of making its way towards the Real Good; but once call it back and collect it upon itself . . . it will find no obstacle in mounting to higher things, in grasping realities.[30]

While one might expect Gregory to laud virginity in this way—as an avenue for "collecting" passion—Coakley points out that he uses the metaphor again when speaking of sex in marriage as "good irrigation" if ordered in relation to God and "so made 'moderate' in comparison with the intensified and unified stream that desire for God demands."[31] Thus Gregory recalls for us that when appetites like sex are thus channeled into the narrow way of discipline, the result is intensification of passion rather than its diminishment.[32] Importantly, for recalling erotic desire as a passion for communion with one another, such a vision means that the transformed married person and the transformed celibate share more in common—join in intimate unity—than the haplessly indulgent spouse or the begrudgingly abstaining celibate.

What a distinctly hopeful yet challenging message for our sexually anxious age! Our worried brother could benefit from a retrieval of Gregory's confidence in God to funnel our appetites so that they become *intensified*, so that we gradually join in God's love of those around us without fear and distraction. The problem with "high libido" is not the intensity of the passion but rather (in Gregory's metaphor) the way it runs amok, flooding tender reeds of vulnerable neighbors and carrying us far afield from the particular relational space we have been given to water as witnesses to God's goodness. Freud's idea of sublimation was not far from this, as when he acknowledges that *eros* must be channeled if civilization is to continue. But secular Freud cannot imagine the immensity of the stream's source, and so he offers a shrunken vision of the sexual life, whereas Gregory knows that the Creator of erotic human creatures holds out a much more enticing, expansive, and passionate vision of the good life.

---

[30] Coakley, *The New Asceticism*, 48–49.
[31] Ibid., 49.
[32] Gregory applauds virginity, then, "*not* on account of its sexlessness, but because of its withdrawal from *worldly* interests—the building up of families, status and honour—and hence its emulation of the changeless life of the Trinity. It is not sex that is the problem, but worldly values. And he sees a good, spiritually productive marriage as almost on a par with celibacy given its equal potential capacity, when desire is rightly 'aimed', to bear the fruits of *leitourgia*, 'service' to others, especially to the poor." See Coakley, *The New Asceticism*, 50; emphasis in original. Our reflections on the temptations of Christ underscore this.

7 Coakley's courage: Reinvigorating theology and opening a way through the sludge of sex-as-usual

It is often said that we worship what we fear. Regardless of where we fall on the spectrum of liberal or conservative, many of us react to our sexual desires—commonly squelching or indulging them. While one proclaims (a bit too loudly) their openness to the erotic's power, another sternly asserts the rules of a God who appears shockingly small and vengeful. Some fear the restraints God would place on our loves; we do not want a God who jealously desires our fidelity as YHWH does. Some fear admission of our desires, refusing to wrest from them the rich formational power that only honest grappling with them provides us. (Or perhaps on both sides of the religious divide there also appears the God who does not much care about our bodies, who washed her hands of this earthy aspect of creatures formed of dust. This may be the most difficult and dangerous of any sensibility to dislodge, as it allows the erotic to float untethered to love Herself and the witness of that love in Christ.) Coakley's gift is her determination to harness the Christian tradition and the biblical witness so that it speaks to this befuddlement and anxiety about sex.

For those like my emailing brother, Coakley's invitation to the transformation of desire in the Triune God means we cannot choose fear of our sexual desires—even when their force is formidable—nor can we choose apathy, cloaking hopelessness for more in an exultation in meager and momentary erotic joys. Instead, she constantly reminds us that God is implicated in our desiring because God, too, yearns for communion with us. While desires come raw and sometimes become vicious and self-serving, God invites us to rip open our lives' longings, however embarrassing. Thus splayed before her in vulnerability and nakedness, we receive like the Song's poets the untamable yet sweet, hot breath of the One who is love.[33]

What does that mean in ordinary time? Fundamentally, it means accepting Augustine's conviction that everything comes from God; even evil is privation and derivative of the good. Unlike Augustine in some sense, we then explore as sacred space our own and others' erotic longings and desires, noting that in consumptive ugliness as well as poignant ache we find fodder for engagement with the living God. It means my emailing brother finds friends who willingly hold his anxiety and assure him of grace; they listen to whatever "extra high" libido means, refusing to shame anyone who so openly claims that God can reform us. In relationships, it means pausing to consider if our love of one another results in deeper love of God and neighbor, or if it distracts us from—or malforms us for—such love. It means acknowledging that we must *learn* to lay aside our cravings for another and practice this through patterns of indulgence and restraint. Dating, married, or celibate, we must all learn new habits, and we join

---

[33] The temptations of Christ remind us of the quality of God's love as untamable, as something not able to be controlled or manipulated; we see this again in Jesus's honest plea but submission to the Father in the garden (Mt. 26:39). Like Jesus we ask for what we need and even for what we desire, but Christ reminds us that our lives are finally determined by God's sense of how we are to participate in the salvation story. Like Jesus, faithfulness feels like a trust fall, a blind drop into the way the Father redeems even affliction for good.

one another in creating spaces of mercy as restoration and as reformation. (It mocks marriage and underrates the difficulty of fidelity to speak and act as if marriage solves the problem of erotic transformation. Rather, such covenants merely determine the overarching shape such transformation must take and may well raise the stakes of our unwillingness to admit a need for it. Arguably the greatest erotic temptation of marriage is the certainty that one has made a terrible mistake when in actuality one has merely seen the other as they are: a mere human, incapable of the feat of meeting our needs even when they diligently seek to do so.)[34]

As for theologians and the erotic, Coakley believes that the task is one of reclamation of our past and creative engagement in the present, all done with the sense that the Spirit has worked among us and continues to do so. For example, we must retrieve the confidence of the church fathers to grapple with the erotic, especially the Song; even if we do not adopt their (sometimes misogynistic) hermeneutical moves, Bernard and Origen heard in this text an invitation into the mysterious, alluring love of God. Why do we often lack such certainty? Why this shyness among theologians to wrestle with the ordinary ways we speak of love among humans as often including an erotic element, yet ignore this aspect when theologizing about "God is love"?

Given that sexuality plays out in clamoring arguments inside and outside the church, we must interrogate what our much-cited affirmation "God is love" means for our friendships. Our unwillingness to stare down our erotic desires and question their significance for our life with God prevents us from developing friendships. While he might seem a strange example to bring in at this juncture, Augustine inspires me in this regard. Augustine's life and his writings are complex and rich. I do not pretend to know all his comments on love and on sexuality, even if much of his sensibility famously filtered into the church in ways Coakley (among others) sees as negative. Despite this and his occasionally awful language about women, I am struck in Augustine's writings by his pathos, including the touching and shameless way he expresses love of his friends. His language would for us be more suited to lovers, and I wonder if we might become people who have overcome our fear and shame enough to reclaim Christian friendship that is likewise deep, affectionate, and unabashedly delighted by another's presence and shattered by their loss. While we claim that we are sexually enlightened, I suspect that it is our shriveled imaginations that force us to frame passionate same-sex or opposite-sex companionship in erotic terms—that is, not in *eros* as deep communion but rather as genitally defined or culturally categorized by labels like "gay." The current US vice president refuses to meet with a woman alone and cites his Christian faith as a reason for this caution. But instead of witnessing to fidelity to Christ, it belies a profound worry that, somehow, *eros* will control, overtake him, and thus friendships

---

[34] I am not claiming all divorce or like "mistakes" are therefore unfaithful. Rather, I am noting the ordinariness of marital disappointment, sometimes interpreted as a mistake in choosing a partner when in reality the error regards the way that all good marriage necessitates erotic transformation that frees the other from the obligation to fulfill us. We think we know this because we can say it; it is quite another thing to "know" this in our bodies, when we are emotionally or erotically left behind. We also are shocked to discover the depth of our own disappointing performances of mundane activities of love. This is precisely where actual love and transformation begins.

such as those Christ forged with Mary Magdalene become impossible.[35] Erotic longing does not press us into the expansive communion of the Song's "undoing" of man and woman's fracture in Genesis, but instead fearfully drives us away from one another and suggests that appetites cannot nourish the joining together apart from marriage that the eschaton promises.

Finally, in all relationships (even in those often not dubbed "erotic") we need to be willing to admit the "not yet"-ness of all our cravings for union. Whether in friendship, fellowship, or covenant, whether in marriages of whatever configuration or whether unmarried, we must speak more often about the inevitability of our loneliness. We may, as Stanley Hauerwas often says, be fortunate enough to be lonely together, such as in good marriages and companionships. But like the Song reminds us, we are meant for communion with God in new bodies, even as our current ones undergo their alteration in readiness for it. If we expose our erotic desire in order to eliminate sexual desire or *eros*, we shall never do so, as it remains a sign of the union to come. Instead, we bear with longing bodies in hope, knowing that its insatiability recalls the reality of divine love still to be revealed in us. In the meantime, we muddle along as those who witness to the God who is love by receiving even an "extra high libido" as a precious clue about our end in the sea of God's *agape*. Thus emboldened, we welcome God's discipline and submit our ordinary appetites for (slow, steady) transformation by her grace.

---

[35] While such a caution *might* make sense if he were an unprincipled or undisciplined teen, his lifelong church attendance should have formed him for freedom in relationships with women. If Pence's reasoning is that he wants to be "above reproach," then why not meet in windowed rooms or open spaces? As it stands, such partitioning seems extreme in a mature man who (it appears) has made a lifelong habit of fidelity. This highlights the bitter and ironic fruit of untrained sexuality in our "free" and "enlightened" culture: women cannot meet alone with Vice President Pence, while we risk sexual comments or even sexual assault if we meet with President Trump.

14

Perfect Obedience, Perfect Love, and the (So-Called) Problem of Heavenly Freedom

James T. Turner, Jr.

1 Introduction

The so-called Problem of Heavenly Freedom (PHF), about which a few recent papers have been written, is a philosophical and theological puzzle generated by three main intuitions.[1] Intuition (1) is the (libertarian) thought that, for a moral agent to have free will, she must be able to choose, in a way that is ultimately up to her, between good and evil actions. Intuition (2) is that libertarian free will is such a great good that, were it to be absent from the heavenly state, this would constitute a qualitative diminution of that state. Intuition (3) is a classic account of the heavenly state such that those in the heavenly state are in a necessarily morally perfect condition. They are "impeccable," where being "impeccable" might be understood as "constitutionally incapable of succumbing to temptation on any given occasion. This suggests that an impeccable person cannot have the capacity to sin."[2] Combining these intuitions leads to the PHF because, purportedly, they imply either that there is no libertarian free will in the heavenly state because those in the heavenly state cannot choose to go wrong with respect to moral actions (and so, sans libertarian free will, the heavenly state is not as great as it could be), or else it is possible for the heavenly redeemed to sin. But both of these disjuncts are often taken to be theologically false, so it becomes incumbent upon Christian thinkers (of

---

[1] James F. Sennett, "Is There Freedom in Heaven?" *Faith and Philosophy* 16, no. 1 (1999): 69–82; Graham Oppy, Yujin Nagasawa, and Nick Trakakis, "The Problem of Heaven," in *Arguing About Gods*, ed. Graham Oppy (Cambridge: Cambridge University Press, 2006), 314–30; Timothy Pawl and Kevin Timpe, "Incompatibilism, Sin, and Free Will in Heaven," *Faith and Philosophy* 26, no. 4 (October 2009): 398–419; Steven B. Cowan, "Compatibilism and the Sinlessness of the Redeemed in Heaven," *Faith and Philosophy* 28, no. 4 (October 2011): 416–31; Timothy Pawl and Kevin Timpe, "Heavenly Freedom: A Reply to Cowan," *Faith and Philosophy* 30, no. 2 (April 2013): 188–97; and Christopher M. Brown, "Making the Best Even Better: Modifying Pawl and Timpe's Solution to the Problem of Heavenly Freedom," *Faith and Philosophy* 32, no. 1 (January 2015): 63–80.

[2] Oliver D. Crisp, *God Incarnate: Explorations in Christology* (London: T&T Clark, 2009), 127.

the libertarian stripe, anyway) to find a way to bring these three intuitions together such that they do not generate the PHF.[3]

Recently, Timothy Pawl and Kevin Timpe have offered joint efforts to provide a rejoinder to the PHF that retains a libertarian account of freedom for both the pre-heavenly redeemed *and* those in the heavenly state. Their arguments advance a libertarian free will cum virtue ethic suggesting that the reason one cannot will to do evil in "Heaven" is because one has, in one's pre-heavenly existence, *freely formed* one's character to such a degree that one simply *cannot* will to do evil. On this view, it is precisely the fact that one's heavenly character has been *freely formed* by one's free choices in one's pre-heavenly existence that makes all of the actions flowing from the formed character libertarianly free in sufficiently important ways to stave off the PHF. Additionally, on their view, one's character being so formed is a necessary requirement for one's having libertarian free will in the heavenly state.[4] Let us call this view P&T. Here are Pawl and Timpe on the matter:

> We think that during pre-heavenly existence a person has the ability to form a moral character which later precludes that person from willing certain things. For instance, neither author of this paper can will to torture an innocent child for a nickel. Our characters are such that we cannot will that; we simply cannot see good reason for engaging in such behavior. . . . We are free in that we can choose to perform morally good actions, but our freely formed characters preclude us from doing morally bad actions insofar as those characters lead us to evaluate reasons for acting, or not acting, in certain ways.

---

[3] For more on how these intuitions combine to create PHF, see the literature noted in note 1. Pawl and Timpe cite Aquinas's *ST* III.18.4 reply to obj. 3 as an affirmation of heavenly freedom ("Incompatibilism, Sin, and Free Will in Heaven," 399, note 2). This citation is not clear to me, for it is a discussion of *Christ's* free will. To be fair, Aquinas does, in this spot, casually mention the state of the "blessed" as a state in which one can "choose with a free choice confirmed in good." But, given its truncated expression (it is not even a full sentence), it strikes me as odd to use this as a proof text for Thomas's approval of heavenly free will. Perhaps another area where Thomas might affirm heavenly freedom is in *ST* Ia.19.10 reply to obj. 2 in which he suggests that, in the same way that God is free even though he cannot do evil, so are we free to choose between, for example, non-sinful opposites (e.g., to sit or not to sit). The idea one might take from this is that, if God is free and cannot sin, then "not being able to sin" does not preclude freedom. Augustine is much clearer on the matter. Cf., *City of God*, ed. Philip Schaff, trans. Marcus Dods (Grand Rapids: Christian Classics Ethereal Library), XXII.30, http://www.ccel.org/ccel/schaff/npnf102.iv.XXII.30.html. Pawl and Timpe effectively quote Augustine to this end at the beginning of their "Incompatibilism, Sin, and Free Will in Heaven."

I should mention that, though Intuition (2) is featured in this literature, *often* it is advanced because freedom's goodness is taken to be salient to the Free Will Defense against the logical problem of evil. This same literature discusses this. For reasons given in the PHF literature for why compatibilist non-libertarian accounts side step the problem altogether, see Cowan, "Compatibilism and the Sinlessness of the Redeemed in Heaven," 416–31. It is possible, though, that compatibilist accounts run into other worse problems, namely, problems trying to get around the logical problem of evil. See Sennett's account in "Is There Freedom in Heaven" and both of the Pawl and Timpe papers listed in note 1.

[4] In what I take to be the original defense against PHF, James Sennett, in his "Is There Freedom in Heaven?," offers a solution that posits a compatibilist notion of freedom in the heavenly state. This is a compatibilist notion of freedom that he takes to be an entailment from the libertarianly free actions of humans while in the pre-heavenly state. See Sennett, "Is There Freedom in Heaven?" 75.

Moreover:

> In heaven, the blessed will be incapable of willing any sin, just as we are incapable of willing the particular sin of torturing an innocent child for a nickel.... This will be because of the character the redeemed have formed in their pre-heavenly existence.... This doesn't mean that they won't be free, however. At the very least... the redeemed in heaven could be derivatively free; that is, even if all the decisions of the blessed in heaven were determined by their characters and the reasons they see for acting in various ways, that by itself wouldn't render them unfree.[5]

Now, P&T has one last important commitment: the freely formed nature of these heavenly characters happens over time and is not something that God can unilaterally effect on the human and still retain her libertarian freedom.[6]

Though I grant that, for a redeemed human to be fit for the heavenly state, a redeemed human's character needs to be such that she can no longer will to do evil actions, I disagree that it is a necessary requirement that this impeccable will and character be formed *by the human* over time. (I assume here that, eschewing Pelagianism, these views trade on a synergistic account of character formation. So, the phrase "by the human" should be understood as consistent with this.) There are two reasons for this disagreement, the first of which points to the impossibility of such human-driven change (even if codriven, assuming, again, synergism). This reason I will call the Impossibility Thesis (IT). An iteration of the IT is offered in Graham Oppy et al.'s explication of their version of the PHF. They state IT in this way:

> I think that this picture is unbelievable [that humans have formed their characters such that they won't sin]. It is not plausible to think that there are—or ever have been—*any* people whose characters are such that, when they die, it is logically impossible for them to make evil choices. It is also not plausible to think that there are—or ever have been—*any* people whose characters are such that, when they die, the features of those characters that bear on any choice that that person might be called upon to make in heaven are as they are *solely* because of libertarian free choices that that person made during his life.[7]

I will comment on and clarify this quote in Section 2. For now, let me briefly state the second reason I am taking issue with the purported necessary requirement that the impeccable character of those in the heavenly state will be freely formed *by the human over time*. The second reason is that, given that the *parousia* of Christ (i.e., Christ's final coming) is at a fixed temporal point in the future, there will be (plausibly) very many redeemed human beings who have died temporally too close to the *parousia* to

---

[5] They use "unfree" as a synonym for "not libertarianly free" (Pawl and Timpe, "Incompatibilism, Sin, and Free Will in Heaven," 409 and 410 respectively).
[6] Pawl and Timpe, "Incompatibilism, Sin, and Free Will in Heaven," 414; Pawl and Timpe, "Reply to Cowan," 188; and Sennett, "Is There Freedom in Heaven?" 73.
[7] Oppy, Nagasawa, and Trakakis, "The Problem of Heaven," 323.

be able fully to develop their characters to be fit for the heavenly state. But, since we have good exegetical reasons for thinking that those alive just prior to Christ's return will immediately enter the heavenly state, their having a freely formed character fit for the heavenly state is not a necessary requirement. Call this second reason Omega Point (OP), which I will explain in Section 3.

In this chapter, then, I will argue both a negative thesis and a positive one. Negatively, I will argue that P&T solutions to the PHF are faulty because they cannot account for the IT and OP problems. Positively, I will argue that a possible solution to the PHF requires an analysis of what it is to love God. To advance these positions, I argue in three stages. First, in Section 2, I draw out the IT by providing a riff on a prima facie theologically informed account of the human being vis-à-vis committing sinful actions. Second, in Section 3, I advance the OP argument, an argument that trades on what is, very plausibly, a theological truth, namely, that those "in Christ" who are not impeccable at the moment prior to Christ's return, will, on His return, be made morally perfect and fit for the heavenly state. Third, in Section 4, I offer a proposal to solve the PHF. The proposal I offer is motivated by a mutual implication Scripture seems to place between loving God and obeying Him. An analysis of this mutual implication helps to show why libertarian free will is not available to the unregenerate. Moreover, it helps to show why libertarian free will is not the *best* kind of free will available to the regenerate. To pump one's intuitions in this direction, I end my proposal by borrowing an analogy offered by Harry Frankfurt. This latter part of Section 4 aims to show why the redeemed will not miss libertarian freedom in the heavenly state. Lastly, in Section 5, I provide some concluding remarks.

2 Impossibility Thesis (IT)

With their version of IT, Graham Oppy et al. preemptively argue against the very *possibility* of a human being developing the sort of moral character that Pawl and Timpe suggest is required for existence in the heavenly state. Now, in the quote given, above, it seems to me that some of Oppy et al.'s language is either too strong or poorly worded. Here is the bit I mean: "It is not plausible to think that there are—or ever have been—*any* people whose characters are such that, when they die, it is logically impossible for them to make evil choices."[8] Now, I cannot see a reason for why the relevant sort of impossibility under discussion is or should be "logical impossibility." I do not know for sure, but I doubt that Pawl or Timpe, for example, would be too concerned about conceding that a redeemed person's sinning in the heavenly state is "logically possible." I conclude this because I suspect that the category of impossibility referred to is not the category of impossibility that is driving the arguments—on either side. Instead, I think the impossibility is one, perhaps, of metaphysical impossibility. And, I take it that this is more likely the case on the assumption that we restrict "logical impossibility" to a disagreement between propositions (e.g., the propositions "that it's

[8] Ibid.

raining" and "that it's not raining" cannot be simultaneously instantiated at the same time and in the same way). So, if Pawl and Timpe were to concede the logical possibility of the heavenly redeemed making evil choices, it would be because the matter does not concern logical (im)possibility. Another way of putting the point is this: *if* they conceded this, it seems likely they might concede it because it is no concession at all, but rather a category mistake.

IT points instead to a problem of *metaphysical* (im)possibility. The question is: Does it violate the *nature* of the heavenly human to commit an evil action (an action for which she is morally blameworthy)? And if so, is it conceivable for humans, who quite naturally commit evil actions, ever to work themselves to a point at which their characters make their committing evil actions *metaphysically impossible*? On my reading, Oppy et al. think *this* is not possible.

Now, I agree with this charge. It too strikes me as unbelievable that a human could affect such a change in herself. Take Jones as a candidate human being. Suppose that we take it as a given that Jones has a human nature by virtue of being a human being. Is it in virtue of being a human—that is, having a human nature—that it is metaphysically impossible for Jones to be able (synergistically) to work herself into an impeccable character? I cannot speak for Oppy et al., but, theologically speaking, I take it that the answer to this question is "no." It seems to me that it is an accidental feature of individual humans that they commit sinful actions. In other words, it does not seem to me that the property of "potentially committing sinful actions" flows out of the *essence* of human nature; it is not part of what it is to be classified as a human. If it were, then the New Creation, being populated with *impeccable* (i.e., not potentially sinful) human beings, would be a metaphysical impossibility. (And so would Christ's impeccability *qua* human.)[9] So, if it is correct or, at least, plausible that the property of "being peccable" is not a part of the nature of human beings, then it is plausible to suggest that Oppy et al.'s argument does not turn on what it means to be human. The argument, instead, turns on whether particular humans have something about them that makes it impossible for them *qua* individual human to transform their characters from morally peccable to morally impeccable.

To attempt to draw out what I mean, consider the following distinctions (what amount to a riff on an Augustinian take on the "nature" of human beings):

SN: Sin nature, unable not to sin
INN: Inaugurated new nature, able not to sin
CNN: Consummated new nature, unable to sin.[10]

---

[9] For a discussion of the impeccability of Christ *qua* human, see Crisp, *God Incarnate*, 122–36.
[10] On what I have labeled "SN," see, for example, Augustine, "A Treatise on Nature and Grace, Against Pelagius," in *St. Augustine: Anti-Pelagian Writings*, ed. Philip Schaff (Grand Rapids, MI: Christian Classics Ethereal Library), chaps. 55–56. For INN and CNN, see, for example, Augustine, "A Treatise on Rebuke and Grace," in *St. Augustine: Anti-Pelagian Writings*, ed. Philip Schaff (Grand Rapids, MI: Christian Classics Ethereal Library), chaps. 33–35. Both texts can be retained here: http://www.ccel.org/ccel/schaff/npnf105.pdf

Now, the "sin nature," to borrow an English translation of a Pauline term, is a post-lapsarian state of all humans (barring Jesus). It is a condition in which humans are unable to refrain from committing evil actions. If this Augustinian riff is correct, this is the condition in which humans find themselves prior to their spiritual regeneration (on my reading of Augustine, this category is exhausted on unbaptized pagans).[11] The "inaugurated new nature" is the condition of the pre-heavenly redeemed, the regenerate; that is, the kind of human Paul deems "new creation" in 2 Cor. 5:17.[12] It is the condition of those "in Christ" that live between the times of Christ's first advent and second. And, finally, the "consummated new nature" is, as the name suggests, the condition of the redeemed human at the consummation of the New Creation; that is, at the *parousia* of Christ. The New Creation is the heavenly state, and it is in *this* state that all humans are morally impeccable. (A small note: I will refrain, so far as possible, from calling this state Heaven, because I do not think the Bible does. Instead, I call it New Creation or the New Heavens and New Earth just so one does not lose sight of the fact that God redeems *this* world.)

Here I need briefly to clarify some terminology. Using a(n) (English translation) biblical term such as "sin *nature*" is potentially ambiguous. For natures are, in the philosophical literature, at any rate, thought of in various, though similar (perhaps synonymous), ways: for example, as the definition of a thing that explains why it is what it is and not something else; as a bundle of properties a thing has, either with respect to its species or with respect to it as an individual, in every possible world; as a thing's essence (and so on). By my lights, SN and INN, at least, plausibly are not like this. They are not like this insofar as they are not a part of the definition of a species. More specifically, they neither individually nor jointly help explain why a thing is classified as a human and not something else. Conversely, in my view, CNN *does* do this—more on this anon. However, individually, all three define a particular *way* in which particular human beings function with respect to actions for which one is morally culpable.

To help make this clearer, consider a rough analogy. To set up the analogy, suppose for argument that human nature—when it functions properly—is designed such that one with a perfectly functioning human nature is unable to sin. Further, consider the human eye and suppose that we make the following distinctions for its "vision nature":

IVN: Impaired vision nature, unable to see objects in a non-blurry way.
CVN: Correctable vision nature (e.g. with contact lenses or eye glasses), able to see objects in a non-blurry way.
PVN: Perfected vision nature (e.g., with laser eye surgery), able only to see objects in a non-blurry way.

---

[11] Cf. Augustine, "A Treatise on the Merits and Forgiveness of Sins, and on the Baptism of Infants," in *St. Augustine: Anti-Pelagian Writings*, ed. Philip Schaff (Grand Rapids, MI: Christian Classics Ethereal Library), Book I, chapters 23, 26, 34, 36, 55. http://www.ccel.org/ccel/schaff/npnf105.pdf

[12] 2 Cor. 5:17: ὥστε εἴ τις ἐν Χριστῷ, καινὴ κτίσις. For arguments on why "καινὴ κτίσις" reflects that those "in Christ" should be understood as "new creation"—as a piece of the coming cosmic-in-scope New Creation—see Douglas J. Moo, "Creation and New Creation," *Bulletin for Biblical Research* 20, no. 1 (2010): 39–60.

Some caveats: First, I am neither an optometrist nor an ophthalmologist, so I have no idea whether this is anything close to an accurate way to describe the visual quality of eye patients. Second, I realize that the syntax associated with CVN and PVN might be ambiguous. For, "able to see objects in a non-blurry way" and "able only to see objects in a non-blurry way" are consistent with "cannot see at all the things that one with IVN can see in a blurry way." On this sort of reading, it is not clear that CVN and PVN are improvements on IVN. But a charitable reading understands that this is not what I mean. What I *do* mean is something like the following: for CVN, one does see, one sees all of what one with IVN sees, and *some* of the objects one sees, one sees in a clear, non-blurry, way. For PVN, one does see, one sees all of what one with IVN and CVN sees, and *all* the objects one sees, one sees in a clear, non-blurry, way. Again, for the sake of the analogy, just assume PVN means whatever the "folk" mean by "20/20 vision."[13] (Recall: this is a *rough* analogy.) The language I use in spelling out these terms—ambiguous as it may be (though, I submit that one is being far too pedantic if one picks on this point)—is used so that it matches closely to the way I have spelled out the "sin nature."

In any case, the idea is that there is a particular way human vision *should* work, when working properly. And plausibly there is a particular way that human nature *should* work, when working properly. So the analogy could run like this: 20/20 vision is to human vision as CNN is to human nature. Another way of putting this is that there is a telos to human vision and a telos to human nature, namely, PVN and CNN respectively.

If that is right, it is clear that neither IVN nor CVN is the telos of human vision, since they are contradictory to it. It is also clear that neither SN nor INN is the telos of human nature, for these are contradictory to it. If so, it follows that one cannot use the particular instances of the SN and INN in particular humans to reason via abstraction to the universal "human being." And, again, that is just a roundabout way of saying that SN and INN are not part of what it is to be human (*Mutatis mutandis* for human vision).

Now, when I suggest that plausibly it is metaphysically impossible for a human with INN to change her character such that she becomes a human with CNN, I mean it in the same way one might plausibly suggest that it is *physically* or *nomologically* impossible that a human with CVN change her vision, by internal effort, such that she becomes a human with PVN. (Note here that the idea is *not* that a human could not change from having CVN to having PVN; rather, it is that a human cannot do this through visual training or exercise.[14] Compare: on P&T, humans can, by repeated habitual action, not merely get more and more virtuous, but get to a point of impeccability, a state in which it becomes *impossible* to do morally blameworthy actions.)[15]

I say all this and I still agree with the overall virtue ethic approach to moral character in which Pawl and Timpe appear to be working. It just seems to me, if it is the case that P&T sorts of human moral development is possible, that it is much more likely that the

---

[13] Here I readily admit that I am one of the "folk."
[14] Again, I am not an eye doctor of any sort. So, just assume this is true for the sake of the analogy.
[15] Pawl and Timpe, "Incompatibilism, Sin, and Free Will in Heaven," 410.

moral improvement of a human with INN is, *at best*, asymptotic on "impeccable." But even given this asymptotic understanding, it strikes me as far-fetched to suggest that there are (barring Jesus), or ever will be, any extant humans with INN that achieve this pre-heavenly level of near moral perfection.

This may be too strong. I suppose it is possible that a Roman Catholic could point to purportedly "sinless" saints, such as Pope John Paul II, for example. Perhaps a member of the Nazarene denomination of Protestantism could point to its purportedly "sinless" ministers.[16] But if these characters are the sort trotted out as evidence for a central premise in rebuttals to the PHF, then so much the worse for these defenses. For indeed, it is very hard to accept the claim that these people are "sinless" in an "impeccable" way. In any case, I suppose the degree to which one can affirm that such people do or will exist (or have existed, bracketing out Christ) is the degree to which one might find the IT misplaced. I, for one, do not think that anyone, except Christ, has ever reached such a sinless state this side of the eschaton. And if that is correct, then IT carries some force.[17]

---

[16] Thanks to Jordan Wessling for this point given in conversation. For Catholics, at least, there might be some equivocation going on with "sinlessness" with respect to premortem humans, even the pope. See Joseph Wawrykow's account in "The Theological Virtues," in *The Oxford Handbook of Aquinas*, ed. Brian Davies and Eleonore Stump (Oxford: Oxford University Press, 2012), 297.

[17] In his interesting paper, "Character-development and Heaven," *International Journal for Philosophy of Religion* 76 (2014): 319–30, dedicated to investigating the "Problem of Heavenly Freedom," Luke Henderson argues that the sort of character-formation requirement set up by Pawl and Timpe implies a debilitating "self-causation." He writes on p. 328:

> If an agent can perform actions such that she eventually construct [sic] a character that causally determines the particular range of moral actions she can perform, such a fact seems to only be true if another general point is true: that agents act because of the way agents are, and agents are responsible for their acts because they are responsible for the way they are. However, such a position seems to entail the counter-intuitive (if not impossible) truth of self-creation, that is, if agents are to be held morally responsible for their actions. The reason such a position leads to self-creation is that an agent can only be responsible for her actions if she is responsible for her character in which the actions originated, but to be responsible for that character, the agent must be responsible for the acts that led to her having that character, and on and on to the agent's very first character; a character which it is implausible to think she formed or created. For those incompatibilists who argue that the blessed will be free and responsible in heaven, because they are responsible for developing a character fit for heaven, this argument would imply that the blessed not only needed to be responsible for the character . . . they cultivated for heaven, but they also needed to be responsible for the prior character . . . they acted from to cultivate the character . . . fit for heaven. However, to be responsible for that character . . . the blessed would have had to be responsible for the prior character . . . and on and on.

Quite obviously, the purported problem is, among other things, one of an infinite regress of characters for which one is supposedly responsible. But this objection seems to me to be a mistake. A libertarian advancing a broadly P&T explanation for heavenly freedom might respond in several ways. For example, in the broadly virtue ethics of Aristotle and Aquinas, it is just part of the scheme that part of the definition of the species "man" is such that, to quote Thomas, "In man's reason are to be found instilled by *nature* certain naturally known principles of both knowledge and action, *which are the nurseries of intellectual and moral virtues*, and in so far as there is in the will a natural appetite for good in accordance with reason" (*ST* IIa.63.1 *respondeo*). In other words, there is a sort of "baseline" character from which one is responsible for cultivating either a virtuous character or a vicious one. If so, this is the regress's stopping point; there is no further explanation needed for the beginning of the character development. For Aristotle's treatment, see Aristotle, *Nichomachean Ethics* III.i.1109b–III.v.1114b25.

3 Omega Point (OP)

I agree that moral character development is possible. I think this is particularly true of those humans with INN. I disagree that a human's free will-developed change from INN to CNN is possible. But, suppose that it is. Suppose that Oppy et al. and I are just wrong about the IT. Even given the possibility of developing a perfect moral character, I deny that such a libertarianly free will-developed character is *necessary* for the free will-retaining impeccable character proper to those in the heavenly state.

In a recent paper, Christopher Brown has already pressed one reason for thinking so. As a counterexample to P&T, he puts forward those humans who "die before the age of reason" and suggests the P&T "solution to the Problem of Heavenly Freedom is ... inconsistent with (what for some, e.g., orthodox Catholics, is) the theological fact that there are perfect persons in heaven who never had a chance to freely contribute to the development of their moral characters."[18] If Brown's reading of Roman Catholic theology is correct, then, at least for Roman Catholics, it is false that it is *necessary* that humans have a character freely formed in their pre-heavenly existence such that they are fit for heavenly existence.

If his claim about what orthodox Roman Catholics believe concerning those who "die before the age of reason" is true, then it does not seem as though a Roman Catholic can advance P&T. For the Protestant, the same is true *if* the Protestant affirms that there are some humans who die without having had the chance to form their characters, yet are morally perfect and free in the heavenly state.

But suppose a Roman Catholic decides to protest on this score; she decides that it cannot be the case—given her intuitions about the relevant connections between pre-heavenly freedom and heavenly freedom—that those who die "before the age of reason" are unilaterally made morally perfect. Suppose the Protestant, having no qualms about protesting Rome, argues from the same intuitions. Even still, there lurks a further problem. To expose this problem, I wish to add to Brown's counterexamples another, perhaps more troubling group: the Kingdom-bound individuals who are alive the second prior to Christ's return (the *parousia*). To begin to see why this is a problem, call the second of Christ's return: T_Ω. And call the second just prior to Christ's return: $T_{\Omega-1}$.

Now, suppose that Smith repents, believes the Gospel, and converts to Christianity at $T_{\Omega-n}$, where "n" denotes a unit of time that is an hour before T_Ω. And assume, for argument, that Smith is baptized at $T_{\Omega-m}$, where "m" denotes a unit of time no earlier than fifteen minutes after $T_{\Omega-n}$. Again, at T_Ω, Christ returns and establishes the New Creation, the heavenly state. So, what happens to Smith, who has just converted and been baptized no earlier than forty-five minutes before the *parousia*? Surely she has not developed her character from brand new INN to CNN. This is particularly true, one would think, if $T_{\Omega-m}$ and $T_{\Omega-1}$ are identical. For I think it is inconceivable that one could freely contribute to one's own character formation "in a moment, in the twinkling of

---

[18] Brown, "Making the Best Even Better," 67.

an eye" (1 Cor. 15:52).[19] And, yet, on a pretty standard reading of 1 Cor. 15:51-52, this kind of transformation is going to happen. Paul seems even to have thought that some of the letter's readers might experience this.[20] There was a palpable expectation that the *parousia* could happen at *any* moment, even as they read the letter![21]

At this point, I wish to frame the above deliverances through the following argument: OP. To begin, however, recall that T_Ω is my designation for the second of the *parousia* and that $T_{\Omega-1}$ is my designation for the second penultimate to the *parousia*. With this in mind, consider:

OP:

(1) If those humans with INN at $T_{\Omega-1}$ will, at T_Ω, be made humans with CNN, then it is false that it is necessary for humans to have a character freely formed in their pre-heavenly existence such that they are fit for heavenly existence.
(2) Those humans with INN at $T_{\Omega-1}$ will, at T_Ω, be made humans with CNN.
(3) Therefore, it is false that it is necessary for humans to have a character freely formed in their pre-heavenly existence such that they are fit for heavenly existence.

It is pretty clear, I think, that, for the P&T defender, the obvious point of attack is premise (2). A straightforward counter would be to run a modus tollens argument and deny that humans with INN at $T_{\Omega-1}$ will, at T_Ω, be made humans with CNN. There are a few ways one might attempt to do this. One way is to propose that those with INN at $T_{\Omega-1}$ go through a temporally extended period of Purgatory before entering into the New Creation as humans with CNN. The idea is that, even after Christ has returned and established the perfected New Creation anticipated in Isaiah 11, 25, 65ff.; Ezekiel 43ff.; Rom. 8:18-25; 1 Cor. 15:24-28, 42-58; Revelation 21 and 22; and others, there will still be some humans who will not have been changed from humans with INN to humans with CNN. Or, to borrow more Pauline terminology, these are humans who will not have been changed from *sōmata psychika* (psyche-powered bodies) to *sōmata*

---

[19] Interestingly, in this passage about what happens at the *parousia*, Paul uses the Greek phrase "ἐν ἀτόμῳ" (a declining of ὁ ἄτομος from which we get "atom") for "moment." This seems to imply some conception of a smallest uncuttable unit. See the next note.

[20] Here is Anthony C. Thiselton on the matter: "God will transform us instantaneously: 'We will all be changed, in a moment, in the twinkling (or blink) of an eye' (15:51-52). The Greek *atomō*, literally 'in an uncut unit,' is the smallest conceivable moment of time; *rhipē* is a rapid movement, and a rapid movement in the eyes is usually a blink. Paul uses one more analogy or metaphor. The trumpet blast (v. 52) is a command to an army that must instantly be obeyed: a sleeping army is awakened to stand on its feet in a flash." See Thiselton, *Systematic Theology* (Grand Rapids, MI: Eerdmans, 2015), 363–64.

[21] Thiselton suggests, despite what some scholars suppose is Paul's "imminent" eschatology—whereby the contention is that Paul believed that Christ would come while he was alive—that Paul had an eschatology of "readiness." In other words, Thiselton believes that Paul had no definitive belief about whether or not the eschaton *would* occur during his lifetime, but he did believe that it *could* and so he, and the church, should be ready (*Systematic Theology*, 354). In any case, regardless of whichever position one takes on the matter, the implication is that Paul believed the eschaton could happen at any moment. (This is because *would* entails *could*.)

pneumatika (Spirit-powered bodies).[22] On this view, those humans with INN at the *parousia* are taken to and through a temporally extended time in Purgatory before they make their way into the New Creation.

This manner of explaining the denial of (2) runs into some potentially interesting problems, however. The foremost problem is that St. Paul, at least, quite clearly believes that the ones to whom he is writing the letter we call "1 Corinthians" would, at Christ's return, be changed (passive voice) *instantly* from *sōmata psychika* to *sōmata pneumatika*. This problem is made more acute given that many—perhaps most—contemporary Pauline exegetes believe that Paul considered the *parousia* to be a temporally immediate possibility.[23] And if it is the case that Christ's *parousia* consummates the New Creation, and that being a part of the New Creation requires that a human have a CNN, then it seems as though Paul believed that some humans with INN, namely his contemporary readers, could, at the *parousia*, instantaneously be changed to humans with CNN.[24] This plausible reading of Paul is potentially troublesome for the deniers of (2) because it implies that a prima facie teaching of Scripture is false. Those that deny (2) in this way, then, should offer some reasons to think either (a) that Paul is not here *teaching* that those alive at the *parousia* will be so changed or else (b) give some other exegetically rooted reason(s) for thinking that this (what I take to be plausible) reading of Paul is incorrect. There is a third option, too: (c) deny that it matters what Paul teaches here. I cannot see that (c) is a live option for Christian theologians, but (a) and (b) potentially offer some wiggle room. So, my case against post-*parousia* Purgatory is not exactly airtight. But I think it does

---

[22] The translation of the Greek terms "*sōma psychikon*" and "*sōma pneumatikon*" is notoriously tendentious (in the main text I have them written in their plural forms to match my syntax). They are often translated into English as "natural/physical body" and "spiritual body" respectively. It seems to me, however, that rendering the adjective "*psychika*" as "natural" is poor. Rendering it "physical" is even worse. Importantly, a growing number of contemporary Pauline exegetes suggest that these terms denote, not the stuff out of which the bodies are made, but the stuff by which the bodies operate (compare: steam engines are not made of steam; they are powered by steam). See, for example, N. T. Wright, *The Resurrection of the Son of God* (Minneapolis, MN: Fortress Press, 2003), 348–52; Murray J. Harris, *Raised Immortal* (London: Marshall, Morgan, and Scott, 1983), 120; Murray J. Harris, "Resurrection and Immortality in the Pauline Corpus," in *Life in the Face of Death*, ed. Richard N. Longenecker (Grand Rapids, MI: Eerdmans, 1998), 153; Thiselton, *Life after Death*, 112; and Thiselton, *Systematic Theology*, 341, 36–63.

[23] As a representative sampling; cf. Wright, *The Resurrection of the Son of God*, 356–57; Thiselton, *Systematic Theology*, 354; Thiselton, *Life after Death*, 98; and Joost Holleman, *Resurrection and Parousia: A Traditio-Historical Study of Paul's Eschatology in 1 Corinthians 15* (Leiden: E. J. Brill, 1996), 72–74, 96–97, 168. I take it that the way I have phrased things is consistent with two competing nuances of this view. See note 21.

[24] It might also be important to note that Paul thought this was possible for himself, too. He uses the first-person plural to discuss the object of Christ's transformative power: "Behold! I tell you a mystery. *We* shall not all sleep, but *we* shall be changed, in a moment, in the twinkling of an eye, at the last trumpet" (1 Cor. 15:51-52; emphasis mine). Now, one might suggest that Paul is an obvious case of a human with CNN. However, I suggest that, given the chronology of this letter and his own testimony, he was not, at the time of writing 1 Corinthians, a human with CNN. Here is how we might know this: Paul wrote this letter before he wrote the letter to the Romans. In the letter to the Romans, Paul still admits to dealing with sin (cf. Rom. 7:15-24). There is disagreement about whether Romans 7 is about Paul, though. See, for example, Craig S. Keener, *The Mind of the Spirit* (Grand Rapids, MI: Baker Academic), 55ff.

place a burden on those that deny (2), by way of post-*parousia* Purgatory, to consider carefully just how to fill in (a) or (b).

Another way to deny premise (2) coherently is to deny that those who are humans with INN at the *parousia* will ever enter into the New Creation, and so they will not be made humans with CNN. This way runs into similar issues as the post-*parousia* Purgatory view. It undercuts a rather plausible reading of St. Paul's joyful proclamation to the Corinthian Christians. For, given this way of negating (2), Paul could not be correct to think that his readers—given the content of his letter, these were clearly humans with INN not CNN—would have entered into the New Creation, had Christ returned at that moment. To put the point another way, this route for denying (2) implies that, knowingly or unknowingly, Paul was misleading his contemporary readers. My putting things this way may strike one as being overly rhetorical but I submit that this is, in fact, an accurate account of things *if* it is the case that those with INN at the moment just prior to Christ's return will not ever enter into the New Creation.

Now, though this view's potential difficulties are similar to the post-*parousia* Purgatory denial of (2), this way of denying (2) seems much worse. For, it implies that Christians *ought not* to hope for the immediate return of Christ. Here is why: I think it is not too implausible to say that most humans, even the supposedly redeemed, do not have CNNs (plausibly none do). And it does not seem that any humans, barring the *parousia* and the immediate relevant changes thereof, will have them any time soon. If so, then Christ's imminent return becomes a terrifying prospect, even for the redeemed. Instead of John the Revelator's "Ἀμήν, ἔρχου κύριε Ἰησοῦ" (Amen. Come, Lord Jesus!) being a prayer of hope and deliverance, it is a curse. Asking for the *parousia* turns out to be a request to banish most of us from the New Creation. Because of this, I cannot see many denying (2) in a way that suggests that humans with INN at the *parousia* will not ever enter the New Creation.

I think that, taken together, the IT and OP provide a strong cumulative case against P&T solutions to the PHF. There are, of course, ways to counter either of these arguments. To rebut IT, one can suggest that all humans who enter into the New Creation have, in their pre-heavenly state, become characteristically similar to those designated "saints" in Roman Catholic tradition. Or, one can suggest that all humans who enter into the New Creation have, in their pre-heavenly state, become characteristically similar to "sinless" Nazarene ministers. Do each of these theologies have conceptual space to add, not just a select few, but *all* of the redeemed? If not, of course, IT has some intuitive force. And, if one does not buy that *any* humans (barring Christ) can or will work themselves (even by God's help) into such a state prior to death, IT seems like a cannon shot through the hull of P&T.

Again, some might try and rebut IT through post-*parousia* Purgatory. But here is where OP heads them off at the pass. The Purgatory person is going to have to provide an account that denies OP's (2) in one of the two ways ([a] or [b]) I have spelled out above. These two options are, in my view, problematic. And so, taking IT and OP together looks like a strong defeater for P&T solutions to the PHF.

4 Perfect obedience and perfect love: A way forward

Is there a solution to the PHF? To try and provide a way forward—a way that *might* appeal to Reformed, (broadly) Arminian, and Roman Catholic views—I wish to revisit my Augustinian nature distinctions and then draw out a connection between obeying God and loving God. Recall the Augustinian nature distinctions as follows:

SN: Sin nature, unable not to sin
INN: Inaugurated new nature, able not to sin
CNN: Consummated new nature, unable to sin

Now, consider some amended forms of these natures couched in the language of obedience:

SN*: Unable to obey God [i.e., perfect and unfailing disobedience][25]
INN*: Able to obey God [i.e., imperfect and failing obedience]
CNN*: Unable to disobey God [i.e., perfect and unfailing obedience]

With these distinctions in mind, suppose that there are different *types* of freedom associated with each nature.[26] Suppose, further, that "to disobey/disobedience" is identical with "to will to do actions for which one is morally blameworthy." If we understand "to disobey/disobedience" in this way, the implication is that *only those with INN** have libertarian free will in the robust sense that they are constitutionally able to choose between willing to disobey *and* willing to obey. A further fall out of the way I have parsed out these natures is that those with SN*, despite appearances to the contrary, cannot do any obedient actions. One might consider those with SN* to be "slaves to sin" (cf. Jn 8:31-38).[27] Contrarily,

---

[25] By "perfect" I mean "complete," not "qualitatively excellent."
[26] What follows is similar to a view advanced by James Sennett in "Is there Freedom in Heaven?" I mark out important distinctions between my view and his below.
[27] Of course, this raises questions surrounding whether "ought" implies "can," and whether or not having an SN is something for which one could be morally culpable. Both of these might well impact ways in which theologians deal with problems surrounding various views on "original sin." These are important issues that have been taken up elsewhere, but I will not enter those debates here. Suffice it to say that if the above arguments are promising, then their conclusions might have important effects on the ways in which Christian theologians think through these other important matters. For an overview of theological reflection on "original sin," see Ian McFarland, "The Fall and Sin," in *The Oxford Handbook of Systematic Theology*, ed. John Webster, Kathryn Tanner, and Ian Torrance (Oxford: Oxford University Press, 2007), 140–59. On Adam's role, see, for example, Peter Enns, *The Evolution of Adam* (Grand Rapids, MI: Brazos Press, 2012), 119ff.; Christopher W. Morgan, "Sin in the Biblical Story," in *Fallen: A Theology of Sin*, ed. Christopher W. Morgan and Robert A. Peterson (Wheaton, IL: Crossway, 2013), 143–56; Moo, "Sin in Paul," in *Fallen: A Theology of Sin*, ed. Christopher W. Morgan and Robert A. Peterson (Wheaton, IL: Crossway, 2013), 120–26. For some theological assessments of the purported implication between "ought" and "can," see, for example, Lynne Rudder Baker, "Why Christians Should Not Be Libertarians: An Augustinian Challenge," *Faith and Philosophy* 20, no. 4 (October 2003): 472; and Gareth B. Matthews, *Thought's Ego in Augustine and Descartes* (Ithaca, NY: Cornell University Press, 2003), 99.

those with INN* have been freed from slavery to sin and disobedience, and given new natures (using "nature" in the way deployed earlier). These are natures whose possessors are no longer *slaves* to sin. These humans can use their libertarian freedom to "fight back" against temptations and desires to do evil. There is a fight, but they are no longer slaves.

Allow me to offer what I take to be an exegetical reason for thinking something like this is the case. Christ and the biblical authors *seem* to suggest that a mutual implication holds between loving God and obeying God. The idea is—at least, if I read the Bible correctly—that obeying God is possible only if one *loves* God, where, as an initial gloss, we can understand love to be what emerges from two interconnected desires: the desire for the teleological good of the beloved (think the *flourishing* of the beloved) and the desire for union with the beloved. If this gloss is near a correct account, then my claim is that those with SN* neither desire God's teleological good nor union with Him.

Here are two quick samples of biblical passages that I think, taken together, provide the mutual implication I suggest above:

Jn 14:15ff:

> [Quoting Jesus]: (15) If you love me, you will keep my commandments. . . . (21) Whoever has my commandments and keeps them, he it is who loves me. . . . (23) . . . If anyone loves me, he will keep my word, and my Father will love him, and we will come to him and make our home with him. (24) Whoever does not love me does not keep my words. And the word that you hear is not mine but the Father's who sent me.

1 Jn 2:1-6:

> (1) My little children, I am writing these things to you so that you may not sin. But if anyone does sin, we have an advocate with the Father, Jesus Christ the righteous. (2) He is the propitiation for our sins, and not for ours only but also for the sins of the whole world. (3) And by this we know that we have come to know him, *if we keep his commandments*. (4) Whoever says "I know him" but does not keep his commandments is a liar, and the truth is not in him, (5) but whoever keeps his word, in him truly the love of God is perfected. By this we may know that we are in him: (6) whoever says he abides in him ought to walk in the same way in which he walked.

I think we can formulate what Jesus says in Jn 14:15-24 and what John says in 1 Jn 2:1-6 into the following conditional claims:

(LG) If one loves God, then one obeys his commandments,

and

(OG) If one obeys God's commandments, then one loves God.

(Note that [LG] and [OG] are consistent with one's disobeying God's commandments. They are not consistent, however, with one's *only* disobeying God's commandments.)

If I have these correct, then the Scriptures suggest that there is a mutual implication between loving God and obeying God. This entails that there cannot be one without the other. From this it follows that those with SN* do not love God, for they are unable to obey God. In other words, those humans with SN* are not *libertarianly free* to love God. And, ipso facto, those who do not love God do not obey God; indeed, they cannot.

Interestingly, if one adopts Thomas Aquinas's account of the theological virtue "charity"—God-directed love—one can make a case for why those with SN* cannot love God. For, only regenerate people are divinely infused with this virtue. As a *theological* virtue, says Thomas, charity is not attainable through actions. It is not like the acquired virtues of temperance or prudence. Its presence in a person marks the regenerative work of the Holy Spirit toward salvation. Those without the Holy Spirit's regenerative work are unable to exercise works of charity, for that virtue is absent in them (and unattainable outside of God's elective grace).[28] I will say more about this below.

On the account of natures I have given, then, the only sort of nature that allows a human *libertarian freedom* for loving God is INN*. Those with INN* can choose to obey God or disobey God. What about those with CNN*? As it turns out, they are not libertarianly free, either. For they *perfectly obey*—in other words—they *perfectly love* God. With their consummated new natures they are impeccable; they cannot do otherwise.

The upshot of these nature-relative freedoms might bring about an unanticipated implication. For they suggest that, though libertarian freedom *is* a great kind of freedom, it is not the *best* kind of freedom. While it allows one to break free from the inability to do non-sinful actions (a great good), it does *not* allow humans *never* to sin. So, its not being a feature of human life in the heavenly state is not a diminution of goods proper to the New Creation. This is because it is not a feature of human beings with CNN*. In other words, it is possibly the case that the redeemed in the New Creation will not miss it. (Compare: second-order goods, like courage, plausibly will not feature in the New Creation, as there is no fear in the New Creation.) With CNN*, humans no longer have to "fight back" against the desire to sin; instead, when Christ returns, *he* will defeat this enemy, like death, in and through the resurrection of the dead and the consummation of New Creation.

I say that libertarian freedom is not the *best* kind of freedom. The reason I am attempting to argue this is because (you might recall) one of the main claims motivating the PHF is the claim that libertarian free will is such a great good that, were it to be absent from the New Creation, it would constitute a diminution of the heavenly state (Recall "Intuition [2]"). Flipping this intuition on its head seems to me the best way to go, for the responses to the PHF that assume that there *is* libertarian freedom in the heavenly state (outlined above) run into serious objections.

---

[28] *ST* IIa.62.1 *respondeo;* IIa.62.2 reply obj. 3; IIa.66.6 *respondeo;* and elsewhere in Thomas; Eleonore Stump, "Love by All Accounts," *Proceedings and Addresses of the American Philosophical Association* 80, no. 2 (November 2006): 27ff; and Wawrykow, "The Theological Virtues," 295–300.

Interlocutor's retort:

It sounds as if we are going to have a clash of intuitions. You say that libertarian freedom's absence from the New Creation is plausibly like the absence of courage, a second-order good. Well, my intuitions *strongly* suggest that libertarian freedom is *vastly* superior to second-order goods. And, as it happens, one of the central motivations for Pawl and Timpe style attempts to solve the so-called Problem of Heavenly Freedom is the powerful intuition that libertarian freedom is a *great* good, a good without which the New Creation would be genuinely diminished. This is why they take great pains to insist that, through libertarianly free choices, one's character can become refined for the New Creation. There is an important causal history in their account that allows for libertarian freedom to continue into the heavenly state *and* provides a way to explain how those in the New Creation are impeccable. Given my strong intuitions about the great goodness of libertarian freedom, why not think that, instead of abandoning their account altogether, we might find some way to amend their account?

My reply: Fixing the P&T account is one way to go, but I do not currently see any ways around the IT and OP problems. Moreover, I am simply not infatuated with libertarian freedom. Here I readily admit that we have something of a clash of intuitions. And, perhaps I have not said enough to pump intuitions toward my conclusion, which is that libertarian freedom is not the *best kind* of freedom. So, let me see if I can do that.

To counter-pump the libertarian's intuitions, I will borrow an analogy from the philosopher, Harry Frankfurt. Now, I take it that he is not a libertarian on free will, so borrowing his analogy to get a libertarian's intuitions pumping toward my conclusion might be a fool's errand. We shall see.

Frankfurt understands love to be, among other things, a certain "configuration of the will . . . [that] shapes the dispositions and conduct of the lover with respect to what he loves, by guiding [the lover] in the design and ordering of his relevant purposes and priorities."[29] I think this is amenable to Thomas's view on charity. Suppose we render it as follows: charity is a certain theological virtue such that the habitual performance of acts in accordance to it further configures the will of the lover so that she more perfectly desires the teleological good of and union with the beloved.[30]

The analogy: Frankfurt says there is an important analogue between love and reason. Both of these capacities are "highly prized features of human nature. . . . Both are sources of what is distinctively humane and ennobling in us."[31] And, what is more, according to Frankfurt, both *bind* humans in certain ways.[32] That is to say, reason *requires* certain things of a human when one attempts to think in accordance with it (e.g., rational thinkers are required not to violate the law of noncontradiction). Nevertheless, one does not feel *constrained*, in any deleterious way, when one is

[29] Frankfurt, *The Reasons of Love*, 42–43.
[30] See note 28.
[31] Frankfurt, *Reasons of Love*, 64–65.
[32] Ibid.

reasoning correctly through a syllogism. By contrast, think of the angst one might feel if, when thinking through a syllogism, one thought that there was no such reasoning-constraint as the law of noncontradiction. At every premise one would have to think: "My! This could be true and false at the same time!" Such a scenario seems one that would fundamentally *stop* the reasoning process. Removing this reasoning-constraint offers not freedom but shackles.

In a similar way, love *requires* certain things of a human, namely (and here I depart from Frankfurt), seeking the teleological good of and union with his beloved. Further, the beloved *captivates* the lover, such that the lover is *compelled* to desire the beloved's teleological good and union with her. Why are such constraints of the mind and of the will good and freeing? To quote Frankfurt:

> The explanation . . . is that an encounter either with volitional or with rational necessity eliminates uncertainty. It relaxes the inhibitions and hesitancies of self-doubt. When reason demonstrates what *must* be the case, that puts an end to any irresolution on our part concerning what we are to believe. . . . Similarly, the necessity with which love binds the will puts an end to indecisiveness concerning what to care about . . . we are liberated from the impediments to choice and action that consist either in having no final ends or in being drawn inconclusively both in one direction and in another.[33]

This last part of the quote is particularly important since, in the case of loving God, what to care about, namely, God, God's purposes, and union with God, are the very things that comprise our own teleological ends.

To further pump the intuitions, consider for a moment whether it is a diminution of heavenly goods if, in the New Creation, all humans will be perfect logicians. Suppose that, in the New Creation, one cannot make mistakes in reasoning. Consider whether you would rather have, in the New Creation, perfect reasoning abilities or whether you would rather retain your ability to make logical mistakes. For that matter, which of these would you rather have *now*? And, would it matter to you if the power to reason perfectly was *given* to you by God rather than it being caused by your having painstakingly worked through logic texts and truth tables? This is an important question because the current solutions to the PHF want there to be some causal story that explains how the narrowed scope of one's freedom is consonant with a robust account of libertarian freedom. I wager that most would answer this question by saying that they would rather have perfect reasoning divinely given to them rather than having to get it through painstaking work. I know I would rather be a perfect reasoner without having to work for it. I am not saying it is *not* good to work for it; I am saying that I would rather *not* have to, that there is a *better* good, namely, that God just gives it to me.

Now consider whether you would rather have, even now, perfect loving abilities or whether you would rather retain your ability to make mistakes in loving. With respect to God, as we have seen, this is the same question as: Would you rather perfectly obey

---

[33] Ibid., 65–66.

God or retain your ability to disobey God? Moreover, would it matter to you if the power to love perfectly was *given* to you by God rather than its being caused by your having painstakingly worked through mistakes in love that caused heartache and broken hearts (or repeated painful conviction of sin)? Again, this question is important for the same reason as above: the current solutions to the PHF want there to be some causal story that explains how the narrowed scope of one's freedom is consonant with a robust account of libertarian freedom. And, I would again wager that most would rather have perfect loving abilities divinely infused rather than gained (if perfection were possible) through heartbreaking efforts. I know I would *much* rather love perfectly *and that* I didn't *have* to work for it. Again, I am not saying that working for it is not good; I am saying there might be a *better* way. The better way, to my mind, is being made a human with the CNN* nature when, at the *parousia*, Christ raises those who are appointed to the resurrection of life (cf. Jn 5:29).

To sum up the analogy here: having one's will be constrained to love perfectly is no untoward diminution of freedom. Furthermore, having God *make* one such that she is a perfect lover and perfect obeyer does not diminish the quality of her experience in the New Creation.

For those well versed in the PHF literature, my proposal might well bring to mind James Sennett's initially proffered solution to PHF. For he suggests, just as I have, that a way to get around PHF is to posit that, though there is libertarian freedom in the pre-heavenly state, there is no libertarian freedom in "Heaven."[34] In Sennett's initial paper, on what he called the "dilemma of heavenly freedom," he offers a "Proximate Conception" of heavenly compatibilist freedom "under which [heavenly] compatibilist free actions are causally dependent on [pre-heavenly] libertarian actions."[35] One can

---

[34] Sennett, "Is There Freedom in Heaven," 75–77. Here I will just provide a caution against using the term "Heaven." I use it here because Sennett uses it. But I think it is a deficient term, for it is not clear if Sennett means a disembodied, intermediate state between death and resurrection or the New Creation in which there is a New Heaven and New Earth (cf. Rev. 21–22). For some biblical-theological reasons for thinking "Heaven" a poor term for denoting the eschatological state, see J. Richard Middleton, *A New Heaven and a New Earth* (Grand Rapids, MI: Baker Academic, 2014). See especially pp. 211–37. See also my "Purgatory Puzzles: Moral Perfection and the Parousia," *Journal of Analytic Theology* 5 (May 2017): 215–17.

[35] Sennett, "Is there Freedom in Heaven?" 75. With his Proximate Conception, Sennett is building upon prior work in the free will literature relevant to, for example, Peter van Inwagen's Consequence Argument against determinism. (Here is a rough sketch of the Consequence Argument: if it is the case that the consequences of the laws of nature and events of the past entail what happens in the future, and it is the case that we are neither responsible for the consequences of the laws of nature nor the events of the past, then we are not responsible for what happens in the future). According to Sennett, if this argument shows anything, it shows that "the notions *free actions* and *determined event* are incompatible." But he continues, "The notion *determined event* is ambiguous. To clear up this ambiguity, I introduce the concepts of *proximate* determination and *remote* determination" (Sennett, "Is there Freedom in Heaven?" 72). Relevant to his Proximate Conception, *proximate* determination happens "just in case the laws of nature and the state of the world at some time immediately prior to the event entail that the event will occur." Remote determination happens in the non-immediate past (Ibid.). So, the idea is, as he puts it, "there is a conception of compatibilist freedom that is consistent with—indeed entails—libertarian freedom: compatibilist free actions are proximately determined actions whose causal histories include proximately undetermined [i.e., not remotely determined] free actions by the same agent" (Sennett, "Is there Freedom in Heaven?" 75). For a detailed explication of (the) Consequence Argument(s), see Peter van Inwagen, *An Essay on Free Will* (Oxford: Clarendon Press, 1986).

see that Sennett attempts to retain a centrally important role for libertarian freedom's effect on the free decisions in the heavenly state. My view is not concerned with doing this. Here is why: Sennett's view *and* P&T require that libertarian free will be a necessary cause of one's impeccable character. On my view, Christ's resurrection power is the jointly necessary and sufficient cause: *Christ* will defeat sinful desires, like he will defeat death, in and through the resurrection of the dead and the consummation of New Creation.

My view suggests that there is no necessary connection between the libertarian choices of those with INN and the sort of freedom attendant to those humans with CNN. This is because Sennett's view, like P&T, is particularly vulnerable to the counterexamples I have highlighted from Christopher Brown's work (e.g., human beings who die before the age of reason). So, I suggest that the *mechanism* for the change, from the freedom proper to INN to the freedom proper to CNN, is the same mechanism for the change from the freedom proper to SN to the freedom proper to INN: God's transformative power. Just as someone cannot give herself an Inaugurated New Nature—it is a work of the Spirit in regeneration—so also someone cannot give herself a Consummated New Nature, as it is a work of God in the resurrection.

5 Conclusion

The PHF forms only if Intuitions (1)–(3) feed into our conception of the heavenly state. Unfortunately for libertarian defenders, the IT and OP arguments seem to provide a strong cumulative case against the best libertarian responses to the PHF. If so, perhaps it is the case that humans do not have libertarian freedom in the heavenly state. All is not lost, however. In Section 4, by borrowing an analogy from Harry Frankfurt and couching perfect obedience in terms of perfect love, I offer a tentative step forward in the discussion that, to my mind, satisfies desires to defend libertarian accounts of free will as a great good for pre-heavenly existence (it is part of what marks out the INN). It also gives us some reason to think that libertarian free will's absence from the New Creation is not, after all, a problem. It is not the *best* kind of free will nor is it required to *get* the best kind of free will.[36]

---

[36] Research for this chapter was completed as part of the Analytic Theology Project at Fuller Theological Seminary, a project funded by a grant from the John Templeton Foundation. Thanks to Oliver Crisp, Jordan Wessling, James Arcadi, Jesse Gentile, and Chris Woznicki for their helpful comments on earlier drafts of this chapter. Thanks also to those who attended the analytic theology seminar at Fuller Seminary in April 2017, at which a previous iteration of this chapter was presented for their helpful feedback.

Contributors

Marilyn McCord Adams[†]
was Distinguished Research Professor at Rutgers University

Erin Dufault-Hunter
Assistant Professor of Christian Ethics, Fuller Theological Seminary

Kent Dunnington
Associate Professor of Philosophy, Biola University

Jeff Jordan
Professor of Philosophy, University of Delaware

R. T. Mullins
Research Fellow, University of St. Andrews

Thomas Jay Oord
Wesley Center Research Scholar, Northwest Nazarene University

Michael C. Rea
Rev. John A. O'Brien Professor of Philosophy, University of Notre Dame

Thomas Talbott
Emeritus Professor of Philosophy, Willamette University

James T. Turner, Jr.
Assistant Professor of Philosophy, Anderson University

Kevin J. Vanhoozer
Research Professor of Systematic Theology, Trinity Evangelical Divinity School

Leigh Vicens
Associate Professor of Philosophy, Augustana University

Adonis Vidu
Professor of Theology, Gordon-Conwell Theological Seminary

Jordan Wessling
Curriculum Development Specialist, Instructional Designer, and adjunct instructor, Fuller Theological Seminary

Sameer Yadav
Assistant Professor of Religious Studies, Westmont College

Index

Adams, Marilyn McCord   56, 84 n.9, 195–8
   on divine love as mighty   119–24
   on divine love as strict   114–15
   on divine love as wide   115–16
   on love embracing horrors   116–19
   on trust   124–6
agapism   199, 201, 206
analytic philosophy; *see* van Inwagen, Peter
angels   110 n.35, 114, 144, 177, 222, 229
Anscombe, Elizabeth   199
Aquinas, Thomas   21–3, 25, 38–9, 44 n.2, 45, 82–4, 85 n.12, 114–15, 131, 136, 166 n.3, 168 n.4, 169–70, 173, 176 n.31, 177, 179–82, 205, 219 n.4, 236 n.3, 242 n.17, 249
Arminius, James   129
Augustine   76, 97–8, 166 n.2, 169–70, 179, 181, 183, 185, 201, 219–20, 227 n.25, 230–2, 236, 239 n.10, 240
Austin, J. L.   158

basic desert   187–9, 191, 196–8
Bavinck, Herman   184
benevolence   16, 23, 64, 82–3, 136
   as distinct from deep love (*see* Jordan, Jeff, on what is a perfect love)
Bernard of Clairvaux   117, 232
Bishop, John   116–17
Bonhoeffer, Dietrich   199
Brown, Christopher   235 n.1, 243, 253
Brümmer, Vincent   8 n.4, 10 n.15, 12
Bundy, Ted   108, 111

Calvin, John   98, 185, 212
Carson, D.A.   8–9, 95 n.27, 151 n.23
Charnock, Stephen   141
classical theism   9, 12, 116 n.11, 129, 132
Coakley, Sarah; *see* Dufault-Hunter, Erin
Coates, Justin   188–91, 194, 198
creation *ex nihilo*   13, 21

Cunningham, Francis   178, 179, 181–2

damnation   97 n.2, 105 n.25, 115; *see also* Talbott, Thomas
Davis, Ellen   221–3
deep love   82–3, 86, 153; *see also* Jordan, Jeff, on what is a perfect love
de la Taille, Maurice   171 n.13, 175
desire for the good of the beloved   44, 47–9, 54, 76, 78, 82, 136–7, 219 n.4, 248
desire for union with the beloved   44–9, 53–5, 57, 76, 78–9, 82, 83, 102, 136–7, 142, 144, 219 n.4, 248
divine punishment   146, 149–51, 154–5, 156, 161
   as divergent from God's love   146
   divine communicative punishment   155–64
   as natural consequences   147–54
   as one with God's love   146
Dodd, C. H.   148, 149 n.15, 150, 151 n.21
Dufault-Hunter, Erin
   on Christ and *eros*   226–9
   conservative and liberal visions about sex   217–18
   eros as desiring God   218–20
   on intensification of desire   229–30
   on Sarah Coakley's theology of *eros*   231–3
   on Song of Songs and *eros*   220–3
   on tending erotic desire   223–6
Duff, R. A.   155–8, 161, 164
Dunnington, Kent
   divine love as regulative ideal   200–1
   on duty as equally legitimate motive of Christian love   205–6
   on duty as the only legitimate motive of Christian love   204–5
   duty-free divine love   201–4
   law and gospel   199, 212

on whether duty is a legitimate motive of Christian love at all   206–7
on whether there is a Christian duty to love   207–10

Edwards, Jonathan   97–8, 105, 111
empathy   99, 133–4, 138, 140, 144
Engelsma, David   105
Equality model of divine love; *see* Jordan, Jeff, on why a perfect love is not an equal love
eros and *agape*   8–9, 220, 223
Evans, C. Stephen   208
evidential argument from evil   81, 90, 92–5
existence of God   64, 92

Faber, F.W.   113, 126
Feuerbachian   8, 35
Frankfurt, Harry   44 n.2, 238, 250–1, 253

God's being
   divine action   10, 30–4, 60, 146, 148, 168, 183, 185
   divine blessedness   128, 130–1
   divine impartiality   84
   divine impassibility   28, 45, 127–9, 131, 135–6, 139–44
   divine omnisubjectivity   128, 131–5, 139–43
   divine perfection   10, 12, 19–20, 46, 48–50, 54–5, 61, 63, 84, 88, 95, 116, 130
   divine personality   43, 51–2, 57–8
   divine simplicity   12, 20, 29, 129
God's love
   ad extra   10, 13, 23, 38, 166, 170–1, 178, 181, 183
   ad intra   13, 22, 27, 37–8, 40, 178 n.36
   as analogous to human love   59, 61, 68, 70–3, 80, 98, 200–1
   as bestowing goodness   24, 56, 114–15
   as contingent   114–15
   as duty-free   201–4
   as effectual   16, 24–6, 30, 119–24
   as equal   49, 61, 84, 98, 108–9, 114–15 (*see also* Equality model; Maximality model)
   as essential *plerosis*   17, 20, 25, 38, 40
   as holy   20–1, 24, 39, 45
   and idealized human love   44, 46–50, 52–3
   as imaging   73–9
   as inclusive   106–7
   and kenosis   11, 13–16, 20, 25–6, 38–9
   as leading to incarnation   20, 79, 89, 120, 229
   as maximal   52, 55, 59, 71, 82–6, 88–9, 94–5, 98–107, 111, 116
   as necessary   13, 35, 38–40
   as not ideal love   50–4
   as partial   90
   as perfect   46–7, 48, 55, 63, 65–6, 68–9, 71–3, 78, 81, 84–5, 88, 90, 116, 127, 142–3, 147
   and providence   10–11, 15–16, 23–5, 41
   as punitive (*see* Wessling, Jordan)
   as regulative ideal for human love   199–201, 204, 206
   as uncontrolling   13, 15, 17, 30, 32–4, 36–7, 39–40
   as wrathful   129–30, 146–52, 146 n.3, 163–4
Gregory of Nyssa   75 n.39–40, 153, 155 n.36, 166 n.2, 215, 220, 227, 229

Hanson, A. T.   148, 149 n.16, 150 n.19–20, 151, 152 n.26
Hartshorne, Charles   10, 120
Henderson, Luke   242 n.17
Hick, John   101, 116
hidden human love   70
Hill, William   177
Hoeksema, Herman   105
Holmes, Arthur   30, 105
Holy Spirit   24, 41, 118, 120, 122–3, 207, 249
   indwelling of (*see* Vidu, Adonis)
horrendous evils   56, 93, 115
horrors; *see* Adams, Marilyn McCord, on love embracing horrors
Howard-Snyder, Daniel   60 n.34, 67 n.19, 70–1, 76, 80 n.63
Hume, David   92

image of God; *see also* Yadav, Sameer, on divine love as imaging
   as *imago Dei* 221
imaginative thought experiment; *see* analytic philosophy
impassibility; *see* God's being, divine impassibility
impeccability; *see* Turner, Jr., James T.
interests
   best interests 59, 74, 83–9, 102–5
   mere interests 84–9, 102–3
   perceived interests 58, 104–5
   real interests 59, 84, 104–5, 107–8

Jenson, Robert 199 n.6, 209, 210 n.24
Jesus Christ 7, 10, 13–14, 17, 20, 25–6, 36, 38, 165, 175, 248
   miracles of 33–4
   resurrection of 17, 33, 119, 209–12, 253
joint attention; *see* shared attention
Jordan, Jeff
   critique of Thomas Talbott 108–11
   on perfect love as partial 90
   on what is a perfect love 81–5
      (*see also* God's love, as maximal)
   on why a perfect love is not a maximal love 85–8
   on why a perfect love is not an equal love 88–90

Kant, Immanuel 202–3, 208, 212
Kierkegaard, Søren 18, 199 n.3, 200–1, 204–6
Koch, Klaus 147–8

Lewis, C.S. 8, 105, 156 n.43, 161 n.50
libertarian free will 235–8, 242 n.17, 247–53
Lombard, Peter 180, 185
Louth, Andrew 201
love of neighbor; *see* Dunnington, Kent
loving personal relationship 75–6, 78, 202
Luther, Martin 98, 174, 184–5

McConnell, Francis 131 n.31, 132 n.37, 143
Mackey, James P. 170, 172, 182

Maximality model of divine love 84, 88, 90, 92, 95; *see also* God's love, as maximal
Mill, J.S. 85
miracles 16, 31–4, 91, 122
Moeller, Charles 185–6
Moltmann, Jürgen 14
moral impeccability 239, 241
Mullins, R.T.
   on the desires of love 136–9
   on divine impassibility 128–31
   on omnisubjectivity 131–5
   on the Unity Problem for divine impassibility 139–44
Murphy, Mark 44 n.2, 47, 53, 76 n.49, 116 n.10, 117 n.10

nonresistant nonbelief in God 63–73, 76–8, 80
Nygren, Anders 9, 46 n.9, 199, 201, 206, 207, 220

Oord, Thomas Jay
   definition of love 11, 27–37
   on problem of evil 12–13, 17, 40–1
   on providence 15–17, 29–31
   on special divine action 31–4
open theism 12, 14, 129, 131
Oppy, Graham 235 n.1, 237–9, 243
Origen of Alexandria 153, 220 n.7, 232
Owen, John 184

Pascal, Blaise 91
Pawl, Timothy 235 n.1, 237 n.6, 238–9, 241, 242 n.17, 250
Peckham, John 9, 10 n.13, 45 n.8
Pereboom, Derk 93–4, 187–91, 196–8
perfect being theology; *see* God's being, divine perfection
personal relationship 43, 63, 65, 67–73, 75–9, 91–2, 94, 202
personal union with a cat 53
Persyk, Ken 116–17
Petavius, Dionysius 171
Pink, Arthur W. 105
Pinnock, Clark 13
Plantinga, Alvin 65, 67, 77 n.54
Plato 9, 76
predestination 115

problem of divine hiddenness 43–6,
    51, 55, 58–61, 63–71, 73, 77, 80–1,
    90–2, 95, 121
problem of evil 23–4, 26, 51, 56–7, 61,
    64–8; *see also* evidential argument
    from evil; Oord, Thomas Jay, on
    problem of evil; skeptical theism;
    theodicy
process theism 10
purgatory 244–6, 252 n.34

Rahner, Karl
    on the indwelling of the Holy
        Spirit 166–7, 172–7, 184
Randles, Marshall 127, 136 n.55, 141
Rea, Michael C.
    on God's love 44–6
    on God's personality (*see* God's being,
        divine personality)
reactive attitudes 187–91, 193–6
relations 10, 12, 19, 22, 25, 27–9, 32, 38,
    40, 60–1, 70, 78, 80, 168, 171, 173,
    183
resentment 187–8
Richard of St. Victor 117
Rowe, William 92–4, 97
Russell, Bertrand 90

salvation 19–20, 36, 56, 58, 97, 105–6,
    117, 162–3, 165–7, 212, 228, 231,
    249
Sanders, John 13, 45 n.6
Scheeben, Matthias Joseph 171–2, 174
Schellenberg, J.L. 43, 45, 57 n.28,
    58 n.31, 63–72, 75 n.43, 76–8, 80,
    90 n.18
Schelling, Friedrich 14
Scotus, John Duns 114–15
Scrutton, Anastasia Philippa 127–30,
    133–6
Sennett, James 235 n.1, 236 n.4, 237 n.6,
    247 n.26, 252 n.34, 253
sex; *see* Dufault-Hunter, Erin
Shabo, Seth 187 n.2, 188–9, 191–4, 198
    Inseparability Thesis 191–3
shared attention 137–8
Shedd, William 129–30
Silverman, Eric 127 n.4, 131 n.28, 136,
    141 n.75

Singer, Irving 1
Singer, Peter 207
skeptical theism 60 n.34, 61, 93 n.26,
    97 n.1
soul 34, 101 n.20, 116, 119, 161 n.50, 165,
    167, 170–2, 174, 176–8, 180, 182,
    184–5, 199, 219, 221 n.9, 223 n.14
speech acts 157–8
Strawson, Peter 187–91, 195, 197
Stump, Eleonore 44 n.2, 45, 63 n.1, 70
    n.25, 128, 136–9, 177–8, 219 n.4,
    242 n.16, 249 n.28
Swinburne, Richard 106, 159 n.49

Talbott, Thomas
    on best interests and mere
        interests 102–4
    on divine love as graded 104–6
    on love as inclusive 106–8
    on maximal divine love and
        incompatible human interests
        99–102
theodicy 13, 25, 41, 56, 61, 67, 93 n.24,
    101, 101 n.20, 116
Timpe, Kevin 188 n.6, 235 n.1, 236–9,
    41–2, 250
Trinity
    divine missions 19, 25, 168–70, 176,
        178–81
    inseparable operations 166, 169–70,
        174
    relation to other Christian
        doctrines 18
    social Trinity 13
Turner, Jr., James T.
    Impossibility Thesis 238–42
    Omega Point 243–46
    on perfect love and perfect obedience
        247–53

universalism 36, 115, 117
Ussher, James 131, 141 n.80

Vanhoozer, Kevin
    on John Webster's account of divine
        love 17–25 (*see also* Webster, John)
    on Thomas Oord's account of divine
        love 11–17
    on two models of love 7–11

van Inwagen, Peter; *see* imaginative thought experiment
Variability model 90, 92, 94–5
Vermigli, Peter Martyr 185
Vicens, Leigh; *see also* resentment; Shabo, Seth, Inseparability Thesis
  on resentment and love 187–98
Vidu, Adonis
  objections to appropriation approach 170–4 (*see also* Rahner, Karl, on the indwelling of the Holy Spirit)
  objections to Rahner's view 174–9
  on the principle of appropriation 167–79
  revised appropriation approach 179–86

Wainwright, William 67 n.19, 76–7, 79 n.61
Ward, Keith 13
Webster, John
  on God's love 18–20
  on God-world relation 23–6
  on plerosis of divine life 20–3
Weil, Simone 203

Wessling, Jordan 4, 50, 52, 55, 58, 72 n.32, 95 n.28, 112 n.37
  arguments for natural consequences view of punishment 150–4
  on divine communicative punishment 155–62
  explanatory advantages of divine communicative punishment 162–4
  explication of natural consequences view of divine punishment 147–50
  on paradigms of God's love and wrath 145–7
William of Ockham 115
Wolf, Susan 50–1, 72–2
Wolterstorff, Nicholas 88 n.15, 132 n.35, 199 n.3, 200–1, 205–7, 211

Yadav, Sameer
  on divine love as imaging 73–9
  on what a loving God might do 68–73

Zagzebski, Linda 120, 132–5, 139–40, 143
Zanchius, Girolamo 128 n.9, 140

www.ingramcontent.com/pod-product-compliance
Lightning Source LLC
Chambersburg PA
CBHW050324020526
44117CB00031B/1723